RUSSIAN
FOLK
EPICS

Folklores and Folk Cultures of Eastern Europe

SERIES EDITOR:
Linda J. Ivanits
Department of Slavic Languages
Pennsylvania State University

Ukrainian Minstrels
And the Blind Shall Sing

Natalie Kononenko

An Anthology of Russian Folk Epics
*Translated with an
Introduction and Commentary by*
James Bailey and Tatyana Ivanova

AN ANTHOLOGY OF

RUSSIAN FOLK EPICS

Translated with an
Introduction and Commentary by

JAMES BAILEY AND
TATYANA IVANOVA

M.E.Sharpe
Armonk, New York
London, England

Library of Congress Cataloging-in-Publication Data

An anthology of Russian folk epics / translated with an introduction and
commentary by James Bailey and Tatyana Ivanova.
p. cm. — (Folklores and folk cultures of Eastern Europe)
Includes bibliographical references.
ISBN 0–87332–640–7 (cloth : alk. paper)
1. Byliny—translations into English. I. Bailey, James, 1929–
II. Ivanova, T.G. (Tat′iana Grigor′evna) III. Series.
PG3114.A6 1998
398.2′0947—dc21
98–17071
CIP

Printed in the United States of America

The paper used in this publication meets the minimum requirements of
American National Standard for Information Sciences—
Permanence of Paper for Printed Library Materials,
ANSI Z 39.48-1984.

EB (c)   10   9   8   7   6   5   4   3   2   1

Dedicated to the memory of
Boris Nikolaevich Putilov

Contents

Foreword

M.E. Sharpe's series on the "Folklores and Folk Cultures of Eastern Europe" endeavors to publish scholarly studies and significant collections of primary texts of East European folklore. *Russian Folk Epics,* the second book in this series, is the fruit of a lengthy collaboration between two eminent scholars, American Slavist James Bailey and Russian folklorist Tatyana Ivanova. It brings together in one volume the best of modern scholarship on the Russian folk epic and a large number of texts of these epics—*byliny*—in a vibrant new translation. *Russian Folk Epics* furnishes the English-speaking world with a single, comprehensive source for the study and appreciation of the Russian oral epic.

Bailey and Ivanova's work is unique among Western studies both in the vast scope of its scholarship and in its meticulous attention to detail. The introduction, opening with the remarkable story of the discovery of a living epic tradition among the peasants of Northern Russia in the mid-nineteenth century, provides a useful overview of the history of collecting and interpreting these texts. Specific information about each epic appears in the thorough commentaries preceding the works themselves.

Perhaps the most valuable aspect of this book—and the one that is sure to bring the greatest enjoyment to readers—is the epics themselves. Many of the texts are translated here for the first time. They constitute a representative cross-section of *byliny* in terms of date of collection (from the eighteenth century into the Soviet era), regional distribution, and performers. In addition to texts from the legendary nineteenth-century male bearers of the folk epic, such as Trofim Riabinin, Bailey and Ivanova have included songs collected from talented women artists, such as Anna Pashkova. The translations strive to keep the "flavor of orality" through adherence to the metric line and the preservation of repetition. The reader can sense that these texts are not from the pen of a particular author, but stem from the collective tradition of the Russian people as transmitted by remarkable, often illiterate, singers. This fine volume of oral epics should delight specialists and general readers alike.

Linda Ivanits, Series Editor

Preface

Some dozen years ago, when I was planning to teach Russian epics in my course on Russian folklore and in another course on epics in the Folklore Program at the University of Wisconsin–Madison, I soon discovered that few translations were available, the main ones being those of Nora K. Chadwick, who brought her collection out in 1932. I decided to start translating more songs myself and at first chose some of those in the fine little volume *Russian Folk Literature* that D.P. Costello and I.P. Foote had published with texts in Russian, a glossary, and notes in English. The project received a real stimulus when a grant to translate Russian epics was awarded by the National Endowment for the Humanities in 1992. This, together with generous support from the Graduate School at the University of Wisconsin, provided funds for a graduate project assistant and for travel to Russia, where I persuaded Tatyana Ivanova to collaborate with me. She is a folklorist at the Institute of Russian Literature (Pushkin House) of the Russian Academy of Sciences in St. Petersburg, is a specialist on Russian epics, for several years has compiled the basic bibliographies of Russian folklore, and teaches courses on Russian folklore at St. Petersburg University. The International Research and Exchanges Board provided travel for her to come to the United States for three weeks to work on the anthology in April 1994.

During the past two or so decades, interest in oral epics has grown considerably, something evidenced by the number of publications that have appeared and by the number of conferences that have been held. This includes the one entitled "Epics and the Contemporary World" that took place April 22 and 23, 1994, at the University of Wisconsin. Unfortunately, the Russian epic has attracted little attention, even though it offers many possibilities for studying oral epics since some three thousand variants were recorded from a living tradition that died out only in the 1960s. Besides this, Russian folklorists have produced many fine studies of the Russian epic in such subjects as the relationship between history and epics, the role of individual performers, the interaction with Western and Eastern epic traditions, the special poetic language of the epics, the textology or quality of the verbal texts, and the melodies employed by the singers. We hope that this anthology and the information it conveys will help to stimulate the interest of non-Russian folklorists in the Russian epic tradition.

We have intended this anthology for those who may be interested in Russian folklore but read no Russian, for students in a course on Russian folklore or in a general course on epics, and for folklorists working in the epic traditions of other peoples in the world. Rather than attempting to provide a contemporary prose translation, we have tried to preserve as much of the special poetic language of Russian epics as possible. This in particular involves observing the identity of the lines and reproducing repetitions, which are so characteristic of oral poetry. We hope that we have been able to convey some sense of the quality of the originals in this respect. The anthology consists of a general introduction to the main features of the Russian oral epic, translations of thirty songs, short introductions to each work, a glossary of terms that have been retained for the sake of "local color," and a selected bibliography of scholarly studies and of the main collections of Russian epics available in English translation and in Russian. The introduction to each song contains explanations of references, interpretations, and the broad plot outline underlying most variants. The main dictionaries that have been consulted in regard to present-day Russian, Old Russian, and dialects have been listed in a separate bibliography. Glossaries that are sometimes attached to collections of epics have also served as an important source for the meaning of unusual folklore words and expressions. The transliteration system of the Library of Congress has been followed in the bibliography, notes, and bibliographic references because libraries in the United States catalogue books by that method. However, a modified system has been used in the translations and in references to them to give readers a more accessible guide to the pronunciation of Russian names and terms. Thus the following substitutions have been made: *ya* for *ia*, *yu* for *iu*, *yo* for *ë*, and sometimes *ye* for *e*.

We express our thanks and appreciation to many people. First of all, to the National Endowment of the Humanities, without whose help this anthology would have never seen the light of day, the International Research and Exchanges Board, the Graduate School at the University of Wisconsin, and the University of Wisconsin for the award of a Halls-Bascom Professorship, which provided special research funds to James Bailey. Second, we would like to thank Dennis Nepveu and Bonnie Harkins, who worked as Project Assistants and helped with bibliography and library materials. Third, we especially wish to thank the many people who have read the manuscript, in one form or another, and who have made many suggestions about improving the anthology: Patricia Arant, Margaret Beissinger, Richard Dauenhauer, V.M. Gatsak, Nikolai Gorelov, Niels Ingwersen, Linda Ivanits, Natalie Kononenko, Yelena Minyonok, T.A. Novichkova, B.N. Putilov, Jeanmarie Rouhier-Willoughby, Uli Schamiloglu, J. Thomas Shaw, and Izaly Zemtsovsky. Fourth, we wish to express our appreciation to Onno Brouwer and his staff at the Cartographic Laboratory, University of Wisconsin, for preparing maps of Russia and of Northwestern Russia. Fifth, we want to convey our gratitude to the people at M.E. Sharpe, Inc., in particular Patricia Kolb, Elizabeth Granda, Ana Erlić, and Dobrochna Dyrcz-Freeman, for their generous help in editing and publishing this anthology. And last of all, we thank the staffs at Memorial Library at the University of Wisconsin, the Russian State Library in Moscow, and the Institute of Russian Literature and the Library of the Russian Academy of Sciences, both in St. Petersburg.

James Bailey
Professor Emeritus
University of Wisconsin–Madison

Tatyana Ivanova
Head of Manuscript Section
Institute of Russian Literature, RAN, St. Petersburg
and Professor, Department of Foreign and Russian Culture
St. Petersburg University

The Russian Oral Epic Tradition: An Introduction

By the middle of the nineteenth century, it was believed that the Russian oral epic tradition had died out.[1] P.N. Rybnikov, who had been sent into administrative exile to the city of Petrozavodsk on Lake Onega in the northwest, was given the job of collecting vital statistics in the area and had to do much traveling, an activity that allowed him to become closely acquainted with the life of the peasants in the region. In a passage that has since been quoted many times by folklorists, Rybnikov writes about how in May 1860 he was caught in a storm on Lake Onega, found shelter on an island, and accidentally discovered that Russian epics (bylinas) were still being sung.

On the island there was a soot-covered *fatera,* a small house where in the summer and fall, during a lull, a contrary wind, or a storm, travelers took cover for the night. Many boats from Zaonezhie were tied up around the dock, and the fatera was crammed full of people. To tell the truth, it was so stinking and dirty that I didn't feel like going in for a rest even though it was very cold outside. I lay down on a sack near a small campfire, made myself some tea in a pan, drank it, ate something from my traveling supplies, and, having warmed myself a little by the fire, gradually fell asleep. Strange sounds woke me up. Before that I had heard many songs and religious verses, but I had never heard such a tune. Lively, whimsical, and cheerful, it at times became faster, at times broke off, and recalled something ancient that people of our time had forgotten. For a long while I didn't want to wake up and to listen closely to the words of the song—it was too tempting to remain under the influence of a completely new impression. Despite my drowsiness, I made out that several peasants were sitting about three steps from me and that a grayish old man with a thick white beard, quick eyes, and a good-natured expression on his face was singing. Squatting by the dying fire, he turned to one neighbor and then to another and sang his song, interrupting it sometimes with a grin. The singer finished and started singing another song. Then I understood that he was singing a bylina about the merchant Sadko, the rich guest. Of course I immediately jumped to my feet, persuaded the peasant to repeat what he had just sung, and took it down from his words. I asked whether he knew anything else. My new acquaintance, Leonty Bogdanovich from the village Seredka of Kizhi District, promised to perform many bylinas for me: about Dobrynya Nikitich, about Ilya Muromets and about Mikhailo Potyk the son of Ivan, about the daring Vasily Buslavyevich, about Khoten Bludovich, about forty pilgrims and one, and about Svyatogor the *bogatyr,* but he knew only incomplete variants and somehow never finished telling the words (Rybnikov 1989, 1: 52–53).

Rybnikov was to learn much more in the following years, but during his first enthusiastic encounter he nevertheless discerned several basic characteristics of the Russian oral epic tradition: the bylinas had survived among the peasants in northern Russia, a close relationship existed between the performers and their audience, epics were sung primarily for entertainment, they were usually performed by a single person, they were sung to a distinct kind of melody, they had no instrumental accompaniment, many subjects or themes existed in variants, and the quality of the singers differed considerably. Rybnikov and his correspondents gathered several hundred bylinas, as well as other kinds of songs, which were published from 1861 to 1867 in four volumes entitled *Songs Collected by P.N. Rybnikov.* Although this collection forms one of the main compilations of Russian epics, the texts have one serious drawback—they were recorded chiefly from a spoken paraphrase rather than from a sung performance.

In the summer of 1871, A.F. Gilferding decided to take a trip to the same area. Much to his own surprise, he returned to St. Petersburg eight weeks later with over three hundred songs. The next summer, in 1872, Gilferding returned to collect epics in another northern area, but he caught typhus and died. The songs he had recorded earlier were published in 1873 in what became an exemplary collection of Russian epics, *Onega Bylinas Recorded by A.F. Gilferding in the Summer of 1871.* Drawing upon Rybnikov's advice and help, Gilferding (1949, 1:

29–84) further expanded knowledge about the epic tradition and its performers. He noticed, for instance, that the rhythm of the verbal text fell apart during a spoken retelling, and he realized that accurate texts could be obtained only from a sung performance. He solved the problem of transcribing the words during singing by having the performers lengthen the pause for a breath at the end of the lines. Gilferding also made another important contribution in his collection: following Rybnikov's idea, he focused attention on the individual singers and their role in the composition of a song. Instead of grouping all epics on the same subject together as had been the practice before him, Gilferding presented them by village and within each village by singer. For each performer he included a biographical sketch about artistic quality, manner of singing, feeling for rhythm, number of songs known, from whom the epics had been learned, and means of livelihood. Gilferding's practice of including such sketches was followed by later collectors; in time this came to form a treasury of information that folklorists to this day draw upon for studying Russian epics. As a consequence, Russian folklorists were among the earliest, if not the first, to devote attention to the performers and to the performance of epics.

Historical Background

Most Russian epics probably originated from the tenth through the fourteenth centuries, mainly during the existence of what has been called Rus, Kievan Rus (Kievan Russia), or the Russian land.[2] Roughly speaking, Kievan Rus extended from near the Baltic Sea in the north to the steppe bordering on the Black Sea in the south, and from the Carpathian Mountains in the west almost to the Volga River in the east. In this period one speaks about the East Slavs, since their division into three linguistic and ethnic groups (Byelorussian, Russian, and Ukrainian) took place only in the fourteenth century. While today Kiev is the capital of Ukraine, it is still regarded as the ancient seat of Russian culture.

The Kievan state was founded in the second half of the ninth century. According to an interpretation espoused by many historians, the origins of the Kievan state were exclusively Slavic. According to another, much disputed, interpretation that is called the "Norman theory," the Kievan state was founded by the Varangians, who have been presumed to have been Scandinavians. This second explanation stems from a legend included in the *Primary Chronicle* under the year 862. Before the founding of the Kievan state, the East Slavs had a tribal organization consisting of twelve tribes that occupied approximately the same territory.

The Russian land consisted of a number of city-states, each ruled by a prince who maintained a personal retinue (*druzhina*), collected tribute, conducted relations with other cities and lands, fostered trade, and was responsible for military affairs. According to a complex system of collateral succession by seniority within generations, the senior member of the princely family became the grand prince in the city of Kiev, while other members received ruling positions in other cities. As time passed, the number of princes increased, competing branches emerged in the family, and seniority became less and less clear. The princes frequently contended with each other for Kiev as well as for other cities, a situation that sometimes led to internecine warfare. As a result, the princes could not present a unified opposition to the Mongols, or Tatars as they have been called in Russian, when they invaded from the east beginning in 1237, devastated many Russian cities, and captured Kiev in 1240, thus bringing an end to the Kievan state.

Owing to its location on the Dnieper River, the city of Kiev became a nexus for the north–south trade route from the Baltic to Constantinople (the "road from the Varangians to the Greeks") and from Western Europe to the east. In 988 during the reign of Vladimir I, who was grand prince from 978 to 1015, Christianity was accepted from the Byzantine Orthodox Church. The high point of Kievan Rus came in the eleventh century during the rule of Yaroslav the Wise who served as grand prince from 1019 to 1054. At this time Kievan Rus is considered to have been culturally, economically, and politically on a level with other countries in medieval Europe. Not only were close trade and diplomatic relations maintained, but intermarriages took place between West European royal families and the families of Russian princes. Despite the close connections with the rest of Europe, Kievan Rus did not share several social and cultural characteristics that are customarily associated with medieval Europe. Kievan Rus did not develop feudalism, did not have serfdom, and had no knights, chivalry, or courtly love poetry. The term "prince" (*kniaz*) referred only to a member of the ruling family and not to the son of a king.

Since Kiev was also on the border between the northern forest zone and the southern steppe (which stretched from the Great Hungarian Plain and the Carpathian Mountains in the west to Mongolia in the east), the history of Kiev was interwoven with the history of the steppe. For centuries the steppe had been not just a highway for nomadic invaders from the east but also the home of local nomadic confederations and states that had political, trade, and even marital ties with Kiev. Several such confederations existed in the steppe during the Kievan period, including the Khazar state (destroyed by Kiev in the tenth century), the Pechenegs, and the Polovetsians (also known as the Cumans). To a large extent Russian epics portray conflicts between these nomadic groups and Kievan Rus from the tenth through the thirteenth centuries.

The other major city was Novgorod, which was located in the northwest on the Volkhov River. The Great Lord Novgorod, as it was addressed, was a trading city that through rivers and lakes had access to the Baltic Sea in the west and to the Volga and the Caspian Sea in the east. The Novgorodians were great sailors and colonizers, eventually settling much of the area around the White Sea and reaching into the Urals and Western Siberia through northern regions. In the thirteenth century, Novgorod developed close trade relations with German cities belonging to the Hanseatic League. The city became independent from the princes, was ruled by an oligarchy, and was noted for its rambunctious assembly called the *veche*. Although Novgorod was not attacked during the Tatar campaigns in the thirteenth century, the city was threatened from the west by the advance of the Swedes and of the Teutonic knights. Russian forces commanded by Prince Alexander Nevsky defeated the Swedes in 1240 and the Teutonic knights in 1242, thus stopping the eastern expansion of these two neighbors.

The Tatar invasion was carried out under the leadership of Batu, a grandson of Genghis Khan. The new Tatar state, which only later was to be called the "Golden Horde," eventually established cities, particularly along the Volga River. These included Kazan, Sarai, and Astrakhan, Sarai becoming the capital. The Tatars were not so much interested in direct control of the Russian populace as they were in receiving tribute, collecting taxes, and imposing levies. Once the Golden Horde accepted Islam, the Tatars did not interfere with the affairs of the Russian Orthodox Church. The Tatar rulers preferred to deal with the Russian princes, recognizing one of them as grand prince by granting him a document called a *yarlyk*. The Russian princes also served as tax collectors for the Tatars. Following the collapse of the

Golden Horde in the fourteenth century, the Moscow princes gradually prevailed over the other Russian princes and began to centralize power around Moscow in the fifteenth century. Tatar domination, also known as the "Tatar Yoke," did not end abruptly but only slowly over a long period of time. Prince Dmitri Donskoi first defeated a Tatar army at Kulikovo Field in 1380, Ivan III renounced Tatar suzerainty and refused to pay tribute in 1480, and Ivan IV, also known as Ivan the Terrible, captured the Tatar cities of Kazan in 1552 and Astrakhan in 1556.

Perhaps the central question about the bylina concerns whether it is an authentic representation of earlier historical periods or an artistic expression of oral literature. Interpretations of the bylina will be covered later, but at this time several features need to be mentioned so as to furnish a context for other topics. Russian epics may absorb and incorporate elements from several different historical epochs. For instance, even though many songs probably reflect conflicts with steppe peoples from the tenth to the thirteenth centuries, particularly with the Polovetsians, the Tatar conquest may have been added as an overlay in such a way that most enemies of Kiev have acquired Tatar names. Contrary to historical fact, Russian heroes always defeat Tatar forces or adversaries in the bylinas. And finally, Prince Vladimir, as he is depicted in epics, does not represent any specific "historical Vladimir" but a generalized "epic Vladimir" around whom Russian heroes are gathered and accomplish their feats.

Epic Cycles, Genres, and Heroes

Scholars employ the term *bylina* for Russian epics, a word that is derived from the past tense of the verb "to be" and implies "something that was." The term was introduced in the 1830s by I.P. Sakharov, a popularizer who took the word from the opening of the medieval Russian literary epic *The Tale of Igor's Campaign*. The singers used the terms *starina* or *starinka,* which come from the adjective meaning old.

Russian epics are customarily divided into three general groups: *Mythological epics,* the *Kievan* or *Vladimir cycle,* and the *Novgorod cycle.* Mythological epics may have originated long before the Kievan state was founded, have no definite historical setting, involve songs about the supernatural and perhaps shamanism, and depict the mysterious figures Svyatogor and Volkh Vseslavyevich. The Kievan or Vladimir cycle consists of songs that comprise the largest group, relate events taking place in or near Kiev, and concern heroes and other

European Russia

people gathered around Prince Vladimir. The Novgorod cycle is devoted to Sadko the *gusli* player and merchant and to Vasily Buslayev,
who rebels against his native city. On the basis of details from everyday life depicted in a song, several scholars have included other epics,
such as "Khoten Bludovich," into the Novgorod cycle (Smirnov and
Smolitskii 1978: 430–33).

Although folklorists disagree about the precise generic classification of Russian epics and their relationship to other narrative songs, they nevertheless delineate several epic subgenres largely according to thematic distinctions (Astakhova 1966: 15–21; Putilov 1968). Generally speaking, the overall chronological development of the bylina may be conceived as beginning with works essentially involving myth and gradually shifting over a period of several centuries to the "factual" historical song that emerged as the Kievan period and then the Tatar period came to an end and ceased to stimulate the creation of new epics. *Heroic epics,* which are concerned mainly with fighting the enemies of Kiev, actually represent a relatively small proportion of the songs in the Russian tradition. Instead, many bylinas involve typical epic themes such as bride taking, confrontations with a monster, or a husband returning home to his wife's wedding. The *bylina-novella* represents an adventure tale in which there is no fighting but only an engaging story. The term *religious verses* (*dukhovnye stikhi*) covers a variety of Biblical and apocryphal stories, medieval church legends, and saints' lives that to one degree or another have been blended with folklore and in some cases have been transformed into a bylina.[3] The term *skomoroshina* refers to a group of satirical songs that are attributed to the Russian medieval minstrels, the skomorokhs, and that in some instances are connected with the bylina. Such songs include the humorous fabliau, parodies of the bylina, and the absurd *nebylitsa* or anti-bylina (Ivleva 1972). The French term *fabliau* refers to a kind of anecdote in verse that especially relates sexual adventures and treats them as low comedy. *Historical songs* became fully developed as a new genre in the sixteenth century, are initially concerned with Muscovite Russia, and relate events about actual historical persons. While the bylina depicts the distant past, the historical song portrays the recent past. *Ballads* constitute a much different kind of narrative than the bylina in regard to length, subject matter, types of characters, rapid pace, and sensationalism (Balashov 1966; Kulagina 1977). Representative examples of all these types of songs have been included in the present anthology in an effort to convey a sense of the diversity existing in the Russian tradition. Even though they do not constitute bylinas, two historical songs and one ballad have been chosen because they form part of the performers' repertory, they are performed to the same melodies, they all are called *starina* by the peasant singers, and they help to bring the features of the bylina itself into sharper relief.

The heroes grouped around Prince Vladimir in Russian epics are called *bogatyry*, larger-than-life figures but nevertheless basically men who for the most part accomplish their deeds as people in the real world and seldom resort to magic. Among the three main bogatyrs, *Ilya Muromets* is the central one and represents the ideal hero for peasant performers in the nineteenth and twentieth centuries. The second is *Dobrynya Nikitich*, who knows how to do things the proper way, is known for his knowledge or courtesy (*vezhestvo*), serves as a diplomat for Prince Vladimir, and represents the dragon slayer in the Russian tradition. The third is *Alyosha Popovich*, who may be regarded as the trickster in the Russian epic since he usually defeats enemies by stealth rather than by strength. Various other heroes and figures are also met from time to time, including the drunkard Vasily Ignatyev, who leaves his nook in a tavern to save Kiev from a Tatar attack; the wealthy "snob" Dyuk, who visits Kiev and finds everything inferior; and the "Don Juan" Churila Plyonkovich, who charms the women at court, much to Vladimir's chagrin. Just as the knights of the Round Table are gathered around King Arthur, so the bogatyrs are grouped around *Prince Vladimir*, who performs no exploits himself. An equally diverse portrait gallery of women includes *Princess Apraxia* as the medieval ideal of feminine beauty ("Dunai"); her sister Nastasia as a *bogatyrka* (a warrior maiden resembling an Amazon—"Dunai"); the epic hero's perceptive mother, who is often named Amelfa Timofeyevna ("Dobrynya and the Dragon"); the wise wife Vasilisa Nikulichna, who cleverly saves her foolish husband from prison ("Stavr"); and Marinka as a sorceress who turns young men into aurochs ("Dobrynya and Marinka"). Princess Apraxia may be Vladimir's wife or daughter. When she is his wife she may be presented negatively ("Alyosha and Tugarin"), but when she is his daughter she is always idealized ("Ilya Muromets and Kalin Tsar"). *Princess Zabava*, who may appear as Vladimir's niece ("Dobrynya and the Dragon"), represents the heroine whom a hero in a magic tale rescues. Prince Vladimir and a few others have a personal retinue called *druzhina*, a form derived from the word for friend (*drug*).

Oral Poetics and Language

The term *epic ceremonialism* is used to describe the poetics of Russian epics or the devices used to compose them. Occasionally a song opens with an interlude called *zapev* that has no connection with the ensuing ory. Although examples occur in "Solovei Budimirovich" and "Vasily Ignatyev," perhaps the most famous one appears in a song from the eighteenth-century collection of Kirsha Danilov (1977: 201).

> High is the height under the heavens,
> Deep is the depth of the ocean-sea,
> Wide is the plain across the whole earth,
> Deep are the pools of the Dniester River,
> Miraculous is the cross of Lebanon,
> Long are the reaches of the Chevylesk River,
> High are the Saracen Mountains,
> Dark are the Brynsk forests,
> Black are the Smolensk swamps,
> And fast are the lower reaches of a river.

An introduction called *zachin* frequently opens an epic. The following illustration occurs in the translated variant of "Ivan Godinovich" and describes a banquet scene at Prince Vladimir's palace where bragging breaks out.

> In the city, in Kiev,
> At gracious Prince Vladimir's,
> There was held, there was held a feast of honor.
> All at the feast ate their fill,
> All at the feast drank their fill,
> All at the feast burst out bragging.
> One bragged about his father and mother,
> Another bragged about his young wife.

Usually a terse, proverb-like ending called *kontsovka* informs listeners that the song is over. The following example taken from "Dobrynya and Alyosha" is revealing because it refers to the calming effect that the performance of a song, perhaps magical in intent, was believed to have on the weather and the sea. This demonstrates one possible function of a bylina among northern singers.

> Since then they've been singing the old song
>   about Dobrynya
> To the blue sea for ensuring calm weather
> And to you good people for listening.

Another poetic feature concerns the *Slavic negative antithesis,* in which a comparison is implied but in a negative form that denies the comparison.[4] In Russian this type of poetic device usually consists of a few lines that a singer may insert at an appropriate point in a song. The following excerpt taken from "Ilya Muromets and Kalin Tsar" provides an example.

> A bright falcon didn't swoop down on the geese,
> on the swans,
> And on the small migratory gray ducks—
> A Holy Russian bogatyr
> Swooped down on the Tatar army.

When performers wish to dwell on a passage, they may expand and ornament it through repetition and parallelism, two of the most prominent stylistic attributes of oral poetry. The following section, which is repeated and rephrased several times in "Ilya Muromets and Kalin Tsar," could be summarized simply as "No one but Ilya Muromets can stand up for Kiev." Albert Lord (1965: 54–55) used the expression *adding style* to describe such passages in which line after line is added, a type of syntax that consists of simple sentences (parataxis) rather than of complex sentences with dependent clauses (hypotaxis).

> "The old Cossack Ilya Muromets isn't alive,
> There's no one to stand up now for the faith
> and for the fatherland,
> There's no one to stand up for God's churches,
> There's no one to stand up for the city of Kiev,
> There's no one to protect our Prince Vladimir
> And Apraxia the Princess!"

Although singers may use such features as repetition or parallelism to slow down the pace of an epic and to induce what is termed *epic retardation,* they nevertheless tend to focus on the main events in a story. Once they finish a high point in the action, they may quickly move to the next high point through *rapid transitions* in time or place. For instance, in "Dobrynya and the Dragon," Dobrynya defeats the dragon in the Saracen Mountains and three lines later meets Prince

Vladimir in Kiev. Or a long period of time may pass, as occurs in "Dobrynya and Alyosha," where Dobrynya has been away from home for twelve years but abruptly returns in time to prevent his wife from marrying Alyosha.

Singers are conscious of an audience's reactions and strive to maintain its attention by using various means to heighten the drama, sharpen contrasts, or produce sudden effects. To recite a good story and to keep their listeners interested, performers particularly like to employ *epic hyperbole*. For instance, when a singer in the song "Volkh Vseslavyevich" says that Volkh, as a child, asks his mother for a mace that weighs 300 poods (10,400 pounds), listeners realize that this is an outrageous statement but understand that Volkh is destined to become a strong warrior. In the same song, Volkh, as a teenager but also as a future chieftain, gathers a *druzhina* of 7,000 instead of the usual number of 30. Such exaggerations exemplify what are termed *epic numbers*. The bylina "Ilya Muromets and Nightingale the Robber" is enclosed within a time frame that forms an overall hyperbole. Ilya leaves home after matins and, after several adventures, including the single-handed defeat of an army near the city of Chernigov and the capture of the monster Nightingale the Robber, arrives in Kiev in time for vespers on the same day. When Nightingale the Robber whistles, all the trees droop, the grasses become entangled, the flowers lose their blossoms, and people lie dead. Hyperbole represents an integral element in the style of the bylina and in the manner of telling a tale.

Since Russian epics were performed orally for a listening audience, they, by the very nature of an oral verbal art, condition and shape the compositional techniques employed by singers in several ways. *Time and plot in the bylina are basically linear*—normally one continuous passage of time is presented in logical sequence without flashbacks, simultaneous actions, or subplots (Likhachev 1967; Putilov 1988: 33–38) because listeners cannot readily grasp such complexities. For a similar reason, relatively few personages play important roles in the plot of a bylina. As a part of their oral presentation, singers use special *tag lines* to inform listeners who is talking to whom in speeches and dialogues. Although present-day readers may be annoyed by a repetition of the phrase "hail to you," which frequently opens tag lines, in oral poetry these words function as a signal telling the audience that a speech is about to be addressed to someone. The abundance of passages involving direct speech also underscores the comparative rarity of indirect speech in the language of Russian epics. The following example of tag lines appears in the song "Dunai."

> Prince Vladimir of capital Kiev spoke:
> "Hail to you, Dobrynya Nikitich!"

During the past several decades, Russian scholars have accomplished much toward the description, analysis, and definition of the language in various genres of Russian folklore, a relatively new discipline that has been named "linguofolkloristics."[5] Some investigators believe that the linguistic idiom of folklore is expressed entirely within the dialectal speech of peasant performers, while others consider that this idiom is supradialectal and represents a special *koine*. Despite such disagreements, most nevertheless concur that the traditional language of Russian folklore forms a distinctive and perceptible subcode of present-day Russian. The tenacity and age of the folklore style is indicated by its presence in some works of Old Russian literature written during the Kievan period. The inclusion of numerous epithet-noun phrases constitutes one of the more obvious stylistic features in Russian folk poetry. A few examples in English translation are *on the blue sea, in the dark forest, the pretty maid, on the fine steed, mother damp earth,* or *young bright falcon.* In regard to the bylina, archaic morphological, syntactic, and lexical items may occur in texts that have been recorded since the middle of the eighteenth century. Such traditional elements lend the language of epics a poetic quality and raised tone that differ considerably from contemporary Russian speech or prose.

In several studies, Patricia Arant (1967; 1990) has demonstrated how the songs of one of the finest Russian singers, T.G. Riabinin, adhere, with some modification, to the formulaic technique that, as Albert Lord discovered, underlies the composition of Serbo-Croatian oral epics. Besides features such as epithet-noun phrases and repetitions that may qualify as formulas or formulaic expressions, Russian epics contain many *commonplaces, pattern scenes,* or, as Lord terms them, *themes* that comprise entire passages (Lord 1965: 68–98). Examples are a hero taking leave of his mother, saddling a horse, entering a council chamber, or bragging at a feast; departure over the wall of a city; depiction of a journey; a hero urging on his horse; battle description; a hero dressing in the morning; the exchange of taunts by adversaries before a fight; two heroes becoming blood brothers; and one combatant asking another for mercy at the end of a fight. Gilferding (1949, 1: 57–58) noted such scenes (or "common places") in the bylina and pointed out how each singer develops an individual expression of these compositional elements and includes them in song after song. Later investigators have shown that performers vary such passages depending on the context and do not repeat them verbatim. Considered on the level of an entire work, the bylinas contain plots or subjects that occur in many epic traditions. A few examples are the birth and childhood of a hero, the fight of a father and son, a battle with a monster, the imprisoned or reluctant hero who at a critical moment emerges to save his city, matchmaking or bride taking, a husband returning after a long absence to his wife's wedding, and a hero's encounter with a sorceress who turns men into animals.

Russian epics predominantly consist of *a single episode* and contain three to five hundred lines, although at times they may exceed a thousand. In other traditions, epics amounting to many thousands of lines often represent *composite epics* that combine several episodes about one hero. On the whole, the Russian tradition did not develop composite songs, but nevertheless some occasionally appear and suggest that an incipient inclination toward composite forms existed (Astakhova 1948: 98–105; Putilov 1988: 15–16, 33–38). For instance, the selected variant of "Dobrynya and the Dragon" has been taken from a song in which several episodes about Dobrynya have been joined together. The version of "Churila Plyonkovich" included here represents a composite of the two episodes about this particular personage, the translated variant of "Sadko" comprises all three episodes about this Novgorodian figure, and the song "Svyatogor" contains both stories about this mythological hero. Length alone is an inadequate basis for judging whether a narrative is an epic. If one considers a group of equally pertinent features—the types of heroes, special poetic language, distinctive melodies, traditional pattern scenes, typical plots, the devices of an oral narrative oriented toward a listening audience, and an epic view of the world—one would have to conclude that for the most part bylinas satisfy these criteria and should be regarded as epics.

Music, Verse, and Performance

Epics recorded in northern Russia in the nineteenth and twentieth centuries were performed essentially by single singers without an instrumental accompaniment.[6] The *gusli,* a stringed instrument that is plucked and resembles a psaltery, is occasionally mentioned as being played by the skomorokhs in the songs themselves, suggesting that such an instrument was perhaps used in the past. A few instances of two and sometimes more singers performing a bylina have been recorded in the Mezen and Pechora regions (Dobrovolskii and Korguzalov 1981: 24, 43). Narrators have their own melodies and ordinarily employ only one, two, or three with their epics, showing that many songs may be sung to the same melody. In some areas the tunes are performed as a kind of recitative, while in others they are sung in a more lyric fashion. The melody and verbal line usually coincide so that *the bylina is stichic,* that is, it is composed line by line; furthermore, the lines are unrhymed, have no stanza form, and most often have a two-syllable ending, or clausula. However, in the Onega area, performers may introduce variations of the melody in such a way that it develops a loose and flexible stanza form. Such musical *tirades* involve a varying number of lines but are not evident in the verbal texts themselves (Dobrovolskii and Korguzalov 1981: 23–24, 29). The rather elastic *long epic line* ranges approximately from nine to seventeen syllables and consists of several verse forms: (1) trochees varying from four to eight feet; (2) three-stress accentual verse having a set number of main stresses per line but a varying number of syllables between them; and (3) meterless verse in which the lines are distinguished only by the clausula (Bailey 1978). The *short epic line* contains mainly eight to ten syllables, has an unrhymed "playful ending," and appears in just a few songs that do not belong to "high epics." Two examples of works composed in the short epic line have been included in the present anthology: "Kostryuk" represents a historical song that parodies a heroic epic, and "The Merchant Terenty" is a comic song involving the skomorokhs.

Collections and Collectors

The earliest collection of Russian epics was attributed to Kirsha Danilov, was compiled in the middle of the eighteenth century, and was published for the first time in 1804 under the title *Ancient Russian Poems Collected by Kirsha Danilov* (Danilov 1977). On the basis of recently discovered documents in the archives of the wealthy Demidov family that lived in the Urals, A.A. Gorelov (1995) concluded that

Kirsha Danilov was indeed a real person, was a trusted and highly respected servant of the Demidov family, was a genuine epic performer, and was a skomorokh. Some twenty-five bylinas appear in Danilov's collection, which contains some of the most archaic texts and includes melodies arranged apparently for violin (Korguzalov 1994).

In the 1830s, P.V. Kireevsky (1808–1856) became interested in collecting folk songs and inspired a group of people to take down and send him texts from many parts of Russia. Only after Kireevsky's death did P.A. Bessonov publish ten volumes entitled *Songs Collected by P.V. Kireevsky* (Kireevskii 1860–74). The bylinas in the first five volumes are important because many were taken down in parts of Central Russia where the epic tradition soon disappeared. S.I. Guliaev (1805–1888), a person of varied interests and abilities, collected folk songs, including epics, in southwestern Siberia near the city of Barnaul in the Altai region. Some of his recordings were included in Kireevskii's compilation, but they were first published as a separate and complete collection only in 1939 (Guliaev 1988). To the already mentioned activities of P.N. Rybnikov (1831–1885) and A.F. Gilferding (1831–1872) it needs to be added that Rybnikov's collection contained 220 texts and Gilferding's 318.

Despite all their merits and the importance of their work, these early collectors in the nineteenth century were amateur folklorists. Around the turn of the century, they were succeeded by professionals who had been trained in the new discipline of folkloristics and who undertook the search for a living tradition in northern regions around the White Sea and along the Kuloi, Mezen, Pechora, and Pinega Rivers.[7] The next stage in the recording of Russian epics began when A.V. Markov (1877–1917) spent the years 1898 to 1899 on the Winter Shore of the White Sea, took down 116 songs, and published them in the volume *White Sea Bylinas Recorded by A. Markov* (Markov 1901). A.D. Grigorev (1874–1945) spent the years 1899 to 1901 on expeditions in Archangel Province and collected 424 texts that he brought out in three volumes under the title *Archangel Bylinas and Historical Songs Collected by A.D. Grigorev from 1899 to 1901* (Grigorev 1904–39). Despite the immense difficulties that traveling in the far north entailed, Grigorev took along a phonograph and recorded the opening lines of about 150 songs. During the years 1901 to 1902, N.E. Onchukov (1872–1942), who had no training in folklore, compiled his collection called *Pechora Bylinas* (Onchukov 1904), which included 101 bylinas from the region along the Pechora River.

Although folklorists discovered no new areas with a living epic tradition after the first decade of the twentieth century, they continued field work by making new recordings in the same places where previous collectors had been. From 1926 to 1928, the twin brothers Iu.M. Sokolov (1889–1941) and B.M. Sokolov (1889–1930) organized three expeditions to Karelia, called them "In the Footsteps of Rybnikov and Gilferding" (Iu.M. Sokolov 1927; B.M. and Iu.M. Sokolov 1932), and published 280 texts in the collection *Onega Bylinas* (Iu.M. Sokolov 1948). On the basis of songs obtained from several expeditions to far northern regions, A.M. Astakhova (1886–1971) compiled the two-volume collection *Bylinas of the North* (Astakhova 1938–51), which contains 232 texts and includes extensive commentary about the songs and performers. In the 1930s one of the centers for the study of Russian folklore was established in the city of Petrozavodsk on Lake Onega. The center published several collections based on archival materials: V. Bazanov, *The Bylinas of P.I. Riabinin-Andreev* (1939); G.N. Parilova and A.D. Soimonov, *Bylinas of the Pudoga Region* (1941); and A.M. Linevskii, *The Singer F.A. Konashkov* (1948). The volume *Russian Epic Songs of Karelia* edited by N.G. Cherniaeva (1981) contains bylinas that had been taken down from 1930 through 1960.

The last stage in the collection of Russian epics took place from the 1940s to the 1960s, when the tradition died out. A.M. Astakhova's volume *Bylinas of Pechora and the Winter Shore* (1961) contains 161 epics, historical songs, and ballads that were recorded in 1942 and from 1955 to 1956. N.P. Kolpakova's collection *The Sung Folklore of Mezen* (1967) includes 54 epics that were taken down in 1958 and 1961.

Epics have also been collected among the Cossacks in southern Russia, in the Urals, and in Siberia, but especially among the Don Cossacks. Unlike the tradition in the far north, Cossack songs were sung by a male chorus, were essentially lyrics, and were relatively short. A.M. Listopadov (1873–1949), the main collector of Don Cossack songs, transcribed hundreds of lyrics and some epics and brought out five volumes entitled *Songs of the Don Cossacks* (1949–54), which included 64 Cossack epics.

During the past three or so decades, several trends have taken place in the publication of Russian epics. One involves providing new and revised editions of older collections and supplying them with detailed commentary, one example being *Songs Collected by P.N. Rybnikov* (Rybnikov 1989–91). Yet another trend concerns collections of songs

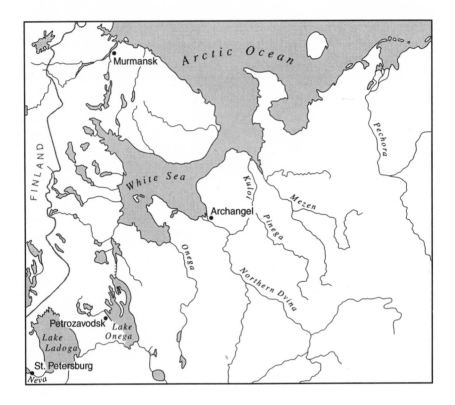

Areas in Northwestern Russia where epics have been recorded

about specific epic heroes or of songs from a single geographic area. Several examples are A.M. Astakhova, *Ilya Muromets* (1958); Iu.I. Smirnov and V.G. Smolitskii, *Dobrynia Nikitich and Alyosha Popovich* (1974) and *Novgorod Bylinas* (1978); and Iu.I. Smirnov, *Russian Epic Poetry of Siberia and the Far East* (1991). The long-cherished dream of Russian folklorists to publish a multivolume compilation of all Russian epics has unfortunately yet to be realized.

The majority of the transcriptions in the nineteenth century were made without the music. Sound recordings, which began to be made in 1896, at first consisted only of fragments and only much later of full texts. In the remarkable compendium *Bylinas: The Russian Musical Epic,* which contains texts, music, and commentary, B.M. Dobrovolskii and V. Korguzalov (1981) have gathered most Russian epics recorded with their melodies. Furthermore, they have distinguished the essential musical features of the regional epic traditions in northern, central, and southern Russia. The Phonogram Archive at the Institute of Russian Literature in St. Petersburg, a major repository of folklore materials, has issued several records of epic performers through the firm "Melodia," one example being *Bylinas of the Russian North* in 1985.

Thanks to the efforts of many collectors, folklorists have accumulated some three thousand texts of Russian epics, of which about two thousand have been published. Approximately sixty to eighty themes or subjects appear in the Russian tradition; they exist in just a few to as many as 150 variants, and in some instances they represent repeated recordings of the same song from the same performer. As a consequence, students of the Russian epic have had an opportunity to trace the development and to study the characteristics of a living tradition over a period of approximately two hundred years. One of the most valuable aspects of the Russian materials as a source for studying oral epics is that the texts have not been adapted to the literary ideals of some particular period nor have they been artificially joined to produce lengthy composite songs, as was the case, for instance, with Elias Lönnrot's publication of the Finnish *Kalevala*.

Performers

Although peasants were the sole bearers of the Russian epic tradition by the time collecting began in earnest in the nineteenth century, several other groups have undoubtedly taken part in the creation, performance, and dissemination of the bylina. Since the institution of court singers was known in medieval Europe and has been commonly encountered in other places where epics have flourished, such singers may be assumed to have existed under similar circumstances in Kievan Rus. As Felix J. Oinas (1984: 32–43; 1987) has indicated, the Kievan prince, princes in other cities, their courts, and their retinues formed an upper class whose ideals—a code of honor, fighting, and hunting—are expressed in the bylina. It is difficult to conceive that peasant singers in Kievan Rus would have had sufficient direct knowledge to depict the details of courtly and urban life appearing in many songs.

The *skomorokhs*, wandering minstrels similar to the medieval French *jongleurs* and the German *Spielmänner*, were also bearers of the epic tradition (Findeizen 1928, 2: 105–70; Zguta 1978), from time to time appear in epics, and probably composed satirical songs termed *skomoroshina* and some novelistic bylinas. In the middle of the seventeenth century during the reign of Tsar Alexei Mikhailovich, state and church authorities started persecuting the skomorokhs; they were forced to leave Moscow and Central Russia and settled in out-of-the-way northern villages where they eventually were assimilated by the peasants. V.N. Tatishchev (1962, 1: 114–15), a Russian historian in the first part of the eighteenth century, reports that he heard skomorokhs perform old songs about Prince Vladimir, Ilya Muromets, Alyosha Popovich, and Nightingale the Robber. By the nineteenth century the skomorokhs had disappeared from Russian culture, but their heritage of songs, including epics, did not disappear—it entered the repertory of peasant singers. Wandering pilgrims (*kaliki perekhozhie*) represent another group that may have served as transmitters of bylinas and may have carried them to distant parts of Russia. They differed from the religious pilgrims who traveled from Kievan Rus to Greece and to the Holy Land in medieval times (Maksimov 1989; Tikhonravov 1898). On the contrary, these "modern pilgrims" were mendicants who performed mainly "religious verses" for alms at churches and monasteries on church holidays or at fairs. Members of this group of people, who in many instances were professionals belonging to special guilds in pre-revolutionary Russia, may have adapted some biblical and religious subjects to the poetics and style of the bylina.

In the introductory essay to his collection, "Olonets Province and Its Folk Rhapsodists," Gilferding (1949, 1: 44) noted that the way a person earned a living had a direct bearing on whether that person might learn and perform epics. In the far northwestern part of Russia, this especially concerned fishing, hunting, and lumbering. Cooperatives called *artels* invited singers to take part as shareholders and to perform epics during breaks in work or during bad weather. The trades of itinerant tailors and shoemakers were also conducive to the singing of epics. However, it needs to be pointed out that women were also fine performers of Russian epics, so that occupation was not the sole inducement for creating a favorable atmosphere and a vibrant tradition.

Collectors not only discovered a number of outstanding performers and several families of singers among northern peasants, but they also were able to delineate "schools" of performers who had had the same teacher. One prime example concerns T.G. Riabinin (1791–1885), who

The singer T.G. Riabinin. Lithograph originally published in the collection by A.F. Gilferding, *Onezhskie byliny, zapisannye Aleksandrom Fedorovichem Gilferdingom*, St. Petersburg, 1873.

was the first of four generations in a family of singers.[8] The elder Riabinin, whom many folklorists consider to have been one of the finest Russian epic singers and from whom Rybnikov and Gilferding collected songs in Olonets Province, learned many of his songs from Ilia Elustafev, who died in the 1830s at the age of ninety and from whom several other performers also had acquired some of their songs. In November and December 1871, Riabinin, invited by Gilferding, came to St. Petersburg and performed his epics before members of the Russian Geographic Society, which at that time was a center for ethnography and the study of folklore. The elder Riabinin passed on his mastery to his son I.T. Riabinin (1844–1908), who in 1893 and 1894 performed in St. Petersburg and Moscow; in 1902 he again gave concerts in the Russian capitals and then visited Kiev, Odessa, Sofia, Belgrade, Vienna, Prague, and Warsaw. Two later members of the family, I.G. Riabinin-Andreev (1873–1926) and P.I. Riabinin-Andreev (1905–1953), also sang bylinas.

In the biographical sketches or commentaries accompanying their collections, transcribers have included remarks about the quality of the singers, particularly in regard to their musical sense, their sensitivity to poetic rhythm, their mastery of the special language of folklore, and their ability to tell a story. Needless to say, only a few exceptionally talented individuals are capable of mastering the composition of what is undoubtedly the most demanding of genres—the oral epic. Collectors and scholars have constantly faced the question of deciding which singers were worth recording and studying. In the field, recorders soon learned that the easiest way to find the finest performers was to seek out the ones with the best reputation among the populace. In order to define differences among performers more precisely, A.M. Astakhova (1938, 1: 70–89), one of the most experienced field collectors and knowledgeable investigators of the bylina, has classified singers into three types: (1) transmitters who simply passed songs on as they had learned them; (2) creators who re-created the songs in their own manner but remained within the tradition; and (3) improvisers who injected much of their own invention into each performance of a song, thus making the text both original and unstable. In Astakhova's opinion, the creators represented the finest singers and furnished the most artistic texts.

Geographic Distribution

One of the main questions about the Russian epic concerns the reason why it originated in Kievan Rus but in the nineteenth and twentieth centuries was discovered only among peasants living in the peripheries of Russia (Zguta 1972). After the East Slavs had separated into three ethnic and linguistic groups in the fourteenth century, one would have anticipated that all would have inherited the Kievan epic tradition. However, this did not occur. Bylinas have not been recorded in the territory of Belarus or of Ukraine, where Kiev has become the capital; furthermore, only a few texts having little artistic merit have been collected in Central Russia. Instead, epics have been found in the outlying areas of Russia in the far north, to the east of Moscow along the Volga River, in the Don region, and in several parts of the Urals and Siberia.

A number of hypotheses have been proposed to explain the disparity between the origin of the bylina in Kievan Rus and the geographic distribution of the genre in recent times.[9] According to one interpretation, the Novgorodians disseminated the epics when they colonized the far northern areas as well as parts of the Urals and Western Siberia. According to another explanation, which takes a comprehensive view of geographic data into account, the bylina was preserved in those areas where a Russian population had close contacts with other peoples, particularly with Finno-Ugric and Turkic groups. For instance, in Zaonezhie, the area to the north and east of Lake Onega, the Karelians have been neighbors with Russians for hundreds of years. In other northern regions, along the middle of the Volga River, and in the northern Caucasus, Russian newcomers have also encountered other ethnic peoples. A similar situation existed in parts of Siberia, which was joined to Russia in the second half of the sixteenth century. Thus a milieu inhabited by other ethnic groups, several of which had their own epic traditions, compelled Russian settlers to become aware of their own identity. For peasants living in Central Russia and having no contact with other peoples, ethnicity was not an issue, but in the peripheral parts of the country, Russian inhabitants were stimulated to sustain their ethnic heritage. Language and folklore played a particularly important role in encouraging and communicating ethnic self-consciousness. In this respect, epic songs about Kievan Rus and Kievan bogatyrs helped a Russian population preserve and transmit memories about Russia's history and culture.

Interpretations of the Bylina

Since the middle of the nineteenth century, Russian folklorists have used a variety of approaches to study the bylina; each in its own way has added to knowledge about the subject and has contributed to an understanding of the genre.[10] Some approaches have followed European trends, and others have been essentially Russian in conception.

Folklorists have sought answers to questions such as the following: When and where was the bylina created? What are the sources of the plots and characters? What have people contributed to its creation and development? What have the main stages in its evolution been over the centuries? What is the relationship of the bylina to history, historical events, and historical personages? Can details of everyday life in a song be ascribed to a particular historical place or period? To what degree have ancient plots, motifs, and characters been transformed into a Kievan setting? How do singers compose oral epics, and do they rely exclusively on memory or improvisation? How does oral literature differ from written literature, and how do the two interact? The approaches surveyed here should be viewed within the context of two factors. First, in the second part of the nineteenth century the study of folklore was only slowly emerging as an independent discipline having its own purposes, subject matter, and methods. Second, a thriving epic tradition furnished Russian scholars with a "living laboratory" that provided a stream of new variants, collections, and information about the singers. As a result, a fortuitous set of circumstances gave scholars both an opportunity and an incentive to seek new interpretations, to test theories, and to propose answers to key questions not only about the bylina but also about oral epics in general. Only the main trends and a few scholars can be mentioned here.

What is termed the *mythological school* actually consisted of a highly varied group of people who not only had widely divergent views but also changed their ideas and approaches considerably over time.[11] These scholars, who were the first to offer a broad interpretation of the Russian epic tradition, elucidated the basic cycles of bylinas and made a distinction between younger and older heroes. These investigators, who were closely familiar with German philology, philosophy, and folkloristics, believed that the tale, the legend, and the epic had emerged over time from an evolution and a transformation of myths. Thus the heroes of Russian tales and epics were related to Slavic mythological figures. For instance, A.N. Afanasev (1826–1871) connected Ilya Muromets with Perun, the Old Russian god of thunder (Afanasev 1865–69, 1: 302–07). Orest F. Miller (1833–1889), who examined Russian epics through the prism of a solar and meteorological myth, believed that in the song "Ilya Muromets and Falconer" the god of thunder (Ilya Muromets the father) engenders and then destroys the storm clouds (Falconer the son) (Orest Miller 1869: 181–85).

In the second half of the nineteenth century, the *theory of borrowing,* which also developed in West European scholarship, succeeded the mythological school and initiated a search for possible Western and Eastern sources. In his work "The Origin of Russian Epics," first published in 1868, V.V. Stasov (1824–1906), the most outspoken advocate of this approach in Russia, asserted that Russian epics contained nothing Russian because their plots, motifs, and characters had been taken from Eastern legends, tales, and epics (Stasov 1894, 3: 948–1260). Furthermore, the bylina did not reflect Russian history, personages, or national spirit. In this regard, Stasov's work was directed against the Slavophils, who idealized medieval Russia, who insisted on the independence of Russian culture from that of Western Europe, and whose ideas played an influential role in Russian society at that time. Vsevolod F. Miller (1848–1913), who later was to become the leading exponent of the Historical School, in an early work concluded that epics about Ilya Muromets had been borrowed from Iranian folklore and that the Russian hero was a transformation of Rustem, the main figure in Iranian narratives (Vs.F. Miller 1892: 117–51). Vsevolod Miller conjectured that the songs of the Polovetsian nomads in the steppe had served as intermediaries between the Iranian and the Russian narratives in the Kievan period.

A.N. Veselovskii (1838–1906), a true comparativist in the study of folklore and literature, has occupied a unique place in the history of Russian folkloristics because he creatively selected, elaborated, and combined elements of the borrowing theory, the migratory theory, and the anthropological school. Using his knowledge of many ancient and modern languages, his vast erudition about many traditions, and his close acquaintance with contemporary works about ethnography, Veselovskii examined and compared plots that existed among various peoples in both oral and written forms. He concluded that an exchange between folklore and written literature took place in both directions. Striving to trace the path of a plot from one ethnic tradition to another within a specific historical setting, Veselovskii focused attention on such items as caravan trade routes, the spread of religious heresies in medieval Europe, and the Crusades. He especially drew upon the concept of "shared trends" and the ideas of the anthropological school, according to which human societies exhibited nearly the same traits at a given stage in their development and evolution. Thus similar motifs and beliefs were conceived to have formed under the influence of universal human psychic laws and of identical conditions in the life of different peoples at different times. For Veselovskii, literature grew out of folklore, which had evolved into separate genres from a primitive syncretism of poetry, dance, and music. The central vision of Veselovskii's research into all forms of written and oral literature concerned what he termed "historical poetics," a subject to which he devoted many of his works.[12]

Although it had begun to develop in the 1860s, by the 1890s the *Historical School* came to dominate the investigation of Russian epics. Vsevolod F. Miller, the acknowledged head of this school, to which many scholars contributed, wrote a lengthy series of articles reflecting the aims of the historical approach and eventually brought them together in his three-volume work *Essays on Russian Folk Literature* (Vs.F. Miller 1897–1924). Since Russian chronicles compiled beginning in the eleventh century contained a wealth of information about the history and life of Kievan Rus, Vsevolod Miller considered a folklorist's main task to be a search in the chronicles for specific people and events, as suggested through personal names, toponyms, and realia, that could have served as an impetus for the creation of a given bylina. For instance, the epic hero Dobrynya Nikitich was identified with the historical Dobrynya who was the uncle of Prince Vladimir I, the baptizer of Kievan Rus. The bylina "Dobrynya and the Dragon" is interpreted as depicting the baptism of Kievan Rus and the triumph of Christianity over paganism. The first part of the song "Dunai" is regarded as having its historical basis in the chronicle story about the abduction of Princess Rogneda of Polotsk and her marriage to Prince Vladimir I. In regard to the problem about how the bylina came to exist among northern peasants, Vsevolod Miller proposed what has become known as the *theory of the aristocratic origin of Russian epics* (Vs.F. Miller 1897–1924, 3: 28–29; Astakhova 1966: 52–56). According to him, court singers in Kievan Rus created the bylina, skomorokhs absorbed the tradition, and, after being banished in the middle of the seventeenth century, they transmitted the songs to northern peasants.

The adherents of the Historical School also turned their attention to migratory plots. Vs.F. Miller, his pupil A.V. Markov, and others, such as M.G. Khalanskii, A.I. Liashchenko, and S.K. Shambinago, claimed that the creation of a bylina resulted from the imposition of a specific historical event on a migratory plot. Thus a particular historical person (Dobrynya) and event (the baptism of Rus in 988) were imposed on the ancient story about dragon slaying. This illustrates a process termed *Kievization*—older epic themes were set in Kievan Rus, acquired Kievan heroes, were adjusted to Kievan life, and were adapted to the poetics and language of the bylina. The members of the Historical School also believed that variants collected from peasants in the nineteenth century represented the last stage in the progressive degradation of the original form that court singers had composed in Kievan Rus. In addition, several scholars have assigned the creation of some bylinas to the Muscovite period of Russian history from the fifteenth through the seventeenth century. For example, M.G. Khalanskii (1885: 187–207) concluded that the song "Dyuk," on the basis of the depicted dress, and customs, and architectural decorations, had been created in Moscow rather than in Kiev.

In the early 1920s, A.P. Skaftymov questioned the basic tenets of the Historical School in his book *The Poetics and Genesis of the Bylinas.* He concluded that the adherents of this school had ignored the aesthetic qualities of the bylina and had treated it basically as an expression of history and historical facts. Skaftymov regarded the epic as a form of oral literature in which certain features occur because they enhance the telling of a story. He pointed out that the hero stands at the center of attention and that everything should heighten the presentation of the hero. Skaftymov coined the term *resonating background* (Skaftymov 1994: 145–46) to explain, for instance, why Prince Vladimir is often portrayed as being passive, incompetent, and even cowardly. This portrayal sets off the hero and produces a contrast that would be nullified if Vladimir were glorified instead. The resonating background further confirms the idea that Prince Vladimir in the bylina is not connected with any of several historical princes having that name but functions as a foil to a hero and represents a generalized figure whom many folklorists refer to as the *epic Prince Vladimir.* Skaftymov's innovative approach shifted emphasis away from studying the bylina as a historical document to studying the bylina as an artistic work of oral literature.

During the Stalinist period, lasting roughly from the end of the 1920s into the 1950s in the Soviet Union, the study and interpretation of Russian folklore were expected to conform to ideological demands (Oinas 1984: 131–79; Zemtsovsky and Kunanbaeva 1997). These conditions are mirrored in Iu.M. Sokolov's textbook *Russian Folklore,* which was published in 1941 and has been translated into English (Iu.M. Sokolov 1950). Among other things, folklorists were compelled to ascribe the creation of all folklore to the "working masses." In regard to epics, efforts were made to have singers adapt the bylina to contemporary life and to compose "new songs" (noviny) about Soviet heroes and leaders. The Historical School was condemned, in particular because it belittled the role of the peasantry in the creation of the Russian epic and attributed the songs to court singers. The comparative method of Veselovskii was also held in disrepute. During this time, folklorists shifted their attention to other, previously little touched upon aspects of the bylina, such as the investigation of regional traditions (A.M. Astakhova, *The Russian Epic in the North*, 1948), schools of singers (V.I. Chicherov, *Schools of Narrators in Zaonezhie*, written toward the end of the 1930s but published only in 1982), and the songs of outstanding individual singers (numerous articles by A.M. Astakhova, V.G. Bazanov, and others). Contrary to the assertions of the Historical School, Astakhova (1938, 1: 7–105; 1948) demonstrated that the bylina did not degenerate or stagnate among northern peasants in the nineteenth and twentieth centuries but continued to evolve and to change in a manner consistent with oral epics. She also noted that peasant singers in the nineteenth and twentieth centuries had created new songs and that they had transformed magic tales and ballads into epics.

A new period in the study of the bylina began toward the end of the 1950s with the appearance of V.Ia. Propp's book *The Russian Heroic Epic* (Propp 1958b). Propp (1895–1970) believed that the bylina, as an artistic phenomenon, had not emerged from factual chronicles but from historically conditioned artistic invention. Propp is not so much against the historical study of the bylina as he is against the equating of the bylina and history. Rather than being derived from specific historical events, an epic is formed through the reinterpretation and transformation of preceding tradition. According to Propp's conception, the Kievan epic developed from an earlier epic that had existed among East Slavic tribes long before the founding of the Kievan state in the second half of the ninth century. Other scholars, such as S.I. Nekliudov and particularly E.M. Meletinskii (1963) in his book *The Origin of the Heroic Epic,* supported Propp's conjecture by elucidating an "archaic epic" that had emerged under similar historical and social conditions in the epic traditions of various peoples, particularly those in Siberia and Central Asia.

Propp's book stimulated the formation of the "historical-typological method," which occupies a prominent place in present-day Russian folklore scholarship. Essentially this method attempts to reconcile the conflict between the study of epics from a historical viewpoint and their study from an artistic viewpoint. The vast factual materials that the followers of the borrowing theory, migratory theory, and Historical School had accumulated have consequently received new illumination. The main goal of the historical-typological method is to recreate and to explain the stages of the historical-folklore process on the basis of typological parallels derived from an examination of the traditions of many peoples. On the one hand, a given plot, motif, or character may be manifested in an earlier or in a later form in one specific ethnic tradition; on the other hand, the totality of materials derived from many ethnic traditions permits the delineation of different stages in the development of the same plot, motif, or character. From this perspective, Russian epics have no *Urtext,* and they are not static but undergo adaptation and reinterpretation as they pass through a succession of historical epochs. A given bylina may, in part or in whole, embody features from the pre-Kievan tribal period, Kievan Rus, the Tatar Yoke, Muscovite Russia, or later peasant life. From this it ensues that each epic presents a special group of problems that have to be studied by examining all available variants. In 1960 V.M. Zhirmunskii formulated the theoretical principles of the historical-typological method in his paper "Epic Creations of the Slavic Peoples and Problems of the Comparative Study of the Epic."[13] B.N. Putilov (1971a) and Iu.I. Smirnov (1974) have applied this approach in their studies of epics in Russian and other Slavic languages. In numerous works, Putilov has performed a leading role in defining and applying the historical-typological method to the investigation of the bylina with an emphasis on its artistic and ethnographic qualities. He has refined the approach with concepts such as the epic subtext, epic knowledge, epic memory, and epic milieu.[14]

Since the 1970s, research on the bylina has been characterized by a polyphony of approaches.[15] In their etymological studies, which draw on sources in many languages and traditions, the linguists V.V. Ivanov and V.N. Toporov have given new life to the mythological school by believing, for instance, that a "fundamental myth" about the "thunderer and his adversary" lies at the basis of the folklore tradition of all Indo-European peoples. In regard to the plots of the bylina, Ilya

Muromets, Dobrynya Nikitich, and Alyosha Popovich are treated as transformations of this myth (Ivanov and Toporov 1974: 166–72). S.N. Azbelev (1982) has continued the approach of the Historical School, which had already been revived in the 1960s by M.M. Plisetskii (1962), B.A. Rybakov (1963), and R.S. Lipets (1969). V.P. Anikin (1984) has proposed that a historical chronology of all variants of an epic can be established, V.M. Gatsak (1989) and F.M. Selivanov (1977; 1990) have studied the artistic side of the bylina and its poetics, and the historian I.Ia Froianov and the folklorist Iu.I. Iudin (1993) have delineated pre-Kievan elements in several epics. Following the lead of A.M. Astakhova (1948: 281–332), Iu.A. Novikov (1995) has shown how the publications of epics in the nineteenth and twentieth centuries provided singers with an alternate way to learn "new" songs. Once songs appeared in print, particularly in cheap popular editions, they eventually made their way to villages where, even in a largely illiterate population, some people were literate and read the texts to performers. In this way the bylina in some cases was transmitted by printed rather than oral means and the traditions of different regions became inter-mixed.

Folklore textology, or the accuracy and reliability of published folk-lore texts, represents another subject that has attracted considerable attention among Russian folklorists in recent decades.[16] During the preparation of new editions of some "classic" collections of Russian epics, compilers have examined the collectors' field notes and manu-scripts and have discovered that discrepancies sometimes exist be-tween them and the printed version. It became apparent that collecting methods and editorial practices affect the texts[17] and that mistakes, distortions, and changes might occur at all stages in the existence of a text, from its transcription in the field to its final realization in print. One of the main temptations has involved the urge to "improve" a text by standardizing the language in accordance with the norms of the contemporary standard language. With justification K.V. Chistov (1963) and B.N. Putilov (1963) have emphasized that a healthy skepti-cism should be maintained toward the accuracy of published folklore works at all stages in their study. It stands to reason that the investiga-tion of epics depends just as much on the reliability of the verbal texts as it does on the performances of the finest singers.

In their investigations of folklore textology, in their studies of indi-vidual songs, and in their preparation of new editions, Russian folklorists employ the textological concepts of *variant* and *version*. Unlike written literature, which for the most part exists only in a single fixed form once it has been printed, by its very nature oral literature in a living tradition constitutes an open-ended and continuous process that has no initial or final form. On the contrary, a given bylina may have been transcribed many times, but its variants, to a greater or lesser degree, always differ. Even repeated recordings of the same epic from the same singer exhibit meaningful divergences; such texts are valuable because their comparison offers insights into the way oral epics are composed and leads toward an understanding of the interaction between memorization and improvisation. The existence of variants, or "multi-forms" as Lord calls them (Lord 1965: 100), carries the implication that there is no "original text" and also that there is no complete or ideal text (Putilov 1976: 191–96; 1988: 149–55). The term version describes significant differences in the plot of a particular epic. Thus the song "Ilya Muromets and Falconer" has been collected in approximately 130 variants expressed in two versions of the plot. In the first, less common version, Ilya encounters the bogatyrka Zlatygorka from a distant alien land, lives with her for a time, and leaves. Falconer, the son she later bears from Ilya, grows up and leaves home to attack an outpost manned by Ilya and other bogatyrs. The Russian epic about a conflict between father and son ends when Ilya kills Falconer. The second version of this song omits all the prehistory to this story and begins with Falconer's appearance at the outpost, but it has the same ending.

Translation

In the introduction to her anthology of Russian epics, which was first published in 1932, Nora Kershaw Chadwick points out that their translation into English began in the middle of the past century. Since she has included a list of earlier translations (Chadwick 1964: 8–9) and T.G. Ivanova (1993b) has made a survey of more recent translations, there is no need to repeat them here.[18] The present anthology has followed the general guidelines that Nora Chadwick laid down: the integrity of the texts is observed, that is, variants are not mixed to produce an "ideally complete song," and the identity of the lines is maintained to preserve a sense of poetry. The purpose of this anthology is to convey what V.M. Gatsak (1977) calls a "folkloristic translation,"

that is, all types of repetition and parallelism have been retained insofar as is feasible. Since the language of the bylina, as would be expected in an orally composed epic, abounds in fixed or nearly fixed
phrases and expressions, a deliberate attempt has been made to translate such elements consistently, although it should be understood that
even they are subject to variation. Because the spoken language of the
performers enters into the idiom of the bylina and because direct
speech is common, some aspects of colloquial English, especially
contractions, have been used when appropriate. It has not been possible to convey the overtones of the hypocoristics (affectionates, dimin-
utives, pejoratives, and augmentatives) that abound in the idiom of
Russian epics because direct English equivalents do not exist. Terms
for Old Russian weights and measures as well as specifically Russian
words (bogatyr and druzhina) have been retained so as to preserve a
certain cultural atmosphere. No effort has been made to reproduce the
rhythm of the original, although the English translation has been made
"rhythmical" but without consistent regularity. The variation in the
length of the lines in Russian has also been maintained. Words or
passages that are ambiguous or do not lend themselves to a ready
explanation occasionally occur in the texts of songs and have been left
as such, although a footnote may be included with a suggested interpretation. The basic purpose has been to provide as readable a translation as possible while preserving as many folklore features of the
original Russian as the English language will permit.

This anthology, as was stated earlier, contains examples of all subgenres comprising the Russian epic and, so as to present a cross section of the singers' repertory, also includes two religious verses, two
historical songs, and one ballad. Texts have been taken from all periods in the recording of the bylina beginning with the eighteenth-century collection of Kirsha Danilov and concluding with several songs
recorded in the 1940s and 1950s. As illustrations of the last phase in
the Russian epic tradition, one song has been selected from T.S.
Kuzmin ("Dyuk") and three from A.M. Pashkova, who was literate
and was influenced by her reading ("Svyatogor," "Ilya Muromets
Quarrels with Vladimir," and "Churila"). The translated epics come
from all main geographic regions where the bylina has been collected.
For the most part, variants have been selected that have not been
translated into English before so that those interested in epics will have
an opportunity to compare variants. In a few instances, this was not

The singer A.M. Pashkova. Sketch from the collecton of G.N. Parilova and A.D. Soimonov, *Byliny pudozhskogo kraia,* Petrozavodsk, 1941.

possible because some songs, such as "Volkh Vseslavyevich" in Kirsha Danilov's collection, exist in a single well-formed variant.

Conclusion

The reading, teaching, and translating of Russian epics over several decades has prompted several overall impressions. The presentation of

Russian epics in a course on oral epics unexpectedly revealed that students grasped the general meaning and the story in Russian songs rather easily. This suggests that Russian epics are accessible to a broad audience and that the "cultural load" for appreciating them is less than it is for the epics of some other traditions. The experience in translating Russian songs has inspired great respect for the performers who in many cases were masters of their language and were fine oral poets. One also comes to understand how deeply epics are infused with cultural allusions, history, beliefs, customs, and myth, so much so that they seem almost inexhaustibly rich and suggestive. One also realizes that oral epics should not be judged by preconceived standards about what an epic should be but by the tradition within which these works have been created.

Notes

1. For general information about Russian epics, see these studies: Astakhova 1966; Chadwick and Chadwick 1936; Iudin 1975; Oinas 1984: 9–31; Propp 1958b; Propp and Putilov 1958: iii–lxiv; Putilov 1971a; 1986; Skaftymov 1994; Iu.M. Sokolov 1950.

2. The presentation of information about Russian history has been based chiefly on two works: Riasanovsky 1993 and Vernadsky 1976.

3. For studies about religious verses, see Fedotov 1935, Selivanov 1995, and Veselovskii 1879–91.

4. Gatsak 1973, Krafčik 1976, and Weiher 1972. J. Thomas Shaw 1996 points out that in English a more precise term for "negative comparison" would be "negative analogy."

5. For a summary and bibliography, see Bailey 1993: 39–41.

6. For works about the melodies sung with Russian epics, see Dobrovolskii and Korguzalov 1981; Korguzalov 1966; and Vasileva 1979, 1989.

7. For a survey of the activities of these folklorists, see Ivanova 1993a.

8. Chettéoui 1942, Chistov 1980: 33–109, and Krinichnaia 1995: 5–45.

9. S.I. Dmitrieva 1975 presents a study of the geographic areas where the various plots of Russian epics have been recorded in the nineteenth and the beginning of the twentieth centuries. In regard to her study, see the comments in Vasilev 1990.

10. For surveys of the different approaches to the study of the bylina, see the items in note 1. It should be added that, actually, a large number of fields present valid approaches to the study of the bylina: archeology, beliefs, ethnography, history, linguistics, music, mythology, oral literature, performance theory, poetics, and versification.

11. For a study of this school, see Toporkov 1997.

12. See the items cited for A.N. Veselovskii in the bibliography. V.M. Zhirmunskii has collected many of Veselovskii's studies in a volume entitled

Historical Poetics (Veselovskii 1940). Zhirmunskii has also included a perceptive introduction and extensive commentary.

13. The piece has been reprinted in a collection of Zhirmunskii's works (1979).

14. Among the items cited in the bibliography, Putilov's main studies are *The Methodology of the Comparative-Historical Study of Folklore* (1976) and *The Heroic Epic and Reality* (1988).

15. For the status of the study of Russian epics in recent decades, see the items in the two bibliographies compiled by T.G. Ivanova 1987; 1993.

16. For a brief summary and references, see Bailey 1993: 112–13.

17. For one example, see Ivanova 1982.

18. The main addition involves the anthology of all genres, *Russian Folklore*, prepared by Alex E. Alexander (1975).

RUSSIAN
FOLK
EPICS

❧ I ❧

EPICS ABOUT THE OLDEST HEROES

✌ 1 ❧

Volkh Vseslavyevich

he bylina "Volkh Vseslavyevich" has been collected seventeen times, but most recordings are incomplete or fragmentary except for the variant selected for translation from the collection of Kirsha Danilov. In this Russian expression of the epic theme about the birth of a hero and his first exploit, a series of motifs is combined in an imaginative way: miraculous birth, rapid growth, unusual strength, a born hunter and warrior, investiture of arms, learning wisdom about shape-shifting, collecting a retinue, becoming a leader, first journey, capturing a city, and defeating an adversary. As often is the case in such stories, Volkh has a supernatural origin, since his human mother conceives him from a serpent. Furthermore, his birth is accompanied by three natural portents: a radiant moon, an earthquake, and the surge of the ocean. These events cause fish, birds, and animals to flee in fear, thus indicating that Volkh will be a hunter. As in magic tales, Volkh grows not by the day but by the hour. He soon speaks, and he asks for armor rather than for diapers: a scene presenting the investiture of arms for a future warrior. As a boy he is taught not only reading and writing but also sly wisdom, or shape-shifting. At the age of twelve, Volkh forms his own druzhina, the number 7,000 being an epic exaggeration for the more traditional multiple of 30, and, as an exemplary chieftain, he supplies his druzhina with food and clothing through his shape-shifting and hunting. In order to scout the hostile Indian Kingdom, Volkh first transforms himself into an aurochs with golden horns, the fierce European wild ox that became extinct in the sixteenth century. Volkh then changes himself into a falcon that swiftly flies to the Indian Kingdom and eavesdrops on the Indian Tsar and his wife. One might assume that she has had a prophetic dream and therefore warns her husband about a future enemy who has been born in Kiev. Volkh flies back to his druzhina and

3

returns with it to besiege the Indian Kingdom, which resembles a city more than an entire country. He uses his magical powers to change himself and his retinue into ants that crawl under the gate, restores his men to their original state, orders them to cut down people of all ages except for 7,000 darling maidens, and confronts his adversary, whom he quickly kills. Volkh becomes tsar and marries the former tsar's wife, the members of his druzhina marry the surviving maidens, and booty from the city is divided among the future townspeople.

The bylina about Volkh, whose name is derived from the word *volkhv,* meaning wizard or sorcerer, has provoked a variety of interpretations (Jakobson 1949; Putilov 1971a: 70–78). This song is generally regarded as being one of the most archaic Russian epics because Volkh is the only Russian hero who performs his feats by magic. His miraculous birth from a human mother and serpent father may reflect totemistic beliefs according to which a person's ancestors were animals. Besides this, Volkh may possess several shamanistic traits, such as his ability to transform himself into a bird, animal, or fish and to move rapidly over long distances. Even though Kiev is referred to several times, all actions actually take place outside of a historical setting in Kievan Rus—Prince Vladimir, his court, and bogatyrs play no role in this bylina. Volkh's mother is a princess, but he is not connected in any way with Prince Vladimir, and he acts as an independent ruler. The motif of the kingdom of India has been ascribed to a written tale that was popular in Byzantium and was later translated into Russian, but in Russian epics references to India are probably fictional and indicate merely a distant, wealthy, and exotic foreign country. This explanation is supported by the fact that in other variants the Golden Horde or the Turkish Sultan may be substituted instead. To some extent, the names appearing in this song reflect the Tatar overlay that exists in many Russian epics: the Indian Tsar has a Tatar name (Saltyk Stavrulyevich, line 94), a reference is made to Batu (line 95), who was the grandson of Ghenghis Khan and was Khan of the Golden Horde (1208–55), and, curiously, the tsar's wife has both Tatar (Azdyakovna) and Christian names (Yelena Alexandrovna).

Several scholars have pointed out possible connections between the figure of Volkh and Prince Vseslav Polotsky (1044–1101), in particular the way this prince is described in the Russian *Primary Chronicle* and in the twelfth-century Russian medieval literary epic *The Tale of Igor's Campaign.* Vseslav, whose name means all glory, was considered to have had a miraculous birth since he was born with a caul on his head—the sign of a future werewolf or vampire. He was long involved in struggles with another Russian prince for the rule of Kiev and was known for his ability to move his army with the speed of a werewolf to surprise his enemies. His wife had a prophetic dream and warned him not to go to Kiev because he would be imprisoned, events that later happened, except that a mob soon freed this popular prince from prison. Volkh's patronymic—Vseslavyevich—indicates that his father's given name was Vseslav. Although the epic Volkh and the historical Vseslav share several characteristics, the origins of the main elements in the bylina are more ancient than Kievan Rus and hence Prince Vseslav.

Kirsha Danilov's variant shows that he had an exceptional talent for composing oral epics. This talent is particularly evident in the triad of natural events that accompany Volkh's birth, the triad of creatures that instinctively try to escape the future hunter, and the expected but incomplete triad of birds and animals but no fish into which he has the ability to change. The step-by-step rapid growth of the future hero, the investiture of his arms, and his concern as a leader for the well-being of his druzhina are all composed in a precise and intricate fashion involving the repetition and parallelism characteristic of oral poetry. The early allusion to the Indian Kingdom (line 15) subtly foreshadows Volkh's conquest of the "country," and the Tsaritsa's prophetic words further enhance the idea that from birth Volkh, as a hero, was fated to defeat the Indian Tsar. The boasts of the Indian Tsar about plundering Kiev and destroying the churches and monasteries provide a motivation and justification for Volkh to make a preemptive attack against the Indian Kingdom.

✎   Volkh Vseslavyevich   ✎

Source: Kirsha Danilov, *Ancient Russian Poems*
(Moscow, 1977), pp. 32–36.

Through the garden, through the green garden,
Walked and strolled the young Princess
Marfa Vseslavyevna,
She jumped from a stone on a fierce serpent.
5   The fierce serpent coiled itself
Around her green morocco leather boot,
And around her silken stocking,
With its tail it beat along her white thigh.
At that time the princess became pregnant,
10   She became pregnant and bore a child.
In the sky the bright moon was shining,
In Kiev a mighty bogatyr was born,
The young Volkh Vseslavyevich.
The damp earth trembled,
15   The famous Indian Kingdom shook,
And the blue sea became rough
Because of the bogatyr's birth,
Of young Volkh Vseslavyevich.
Fish went to the bottom of the seas,
20   Birds flew high in the skies,
Aurochs and deer went beyond the mountains,
Hares and foxes went into thickets,
Wolves and bears went into fir groves,
Sable and marten went into stands of trees.
25   And when Volkh was one and a half hours old,
Volkh spoke like thunder roars:
"Hail to you, my lady and mother,
Young Marfa Vseslavyevna!
Don't swaddle me in scarlet diapers,
30   Don't gird me with silken bands,
But swaddle me, mother,
In strong steel armor,

And on my reckless head put a golden helmet,
In my right hand—a mace,
35   A heavy leaded mace,
The mace should weigh three hundred poods."
    And when Volkh was seven years old,
His mother sent him to study reading and writing—
Reading came easily to Volkh.
40   His mother sat him down to write with a pen—
Writing came easily to him.
    And when Volkh was ten years old,
At that time he was taught several wisdoms:
The first wisdom he studied—
45   Was how to turn himself into a bright falcon,
The second wisdom Volkh studied—
Was how to turn himself into a gray wolf,
The third wisdom Volkh studied—
Was how to turn himself into a bay aurochs with
        golden horns.
50   And when Volkh was twelve years old,
He started gathering himself a druzhina,
He gathered a druzhina for three years,
He collected a druzhina of seven thousand.
Volkh himself was fifteen years old,
55   And all his druzhina was fifteen years old.
    A great rumor then reached
The capital city of Kiev.
The Indian Tsar was preparing himself,
He was bragging and boasting,
60   He wanted to plunder the city of Kiev,
And to send God's churches up in smoke
And to ravage the venerable monasteries.
But at that time Volkh was shrewd,
With all his brave druzhina
65   He set out on a campaign
To the famous Indian Kingdom.
    The druzhina slept, but Volkh didn't sleep,
He turned himself into a gray wolf,
He ran and dashed through the dark forests
        and dense trees,

70   He slaughtered the horned elk,
        He gave no quarter to the wolf or bear,
        And sables and snow leopards were his
                favorite morsel,
        He didn't scorn hares and foxes.
        Volkh gave his brave druzhina food and drink,
75   He shod and dressed his good youths,
        They wore sable coats
        And had leopard coats as spares.
                The druzhina slept, but Volkh didn't sleep,
        He turned himself into a bright falcon,
80   He flew far away to the blue sea,
        He slaughtered geese and white swans,
        He gave no quarter to small gray ducks.
        He gave his brave druzhina food and drink,
        And all his dishes were varied,
85   Varied and tasty dishes.
                And Volkh started practicing sorcery.
        "Hail to you, my daring good youths!
        There aren't too many or too few of you—
                seven thousand,
        But brothers, do you have a person,
90   Who would turn himself into a bay aurochs,
        Who would run to the Indian Kingdom,
        Would find out about the Indian Kingdom,
        About Tsar Saltyk Stavrulyevich,
        About his reckless head as one of Batu's clan?"
95   As a blade of grass would flatten out,
        So all his druzhina bowed down,
        The daring good youths answered him:
        "Except for you, our Volkh Vseslavyevich,
        We don't have such a youth."
100   Then Vseslavyevich turned himself
        Into a bay aurochs with golden horns,
        He started running to the Indian Kingdom,
        He made his first bound for a whole verst,
        But no one could see his second bound.
105   He turned himself into a bright falcon,
        He started flying to the Indian Kingdom,

And he arrived in the Indian Kingdom,
And he perched on the white-stone palace,
On the royal palace,
110   And on the window with a wooden frame
Of the Indian Tsar.
Violent winds were blowing over the crusted snow,
The Tsar was conversing with the Tsaritsa.
    The Tsaritsa Azdyakovna spoke,
115   The young Yelena Alexandrovna:
"Hail to you, my famous Indian Tsar!
You wish to prepare for war against Rus,
But you don't know and aren't acquainted with
        one thing—
In the sky a bright moon was shining,
120   And in Kiev a mighty bogatyr was born,
An opponent for you, my Tsar."
    At that time Volkh was shrewd—
Sitting on the window with a wooden frame,
He heard the words they said,
125   He turned himself into an ermine,
He ran through the basements and through
        the cellars,
And through the high chambers,
He bit through the strings of the taut bows,
He pulled out the iron tips of the tempered arrows,
130   From the arms, from the firearms,
He jerked out the flints and ramrods,*
And he buried everything in the ground.
    Volkh turned himself into a bright falcon,
He rose up high in the skies,
135   He flew far away to the open field,
He flew to his brave druzhina.
The druzhina was sleeping, but Volkh
        didn't sleep,
He woke up his daring good youths:
"Hail to you, my brave druzhina!

---

*Obvious anachronisms.

140   It's not time to sleep, it's time to get up,
Let's go to the Indian Kingdom!"
       And they came to the white-stone wall,
The white-stone wall was strong,
The gates of the city were made of iron,
145   All the hinges and bolts were made of copper,
Guards were standing there night and day,
The threshold was made of expensive walrus tusk,
Intricate notches had been carved,
But only a tiny ant could pass through the notches.
150   All the youths became despondent,
They became despondent and sad,
They spoke these words:
"We'll lose our heads in vain,
How can we pass through the wall?"
155   Young Volkh was shrewd.
He turned himself into a tiny ant
And turned all his good youths into tiny ants,
They passed through the white-stone wall
And the youths then stood on the other side
160   Inside the famous Indian Kingdom.
He turned them all into good youths,
They stood there with their fighting gear.
       He gave all his youths an order:
"Hail to you, my brave druzhina!
165   Go through the Indian Kingdom,
Cut down the young and old,
Don't leave any for posterity in the kingdom,
Only choose and leave,
Not too many and not too few—
170   Seven thousand darling pretty maids!"
       And his druzhina went through the Indian Kingdom,
And it cut down the young and old,
And only chose and left
Darling pretty maids.
175   And Volkh himself went into the palace,
Into the royal palace,
To the Tsar, to the Indian Tsar.
The doors of the palace were made of iron,

The hinges and hasps were made of gilded steel.
180   Then Volkh Vseslavyevich spoke:
"Although I might hurt my foot, I have to break down
      the doors!"
With his foot he kicked the iron doors,
He broke all the steel hasps.
He took the Tsar by his white hands,
185   The famous Indian Tsar,
Saltyk Stavrulyevich.
Volkh then spoke these words:
"One doesn't kill or execute tsars like you."
Grabbing him, Volkh struck him against the
      brick floor,
190   He smashed him into pieces of shit.
      Then Volkh himself became tsar,
And took the Tsaritsa Azdyakovna in marriage,
The young Yelena Alexandrovna.
And his brave druzhina
195   Married all those maids.
Then young Volkh became tsar,
And his druzhina became the townspeople.
He rolled out barrels of gold and silver,
And divided steeds and cows into herds,
200   And gave each person one hundred thousand coins.

‹ 2 ›

Svyatogor

Svyatogor appears mainly in two subjects among Russian epics. In the first one, he finds a bag that is too heavy for him to lift and sinks into the ground; in the other one he comes across a coffin, lies down in it to try its size, and becomes trapped. Both stories end with the death of the hero, something that rarely happens in Russian epics. Although the first subject has been recorded six times and the second fifty times, many of the texts are composed in prose rather than in verse, a feature that perhaps shows how these songs were being forgotten or else reflects the gradual decline of the Russian epic tradition. Moreover, the narratives tend to be terse and are not highly developed. The translated variant represents a composite of both subjects, the first ending at line forty-four and concluding with the rescue of Svyatogor by his horse rather than with his death.

Few Russian epics have prompted as many different interpretations as those about Svyatogor, a situation that probably results from the mysterious and apparently incomplete nature of the stories themselves (Mazon 1932; Smolitskii 1972). The basic question concerns the reason why Svyatogor, whose name means "Holy mountain," is fated to die. Is he being punished for misdeeds, and, if so, what precisely is he guilty of? In the songs, Svyatogor is associated with distant mountains such as Mount Ararat in eastern Turkey near the Armenian border, the Mount of Olives in the Holy Land, and the Holy Mountains, which may refer to Mount Zion in the Holy Land or to Mount Athos in Greece. During the Middle Ages, Russian Orthodox pilgrims often visited Mount Athos, where many monasteries exist to this day. Svyatogor's outward appearance alone sets him apart from the ordinary human world. He is a giant (his shoulders are two yards wide), he possesses fantastic strength, he shakes the earth when he walks, he is at home only in the mountains and not in the open field, he is impervious to Ilya's blows with a club weighing forty poods, and he easily picks up Ilya and his horse to put them in his pocket.

Most folklorists agree that Svyatogor represents an "older" type of hero than the "younger" heroes such as Dobrynya Nikitich, Alyosha Popovich, and Ilya Muromets. Consequently, the songs about Svyatogor are believed to signify a change of generations among epic heroes. This distinction emerges most clearly in the second subject, where Ilya, when he appears in the work, forms an implicit contrast and comparison. Svyatogor is a "loner," he does not belong to any ethnos, he accomplishes nothing that benefits a particular group of people, he exists outside any national or historical setting, and he, as a member of a doomed generation of giants, may vaguely reflect mythological beliefs or primeval natural elements. In contrast, Ilya Muromets is a hero of the new generation, he belongs entirely to the human world, he is an ordinary person who nevertheless has unusual strength, he lives during the historical epoch of Kievan Rus, and, as a "Holy Russian" bogatyr, he is closely connected with his ethnos. In Kievan Rus heroism was determined not solely by physical strength but by the goals that this strength served. Svyatogor never finds any practical application for his enormous strength, and he never performs any heroic exploits. Thus in the epic consciousness of the singers, Svyatogor is not a Kievan hero.

The saddlebag or the "skomorokh's little bag" that Svyatogor finds but cannot lift has especially attracted the attention of scholars, who have tried to explain this suggestive but obscure symbol. Some connect the bag with a preceding episode in the epic biography of Svyatogor and with a widely occurring motif that involves a religious and moral judgment of someone who challenges God or death. In some variants, Svyatogor boasts that he could lift the entire earth if he could find a place to support him. The fateful bag, which constitutes both a test and a lesson for Svyatogor, symbolizes the weight of the whole earth, which even a giant cannot lift. If the epic is interpreted as containing a hidden moral story, Svyatogor's words represent arrogant and unrestrained bragging, for which he is punished. In the end, Svyatogor may come to understand his guilt and to accept his fate when he says "It's certain that death has come to me." A similar course of events occurs in South Slavic epics where God, having heard the boasting of a hero, sends him an angel with a bag whose weight is equal to that of the earth.

A common epic motif appears in the second subject: two bogatyrs accidentally meet in the open field; both are looking for a fight, and they end their ensuing duel by becoming sworn brothers. However, in the translated variant something different initially happens because Svyatogor is asleep on his horse and is not seeking someone to cross swords with. This infuriates Ilya, who tries in vain to strike Svyatogor three times. Svyatogor finally complains about biting flies, picks Ilya up by the hair, and puts him and his horse in his pocket. Rather than fighting a duel, Ilya wisely says that he wants to become a sworn brother with Svyatogor. The following episode about finding and measuring a coffin is connected with the fate of a hero in many traditions and demonstrates that even such a giant as Svyatogor cannot escape death. The transfer of strength from one person to another through breath represents another motif in folklore. In the Russian epic, after realizing that his fated time has come, Svyatogor offers to transfer part of his strength to a member of the younger generation of heroes, that is, to Ilya Muromets. In the translated variant, Ilya refuses to accept even a little power because he fears he would become a giant too heavy for the earth to bear.

The bylina about Svyatogor contains several motifs that are widespread in world folklore. The song contains several biblical references, in particular to Samson, whose name appears in some variants, is related to medieval tales about a quarrel with death; and, in the Russian folklore tradition, shares elements with the genre called "religious verses," which are devoted to religious and moral themes. This especially concerns the main character in the song "Anika the Warrior": all his life he has robbed, pillaged, destroyed, and killed, and in the end he attacks even death itself.

E.P. Rodina collected this epic in 1938 in the Pudoga Region of Karelia from the outstanding woman performer A.M. Pashkova.

∽ Svyatogor ∾

Source: G.N. Parilova and A.D. Soimonov,
Bylinas of the Pudoga Region (Petrozavodsk, 1941), pp. 98–102.

Not far, not far away in the open field
A cloud of dust was swirling,
Dust was swirling in a column,
A good youth appeared in the field,
5   Svyatogor, the mighty Russian bogatyr.
Svyatogor had a steed like a fierce wild animal,
The bogatyr's shoulders were more than
          two yards wide,
He was riding in the field and was amusing
          himself,
He was throwing his steel mace
10   Higher than the towering forest,
But lower than the moving clouds.
His mace would fly away
High up in the skies,
When the mace would come down,
15   He'd catch it with one hand.
     Svyatogor the bogatyr came across
A skomorokh's* little bag in the open field.
He didn't dismount his good steed,
He wanted to lift the bag with his whip,
20   But the little bag wouldn't be moved.
Svyatogor dismounted his good steed,
He took the little bag with one hand,
But the little bag wouldn't be budged.
He took it with both his hands,
25   He strained with all his bogatyr's strength,
He sank into the mother damp earth up
          to his knees,
But the little bag wouldn't be budged,

---

*It is not clear how the skomorokhs are connected with the bag.

It wouldn't be budged and couldn't be lifted.
Svyatogor said to himself:
30   "I've ridden much around the world,
But I've never seen such a wonder,
The little bag won't be budged,
It won't be budged and can't be lifted,
It won't give way to my bogatyr's strength."
35   Svyatogor spoke these words:
"It's certain that death has come to me,
       Svyatogor."
And he implored his steed:
"Hail to you, my faithful bogatyr's steed!
Now come save your master."
40   He took ahold of the silver bridle,
He took ahold of the gilded girth,
He took ahold of the silver stirrup.
His bogatyr's steed then strained itself,
And it pulled Svyatogor out of the damp earth.
45   Then Svyatogor mounted his good steed
And rode through the open field
Toward the Ararat Mountains.
Svyatogor became tired and worn out
From the skomorokh's little bag
50   And he fell asleep on his good steed,
He fell asleep with a bogatyr's deep sleep.
       From far, far away, from the open field,
Came riding out the old Cossack Ilya Muromets,
Ilya Muromets, the son of Ivan.
55   He saw Svyatogor the bogatyr:
"What kind of wonder do I see in the open field—
A bogatyr is riding on a good steed,
The steed under the bogatyr is like a fierce
       wild animal,
And the bogatyr is sleeping very soundly."
60   Then Ilya shouted in a shrill voice:
"Hail to you, my daring good youth!
Are you making fun of me, youth?
Are you sleeping or just pretending, bogatyr?
Aren't you trying to trick me, the old one?

65   I can give you an answer in kind."*
      There was no answer from the bogatyr.
      Ilya shouted even louder than before,
      Louder than before, in a shrill voice—
         There was no answer from the bogatyr.
70   Ilya's bogatyr rage flared up,
      The rage of the old Cossack Ilya Muromets.
      Then he took his steel mace,
      He struck the bogatyr on his white chest,
      But the bogatyr kept sleeping and didn't
         wake up.
75   Then Ilya Muromets grew angry,
      He rode out into the open field
      And with a running start he struck the bogatyr
      Even harder than before with his steel mace—
      The bogatyr kept sleeping and didn't wake up.
80   Then the old Cossack Ilya Muromets grew
         angry,
      He took his traveling club,
      It wasn't a small club but weighed forty poods,
      He made a running start from the open field
      And struck the bogatyr on his white chest,
85   Ilya injured his right hand.
         Then the bogatyr on the steed woke up,
      The bogatyr spoke these words:
      "Oh, how badly Russian flies can bite!"
      The bogatyr glanced to his right,
90   Then he saw Ilya Muromets,
      He took Ilya by his yellow curls,
      He put Ilya in his pocket,
      Ilya together with his bogatyr's horse,
      And he started riding to the holy mountains,
95   To the holy Ararat Mountains.
      He rode all day until evening,
      He rode the whole dark night until morning,
      He rode a second day until evening,

---

*Ilya is willing to fight or talk but suspects that Svyatogor is feigning sleep to gain an advantage.

He rode the whole dark night until morning,
100 And on the third day
His bogatyr's steed started stumbling.
        Svyatogor spoke to his good steed:
"Oh you food for wolves and bag of grass,
You dog, why are you stumbling?
105 Can't you walk, or don't you want to carry me?"
        The faithful bogatyr's steed then spoke,
It spoke in a human voice:
"Please forgive me, master,
Please let me say a few words.
110 Three whole days without resting my legs
I've been carrying two mighty Russian
                bogatyrs,
And as a third a bogatyr's steed."
        Then Svyatogor the bogatyr felt
That he had something heavy in his pocket.
115 He took Ilya by his yellow curls,
He put Ilya on the damp earth
Together with his bogatyr's steed.
He started asking him and questioning him:
"Tell me, my daring good youth,
120 What land and what country are you from?
If you're a Holy Russian bogatyr,
Then let's go riding to the open field,
Let's test our bogatyr's strength."
        Ilya spoke these words:
125 "Hail to you, my daring good youth!
I can see your great strength,
I don't want to fight with you,
I wish to become a sworn brother with you."
        Svyatogor the bogatyr agreed,
130 He dismounted his good steed,
And then they pitched a white tent,
And they let their steeds go to the green
                meadows.
They hobbled them for the green meadows.
They got together in the white tent,
135 They told each other stories about themselves,

They exchanged golden crosses,
They became sworn brothers,
They embraced and kissed each other.
Svyatogor the bogatyr would be the big brother
140 And Ilya Muromets would be the little brother.
Then they took part in a meal,
They carved up a white swan
And they lay down in the tent to take a rest.
And they didn't sleep a short or a long time—
        just three whole days,
145 On the fourth day they woke up,
They set off along the road and along the path.
They saddled their good steeds,
They didn't ride to the open field,
But they rode to the holy mountains,
150 To the holy Ararat Mountains.
They galloped up to the Mount of Olives,
They saw a wondrous wonder,
A wondrous wonder and a marvelous marvel.
There on the Mount of Olives
155 Was lying an oaken coffin.
The bogatyrs dismounted their steeds,
They bent down over the coffin.
    Svyatogor spoke these words:
"Who's destined to lie in this coffin?
160 Listen, my little brother,
Lie down in the coffin and measure yourself,
Find out whether this oaken coffin fits you."
    Ilya Muromets obeyed
His big brother immediately,
165 Ilya lay down in the oaken coffin.
The coffin didn't fit Ilya,
It was too long in length and too wide in width,
And Ilya got out of the coffin.
Svyatogor the bogatyr lay down in the coffin,
170 The coffin fitted Svyatogor,
It was his size in length and just right in width.
    Svyatogor said to Ilya Muromets:
"Hail to you, Ilya, my little brother!

Please close the oaken lid,
175   I'll lie awhile in the coffin and admire it."
        When Ilya closed the oaken lid,
        Svyatogor said these words:
        "Hail to you, Ilya Muromets!
        The air's too heavy for me to lie in the coffin
180   And the air's too stifling for me to breathe,
        Please open the oaken lid,
        Please give me some fresh air."
        The lid couldn't be lifted,
        It wouldn't open even a crack.
185   Svyatogor said these words:
        "Smash the lid with your sharp saber."
        Ilya obeyed Svyatogor,
        He took his own sharp saber,
        He struck the oaken coffin.
190   Wherever Ilya Muromets would strike
        Iron hoops would appear.
        Ilya struck all up and down—
        The iron hoops kept on appearing.
        Svyatogor spoke these words:
195   "Hail to you, my little brother, Ilya Muromets!
        It seems to be the end for me, the bogatyr,
        Please bury me in the damp earth,
        Please take my bogatyr's steed,
        Please bend down to the oaken coffin,
200   I'll breathe in your white face,
        So that your strength will grow."
        Ilya spoke these words:
        "I have streaks of gray on my head,
        I don't need your strength,
205   I have strength enough of my own.
        If my strength were to grow,
        The mother damp earth wouldn't bear me.
        And I don't need your bogatyr's horse,
        My shaggy old Burushko
210   Has served me loyally and truthfully."
        Then the brothers said farewell,
        Svyatogor stayed lying in the damp earth,

And Ilya Muromets rode through Holy Russia,
To the city, to the city of Kiev,
215   To the gracious Prince Vladimir.
Ilya told the story about the wondrous wonder,
How he buried Svyatogor the bogatyr
On the Mount of Olives.
       A song of praise has been sung to Svyatogor,
220   And praise has been given to Ilya Muromets,
And with this the epic has come to an end.

II

KIEVAN CYCLE

Epics About Ilya Muromets

3

Ilya Muromets and Nightingale the Robber

*A*s the central figure in the Russian epic tradition, Ilya Muromets is the subject of more songs and has a more complete epic biography than any other bogatyr (Astakhova 1958: 393–419). His appearance as "Ilyas von Riuzen" in several German and Scandinavian sagas dating from the twelfth and thirteenth centuries reveals that he was an established hero by that time in Kievan epics. Since that period the characteristics of Ilya Muromets as an epic hero have undoubtedly changed. For example, even though he is frequently referred to as an "old Cossack," folklorists believe that this appellation appeared in the sixteenth or seventeenth century. They also note that the adjective "old" does not indicate age but rather respect, experience, and seniority. The image of Ilya appears to have evolved further in the nineteenth century when peasant performers started emphasizing his peasant background. The importance of Ilya Muromets in Russian culture is also shown by the fact that his relics were long believed to lie in a Kiev monastery and that he appeared in many tales circulated in chapbooks in the eighteenth and nineteenth centuries.

The song "Ilya Muromets and Nightingale the Robber" has been recorded 132 times and is one of the most popular Russian epics. Singers may more accurately call this bylina "The First Journey of Ilya Muromets" because in it he leaves his village of Karacharovo near the city of Murom (the names vary), performs his first exploits, and for the first time comes to Kiev, where he is accepted as a bogatyr at Prince Vladimir's court. The events in other songs about Ilya largely do not follow any chronological order: "Ilya and Idolishche," "Ilya and the

Highwaymen," "The Three Journeys of Ilya Muromets," "Ilya Muromets and Falconer," "Ilya Muromets's Fight with Dobrynya," "Ilya Muromets Quarrels with Prince Vladimir," and "Ilya Muromets and Kalin Tsar." However, the earliest part of this hero's biography appears in a work entitled "The Cure of Ilya Muromets," where Ilya is presented as the son of peasants and lies paralyzed on a stove for thirty years. He is miraculously cured by several passing pilgrims whom he befriends and who give him something special to drink. Ilya then helps his parents clear a field by uprooting whole trees and, realizing that he now has the strength of a bogatyr, he leaves home on his first journey. From the mysterious pilgrims Ilya also learns that he is not fated to die in battle. "The Cure of Ilya Muromets" probably is a relatively recent work, is composed in prose instead of verse, and reflects the attempt by singers to complete Ilya's epic biography by describing his childhood and peasant origin.

Although the confrontation with Nightingale the Robber forms the core of this epic, three conflicts actually occur: the battle near the city of Chernigov, the clash with Nightingale, and disbelief about Ilya's exploits at Vladimir's court (Propp 1958b: 237–86; Skaftymov 1994: 112–27). The work as a whole forms an extended temporal hyperbole—Ilya leaves home after matins and wants to be in Kiev for vespers. Furthermore, the action may take place on Easter Sunday and may involve Ilya's vow not to shed blood on a religious holiday. In the translated variant, these background features fade away since Ilya goes directly to Vladimir's court rather than to church after arriving in Kiev.

During the first conflict, Ilya frees the besieged city of Chernigov, which is located about a hundred miles north of Kiev and for which several names may be substituted. The ethnic origin of the hostile force is not clear, although in some recordings Tatars or Lithuanians may be mentioned. Most likely this part of the song concerns conflicts with the Pechenegs, Khazars, or Polovetsians, since these groups were the main opponents of Kievan Rus from the tenth through the twelfth centuries.

The second conflict in the bylina about Nightingale the Robber involves a hero's fight with a monster, a theme that also appears in the Russian epics "Dobrynya and the Dragon," "Alyosha and Tugarin," and "Ilya Muromets and Idolishche." Such monsters are mythological in origin, but in the Russian tradition they represent a fantastic hybrid of zoomorphic and anthropomorphic characteristics that lose their distinctiveness, become more humanlike, and may receive Turkic or Tatar names. Nightingale's various possible patronymics (Rakhmatovich or Odikhmantevich) are examples of this last tendency. The strange "Black Swamp," the sometimes magical "cross of Lebanon," and the river "Smorodina," near which heroes in Russian folklore may meet their adversaries, suggest a group of ominous boundary markers for the otherworld and heighten the mythological associations of Nightingale. Despite these details, the description of Nightingale remains vague. Although the noun nightingale (*solovei*) was used as a personal name in Kievan Rus, in this instance the word nevertheless implies something avian. Nightingale flies, sits in a tree, has a nest, and is brought down as wild game; at the same time, he has a human family and accepts a goblet of wine with his hands. His main talent as a monster is his ability to utter a shriek that devastates everything around him. Even though this song also involves the epic theme about a "roadblocker," Nightingale, despite his nickname, is not actually a "robber" or "highwayman," a subject that is developed separately in the bylina "Ilya and the Highwaymen."

The third conflict arises after Ilya arrives in Kiev. He is met with skepticism because Vladimir and his court do not believe that he could have defeated the unknown force surrounding Chernigov and that he could have passed by Nightingale the Robber on the short road to Kiev without a struggle. Besides this, Vladimir insults Ilya by calling him a "peasant bumpkin" and a liar, words that set the stage for another song entitled "Ilya's Quarrel with Vladimir." In the chosen variant, Ilya takes Vladimir and his boyars to see Nightingale, who, after being asked to perform with a half-shriek, scares everyone with a full shriek and wrecks neighboring buildings. The bylina usually ends when Ilya executes Nightingale. Thus Ilya becomes recognized as a bogatyr in Kiev, and, through his symbolic clearing of the road to Kiev, he becomes a uniter and defender of Kievan Rus. Ilya's character is clearly delineated as that of a bogatyr who is courageous, deals calmly with difficult situations, is not distracted by personal animosity, and has a strong sense of duty to the Russian land.

The bylina "Ilya Muromets and Nightingale the Robber" reflects a transitional period in the Russian epic tradition when mythological features were blended with historical features. The glorification of a hero who has defeated a monster no longer could satisfy the artistic sense of singers. As a result, a struggle with a monster was losing its heroic appeal, and only a person who fought a real historical opponent could become a bogatyr. Thus the mythological Nightingale acquires partial human characteristics and a Turkic patronymic; the hostile force near Chernigov dimly suggests struggles with the historical adversaries of Kievan Rus. The conflict between the peasant Ilya Muromets and Prince Vladimir and his boyars can be regarded as being a more recent modification of this bylina as it has gradually been adapted to changing social and historical circumstances.

A.F. Gilferding recorded the translated variant in 1871 in Kizhi District of Olonets Province from one of the most talented Russian singers, T.G. Riabinin, who founded an epic dynasty that lasted four generations.

Ilya Muromets
and Nightingale the Robber

Source: A.F. Gilferding, *Onega Bylinas*, 4th ed., vol. 2 (Moscow, 1950), no. 74.

From the city of Murom,
From the village of Karacharovo,
Rode a daring and stout good youth.
He attended matins in Murom,
5   He wanted to be in time for vespers in the
          capital city of Kiev.
     He rode up to the famous city of Chernigov.
Near the city of Chernigov
A vast army had been assembled,
A vast army as black as a black raven.
10   No one walked past there on foot,
No one rode past there on a good steed,
No bird, no black raven flew past,
No gray animal scoured past.
     Ilya rode up to this great army,
15   He attacked this great army,
He trampled it with his steed and jabbed it
          with his spear,

He defeated this great army.
He rode up to the famous city of Chernigov,
The men of Chernigov came out
20 And opened the gates to the city of Chernigov,
They invited Ilya to become voyevoda in
        Chernigov.
    Ilya spoke these words to them:
"Hail to you, my men of Chernigov!
I won't become voyevoda in Chernigov.
25 Point out for me the straight-traveled road,
The straight-traveled road to the capital city
        of Kiev."
    The men of Chernigov spoke to him:
"Hail to you, our daring stout good youth,
Famous Holy Russian bogatyr!
30 The straight-traveled road is filled with fallen wood,
The road is filled and is overgrown with grass,
Along that straight-traveled road
No one has passed on foot,
No one has ridden past on a good steed.
35 By that Swamp, by that Black Swamp,
By that birch, by that crooked birch,
By that stream, by Smorodina,
By that cross, by that cross of Lebanon
Sits Nightingale the Robber in a damp oak,
40 Sits Nightingale the Robber, Odikhmanty's son.
Nightingale whistles like a nightingale,*
He screams, the villain robber, like a wild animal,
And from the whistle of a nightingale,
And from the scream of a wild animal
45 All the grasses and meadows become entangled,
All the azure flowers lose their petals,
All the dark woods bend down to the earth,
And all the people there lie dead.
The straight-traveled road is five hundred versts,
50 But the round-about road is a whole thousand."

---

*This redundant combination results because singers sometimes include a nightingale whistle as one element in the description of a monster.

Ilya urged on his bogatyr's good steed,
He rode along the straight-traveled road.
His bogatyr's good steed
Jumped from mountain to mountain
55   And bounded from hill to hill,
It leaped across small streams and lakes.
He rode up to the stream Smorodina,
Up to that Swamp, up to that Black Swamp,
Up to that birch, up to that crooked birch,
60   Up to that cross, up to that famous Lebanese
            cross.
Nightingale whistled like a nightingale,
The villain robber screamed like a wild animal
So that all the grasses and meadows became
            entangled,
The azure flowers lost their petals,
65   All the dark woods bent down to the earth.
        His bogatyr's good steed
Stumbled against some roots.
The old Cossack Ilya Muromets
Took his silken whip in one white hand
70   And he beat his steed on its strong ribs.
Ilya spoke these words:
"You food for wolves and bag of grass!
Don't you want to walk or can't you carry me?
Dog, what are you stumbling against some
            roots for?
75   Haven't you heard the whistle of a nightingale?
Haven't you heard the scream of a wild animal?
Haven't you felt the blows of a bogatyr?"
        Then the old Cossack Ilya Muromets
Took his taut supple bow,
80   He took it in his white hands,
He stretched the silken string,
He laid on a tempered arrow,
Then he shot it at Nightingale the Robber,
He knocked out Nightingale's right eye and
            temple,
85   He dropped Nightingale to the damp earth,

He tied him to his right steel stirrup,
He carried him through the famous open field,
He carried him past Nightingale's nest.
    In Nightingale's nest
90   There happened to be three daughters,
His three beloved daughters.
The oldest daughter was looking out the window
        with a wooden frame,
She spoke these words:
"Our father's riding through the open field,
95   He's riding a good steed,
He's carrying a peasant bumpkin
Who's fastened to his right stirrup."
    His second beloved daughter took a look,
She spoke these words:
100   "Father's riding through the plain, the
        open field,
He's carrying a peasant bumpkin
Who's fastened to his right stirrup."
    The youngest beloved daughter took a look,
She spoke these words:
105   "A peasant bumpkin is coming,
The peasant is riding a good steed,
He's carrying our father on a stirrup,
Our father's fastened to a steel stirrup,
His right eye and temple have been knocked out."
110   She spoke these words:
"Hail to you, our beloved husbands!
Please take your hunting spears,
Please run into the plain, the open field,
Please kill the peasant bumpkin."
115   Their beloved husbands
Are Nightingale's sons-in-law,
They grabbed their hunting spears,
They ran into the open field
Toward the peasant bumpkin,
120   They wanted to kill the peasant bumpkin.
    Nightingale the Robber, Odikhmanty's son,
        then spoke to them:

"Hail to you, my beloved sons-in-law!
Throw down your hunting spears,
Invite the peasant bumpkin,
125 Invite him into Nightingale's nest,
Feed him tasty food,
Give him mead to drink,
Present him with precious gifts."
The sons-in-law of Nightingale
130 Threw down their hunting spears,
They invited the peasant bumpkin
Into Nightingale's nest.
The peasant bumpkin didn't listen,
He kept on riding through the famous open field
135 Along the straight-traveled road to the
capital city of Kiev.
He came to the famous capital city of Kiev
And went to the wide courtyard of the famous
Prince.
Vladimir the Prince had left God's church,
He had gone to his white-stone palace
140 To his hall, to his dining hall.
They had sat down to eat, to drink, and to take
bread,
To take bread and to have dinner.
The old Cossack Ilya Muromets
Left his steed in the middle of the courtyard,
145 He entered the white-stone palace,
He passed into the dining hall,
He flung the door wide open,
He crossed himself as was prescribed,
He made bows as was instructed,
150 He bowed low in three directions, then in a
fourth,
In particular to Prince Vladimir himself,
Ilya also bowed to all Vladimir's subject princes.
Vladimir the Prince then questioned the youth:
"Please tell me where you're from, stout good
youth,
155 What name do they call the youth by,

What patronymic do they honor the daring
    youth by?"
The old Cossack Ilya Muromets spoke:
"I'm from the famous city of Murom,
From the village of Karacharovo,
160   I'm the old Cossack Ilya Muromets,
Ilya Muromets, the son of Ivan!"
Vladimir spoke these words to him:
"Hail to you, old Cossack Ilya Muromets,
Did you leave from Murom a long time ago
165   And by which road did you ride to the capital
    city of Kiev?"
Ilya spoke these words:
"Hail to you, our famous Vladimir of capital
    Kiev!
I attended Christ's matins in Murom
And I wanted to be in time for vespers in the
    capital city of Kiev.
170   Then my journey was delayed.
I rode along the straight-traveled road,
Along the straight-traveled road I rode past the
    city of Chernigov,
I rode past that Swamp, past that Black Swamp,
Past that famous stream Smorodina,
175   Past that famous crooked birch,
I rode past that famous Lebanese cross."
Vladimir spoke these words to him:
"Hail to you, my peasant bumpkin!
Peasant, you lie before my eyes,
180   Peasant, you mock me before my eyes!
Since an army of great number has been
    assembled
Near the famous city of Chernigov,
No one has walked past on foot,
And no one has ridden past on a good steed,
185   No gray beast has scoured past there,
No bird, no black raven has flown past.
By that Swamp, by that Black Swamp,
By that famous stream, by Smorodina,

By that birch, by that crooked birch,

190   By that cross, by that Lebanese cross
Sits Nightingale the Robber, Odikhmanty's son.
When Nightingale whistles like a nightingale,
When the villain robber screams like a wild
        animal,
Then all the grasses and meadows become
        entangled,

195   The azure flowers lose their petals,
All the dark woods bend down to the earth,
And all the people there lie dead."
      Ilya spoke these words to him:
"Vladimir, Prince of capital Kiev!

200   Nightingale the Robber is in your courtyard,
His right eye and temple have been knocked out,
And he's fastened to a steel stirrup."
      Then Vladimir, Prince of capital Kiev,
Quickly stood up on his nimble feet,

205   He threw his marten coat on one shoulder,
Then he threw his sable hat on one ear,
He went to his wide courtyard
To look at Nightingale the Robber.
Vladimir the Prince then spoke these words:

210   "Whistle, Nightingale, like a nightingale!
Scream, dog, like a wild animal!"
      Nightingale the Robber, Odikhmanty's son, then
        spoke to him:
"Prince, I didn't eat dinner today with you,
You aren't the one I want to listen to,

215   I ate dinner with the old Cossack Ilya Muromets,
I want to listen to him."
      Vladimir, Prince of capital Kiev, spoke:
"Hail to you, old Cossack Ilya Muromets!
Order Nightingale to whistle like a nightingale,

220   Order him to scream like a wild animal."
      Ilya spoke these words:
"Hail to you, Nightingale the Robber,
        Odikhmanty's son!
Whistle just half a nightingale's whistle,

Scream just half a wild animal's scream."
225   Nightingale the Robber, Odikhmanty's son,
             then spoke to him:
"Hail to you, old Cossack Ilya Muromets!
My bloody wounds have opened,
And my sweet lips won't move,
I can't whistle like a nightingale,
230 I can't scream like a wild animal.
Please order Prince Vladimir
To pour me a goblet of green wine,
When I drink a goblet of green wine,
My bloody wounds will disappear,
235 And my sweet lips will part.
Then I'll whistle like a nightingale,
Then I'll scream like a wild animal."
      Ilya spoke to Prince Vladimir:
"Vladimir, Prince of capital Kiev!
240 Go to your hall, to your dining hall,
Please pour a goblet of green wine,
Not a small chalice but a bucket and a half,
Please bring it to Nightingale the Robber."
      Then Vladimir, Prince of capital Kiev,
245 Quickly went to his dining hall,
He poured a goblet of green wine,
Not a small chalice but a bucket and a half,
He mixed it with mellowed mead,
He brought it to Nightingale the Robber.
250 Nightingale the Robber, Odikhmanty's son,
Accepted the goblet from the Prince with one
             hand,
Nightingale drank the goblet in one draught,
Nightingale then whistled like a nightingale,
The Robber screamed like a wild animal.
255 The cupolas on the palaces were twisted,
And the windows in the palaces were shattered
From the nightingale's whistle,
And all the people there lay dead.
Vladimir, Prince of capital Kiev,
260 Took cover under his marten coat.

Then the old Cossack Ilya Muromets
Quickly mounted his good steed,
He took Nightingale to the open field
And he cut off his reckless head.
265   Ilya spoke these words:
"You've whistled enough like a nightingale,
You've screamed enough like a wild animal,
You've made enough fathers and mothers cry,
You've made enough young wives widows,
270   You've made enough little children orphans."
Since then a song of praise has been sung to
    Nightingale,
A song of praise has been sung to him for
    ever after.

4

Ilya Muromets and Falconer

*T*he bylina about "Falconer" is devoted to the age-old story about the fight of a father and a son. The Persian "Sorab and Rustem" as retold by Firdausi, the German "Hildebrandslied," and the Armenian "David of Sassoun" are other well-known examples of this traditional epic theme. Although the Russian realization of this subject has been attributed to Eastern or Western sources, it seems to be unique in several respects and always ends with the death of the son (Putilov 1971b: 83–90).

The song about the conflict between Ilya Muromets and his son Falconer has been collected 130 times and is one of the most popular Russian epics. Two basic versions of the plot can be distinguished among the variants. The less common first version begins with a description of how Ilya meets, fights, and subdues a maiden warrior, or bogatyrka. He may marry her and may live with her for awhile but leaves after giving her tokens of recognition for their future child, such as a cross for a son or a ring for a daughter. After a son is born and grows up rapidly like a future epic hero, he may ask or force his mother to reveal the name of his father. Even though she may warn him not to fight his father, Falconer leaves his home and finds Ilya at an outpost where they fight until Ilya finally recognizes his son and accepts him. Later the son tries to kill his sleeping father but is killed by him instead.

Depending on the variant, the mother may have several names, two of which, "Zlatygorka" (Golden Mountain) or "Semigorka" (Seven Mountains), have mythological implications. She is also addressed with the word *baba,* which is derogatory in today's standard Russian but means wife or woman in peasant speech. As in the translated variant, the opening emphasizes the mother's foreign origin, her association with the distant sea and mountains, and the mysterious but magical "Latyr stone," a legendary altar stone that is often mentioned in Russian songs. These allusions, along with the color gold, suggest that the mother has connections with the otherworld and with the supernatural. The son may be nameless, or he may have various names, the most frequent being "Falconer," which at one time may have been a rank at court. In Russian epics, an affair or marriage between a bogatyr and a foreign woman involved with the supernatural usually ends disastrously for one or both parties.

The second version of the song opens at an outpost on the frontier with the "open field," or steppe, where bogatyrs stand guard against attacks by enemies of the Kievan state. Falconer comes as such an opponent (lines 121–33) and challenges the Russian heroes. Among them are Dobrynya, Alyosha, Ilya, and Dolgopoly, the last being a rarely met bogatyr whose name means "long skirts," as in the tails on a coat. After they discuss who should confront the stranger, Ilya decides to take up the challenge to fight Falconer, who is described almost with the same words as Nightingale the Robber (lines 168–75). A lengthy battle takes place with sabers, spears, and maces and is followed by hand-to-hand fighting in which Falconer overcomes Ilya. After he prays for and receives divine intervention, Ilya regains his strength, defeats Falconer, repeatedly asks his name, and finally recognizes his son. After an apparent reconciliation, Falconer goes home, kills his mother, and returns to kill his father. Falconer finds Ilya sleeping and hurls a spear at him, but Ilya, protected by the cross he is wearing, wakes up and kills his son.

The motivation for Falconer's determined and aggressive actions is not clear. On this point the epic is both terse and objective and conveys no inner feelings experienced by the main characters. Why does Falconer seek his father? Where does he really come from? Why don't father and son recognize each other? Why does Falconer kill his mother and then try to kill his father? According to one explanation of the subtext underlying these events, this bylina reflects the clash of two different epochs, that is, a matriarchy and a patriarchy (Avizhanskaia 1947). Under a matriarchy, marriages were exogamous (the husband and wife belonged to different groups); marriages were matrilocal (they lived on the territory of the wife's group); marriages were matrilineal (children belonged to the mother's group and often did not know their father); or marriages were intentionally short. With the advent of a patriarchal age, such transient marriages were condemned, and children with an unknown father were considered illegitimate. According to this viewpoint, the Russian presentation of a conflict between father and son contains features of a matriarchal society that are judged negatively by the standards of a patriarchal society. Falconer is deeply offended by his illegitimate birth and, with great malice and perhaps hatred, seeks to take revenge on both parents. Thus a son's ignorance of his father leads to fatal consequences. However, many investigators of the Russian epic do not accept such an interpretation, citing the lack of evidence to prove the existence of a matriarchy among the East Slavs.

The Russian expression of a human story about the reunion of an absent father and his son ends with the son's death, is adapted to the father's viewpoint, is turned into a Kievan epic, and includes one of the main Russian heroes as the father. Falconer comes with the intention of killing all the bogatyrs, ravaging Kiev with its churches and monasteries, beheading Prince Vladimir, and taking Princess Apraxia in marriage, characteristics that are usually associated with enemies of Kiev such as Kalin Tsar. In one line of the selected variant (231), Ilya specifically calls Falconer an "infidel Tatar." The bylina portrays Falconer as immoral and Ilya as a hero who, by killing his own son, justifiably destroys an opponent of Kiev. In a tragic outcome that is unusual in the Russian epic tradition, Ilya has the choice of defending the Russian land against an adversary or of accepting his son. In the end, Ilya does not hesitate and stands up for the Kievan state, just as he always does in other songs.

The same theme has been realized in another Russian song, the rare bylina "Saul Levanidovich," in which the father stays away from home for a long time because he has been taken prisoner. The son, who was born during his father's absence, goes looking for him and runs into a hostile army that sends out a bogatyr to challenge him. This turns out to be the captive father who, during the ensuing duel, recognizes his son and is reconciled with him. In this particular song, a traditional conflict has been changed into an adventure story. The enmity between father and son is based on a misunderstanding that is explained and does not lead to a fatal conclusion. Thus the songs "Ilya Muromets and Falconer" and "Saul Levanidovich" offer two different interpretations of a common plot in oral epics.

A.D. Grigorev transcribed the translated variant in 1901 on the Mezen River in Archangel Province from the singer I.A. Chupov, who combines the two versions of this bylina in his rendition.

The Birth of Falconer, His Departure, and His Fight with Ilya Muromets

Source: A.D. Grigorev, *Archangel Bylinas and Historical Songs*, vol. 3
(St. Petersburg, 1910), no. 368.

To the sea, to the blue sea,
To the blue and the cold sea,
To the stone, to the Latyr stone,
To that baba, to Zlatygorka,
5   Strolled and walked a daring good youth,
By name the old Cossack Ilya Muromets.
Ilya walked and strolled to her twelve years,
He begot a beloved child by her.
He planned, the old one, to ride to the open
       field,
10   He started telling Zlatygorka,
Telling her and firmly instructing her,
He left her his wondrous cross,
He also left a golden ring from his hand:
"Hail to you, my baba Zlatygorka!
15   If you bear a son, give him the wondrous cross,
If you bear a daughter, give her the golden ring."
Then the old Cossack rode to the open field.
      Neither much nor little time passed since then.
That baba, that Zlatygorka,
20   Gave birth to the young Falconer.
Falconer didn't grow by the year but by the
      hour.
What people become in the world at seventeen
      years,
Our Falconer became at seven years.
      Falconer became twelve years old.
25   Then he started going out on the main porch,

He started looking and observing through a
    spyglass.*
First he looked along the open field,
Second he looked along the blue sea,
Third he looked at a steep hill,

30   Last he looked at the capital city of Kiev.
He planned to go and capture the beautiful
    city of Kiev.
He asked his mother for her blessing:
"Mother, please give me your blessing,
For me, a good youth, to ride to the open field."

35   His mother gave him her blessing,
His dear mother gave it to him and she told him:
"You'll go, my child, to the open field,
You'll come across an old man in the open field.
The beard of the old man will be all gray,

40   The head of the old man will be all white,
The steed under the old man will be all white,
The tail and mane of the steed will be all black.
Don't ride up to that old man,
Don't ride up to that old man, but dismount
    your steed.

45   Don't walk up to that old man,
But bow low to that old man.
That old Cossack is your dear father."
Falconer was offended by this,
He took it for an insult, for a great insult.

50   Then Falconer dressed himself in colorful
    clothing,
He put on a bogatyr's armor.
Then Falconer led out his good steed,
Falconer saddled and bridled his good steed,
On his steed he laid some saddle cloths,

55   On the saddle cloths he laid felt blankets,
On the felt blankets he put a Circassian saddle
With twelve silken girths,

---

*An anachronism that often appears in Russian epics.

He laid the thirteenth girth across the backbone,
Across the horse's spine.

60   Then Falconer mounted his good steed.
People didn't see Falconer mounting his
            steed—
All they saw was Falconer stepping in the
            stirrups.
But they couldn't see the bogatyr's departure—
All they saw was dust rising in the field,

65   Dust was swirling and smoke was rising in a
            column.
        Then Falconer rode out in the open field,
He rode around the open field.
He rode in the field and enjoyed himself,
He amused himself with Tatar games.

70   He cast his spear through the skies,
He'd throw it with his right hand, and he'd
            catch it with his left.
He recited a charm over his spear:
"Just as I so easily master you now, my spear,
So easily am I to master the old Cossack."

75   And in the morning, in the early morning,
After the bright sun had risen,
Then the old Cossack came out of his white tent.
He glanced and looked through his spyglass.
First he looked at the capital city of Kiev,

80   Second he looked through the open field,
He caught sight of an enemy in the open field.
Then the old Cossack entered his white tent:
"Hail to you, my daring good youths!
You've slept enough, it's time for you to get up,

85   It's time for you to get up, it's time to go riding,
We really have to ride to the open field,
A daring good youth is riding in the field.
        Our Ivashka Dolgopoly could go riding,
He'd be a strong kid among us,

90   He's a strong but clumsy kid,
He'd lose his reckless head in vain.

Our Alyosha Popovich could go riding,
He'd be a weak kid among us,
But he's a quick-tempered kid in mind and
      reason,
95   He'd lose his reckless head in vain.
Our Dobrynya, Nikita's son, could go riding,
He'd be a strong kid among us,
He'd be a strong and savvy kid,
He'd be a savvy and courteous kid,
100   He could ride out and meet the good youth,
He could approach him,
He could pay our respects to the good youth."
     Then Dobrynya started equipping himself,
He put ringed mail on himself,
105   He put on colorful clothing,
He put on a bogatyr's armor.
     Then Dobrynya went out of the white tent,
Then Dobrynya came out of the white tent,
Dobrynya saddled and bridled his good steed,
110   Dobrynya mounted his good steed,
Dobrynya rode to the open field.
Then Dobrynya rode out in the open field,
He came across Falconer in the open field.
He came across him and approached him,
115   Dobrynya dismounted his good steed,
He bowed low to that good youth:
"Greetings to you, my daring good youth!
What city and what land are you from?
Who are your father and mother?
120   Youth, what name do they call you by,
What patronymic do they honor you by?
And where are you going and where are you
      making your way?"
     Then the daring good youth answered:
"I'm riding to your famous and beautiful city
      of Kiev,
125   I'll seek out you Russian bogatyrs,
I'll cut down you bogatyrs with my saber,

I'll include you bogatyrs in my list,*
I'll toss you in the fast stream,
I'll trample the old Cossack with my steed,
130   I'll cut off Prince Vladimir's head,
And I'll take Princess Apraxia in marriage,
I'll burn down the whole city of Kiev,
I'll send all God's churches up in smoke."
Then Dobrynya mounted his good steed,
135   Dobrynya rode to the white tents,
Dobrynya came to the white tents,
Then Dobrynya entered a white tent,
Then Dobrynya spoke these words:
"Hail to you, old Cossack Ilya Muromets!
140   I'm no match for the youth riding there in the field,
I'm no match for him, I'm not his equal.
He's riding from the sea, from the blue sea,
He's riding from the blue and cold sea,
He's riding from the stone, from the Latyr stone,
145   He's riding from that baba, from Zlatygorka.
They call him the young Falconer.
He's riding to our famous and beautiful city of Kiev,
He wants to seek out us bogatyrs,
He wants to cut us bogatyrs down with his saber,
150   He wants to include us bogatyrs in his list,
He wants to throw us into the fast stream,
To trample you with his steed, old Cossack,
And to cut off Prince Vladimir's head,
And to take Princess Apraxia in marriage,
155   He wants to burn down the whole city of Kiev,
And to send all God's churches up in smoke."
Then the old Cossack was offended,
He took this for an insult, for a great insult.
Then the old Cossack started equipping himself,
160   Ilya quickly started getting ready.
He put ringed mail on himself,
He put on colorful clothing,

---

*This is probably a list of defeated enemies.

He took along all a bogatyr's gear.
Then the old Cossack went out of the white tent,
165   The old Cossack saddled and bridled his good
            steed,
The old Cossack started riding to the open field,
He came across Falconer in the open field.
Then Falconer roared like a wild animal,
Then Falconer whistled like a nightingale,
170   Then Falconer hissed like a snake.
Then the mother damp earth shook,
Then the damp oaks were bent over
And their tops were intertwined with their trunks,
And the dry oaks were snapped,
175   Ilya's good steed fell on all fours.
        The old one beat his steed on its strong ribs,
The old one repeated to his steed:
"Hail to you, my steed, you bag of grass!
Haven't you heard the roar of a wild animal,
180   Haven't you heard the hiss of a snake,
And the whistle of a nightingale?"
        Then Ilya's steed grew angry,
The steed flew above the damp earth.
It came across Falconer in the open field,
185   It came across him and approached him,
The old one spoke these words himself:
"Hail to you, my daring good youth!
Without shooting the bright falcon, you
            pluck it;
Without killing the good youth, you ride and brag."
190   Then two thunder clouds didn't collide—
Two strong bogatyrs came together.
They came together with sharp sabers,
Their sharp sabers were nicked,
They didn't wound each other in this fight.
195   They came together with Tatar spears,
The tips of their spears were bent,
They didn't wound each other in this fight.
They came together with battle maces,
Their battle maces were broken,

200   They didn't wound each other in this fight.
      Then the youths dismounted their good steeds,
      And they grappled in heavy fighting, hand-to-hand,
      And they fought a day from morning to evening,
      And from evening they fought to midnight,
205   And from midnight they fought to daylight,
      And in all they fought three days and nights.
            Then by Falconer's good luck,
      And by Ilya's bad luck,
      The old one's right leg gave way,
210   The old one's left leg slipped,
      And then the old Cossack fell on the damp earth.
      Falconer jumped on Ilya's white chest,
      He didn't ask his name or patronymic,
      He didn't ask about his family or about his
                  bravery,
215   He took his sharp knife out of its sheath,
      He undid Ilya's carved buttons,
      He wanted to rip open Ilya's white chest,
      He wanted to see Ilya's ardent heart.
            Then the old Cossack was offended,
220   He took it for a great insult.
      Then the old Cossack Ilya Muromets prayed:
      "Hail to you, Most Merciful Saviour,
      God's Most Holy Mother, Mother of God!
      Didn't I stand up for the Orthodox faith?
225   Didn't I stand up for God's churches?
      Didn't I stand up for the Christian monasteries?
      Didn't I stand up for the famous and beautiful
                  city of Kiev?
      They said that death was not foretold for the old
                  one in the field,
      But death will probably come to the old one now.
230   Don't allow me, Lord, to be defeated
      By an infidel Tatar in the open field."
      The old one's strength then grew,
      Then his strength grew two- and threefold,
      Two- and threefold it grew, exactly fivefold.

235 He shoved off and pushed aside Falconer from
　　　　　　　his white chest,
　　　　He jumped on Falconer's white chest,
　　　　He spoke these words himself:
　　　　"Hail to you, my daring good youth!
　　　　What city and what land do you come from,
240 Who's your father and who's your mother?
　　　　What name, my youth, do they call you by,
　　　　What patronymic do they honor you by?"
　　　　　　　Then the daring good youth answered:
　　　　"Hail to you, old elder!
245 When I was on your white chest,
　　　　I didn't ask your name or your patronymic,
　　　　I didn't ask about your family or about your
　　　　　　　bravery,
　　　　I took my sharp knife out of its sheath,
　　　　I wanted to rip open your white chest,
250 I wanted to look at your ardent heart."
　　　　　　　The old Cossack spoke to him a second time:
　　　　"Tell me, youth what name do they call you by?"
　　　　The daring good youth answered him:
　　　　"When I was on your white chest,
255 I didn't ask your name or patronymic,
　　　　I wanted to rip open your white chest."
　　　　　　　The old Cossack Ilya Muromets spoke to him:
　　　　"You tell me, youth, what name do they call
　　　　　　　you by,
　　　　What patronymic do they honor you by?"
260 Then the young Falconer answered:
　　　　"I'm from the sea, from the blue sea,
　　　　I'm from the blue and cold sea,
　　　　I'm from the stone, from the Latyr stone,
　　　　I'm from that baba, from Zlatygorka,
265 And they call me the young Falconer."
　　　　　　　Then the old Cossack stood up on his nimble
　　　　　　　feet,
　　　　He took Falconer by his white hands,
　　　　He stood Falconer on his nimble feet,

He kissed him on his sweet lips.
270 He spoke these words himself:
"I'm really your dear father."
Then the youths mounted their good steeds,
Then they rode to the white tents,
They came to the white tents,
275 Then the youths entered a white tent,
They drank three days and nights in the white tent.
    Then Falconer rode to the open field,
To the sea, to the blue sea,
To his mother, to his dear mother.
280 His dear mother caught sight of him,
She came out on the main porch
And met Falconer from the open field,
She met Falconer by the main porch.
Then Falconer dismounted his good steed,
285 He put her to death, he cut off her reckless head.
    Neither much nor little time has passed since then,
He rode again to the open field,
He came across a white tent in the open field.
The old Cossack Ilya Muromets was sleeping
        in the tent.
290 Falconer didn't enter the white tent,
Then he took his sharp spear,
He threw it at the old one's white chest,
The spear flew and struck the old one's
        wondrous cross.
Then the old Cossack Ilya Muromets woke up,
295 The old Cossack jumped out of the white tent,
He grabbed Falconer by his combed curls,
He threw him high in the heavens,
He threw Falconer up but didn't catch him,
Then Falconer fell on the damp earth.
300   And since then songs of praise have been sung
        to Falconer,
Songs of praise have been sung and old songs
        have been sung to Falconer.

✍ 5 ❧

Ilya Muromets
and Kalin Tsar

he song "Ilya Muromets and Kalin Tsar" is one of the
few Russian epics that concerns the struggle with the
Tatar Golden Horde from the thirteenth through the fifteenth centuries. This bylina is so closely connected with several others, especially "Battle on the Kama" and "Ilya Muromets, Yermak, and
Kalin Tsar," that they all are usually examined together as different
realizations of the same subject. Although they vary considerably in
their details, the three main versions of this song essentially relate how
a Tatar army commanded by Kalin Tsar approaches the city of Kiev
and how this force is defeated either by Ilya Muromets alone or by a
group of bogatyrs whom he rallies to defend the city (Propp 1958b:
301–54).

The epic "Ilya Muromets and Kalin Tsar," which has been recorded
eighty times, may open with a description of an enormous Tatar army
near Kiev or, as does the variant selected for this anthology, may relate
how Prince Vladimir has put Ilya in a dungeon and has left him to die
by starvation. The circumstances behind this initial situation can be
understood only by referring to the song "Ilya Quarrels with Vladimir," which presents the reasons for Ilya's "rebellion" against Vladimir and for Ilya's imprisonment. Apraxia, who may be Vladimir's
wife, daughter, or niece, is far more perceptive about future misfortune
than he is. She secretly takes care of Ilya because she foresees how he
alone will be able to save Kiev at some future time. Only after the
Tatars have approached Kiev and have issued an ultimatum does Vladimir regret his action. When Apraxia tells him that Ilya is alive,
Vladimir frees Ilya and asks him to stand up for Kiev, his Prince, and

49

Princess Apraxia. Ilya, without complaining but also without forgiving Vladimir, immediately rides to the camp of twelve Russian bogatyrs headed by his godfather, Samson Samoilovich, a figure rarely appearing in Russian epics and then only as the head of a group of bogatyrs. These absent heroes had left Kiev because Vladimir had imprisoned Ilya and because the prince had favored the boyars over them. Despite Ilya's pleas, the other bogatyrs refuse to help him. He starts fighting the Tatar army alone, eventually falls with his horse into one of the traps or ditches that the Tatars had dug to protect their flanks from attacks by horsemen, and is captured. Kalin Tsar offers the Russian hero honorable service with the Tatars, but Ilya rejects this enticing proposition, frees himself, and begins fighting again. In the selected variant Ilya finally persuades the other bogatyrs to help only by resorting to magic; he utters an incantation over an arrow (lines 531 to 538) and shoots it so that it grazes the chest of his godfather, Samson Samoilovich. In some variants Kalin Tsar is killed by the Russian bogatyrs; in others the Tsar escapes with the remnants of his army and makes a pledge never to attack Kiev again; and in yet others, including the translated song, Kalin Tsar is captured, is taken to Prince Vladimir, and promises to pay tribute ever after. In variants opening with Ilya in a dungeon, this bylina constitutes the Russian expression of the epic story about an imprisoned or reluctant hero who at the last minute emerges to save his people from an enemy assault. Achilles in the *Iliad* represents one example of this theme.

Efforts have been made to ascribe the origin of the song "Ilya Muromets and Kalin Tsar" to a precise historical event (Azbelev 1971). Many folklorists in the nineteenth century believed that the defeat of the Russian forces in 1223 on the River Kalka, the first clash between Kievan Rus and the Tatars, has been reflected in this bylina. Other scholars associate this epic with the Battle of Kulikovo Field, which took place in 1380: the Tatar Khan Mamai with an army of 200,000 men was met on the upper reaches of the Don River by the Muscovite Prince Dmitri Donskoi and his army. The rout of Mamai's forces constituted the first time that the Russians defeated the Tatars and also marked the beginning of the liberation of Rus from the Tatar Yoke. V.Ia. Propp and others have cast doubt on the connection of this song with a specific historical event, emphasizing that Russian epics are not concerned with particular victories or defeats but with a broad portrayal and interpretation of one epoch. Contrary to historical facts, singers related Russian victories over the Tatars even when such victories had not occurred. Furthermore, the bylina "Ilya Muromets and Kalin Tsar" may have been based on epics that depicted earlier conflicts of Kievan Rus with the Khazars, Pechenegs, and Polovetsians. Thus, according to their "epic consciousness" and their knowledge of the epic tradition, singers adapted battles, such as those on the River Kalka or in Kulikovo Field, to patterns already existing in Kievan epics.

A few other details in this song need to be clarified. The head of the Tatar army is often called "the Dog Kalin Tsar," perhaps because the dog was a totem for some Tatar clans. In Russian epics it is not always clear whether the performers attach a pejorative meaning to the noun "dog" or simply use it as part of the Tatar Tsar's name. In the present translation, the word has been treated as a proper name. It should be added that in Turkic languages the word *kalin* means thick, stout, stocky, or fat and suggests that Kalin Tsar is a "fat glutton." This negative characteristic is much more clearly developed in the figure Tugarin in the bylina "Alyosha Popovich, His Squire Yekim, and Tugarin." Kalin Tsar has not been clearly linked with a particular historical personage. The description of the Tatar army, which is so huge that Ilya cannot find its "end or edge," parallels passages in Russian chronicles about the overwhelming size of a Tatar army, such as the one led by Batu, who captured Kiev in 1240. The Tatar messenger is instructed to offend Russian sensibilities deliberately by not tying up his horse, by entering the council chamber without announcement, by not bowing to the icons, Prince Vladimir, and his court, and by throwing down a written ultimatum. Historically the Tatars, after approaching a city, sent messengers demanding the city's unconditional surrender. While the letter itself may reflect the later Tatar practice of granting privileges to a Russian prince in a document called the *yarlyk,* the Russians themselves at this time had messengers deliver verbal rather than written messages.

The bylina "Ilya Muromets and Kalin Tsar" also presents a remarkable character study of Ilya Muromets. Instead of expressing bitterness and anger about his imprisonment to Prince Vladimir, Ilya leaves without any reconciliation and deals with the most pressing matter—the defense of Kiev. Initially he scouts the immense Tatar force and looks for the bogatyrs who left Kiev. Even though he fails to persuade them to fight and his horse delivers a prophetic warning, Ilya single-handedly confronts the hostile army. After Ilya's capture, Kalin Tsar offers him everything that Prince Vladimir had never awarded him or the other bogatyrs, but Ilya, always a patriot, refuses the offer. He is not interested in holding a grudge against Prince Vladimir—the protection of Kiev, Christianity, and the Russian land outweighs such personal concerns. Ilya shows no hesitation or doubts about what needs to be done—his actions reveal his inner character and, ultimately, his unexpressed but implied disapproval of Prince Vladimir's conduct. Ilya's patience, his slowness to be offended, his calm ability to deal with adversity, his sense of duty, and his willingness to work for the common good may perhaps reflect the ideals of peasant singers who regarded Ilya as someone to be imitated in real life.

A.F. Gilferding collected the song chosen for translation in 1871 in Kizhi District of Olonets Province from the singer T.G. Riabinin. His variant offers a fine illustration of how singers use repetition and traditional pattern scenes, such as the saddling of a horse, to compose an oral epic.

↩ Ilya Muromets and Kalin Tsar ↪

Source: A.F. Gilferding, *Onega Bylinas,* 4th ed., vol. 2
(Moscow, 1950), no. 75.

When Vladimir, Prince of the capital Kiev,
Became angry at the old Cossack Ilya Muromets,
He imprisoned Ilya in a deep dungeon,
In a cold and in a deep dungeon
5   For a time and period of three years.
The famous Prince Vladimir
Had a single daughter.
She saw this wasn't a trifling matter
That Vladimir, Prince of capital Kiev,
10   Had imprisoned the old Cossack Ilya Muromets
In a dungeon, in a cold dungeon.
He alone could stand up for the faith and for the
         fatherland,
He alone could stand up for the city of Kiev,

He alone could stand up for the cathedral churches,
15   He alone could protect our Prince Vladimir,
He could protect Apraxia the Princess.
She ordered duplicate keys to be made,
She relied on secret people,
She ordered featherbeds and down pillows
20   To be taken to the cold dungeon,
She ordered warm blankets to be taken there,
She ordered good food to be delivered there,
And clothing to be changed again and again
For the old Cossack Ilya Muromets.
25   But Vladimir the Prince didn't know about this.
          And then the Dog Kalin Tsar became enraged against
               the city of Kiev
And wanted to ravage the capital city Kiev,
To cut down all the commoners and simple people,
To send all God's churches up in smoke,
30   To cut off the heads of Prince Vladimir
And of Apraxia the Princess.
The Dog Kalin Tsar dispatched a messenger,
A messenger to the capital city Kiev,
And he gave him an urgent letter,
35   And he charged the messenger:
"When you arrive in the capital city Kiev,
Then in the capital Kiev, messenger,
You'll go to the famous Prince Vladimir,
You'll go to his wide courtyard
40   And you'll dismount your good steed,
You'll release your steed in the messenger's courtyard,
You'll go to the white-stone palace,
You'll go through the white-stone palace,
You'll go into his dining hall,
45   You'll swing the door wide open.
Don't take the shako off your head,
Go up to the oaken table,
Stand opposite Prince Vladimir,
Place the letter on the golden table,
50   Say to Prince Vladimir:
'Vladimir, Prince of capital Kiev!

Take the urgent letter
And see what's written in the letter,
And see what's printed in the letter.*

55 Clean up all the archer's streets
And all the large princely courtyards.
All around the city of Kiev,
All along the wide streets,
All along the princely lanes,

60 Place sweet intoxicating drinks,
So that barrel will stand close to barrel,
So that the Dog Kalin Tsar will have something to
        stand by
With his troops, with his many troops,
In your city, in Kiev.' "

65   Then Vladimir, Prince of capital Kiev,
Took the urgent book,†
He unsealed the letter,
He saw what was written in the letter,
He saw what was printed in the letter,

70 And that he was ordered to clean the archer's streets
And the large princely courtyards,
To place sweet intoxicating drinks
All along the wide streets
And all along the princely lanes.

75   Then Vladimir, Prince of capital Kiev,
Saw this wasn't a trifling matter,
Not a trifling matter but a serious one,
And Vladimir the Prince sat down on a red chair.
He wrote an obedient letter:

80   "Hail to you, Dog Kalin Tsar!
Give me a time and period of three years,
Of three years and of three months,
Of three months and also of three days.
I'm to clean the archer's streets

---

*These actions are intended to offend Russian sensibilities about a ritual that
people perform when entering a council or feast—they bow to the icons, to Prince
Vladimir, and to the whole court.

† The singer should have said "letter" and corrects himself in the next line.

85 And all the large princely courtyards,
 I'm to distill sweet intoxicating drinks
 And to place them all around the city of Kiev
 And all along the wide streets,
 All along the famous princely lanes."
90 He sent off this obedient letter,
 Sent it off to the Dog Kalin Tsar.
  And the Dog Kalin Tsar
 Gave him a time and period of three years,
 Of three years and of three months,
95 Of three months and also of three days.
 Day after day sped past as fast as rain comes down,
 And week after week sped past as fast as a river runs,
 There passed the time and period of three years,
 Of three years and of three months,
100 Of three months and also of three days.
 Then the Dog Kalin Tsar rode up,
 He rode up to the city of Kiev
 With his troops, with his many troops.
  Then Vladimir, Prince of capital Kiev,
105 Walked up and down his hall,
 He shed bitter tears from his bright eyes,
 The Prince wiped his eyes with a silk kerchief,
 Prince Vladimir spoke these words:
 "The old Cossack Ilya Muromets isn't alive,
110 There's no one to stand up now for the faith and for
   the fatherland,
 There's no one to stand up for God's churches,
 There's no one to stand up for the city of Kiev,
 There's no one to protect our Prince Vladimir
 And Apraxia the Princess!"
115 His beloved daughter spoke these words to him:
 "Hail to you, my father—Vladimir, Prince of capital
   Kiev!
 The old Cossack Ilya Muromets is alive,
 He's alive in the cold dungeon."
  Then Vladimir, Prince of capital Kiev,
120 Quickly took the golden keys
 And went to the cold dungeon,

He quickly unlocked the cold dungeon
And went up to the iron grating,
He opened the iron grating.
125   There the old Cossack Ilya Muromets
Was sitting in the dungeon—he hadn't aged.
Feather beds and down pillows,
And warm blankets had been brought there,
Good food had been delivered there,
130   And his clothing had been changed.
Vladimir took Ilya by his white hands,
By his rings, by his gilded rings,
He led Ilya from the cold dungeon,
He brought him into the white-stone palace,
135   He stood Ilya across from himself,
He kissed him on his sweet lips,
He took him behind the oaken tables,
He seated Ilya beside himself,
And he gave him tasty food,
140   And he gave him a drink of mead,
And he spoke these words to Ilya:
"Hail to you, old Cossack Ilya Muromets!
Our city of Kiev has been surrounded,
The Dog Kalin Tsar has encircled our city of Kiev
145   With his troops, with his many troops.
Please stand up for the faith and for the fatherland,
And please stand up for the famous city of Kiev,
And please stand up for the mothers, for God's
           churches,
And please stand up for Prince Vladimir,
150   And please stand up for Apraxia the Princess!"
       Then the old Cossack Ilya Muromets
Walked out of the white-stone palace,
He walked through the city of Kiev,
He walked into his white-stone palace,
155   He asked to see his favorite squire,
He walked with his favorite squire
To his famous courtyard, to his wide courtyard,
He went into the stalls in the stable,
He looked at his bogatyr's good steed.

160   Ilya spoke these words:
"Hail to you, my favorite squire,
My humble faithful servant!
You've kept my bogatyr's steed very well!"
Ilya kissed him on his sweet lips.

165   Ilya led his good steed out of the stalls in the stable
To that famous courtyard, to that wide courtyard.
Then the old Cossack Ilya Muromets
Started saddling his good steed.
He laid a saddle cloth on the steed,

170   On the saddle cloth he laid a felt blanket,
He put on a silken saddle cloth,
On the saddle cloth he added an undercloth,
On the undercloth he put a Circassian saddle,
But the Circassian saddle didn't hold

175   And he tightened the twelve silk girths,
And he drew in the steel pins,
And he put on the steel stirrups,
And he put on the buckles of red gold—
Not for beauty or for pleasure

180   But always for a bogatyr's strength.
The silk saddle girths would stretch but wouldn't tear,
The steel and iron would bend but wouldn't break,
The buckles of red gold
Would get wet but wouldn't tarnish.

185   And then Ilya mounted his good steed,
He took along his sturdy bogatyr's gear.
First he took a steel mace,
Second he took a Tatar spear,
And he also took his sharp saber,

190   And he also took his traveling club,
And he rode out of the city, out of Kiev.
      Ilya rode out to the open field
And he rode up to the Tatar troops
To look at the Tatar troops.

195   A force of great number had been assembled.
As from a human scream,
As from a horse's neighing,
The human heart became depressed.

Then the old Cossack Ilya Muromets
200   Rode through the plain, the open field,
He couldn't find the end or edge of the army.
He leaped on a high hill,
He looked in three directions and then in a fourth,
He looked at the Tatar army,
205   He couldn't see the end or edge of the army.
And he leaped on another hill,
He looked in three directions and then in a fourth,
He couldn't see the end or edge of the army.
He came down from that high hill,
210   He rode through the plain, the open field,
And he leaped on a third high hill,
He looked in an easterly direction.
He saw in the easterly direction,
He saw there some white tents,
215   Some bogatyrs' steeds were standing by the white tents.
He came down from that high hill
And he rode through the plain, the open field,
Ilya came to the white tents,
Ilya dismounted his good steed
220   By the tents, by the white tents.
The bogatyrs' steeds were standing there,
They were standing by one white tent,
They were eating the finest grain.
        Ilya spoke these words:
225   "I should try my greatest luck."
He snapped the silken reins
On his bogatyr's good steed,
He urged his steed to go to the white tent:
"Will the bogatyrs' steeds allow
230   My bogatyr's steed to come up
To the tent, to the white tent,
To eat the finest grain?"
His good steed went boldly up to the tent,
It went to eat the finest grain.
235   The old Cossack Ilya Muromets
Went to the white tent.
Ilya Muromets came to the white tent,

In the white tent were twelve bogatyrs,
All were Holy Russian bogatyrs,
240   They'd sat down to take part in a meal,
They'd sat down to have their dinner.
       Ilya spoke these words:
"Good appetite, Holy Russian bogatyrs,
And to you, my godfather,
245   Samson Samoilovich!"
       His godfather spoke to him:
"Please come, beloved godson,
Old Cossack Ilya Muromets,
And sit down to have dinner with us."
250   And Samson stood up on his nimble feet,
He greeted Ilya Muromets,
They greeted and they kissed each other,
They seated Ilya Muromets at their table
To take part in their meal.
255   There were twelve bogatyrs—
Ilya Muromets was the thirteenth.
They ate, they drank, and they had dinner,
They came out from behind the oaken table,
They prayed to the Lord God.
260   The old Cossack Ilya Muromets spoke to them:
"My godfather, Samson Samoilovich,
And you, mighty Russian bogatyrs!
Please saddle your good steeds,
Please mount your good steeds,
265   Please ride to the plain, the open field,
Near the famous capital city Kiev.
The Dog Kalin Tsar has come
Near our city, near Kiev,
He's come with his many troops.
270   He wants to ravage the capital city Kiev,
He wants to cut down all the commoners and simple
          people,
He wants to send all God's churches up in smoke,
He wants to cut off the reckless heads
Of Prince Vladimir and Apraxia the Princess.
275   Please stand up for the faith and for the fatherland,

Please stand up for the famous capital city Kiev,
Please stand up for God's churches,
Please protect our Prince Vladimir
And Apraxia the Princess!"
280   Samson Samoilovich spoke to him:
"Hail to you, my beloved godson,
Old Cossack Ilya Muromets!
We won't saddle our steeds,
And we won't mount our good steeds,
285   We won't ride to the famous open field,
We won't stand up for the faith and for the fatherland,
We won't stand up for the capital city Kiev,
We won't stand up for the mothers, for God's churches,
We won't protect our Prince Vladimir
290   And also Apraxia the Princess.
He has many princes and boyars,
He feeds them, gives them drink, and rewards them,
But we get nothing from Prince Vladimir."
       The old Cossack Ilya Muromets spoke:
295   "Hail to you, my godfather,
Hail to you, Samson Samoilovich!
This matter of ours will turn out badly,
The Dog Kalin Tsar will ravage the city of Kiev,
He'll cut down all the commoners and simple people,
300   He'll send all God's churches up in smoke,
He'll cut off the reckless heads
Of Prince Vladimir and Apraxia the Princess.
Please saddle your good steeds
And please mount your good steeds,
305   Please ride to the open field near the city of Kiev,
And stand up for the faith and for the fatherland,
And stand up for the famous capital city Kiev,
And stand up for God's churches,
Please protect our Prince Vladimir
310   Together with Apraxia the Princess."
       Samson Samoilovich spoke these words:
"Hail to you, my beloved godson,
Old Cossack Ilya Muromets!
We won't saddle our steeds,

315   And we won't mount our good steeds,
       We won't ride to the famous open field,
       We won't stand up for the faith and for the fatherland,
       We won't stand up for the capital city Kiev,
       We won't stand up for the mothers, for God's churches,
320   We won't protect our Prince Vladimir
       And also Apraxia the Princess.
       He has many princes and boyars,
       He feeds them, gives them drink, and rewards them,
       But we get nothing from Prince Vladimir."
325   The old Cossack Ilya Muromets spoke:
       "Hail to you, my godfather,
       Hail to you, Samson Samoilovich!
       This matter of ours will turn out badly.
       Please saddle your good steeds
330   And please mount your good steeds,
       Please ride to the open field near the city of Kiev,
       And stand up for the faith and for the fatherland,
       And stand up for the famous capital city Kiev,
       And stand up for God's churches,
335   Please protect our Prince Vladimir
       Together with Apraxia the Princess."
         Samson Samoilovich spoke to him:
       "Hail to you, my beloved godson,
       Old Cossack Ilya Muromets!
340   We won't saddle our steeds,
       And we won't mount our good steeds,
       We won't ride to the famous open field,
       We won't stand up for the faith and for the fatherland,
       We won't stand up for the capital city Kiev,
345   We won't stand up for the mothers, for God's churches,
       We won't protect our Prince Vladimir
       And also Apraxia the Princess.
       He has many princes and boyars,
       He feeds them, gives them drink, and rewards them,
350   But we get nothing from Prince Vladimir."
         Then the old Cossack Ilya Muromets
       Saw that Samson wasn't happy with the matter,
       Ilya went out of the white tent,

He went to his bogatyr's good steed,
355   He took it by the silken reins,
He led it away from the white tent
And from the finest grain.
Ilya mounted his good steed,
Then he rode through the plain, the open field,
360   And he rode up to the Tatar troops.
A bright falcon didn't swoop down on the geese, on
     the swans,
And on the small migratory gray ducks—
A Holy Russian bogatyr
Swooped down on the Tatar army.
365   He urged on his bogatyr's steed,
He rode through the Tatar army.
He trampled the army with his steed,
He trampled it with his steed and jabbed it with his
     spear,
He slaughtered this great army,
370   He slaughtered this army as though mowing grass.
     His bogatyr's good steed
Proclaimed in human language:
"Hail to you, my famous Holy Russian bogatyr!
Although you've attacked this great army,
375   You can't defeat this great army.
The Dog Kalin Tsar has assembled,
He's assembled an army of great number,
And he has strong bogatyrs,
He has daring polyanitsas.*
380   The Dog Kalin Tsar
Has made three deep traps
In the famous plain, in the open field.
When you ride through that plain,
     that open field,
You'll slaughter that great army.
385   When we fall into those deep traps,
I'll jump out of the first trap

---

*The word *polyanitsa* can mean hero (bogatyr) or warrior maiden (bogatyrka), but here it implies other "heroes."

And I'll lift you out of it.
When we fall into the second trap,
I'll also jump out of it
390 And I'll lift you out of it.
When we fall into the third deep trap,
Then I'll jump out myself,
But I won't be able to lift you out of it,
You'll stay in the deep trap."
395　　The old Cossack Ilya Muromets
Wasn't happy with this matter,
And he took his silken whip in his white hands,
He beat his steed on its strong ribs.
He spoke these words to his steed:
400 "Hail to you, you traitorous dog!
I feed you, give you drink, and take care of you,
But you want to leave me in the open field
In a trap, in a deep trap!"
　　And Ilya rode through the plain, the open field,
405 Into that army, into that great army.
He trampled it with his steed and jabbed it with his
　　　　spear,
And he slaughtered the army as though mowing grass.
Ilya's strength didn't diminish.
He fell into a trap, into a deep trap,
410 His good steed jumped out of it,
It jumped out and lifted Ilya out of it.
And he urged on his bogatyr's steed
Through the plain, the open field,
Into that army, into that great army,
415 He trampled it with his steed and jabbed it with his
　　　　spear,
And he slaughtered the army as though mowing grass.
Ilya's strength didn't diminish,
Ilya sat on his good steed and didn't look tired.
　　And he fell with his bogatyr's steed,
420 And he found himself in the second trap,
His good steed jumped out of it
And lifted Ilya out of it.
And he urged on his bogatyr's steed

Through the plain, the open field,
425   Into that army, into that great army,
He trampled it with his steed and jabbed it with his
      spear,
And he slaughtered the army as though mowing grass.
Ilya's strength didn't diminish,
Ilya sat on his good steed and didn't look tired.
430   And he found himself in the third trap,
He fell with his steed into the deep trap.
His bogatyr's good steed
Also jumped out of the third trap,
But it couldn't lift Ilya out of it,
435   Ilya slipped off his good steed,
And he stayed in the deep trap.
      The infidel Tatars came
And they wanted to capture the good steed.
Ilya's bogatyr steed
440   Didn't let itself fall into their white hands,
The good steed escaped to the open field.
Then the infidel Tatars came,
And they fell on the old Cossack Ilya Muromets,
They fettered his nimble feet,
445   And they tied up his white hands.
      The Tatars spoke these words:
"We should cut off his reckless head."
      Other Tatars spoke these words:
"We shouldn't cut off his reckless head,
450   We should take Ilya to the Dog Kalin Tsar—
Let him do what he wants with Ilya."
      They took Ilya through the open field
Toward the canvas tents,
They took him to one canvas tent,
455   They took him to the Dog Kalin Tsar,
They stood him opposite the Dog Kalin Tsar.
      The Tatars spoke these words:
"Hail to you, our Dog Kalin Tsar!
We've captured the old Cossack Ilya Muromets
460   In the traps, in the deep traps,
And we've brought him to you, to the Dog Kalin Tsar—

Do with him what you want."
     Then the Dog Kalin Tsar spoke these words to Ilya:
"Hail to you, old Cossack Ilya Muromets!

465   Like a young pup, you've set upon my great army—
How can you alone defeat my great army!
Please unshackle Ilya's nimble feet,
Please untie Ilya's white hands."
And they unshackled his nimble feet,

470   And they untied his white hands.
     The Dog Kalin Tsar spoke these words:
"Hail to you, old Cossack Ilya Muromets!
Please sit down with me at my table,
Please eat my tasty food,

475   Please drink my drinks of mead,
And please put on my expensive clothes,
And please use my golden treasure,
Use my golden treasure for your needs,
Please don't serve your Prince Vladimir,

480   Please serve the Dog Kalin Tsar."
     Ilya spoke these words:
"I won't sit down with you at the same table,
I won't eat your tasty food,
I won't drink your drinks of mead,

485   I won't wear your expensive clothes,
I won't use your countless golden treasure,
I won't serve you, Dog Kalin Tsar.
I'll still serve the faith and fatherland,
I'll stand up for the capital city Kiev,

490   I'll stand up for the Lord's churches,
I'll stand up for Prince Vladimir
And for Apraxia the Princess."
     Then the old Cossack Ilya Muromets
Went out of the canvas tent,

495   He went away to the plain, the open field.
The infidel Tatars started pressing him,
They wanted to capture the old Cossack Ilya Muromets.
The old Cossack Ilya Muromets
Didn't happen to have his sturdy gear with him,

500   He had nothing to resist the Tatars with.

The old Cossack Ilya Muromets
Saw this wasn't a trifling matter.
He grabbed a Tatar by the legs,
Then he swung the Tatar,
505   He slaughtered the Tatars with a Tatar,
And the Tatars ran from him.
And he passed through all the Tatar army,
He came out in the plain, the open field,
He threw the Tatar aside.
510   Then he walked through the plain, the open field,
He didn't have his bogatyr's steed with him,
He didn't have his sturdy gear with him.
Ilya gave a bogatyr's whistle,
His good steed heard him in the open field,
515   It came running to the old Cossack Ilya Muromets.
Again the old Cossack Ilya Muromets
Mounted his good steed
And rode through the plain, the open field,
He leaped on a hill, on a high hill,
520   He looked in an easterly direction.
In the easterly direction,
Bogatyrs' good steeds were standing
By some tents, by some white tents.
Then the old Cossack Ilya Muromets
525   Dismounted his good steed,
He took his taut supple bow in his white hands,
He stretched the silken bowstring,
He laid on a tempered arrow,
And he released the arrow into the white tent.
530   Ilya spoke these words:
" 'Fly, tempered arrow,
Fly, arrow, into the white tent,
Take the roof off the white tent,
Fall, arrow, on the white chest
535   Of my godfather,
And slide along his white chest,
Make a little scratch,
A little scratch but not a big one.'
He's sleeping there and taking his ease,

540 And I alone can do little here."
        And he released the silken string,
     He released the tempered arrow.
     The tempered arrow whistled
     Into the famous white tent,
545 It took the roof off the white tent,
     The arrow fell on the white chest
     Of Samson Samoilovich.
     The arrow slid along his white chest,
     It made a very small scratch.
550   Then the famous Holy Russian bogatyr
     Samson Samoilovich
     Woke up from his deep sleep,
     He cast his bright eyes around—
     The roof had been taken off the white tent,
555 The arrow had flown along his white chest,
     It had made a scratch on his white chest.
     He quickly stood on his nimble feet.
        Samson spoke these words:
     "Hail to you, my famous Holy Russian bogatyrs!
560 Please quickly saddle your good steeds!
     Please mount your good steeds!
     From my beloved godson
     Unwanted gifts have flown to me,
     A tempered arrow came flying
565 Through my famous white tent,
     It took the roof off the white tent,
     The arrow slid along my white chest,
     It gave me a scratch on my white chest,
     It gave me only a small scratch but not a big one.
570 The cross on my chest served me well,
     A cross of six poods on my chest.
     If there hadn't been a cross on my chest,
     The arrow would have torn off my reckless head."
        Then all the Holy Russian bogatyrs
575 Quickly saddled their good steeds,
     And the youths mounted their good steeds,
     And rode through the plain, the open field,
     Toward the city, toward Kiev,

Toward those Tatar forces.
580   From that hill, from that high hill,
The old Cossack Ilya Muromets observed,
The bogatyrs were riding through the open field,
They were riding on their good steeds.
And Ilya came down from that high hill,
585   And he rode up to the Holy Russian bogatyrs:
There were twelve bogatyrs—Ilya was the thirteenth.
And they came to the Tatar army,
They urged on their bogatyrs' steeds,
They slaughtered the Tatar army,
590   Then they trampled all the great army,
And they came to a canvas tent,
The Dog Kalin Tsar was sitting in the canvas tent.
       The Holy Russian bogatyrs spoke:
"We should cut off the reckless head
595   Of the Dog Kalin Tsar."
       The old Cossack Ilya Muromets spoke:
"Why cut off his reckless head?
Let's take him to the capital city Kiev
To the famous Prince Vladimir."
600   They brought him, the Dog Kalin Tsar,
To the famous city of Kiev,
To the famous Prince Vladimir,
They brought the Dog Kalin Tsar to the white-stone palace,
To the famous Prince Vladimir.
605   Then Vladimir, Prince of capital Kiev,
Took the Dog by his white hands
And seated him at the oaken tables,
He gave him tasty food
And gave him a drink of mead.
610   The Dog Kalin Tsar spoke these words to him:
"Hail to you, Vladimir, Prince of capital Kiev!
Don't cut off my reckless head!
Let's sign solemn agreements with each other,
I'll pay you tribute for ever after,
615   I'll pay it to you, Prince Vladimir!"
       Since then a praise has been sung to this old song,
At this place the old song has come to an end.

6

Ilya Muromets Quarrels with Prince Vladimir

*U*nlike most Russian epics, this song focuses on social differences involving a conflict between Prince Vladimir and the aristocratic boyars on the one hand, and the bogatyr Ilya Muromets on the other hand (Propp 1958b: 289–301). This bylina may represent a further development of motifs that are only alluded to in several other songs. In "Ilya Muromets and Nightingale the Robber," the prince and boyars are openly skeptical about Ilya's exploits and are scornful about his peasant origin. In the beginning of some variants of "Ilya Muromets and Kalin Tsar," Ilya has been imprisoned by Prince Vladimir and, since all bogatyrs have left Kiev in protest, none are left to protect the city against the attack of Kalin Tsar. In these two songs (Nightingale the Robber and Kalin Tsar), social tension forms the background against which a struggle takes place with an external enemy. In contrast, social conflicts in which no external enemy is present lie at the basis of the song "Ilya Muromets Quarrels with Prince Vladimir." The advancement of social differences to the foreground suggests that this work came into existence toward the end of the sixteenth century or during the seventeenth century, when Russia was in social turmoil and when peasant uprisings and Cossack disturbances were common. Whatever the actual time of its origin may have been, this epic probably appeared later than those about the Tatar conquest and domination. Twenty-seven variants of this bylina have been recorded.

Although the texts of the song "Ilya Muromets Quarrels with Prince Vladimir" are more unstable than those of most other Russian epics, two general versions can be distinguished. In the first, the conflict between Ilya Muromets and Prince Vladimir takes place for a variety of reasons. Vladimir may not seat the hero in an honored place at a feast; he may also award the princes and boyars with gold and silver but may instead give Ilya a worn Tatar fur coat. As a result, Ilya causes an uproar and leaves the feast. In the conclusion of some recordings Prince Vladimir and Ilya are reconciled, but in others the Prince puts Ilya in a dungeon to die from starvation. Since it is precisely at this point that some variants of the epic about Kalin Tsar begin, it is understandable why singers sometimes combine these two songs (the quarrel with Vladimir and Kalin Tsar). In the second version of this bylina, Ilya is not invited to a feast at Prince Vladimir's court and instead holds his own competing regalement for the lower classes. In the end, Vladimir usually invites Ilya to a banquet where they become reconciled. The translated song belongs to the second version but does not end with a reconciliation.

Feasts at the court of a prince in Kievan Rus were not simply a form of entertainment. They also provided a prince with the opportunity to have personal contacts with his retainers and subjects and functioned as a council where important decisions of state were made. Feasts lie at the center of the quarrel between Ilya and Vladimir. When Ilya is not seated in a place of honor or is not invited, he perceives this as a sign that Vladimir has removed all bogatyrs from his council in favor of the "fat-bellied boyars" and "rich merchants." Ilya is so upset by Vladimir's neglect of the bogatyrs who defend Kiev from its enemies that he "rebels" by seeking companions among "tavern riff-raff," "village bumpkins," "tradesmen," and "bast-wearing peasants." Furthermore, he commits sacrilege when he shoots down golden and silver crosses from churches and then sells the metal to buy drinks for his "guests."

E.S. Shoimer collected the translated variant in 1939 in Pudoga Region of Karelia from the woman epic singer and lamenter A.M. Pashkova. Although other performers usually relate how Prince Vladimir sends only Dobrynya on a "peace mission" to Ilya, Pashkova expands this episode to include four people, in some instances treats them humorously, and inserts "realistic" details about them. Vaska Dolgopoly (long skirts or tails on a coat) is made so drunk by the wily Ilya that he cannot find his way back to Vladimir's palace. Alyosha, because of his scorn for the "tavern riff-raff," is hit three times by the insulted Ilya, who calls him a "priest's dog" (line 151), a reference to

Alyosha's patronymic (Popovich), meaning the son of a priest (*pop*). The "epic dandy" Churila forgets his "faithful service" and instead amuses himself with women in "Marinka's Lane," perhaps a "red-light district" and an allusion to the enticing sorceress Marinka in the song "Dobrynya and Marinka." Dobrynya, after he approaches carefully and speaks softly, is accepted and joins Ilya's feast only because he and Ilya are sworn brothers. Despite his outward anger, Ilya is in control of the situation and, in his customarily calm and reasoned way, adroitly deals with each successive "envoy" from Prince Vladimir.

Pashkova concludes her variant of the bylina with a paraphrase of the last three lines from a poem entitled "Ilya Muromets" by the poet A.K. Tolstoy (1817–1875). Her rendition of the bylina about Ilya's rebellion against Prince Vladimir is an example of a song recorded during the last stages of the Russian epic tradition and, since she was literate, reflects the influence of written literature on oral poetry.

Ilya Muromets Quarrels with Prince Vladimir

Source: G.N. Parilova and A.D. Soimonov,
Bylinas of the Pudoga Region (Petrozavodsk, 1941), no. 2.

In the city, in the city of Kiev,
At gracious Prince Vladimir's,
There was a banquet and a feast of honor.
Vladimir of capital Kiev had summoned
5   The princes and the boyars of Kiev,
All the mighty Russian bogatyrs,
And all the daring polyanitsas,
But Vladimir of capital Kiev didn't invite
The old Cossack Ilya Muromets
10   To that feast of honor.
     Ilya grew angry and became enraged,
He went out into the wide courtyard,
He tightened his taut supple bow,

He adjusted his tempered arrows,
15   He walked through the city,
He walked through Kiev,
He shot at God's churches,
He broke the crosses off the churches,
He shot off the golden cupolas,
20   He pulled the clappers out of the bells.
Ilya went to the drinking houses,
Ilya spoke these words:
"Please come outside, you tavern riff-raff,
On the square, on Archer's Square!*
25   Pick up the golden cupolas,
Pick up the silver crosses,
Take them to the drinking houses,
And sell the silver and the gold.
First buy some barrels of green wine,
30   And second buy some barrels of heady beer,
And third buy some barrels of sweet mead."
Then the tavern riff-raff
Very quickly left the drinking houses,
They picked up the silver and the gold,
35   They sold them in drinking houses.
First they rolled out the barrels of green wine,
Second the barrels of heady beer,
And third the barrels of sweet mead.
Ilya Muromets, the son of Ivan,
40   Shouted in a loud voice:
"You drunkards and you sots!
Gather on Archer's Square,
Gather, you tradesmen from Archer's Square,
Gather, you village men,
45   You wearers of bast shoes and overalls,
Men as well as women!
Come to Ilya's feast of honor!
I'll feed you until you're full,

---

*The name "archer's square" may be an anachronism, since only later, in Muscovite Rus during the seventeenth century, were some sections of cities inhabited by "archers," who comprised the military of the time.

I'll give you drinks until you're drunk."
50   Then there came together and gathered
All the drunkards and all the sots,
All the tradesmen from Archer's Square,
All the village men,
All the wearers of bast shoes and overalls,
55   Men as well as women,
At Ilya Muromets' feast of honor.
Ilya Muromets, the son of Ivan,
Stood and measured out wine with a dipper.
        The prince's servants heard about this,
60   They ran to the white-stone palace,
And they spoke to Prince Vladimir:
"Hail to you, our Sun, Vladimir of capital Kiev!
You're eating, drinking, and enjoying yourself,
But you don't know the trouble hanging over
        Kiev.
65   The old Cossack Ilya Muromets
Has flown off the handle and has started
        showing off,
He's broken the crosses off the churches,
He's shot off the golden cupolas,
He's pulled out all the clappers of the bells,
70   He's rolled out barrels of wine on the square,
He's been regaling the tavern riff-raff
And all the village poor."
        Then Vladimir, Prince of capital Kiev,
Threw a marten coat on one shoulder
75   And a sable hat on one ear,
He took a spyglass with him,
He went out on the upper balcony,
He looked at Archer's Square,
Where Ilya was regaling himself with the poor.
80   Vladimir of capital Kiev spoke:
"Hail to you, my princes and my boyars!
Consult with me and take counsel with me
About how to calm down Ilya and to appeal to
        his conscience,
And how to invite him to my feast of honor.

85   I myself don't feel like going
        And it's not proper to send the Princess.
        Should we send someone as a summoner?
            The princes and the boyars spoke:
        "Let's send Vaska Dolgopoly."
90   Then Vaska jumped up from behind an
                oaken table
        And ran to the Cossack Ilya Muromets.
        Vaska spoke these words:
        "Ilya Muromets, the son of Ivan!
        I've come from Prince Vladimir
95   As an envoy and as a summoner.
        Please let's go to his feast of honor."
            The Cossack Ilya Muromets spoke:
        "Hail to you, Vaska Dolgopoly!
        Please drink a goblet of green wine."
100   Vaska Dolgopoly was glad to take it.
        Ilya Muromets, the son of Ivan,
        Poured him a goblet of green wine,
        Not a small chalice but a bucket and a half,
        By weight it weighed a pood and a half.
105   Vaska took it with one hand,
        He drank the goblet in one draught.
        Then Vaska started showing off,
        He played up to Ilya Muromets:
        "Ilya Muromets, the son of Ivan!
110   You have some excellent wine,
        I drank a goblet, but my soul burns for another."
            Then Ilya Muromets poured
        A second goblet of green wine,
        He mixed it with mellowed mead,
115   He offered it to Vaska Dolgopoly.
        Then Vaska took it with one hand,
        He drank the goblet in one draught.
        After he'd drunk the goblet, he couldn't
                stand up.
            Ilya spoke these words:

120   "Hail to you, my tavern riff-raff!
Take Vaska by his white hands,
By his white hands and under his arms,
Accompany Vaska through Kiev,
Take him to the prince's courtyard,
125   So that the Kievans won't laugh at Vaska."
     Then the tavern riff-raff
Grabbed Vaska under the arms,
They accompanied Vaska through Kiev
To the prince's courtyard,
130   They let Vaska go and then returned.
Vaska Dolgopoly
Stumbled over his long skirts,
He flopped around the prince's courtyard,
But he couldn't make it to the white stone
        palace.
135   Vladimir of capital Kiev spoke:
"Please let's send a summoner—
Alyosha Popovich."
     Then Alyosha got dressed,
He set out as a summoner
140   To summon the Russian bogatyr,
The old Cossack Ilya Muromets,
To Vladimir's feast of honor.
     Alyosha the priest's son spoke:
"That's no daring honor or praise
145   For a mighty Russian bogatyr
To sit with tavern riff-raff and with the poor!
Please let's go to the feast of honor,
To our Sun, to Prince Vladimir."
     Ilya Muromets grew angry and became enraged,
150   Ilya jumped on his nimble feet:
"Hail to you, smart aleck and priest's dog!
You're not the one to teach and lecture me!"
Ilya struck him on his bogatyr's shoulders
Once, twice, and even a third time.
155   Alyosha bent over and buckled a little,

As though he'd become drunk at a feast of
    honor.
    When he came to Prince Vladimir,
Alyosha spoke these words to him:
"Ilya regaled me with all his might,
160   I barely made my way to the prince's courtyard."
    Vladimir of capital Kiev spoke:
"Hail to you, Churila Plyonkovich!
Please perform a faithful service for me, the
    Prince,
Please go as a summoner,
165   Invite the Cossack Ilya Muromets
To my princely feast."
    Then Churila very quickly
Dressed and prepared himself,
He put on shirts and shirtfronts,
170   He perfumed himself and oiled his hair,
He set out on his way.
While Churila was walking through Kiev,
He turned into Marinka's Lane,
He amused himself a little with the girls,
175   He amused himself a little with the priests'
    wives,
He forgot about Prince Vladimir.
    Vladimir, Prince of capital Kiev,
Walked around his palace and pouted,
He was expecting Ilya and Churila.
180   The day was getting on toward evening,
But Churila didn't return with Ilya.
Vladimir of capital Kiev spoke:
"Hail to you, Dobrynya Nikitich!
Please perform a faithful service for me,
185   A faithful and devoted service.
Please go as a summoner
To the old Cossack Ilya Muromets,
Please invite him to my feast of honor."
    Then Dobrynya, our dear Nikitich,

190   Didn't put on his sable coat,
And didn't put on his down hat.
Very quickly and with greatest haste
He ran through the city of Kiev
To that square, to Archer's Square,

195   He stopped and started thinking:
"Which side should I approach
My own sworn brother from,
The old Cossack Ilya Muromets?"
    Ilya Muromets, the son of Ivan,

200   Was sitting at a wooden table,
At a roughly finished wooden table.
Others were sitting all around,
The drunkards and sots were sitting there,
All the tavern riff-raff were sitting there,

205   And the village peasants were sitting there.
On their roughly finished tables
They had many tasty dishes,
They ate until they were full,
They drank until they were drunk.

210   Then Dobrynya, our dear Nikitich,
Very quickly approached the tables
And he spoke his words very softly:
"Greetings to you, my own sworn brother!
You're my big brother, Ilya Muromets,

215   I've come to you from Prince Vladimir.
Please let's go to his feast of honor."
    Then Ilya Muromets, the son of Ivan, spoke:
"If you weren't my own sworn brother,
I'd regale you as I did Alyosha Popovich,

220   But please sit down with us at the roughly
        finished tables.
For the first time I've held a feast of honor,
I haven't summoned any princes and boyars to
        the feast,
But I've gathered all the poor and all the
        peasants,

And all the tavern riff-raff."
225   Then Dobrynya Nikitich sat down
At the roughly finished table.
They ate until they were full,
They drank until they were drunk—
They weren't in any hurry to go to Vladimir.
230   Then the old Cossack Ilya Muromets spoke:
"I don't care for the prince's courtyard,
I don't like feasts,
I'm not a finicky man,
As long as there is a morsel of bread."

Epics About Dobrynya

Dobrynya and the Dragon

obrynya Nikitich is the central figure in several songs, from which four have been selected for this anthology: "Dobrynya and the Dragon," "Dobrynya and Marinka," "Dobrynya and Vasily Kazimirovich," and "Dobrynya and Alyosha." In them Dobrynya is depicted as a diplomat entrusted by Prince Vladimir with special missions; he is a musician and chess player, an archer and wrestler, and is noted for his special "knowledge" or "courtesy." Above all, Dobrynya represents the "dragon slayer" in the Russian tradition (Propp 1958b: 179–206; Putilov 1971a: 31–53). He is often considered to have come from the city of Ryazan southeast of Moscow, but his social origin is not presented consistently.

"Dobrynya and the Dragon" is one of the most complex and popular Russian epics, having been collected over seventy times. The song belongs to a group of Russian epics involving a hero's fight with a monster: "Alyosha Popovich and Tugarin," "Ilya Muromets and Nightingale the Robber," and "Ilya Muromets and Idolishche." The bylina about Dobrynya offers the clearest description of a dragon, because Tugarin, Nightingale, and Idolishche are hybrid creatures that, to varying degrees, have anthropomorphic traits. Many features customarily associated with a dragon in other traditions appear in the song about Dobrynya: Zmei Gorynishche (literally "Dragon, the Son of a Mountain") flies, has as many as twelve trunks or heads, lives in a cave in the mountains (the Saracen Mountains), is associated with water (the Puchai River), breathes fire (it threatens to burn Dobrynya), and kidnaps women (it abducts Vladimir's niece Zabava Potyatichna). These motifs are realized in different ways in other genres: in the magic tale where the hero rescues a woman and marries her; in religious verses, particularly those about Saint George and the dragon, and about Fyodor Tiron, who saves his mother from a dragon; and in saints' lives and legends. In epics and magic tales, the dragon knows that it is destined to die at the hand of a particular person.

The Russian song often begins with a description of Dobrynya's childhood, showing how he is brought up by his mother alone and how, as a boy, he kills baby dragons. Eventually he decides to leave home on his first journey for no clear reason, without his mother's blessing, and despite her warning not to go near the Puchai River. At the river he may also be warned by three women washing clothes not to go bathing naked in the river, the second prohibition that Dobrynya violates and one that also occurs in the bylina "Vasily Buslayev Travels to Jerusalem." The Puchai River is an ominous place and resembles the fiery river marking the boundary between two worlds in magic tales. When the dragon appears, Dobrynya has no weapons to defend himself with but accidentally finds a "hat of the Greek land," a hat that medieval religious pilgrims wore after visiting Mount Athos in Greece or the Holy Land. Dobrynya uses this "religious" object to overcome his opponent. Singers have forgotten the original meaning of this hat and often treat it as some kind of weapon. After Dobrynya defeats the dragon, it pleads for mercy and asks him to sign a "nonaggression pact." Dobrynya accepts the agreement, but the dragon immediately breaks it by flying to Kiev and kidnapping Prince Vladimir's niece Zabava Potyatichna. (In present-day Russian, the noun *zabava* means game, fun, or amusement.) Dobrynya goes to court in Kiev, where, even though he still has not been recognized as a bogatyr, Prince Vladimir gives him the task of rescuing Zabava. Dobrynya then relates a "complaint" about his fate to his mother, who consoles him with words about his talent for "courtesy." Displaying an epic mother's insight into her son's future, she gives him a magical whip and advice about how to encourage his horse. In the ensuing encounter, Dobrynya fights the dragon for three days and despairs of winning when a voice from heaven tells him to continue. While he is wallowing in dragon blood that the mother damp earth refuses to accept, the voice from heaven tells Dobrynya to utter an incantation and to stick his spear in the ground, thus allowing the earth to "swallow" the dragon's blood. These motifs are also encountered in religious verses about Saint George or Fyodor Tiron. Dobrynya releases numerous captives, including Zabava, whom he may take back to Kiev but whom he never marries. Russian singers sense that the dragon-slaying story is incomplete unless the hero marries the rescued woman. However, they are reluctant to include such an episode and may invent explanations, such as that Dobrynya is a peasant and therefore is an unsuitable match for the aristocratic Zabava. At this point in many recordings singers insert an episode about how Dobrynya entrusts Zabava to Alyosha Popovich, encounters the polyanitsa or bogatyrka Nastasia, and marries her instead.

The chosen variant was recorded from the singer P.L. Kalinin and appears in a composite bylina containing three episodes about Dobrynya. Kalinin omits the opening about Dobrynya's childhood and begins directly with Dobrynya's departure from home. In Russian the word for dragon (*zmei*) is masculine in gender, and the related word for snake or serpent (*zmeia*) is feminine in gender. As sometimes happens, Kalinin uses both words, with the result that the dragon's gender varies. The concluding episode about Dobrynya's marriage contains a fine example of epic hyperbole—Dobrynya hits the polyanitsa three times with his club, and she compares the blows to mosquito bites. Although relationships with women from another land or world frequently end badly for either or both people in Russian epics, Nastasia is not a sorceress and has no supernatural powers. The final section is closely connected with the song "Dunai," where Dunai fights the bogatyrka Nastasia, subdues her, and marries her, with fatal consequences for both of them.

Several interpretations have been proposed for this bylina, which actually consists of two episodes. The first is mythological in nature, involves the hero's first exploit and fight with an adversary, and is both timeless and placeless. The second concerns Prince Vladimir and the rescue of his niece as well as numerous "Russian captives" from a dragon that is depicted as an enemy of Kiev. In this way the song conveys a sense of a particular historical time and place. Members of the Historical School have expressed the view that Dobrynya, which was a common name in Kievan Rus and occurs in Old Russian chronicles, was the uncle of Vladimir I (Vs.F. Miller 1892: 32–54). During his rule as Kievan prince (980–1015), Christianity was accepted from Byzantium in 988 and a mass baptism of the Kievan population took place, according to one legend, in the Pochaina River in Kiev. Vladimir I was also known for casting down the pagan idols at this time in Kiev. Somewhat earlier, Dobrynya and Putyata, a voyevoda (a military leader or governor of a city) and perhaps the father of Zabava Potyatichna, reputedly Christianized Novgorod by fire and sword. On the basis of such information, the epic is regarded as symbolizing the acceptance of Christianity in Kievan Rus and the victory of Christianity over the "dragon of paganism." The hat of the Greek land, the voice miraculously speaking from the heavens, and the prohibition against bathing naked in a holy river, such as the River Jordan in the Holy Land, are cited to support this interpretation. Other scholars have pointed out that the theme of dragon slaying is ancient, existing long before the appearance of Christianity. Furthermore, few religious symbols really occur in the epic, the Puchai River is fraught with danger and represents the abode of the dragon, and several magical elements are present. These are the whip of seven silks that Dobrynya's mother gives him and the horse Burko that Dobrynya has inherited from his father and grandfather.

A.F. Gilferding recorded the variant selected for translation in 1871 in Povenets District of Olonets Province from the singer P.L. Kalinin.

↩ Dobrynya and the Dragon ↪

Source: A.F. Gilferding, *Onega Bylinas,* vol. 1
(Moscow and Leningrad, 1949), no. 5, pp. 130–44.

Dobrynya's mother was speaking to him,
Dobrynya Nikitich's mother was instructing him:
"Hail to you, my darling Dobrynya, Nikita's son!
Don't ride to the Saracen Mountains,
5   Don't trample little baby dragons there,
Don't rescue Russian captives there,
Don't go bathing in the mother* Puchai River.
That river is ferocious,
It's a ferocious and an angry river,
10   Fire blazes from the first current,
Sparks shower from the second current,
Smoke rises in a column from the third current,

---

* The word "mother," as a token of respect and affection, is often used as a noun of address.

Smoke rises in a column mixed with flames."
The young Dobrynya, Nikita's son,
15   Didn't listen to his parent, to his mother,
The honorable widow Ofimya Alexandrovna.
He rode to the Saracen Mountains,
He trampled little baby dragons there,
He rescued Russian captives there.
20   Dobrynya was bathing in the Puchai River,*
Dobrynya himself then said:
"Dobrynya's mother spoke to him,†
Dobrynya Nikitich's dear mother instructed him:
'Don't ride to the Saracen Mountains,
25   Don't trample little baby dragons there,
Don't go bathing, Dobrynya, in the Puchai River.
That river is ferocious,
It's a ferocious and an angry river,
Fire blazes from the first current,
30   Sparks shower from the second current,
Smoke rises in a column from the third current,
Smoke rises in a column mixed with flames.
That mother Puchai River
Is like a torrent of rain water in a gully.' "
35   Dobrynya didn't have time to say a word—
Fire blazed from the first current,
Sparks showered from the second current,
Smoke rose in a column from the third current,
Smoke rose in a column mixed with flames.
40   Then the accursed dragon emerged,
A dragon with twelve trunks:
"Hail to you, my young Dobrynya, Nikita's son!‡
If I want I'll devour Dobrynya whole,
If I want I'll crush Dobrynya with my trunks,
45   If I want I'll carry Dobrynya off as a captive."
Dobrynya, Nikita's son, then spoke:

---

*The singer omits a description of Dobrynya's journey to the Puchai River.
†The singer sometimes has Dobrynya speak about himself in the third person.
‡As in Russian magic tales, the supernatural adversary always knows and expects the hero.

"Hail to you, accursed dragon!
If you had captured Dobrynya,
Then you could brag about Dobrynya,
50   But now Dobrynya isn't in your hands."
            Then Dobrynya dove in near one shore,
Dobrynya came up on the other shore.
Dobrynya didn't have a good steed,
Dobrynya didn't have a sharp spear,
55   Dobrynya had nothing to manage with.
Then Dobrynya himself was horrified,
Dobrynya himself then said:
"It's obvious that the end has come now for Dobrynya!"
            A hat of the Greek land was lying there,
60   The hat weighed more than three poods.
He struck the dragon's trunks,
He shoved away the dragon's twelve trunks,
He pressed the dragon down with his knees,
He grabbed a knife and dagger,
65   He wanted to rip open the dragon.
            Then the dragon implored him:
"Hail to you, my darling Dobrynya, Nikita's son!
Dobrynya, be my big brother
And I'll be your little sister.
70   Let's take a solemn vow:
You're not to ride to the Saracen Mountains,
You're not to trample little baby dragons,
You're not to rescue Russian captives.
I'll be your little sister:
75   I'm not to fly to Holy Russia,
I'm not to take any more Russian captives,
I'm not to carry away any Christian people."
            Dobrynya relaxed his bogatyr's knees.
Then the dragon acted cunningly,
80   Then the dragon coiled up from under his knees,
Then the dragon flew away to the grassy steppes,
And the young Dobrynya, Nikita's son,
Started walking to the city of Kiev,
To the gracious Prince, to Vladimir,
85   To his parent, to his mother,

To the honorable widow Ofimya Alexandrovna.
   And Dobrynya bitterly complained:
"Dobrynya doesn't have a good steed,
Dobrynya doesn't have a sharp spear,
90   Dobrynya has nothing to ride on to the open field!"
   Vladimir of capital Kiev spoke:
"The evening sun is setting now,
Our feast of honor is in full swing,
But I, Vladimir, am not having a good time
95   Because of my beloved niece,
Young Zabava, Potyata's daughter.
The accursed dragon flew here,
The dragon flew through the city of Kiev.
Zabava, Potyata's daughter, was going
100   With her nurses and her maids
For a walk in the green garden.
The accursed dragon then swooped down
Toward the mother earth, toward the damp earth.
While Zabava, Potyata's daughter,
105   Was walking in the green garden,
The dragon grabbed her with its trunks
And carried her away into the dragon's cave."
   Two mighty Russian bogatyrs were sitting there:
Alyosha Levontyevich was sitting there
110   And secondly Dobrynya, Nikita's son.
Vladimir of capital Kiev spoke:
"You mighty Russian bogatyrs!
Hail to you, Alyosha Levontyevich!*
Can you get Zabava, Potyata's daughter,
115   From the cave, from the dragon's cave?"
   Alyosha Levontyevich then spoke:
"Hail to you, our Sun, Vladimir of capital Kiev!
I've heard in this wide world,
I've heard from Dobrynya Nikitich
120   That Dobrynya is the dragon's sworn brother.
The accursed dragon would give up

---

* The singer should also have included Dobrynya.

Zabava, Potyata's daughter,
To the young Dobrynya Nikitich
Without a battle and without a fight and bloodshed."
125   Vladimir of capital Kiev spoke:
"Hail to you, my darling Dobrynya, Nikita's son!
Please get Zabava, Potyata's daughter,
From the dragon's cave.
If you don't get Zabava, Potyata's daughter,
130   I'll order Dobrynya's head cut off."*
        Then Dobrynya hung his reckless head,
He lowered his bright eyes
Down toward the floor, toward the brick floor.
Dobrynya said nothing in answer to Vladimir.
135   Dobrynya stood up on his nimble legs,
He paid Vladimir great appreciation
For the cheerful banquet.
He went to his parent, to his mother,
To the honorable widow Ofimya Alexandrovna.
140   Then his parent, his mother, met him,
Then she spoke to Dobrynya herself:
"My dear child, why aren't you cheerful?
Why has my dear child hung his reckless head?
Hail to you, my young Dobrynya, Nikita's son!
145   Didn't you find the dishes suitable?
Or didn't you find the drinks appropriate?
Or did some fool then mock you?
Or did some drunkard call you by a nasty name?
Or did they pass you over with a goblet?"
150   Dobrynya, Nikita's son, then spoke,
Then he spoke to his parent, to his mother,
The honorable widow Ofimya Alexandrovna:
"Hail to you, my honorable widow, Ofimya
                Alexandrovna!
I found the dishes suitable,
155   And I found the drinks appropriate,
I wasn't passed over there with a goblet,

---

*Although in Russian magic tales a hero is often threatened with punishment if he
fails to carry out a task, in epics such a motif is rarely encountered.

And a fool didn't mock me,
And a drunkard didn't call me by a nasty name.
Our Sun, Vladimir of capital Kiev,
160   Imposed a great service on me—
I have to get Zabava, Potyata's daughter,
From the cave, from the dragon's cave.
But now Dobrynya doesn't have a good steed,
But now Dobrynya doesn't have a sharp spear,
165   He has nothing to go with to the Saracen Mountains
To the dragon, to the accursed dragon."
      Then his parent, his mother, spoke to him,
The honorable widow Ofimya Alexandrovna:
"Now, my dearest child,
170   Young Dobrynya Nikitich!
Pray to God and lie down to sleep,
The morning will be wiser than the evening,*
Tomorrow will be a better day for us.
Go to the stalls, to the stalls in the stable,
175   Take a steed from the stalls in the stable—
Your father's and your grandfather's steed is there,
Burko has been standing there for fifteen years,
His legs are covered up to the knees in manure,
The door is filled up to the middle with manure."
180   Then Dobrynya, Nikita's son,
Went to the stalls, to the stalls in the stable,
He jerked the door out of the manure,
The steed jerked its legs out of the manure,
And then Dobrynya Nikitich took it,
185   Dobrynya took the good steed
By the bridle, by the braided bridle,
He led the steed out of the stalls in the stable,
He fed the steed the finest wheat,
He gave the steed some mead to drink.
190   Dobrynya then lay down to sleep on a large hay wagon.
He got up very early in the morning,
He washed himself very clean,

---

*A Russian proverb meaning "sleep on it."

He dressed himself very well,
And he saddled his good steed.
195   He put saddlecloths on saddlecloths,
He put felt blankets on the saddlecloths,
He put a Circassian saddle on the felt blankets,
And then Dobrynya mounted his good steed.
Then his parent, his mother, saw him off,
200   The honorable widow Ofimya Alexandrovna.
At his departure she gave him a whip,
She gave him a Shemakhan whip
Made of seven kinds of silk.
        And she instructed Dobrynya:
205   "Hail to you, my darling Dobrynya, Nikitich's son!
Here's a Shemakhan whip for you.
You'll go to the Saracen Mountains,
You'll trample little baby dragons,
And you'll rescue Russian captives.
210   If your Burko can't gallop
And can't shake the baby dragons off his feet,
Lash your Burko between his ears,
Lash him between his ears and between his legs,
Lash him between his legs, between his rear legs.
215   Say these words yourself to Burko:
'Burko, now start galloping
And shaking the baby dragons off your feet!' "
Then she said goodbye and returned back home.
        Then people saw Dobrynya mounting his horse,
220   But they didn't see the daring Dobrynya riding.
He didn't ride along the roads or through the gates,
He went over the city wall
And past the corner tower,
He rode to the Saracen Mountains.
225   He trampled little baby dragons,
And he rescued Russian captives.
The baby dragons gnawed at Burko's fetlocks
So that Burko couldn't gallop.
Then Dobrynya became horrified on his steed—
230   Now the end had come for Dobrynya!
He remembered his mother's instructions,

He stuck his hand in his deep pocket,
He pulled out his Shemakhan whip
Which was made of seven kinds of Shemakhan silk,
235 He lashed his Burko between his ears,
He lashed him between his ears and between his legs,
He lashed him between his legs, between his rear legs.
He said these words to Burko:
"Hail to you, my Burko, now start galloping
240 And shaking the baby dragons off your feet!"
His Burko started galloping
And shaking the baby dragons off his feet,
He trampled all the little baby dragons,
He rescued the Russian captives.
245 Then the accursed dragon emerged
From the cave, from the dragon's cave
And then she spoke to Dobrynya herself:
"Hail to you, my darling Dobrynya Nikitich!
You've violated your solemn vow,
250 You've come to the Saracen Mountains
To trample my little baby dragons."
Then Dobrynya Nikitich spoke:
"Hail to you, accursed dragon!
Did I violate my solemn vow
255 Or did you, accursed dragon, violate yours?
Why did you fly through the city of Kiev
And carry away Zabava, Potyata's daughter?
Surrender Zabava, Potyata's daughter,
Without a battle and without a fight and bloodshed!"
260 The dragon wouldn't surrender her without a battle
        and without a fight and bloodshed,
The dragon started a battle and big fight,
And much shedding of blood with Dobrynya.
    He fought with the dragon for three whole days,
But he couldn't kill the accursed dragon.
265 Finally Dobrynya wanted to ride away—
A voice from the heavens then announced to Dobrynya:
"Hail to you, my young Dobrynya, Nikita's son!
You've fought with the dragon for three whole days—
Fight with the dragon for three more hours."

270   Then Dobrynya fought for three more hours,
And he killed the accursed dragon.
The dragon spilled its blood,
The blood flowed down the mountain from east to west,
But then the mother damp earth
275   Wouldn't swallow the dragon's blood.
Dobrynya was standing in blood for three whole days,
Dobrynya was sitting on his steed and was horrified,
Then Dobrynya wanted to ride away.
      A voice from the heavens again announced to Dobrynya:
280   "Hail to you, my young Dobrynya, Nikita's son!
With your Tatar spear
Strike the mother damp earth,
And recite a charm to the earth."
      Then he struck the damp earth,
285   And he recited a charm to the earth:
"Open wide, mother damp earth,
In all directions, in all four directions!
Swallow all the dragon's blood!"
The mother damp earth opened wide
290   In four directions, in all four directions,
It swallowed the dragon's blood.
      Dobrynya dismounted his good steed
And went through the caves, through the dragon's caves,
From the caves, from the dragon's caves,
295   He led out the Russian captives.
He led out many princes and sons of princes,
He led out many kings and sons of kings,
He led out many daughters of kings,
He led out many daughters of princes
300   From the caves, from the dragon's caves,
But he couldn't find Zabava, Potyata's daughter.
He passed through many of the dragon's caves
And he entered the last cave,
There he found Zabava, Potyata's daughter,
305   In the last of the dragon's caves.
He led out Zabava, Potyata's daughter,
From the dragon's cave,
He led Zabava out to the wide world.

He spoke to the kings and sons of kings,
310   He spoke to the princes and sons of princes,
And to the daughters of kings
And to the daughters of princes:
"No matter where you've come from,
You all should go to your own countries,
315   And you all should leave for your own places—
The accursed dragon won't touch you any more.
The accursed dragon has been killed,
And the dragon's blood has passed
Down the mountain from east to west.
320   No longer will the dragon carry away Russian captives
And Christian people.
The dragon has been killed by Dobrynya,
And the dragon's life has now been ended."
        Then Dobrynya mounted his good steed,
325   He took Zabava, Potyata's daughter,
He seated Zabava on his right thigh,
And then Dobrynya started riding through the open field.
        Zabava, Potyata's daughter, spoke:
"For your service, for your great service,
330   I now should call you father,
But I cannot call you so, Dobrynya!
For your service, for your great service,
I should call you my own brother,
But I cannot call you so, Dobrynya!
335   For your service, for your great service,
I should call you my beloved friend,
But, Dobrynya, you can't fall in love with me!"
        Dobrynya, Nikita's son, then spoke
To the young Zabava, Potyata's daughter:
340   "Hail to you, my young Zabava, Potyata's daughter!
You are of princely birth,
I am of peasant birth.
We can't call each other beloved friend."
        Dobrynya carried her through the open field,
345   In the open field he came across hoofprints,
Horse's hoofprints,
The earth had been broken into clods.

Dobrynya, Nikita's son, then rode
Along those horse's hoofprints.
350   Then he saw Alyosha Levontyevich:
"Hail to you, Alyosha Levontyevich!
Take Zabava, Potyata's daughter, from me,
I've been carrying Zabava honorably,
Alyosha, take her from me honorably.
355   Please don't shame her white face—
If you shame her white face
And if she complains to me,
Then the next day I'll cut off Alyosha's head!
Please take her to Vladimir honorably,
360   To our Sun, to the Prince of capital Kiev."
He sent Zabava, Potyata's daughter,
With Alyosha Levontyevich,
He rode himself along the horse's hoofprints.
He came across a bogatyr in the open field,
365   The bogatyr was sitting on a good steed,
The bogatyr was wearing woman's clothing.
Dobrynya, Nikita's son, then spoke:
"This isn't a bogatyr on a good steed,
This seems to be a daring polyanitsa,
370   Some kind of maid or woman!"
And Dobrynya then rode toward the bogatyr,
He struck the polyanitsa on her reckless head,
The polyanitsa kept on sitting—she didn't budge,
And the polyanitsa didn't glance around.
375   Dobrynya sat on his steed—he was horrified,
Dobrynya rode away from the bogatyr,
From that polyanitsa, from that daring polyanitsa:
"Dobrynya seems to have his old boldness,
But Dobrynya doesn't seem to have his former strength!"
380   A damp oak was standing in the open field
And was a human girth around.
Dobrynya then rode toward the damp oak
To test his bogatyr's strength.
When Dobrynya struck the damp oak,
385   He smashed the whole oak into splinters.
Dobrynya sat on his steed—he was horrified:

"Dobrynya seems to have his old strength,
But Dobrynya doesn't seem to have his former boldness!"
    Dobrynya, Nikita's son, then made a run
390   On his steed, on his good steed,
Toward that polyanitsa, toward that daring polyanitsa,
He struck the polyanitsa on her reckless head,
The polyanitsa kept on sitting on her steed—she didn't budge,
And the polyanitsa didn't glance around.
395   Dobrynya sat on his steed—he was horrified:
"Dobrynya seems to have his former boldness,
But Dobrynya doesn't seem to have his old strength,
Dobrynya wore himself out fighting the dragon."
    He rode away from the polyanitsa, from the daring polyanitsa,
400   A damp oak was standing in the open field,
It was two human girths around.
Dobrynya then rode toward the damp oak,
When Dobrynya struck the damp oak,
He smashed the whole oak into splinters.
405   Dobrynya sat on his horse—he was horrified:
"Dobrynya seems to have his old strength,
But Dobrynya doesn't seem to have his former boldness!"
    Dobrynya burst into a rage at his good steed,
    And Dobrynya for the third time made a run
410   Toward that polyanitsa, toward that daring polyanitsa,
And he struck the polyanitsa on her reckless head.
The polyanitsa kept on sitting on her steed—she budged,
And the polyanitsa glanced around,
The daring polyanitsa spoke:
415   "I thought the Russian mosquitoes have been biting,
But actually Russian bogatyrs have been snapping!"
    Then she grabbed Dobrynya by his yellow curls,
She pulled Dobrynya down from his steed,
And then she lowered Dobrynya into a deep bag,
420   Into a bag, into a leather bag.
And her good steed started carrying it,
The steed started carrying it through the open field,
Her good steed proclaimed:
"Hail to you, my daring polyanitsa,
425   Young Nastasia, Nikula's daughter!

I can't carry two bogatyrs—
This bogatyr is equal to you in strength,
This bogatyr has double your boldness."
    The young Nastasia, Nikula's daughter,
430   Then lifted the bogatyr out of the leather bag,
And she spoke to the bogatyr herself:
"If the bogatyr is old and savvy—
Then I'll call him father.
If the bogatyr is young,
435   And if the bogatyr pleases me,
I'll call him my beloved friend.
If the bogatyr doesn't please me,
I'll put him on one palm, I'll squeeze him with the other,
And I'll turn him into an oatmeal pancake."
440   Then she noticed Dobrynya Nikitich:
"Greetings to you, my darling Dobrynya, Nikita's son!"
    Dobrynya, Nikita's son, then spoke:
"Hail to you, my daring polyanitsa!
How did you know me just now?
445   I've never seen you before."
    "I've often been in the city of Kiev,
I've seen you, Dobrynya Nikitich,
But you couldn't have known me from anywhere,
I'm the daughter of the Lithuanian king,
450   The young Nastasia, Nikula's daughter.
I rode to the open field to look for a fight
And to seek a husband equal to me.
If you'll take me in marriage, Dobrynya,
I'll let you go alive, Dobrynya,
455   But you must take a solemn vow with me.
If you don't take a solemn vow—
I'll put you on one palm, I'll squeeze you from above with the other,
And I'll turn you into an oatmeal pancake."
    "Hail to you, my young Nastasia, Nikula's daughter!
460   Let me go alive,
I'll take a solemn vow,
I'll accept the golden crowns with you, Nastasia."
    Then they took a solemn vow.
They started riding to the city of Kiev,

465 To the gracious Prince, to Vladimir.
Then they came to the city of Kiev,
To the gracious Prince, to Vladimir.
Then Dobrynya, Nikita's son,
Came to his parent, to his mother,

470 To the honorable widow Ofimya Alexandrovna,
And his parent, his mother, met him.
The honorable widow Ofimya Alexandrovna,
She asked Dobrynya herself:
"Who have you brought with you, Dobrynya, Nikita's son?"

475 "Honorable widow, Ofimya Alexandrovna,
My parent and my mother!
I've brought a bride for myself,
The young Nastasia, Nikula's daughter,
I'm to accept the golden crowns with her, with Nastasia."

480 They departed to the gracious Prince, to Vladimir,
And they entered the hall, the dining hall.
Dobrynya crossed himself as was prescribed,
He bowed and paid his respects
In four directions, in all four directions,

485 To the prince and to his princess in particular.
"Greetings to you, our Sun, Vladimir of capital Kiev!"
"Greetings to you, Dobrynya, Nikita's son!
Who have you brought with you, Dobrynya Nikitich?"
Dobrynya, Nikita's son, then spoke:

490 "Hail to you, our Sun, Vladimir of capital Kiev!
I've brought a bride for myself,
Nastasia and I are to accept the golden crowns."
The banns about them were published,
She was brought into the Christian faith,

495 Then he and Nastasia accepted the golden crowns,
And he and Nastasia started spending their lives together.

‹› 8 ‹›

Dobrynya and Marinka

he song "Dobrynya and Marinka" is a story about a supernatural witch, enticing courtesan, alluring sorceress, or enchanting shaman who uses her magical powers to turn an epic hero into an animal. In many cases his mother or sister, who possesses even stronger magic, forces the sorceress to turn the hero back into a human being. There are many variations on this theme in magic tales and in epics, perhaps the most notable one appearing in the tenth book of *The Odyssey,* where the goddess Circe transforms some of Odysseus's men into pigs. What may be involved is an ancient story about a temptress or a seductive woman who acts in a sexually provocative manner. The variants of the Russian song about Dobrynya and Marinka, of which some seventy have been recorded, differ greatly. For this reason, a summary of the basic motifs that occur is presented with the understanding that no single recording contains all of them. It should be mentioned that the very form of the name "Marinka" instead of the usual "Marina" is derogatory in Russian folklore and is often associated with a witch.

In the beginning, Dobrynya may be described as having served at Vladimir's court in the positions of steward, cupbearer, and gatekeeper for three years each. When his service is finished after nine years, he is free to roam the city of Kiev, but before he starts, his mother, who has the customary ability of an epic mother to foresee trouble for her son, warns him not to go to Marinka's street because she is a sorceress and has turned nine young men into aurochs (the extinct European wild ox). Dobrynya, as is typical for an epic hero, accepts the dare and goes anyway. He may take along his bow and arrows, just as though he were setting out on a journey to hunt, even though he actually stays within the city. At Marinka's palace he sees a pair of doves, usually a symbol of lovers, and he shoots an arrow that misses the doves but that

98

lands in Marinka's palace and may kill her lover Zmei Gorynych or Tugarin. They are dragon-like figures that Dobrynya or Alyosha fight in other epics. Dobrynya insists on retrieving his arrow, insults Marinka, who may offer herself in marriage, and leaves. Then Marinka cuts out pieces of the wooden floor where he stood and burns them in a stove while reciting an incantation to make Dobrynya fall in love with her. In many variants, the incantation resembles actual love charms, one brief example of which may be quoted from the collection of L.N. Maikov (*Great Russian Incantations* [St. Petersburg, 1868], no. 5).

> In the name of the Father and Son and Holy Ghost, amen. In the stove a fire burns, the wood burns, and blazes, and smolders. So should God's man, slave (name), smolder and burn for God's woman, slave (name), every day, every hour, always, now and eternally. For ever and ever, amen.

Although Marinka's actual magic words are not included in the translated song, the desired response is achieved. Dobrynya returns to her as a compliant lover whom she transforms into a wild animal such as an aurochs with golden horns, a mysterious creature that occasionally appears in Russian folklore. Singers offer various explanations about how Dobrynya's mother or sister finds out what has happened to him, one being that Marinka boasts about her prowess during a feast at Prince Vladimir's. A female relative, who has superior magical powers, comes to Marinka, demands that she restore Dobrynya to his human form, and threatens to turn Marinka herself into an animal. Marinka gives in to the more compelling sorceress, turns herself into a magpie, flies to the open field, lights on Dobrynya, and promises to return him to his normal state if he will marry her. Dobrynya agrees, but once he is married to Marinka he claims his authority over her and kills her much as Ivan Godinovich kills his unfaithful wife in the bylina by that name.

One can only guess as to the precise reason why Dobrynya wants to go to Marinka and what their relationship has been. One interpretation is that the subtext may concern the traditional epic theme of bride taking or a marriage proposal on Dobrynya's part, in which case the arrow represents a courtship symbol (Putilov 1972: 5–11). However, this is not a magic tale with a happy ending after the hero returns home with his bride from the otherworld—this is an epic. As usually happens when a Russian bogatyr becomes involved with a woman having supernatural powers, either or both meet a disastrous end. Also, when a woman exceeds the bounds of accepted behavior in Russian epics, she is punished, most often by death. Curiously Dobrynya invites Christian priests to perform a ritual to ensure that such an evil being is destroyed once and for all—they burn Marinka's body and scatter the ashes. The discovery of small snakes in Marinka's joints reveals her essential evil nature and give additional justification for her execution. Another interpretation of this perplexing song is that Russian singers have taken an ancient plot about a witch enchanting a hero and have adapted it to the pattern of a Kievan heroic epic. Thus singers connect the story with one of the main Russian bogatyrs, send Dobrynya off on a journey even though he remains within Kiev, motivate his visit to Marinka and the shooting of the doves by saying that he is going on a hunt, introduce the dragon lovers, and in some variants describe how Marinka boasts at a feast.

Some members of the Historical School, as part of their effort to find specific historical sources for events and personages in Russian epics, have looked upon Marinka as representing Marina Mniszek, the Polish Catholic wife of False Dmitry I (the monk Gregory Otrepev), who briefly ruled Moscow as tsar from 1605 to 1606 during the Time of Troubles (1598–1613). Because of her turbulent life and love adventures, Marina Mniszek has been depicted in legends and historical songs as a sorceress who could change herself into a magpie (Vs.F. Miller 1897–1924, 1: 153–59).

However the bylina about Dobrynya and Marinka may be interpreted, the motivation for certain actions remains obscure, and the adaptation to the Kievan epic tradition is only partially realized.

A.F. Gilferding collected this variant from the singer I. Eremeev in Olonets Province during the summer of 1871.

✔ Dobrynya and Marinka ✘

Source: A.F. Gilferding, *Onega Bylinas,* vol. 2
(Moscow and Leningrad, 1950), no. 163.

In the capital city, in Kiev,
There lived the young Dobrynya Nikitich.
Dobrynya liked to go hunting,
To hunt like a young man,
5   Like a young man and bogatyr.
He got up very early in the morning,
He washed himself very thoroughly,
He dressed himself very handsomely,
He saddled his good steed
10   With his Circassian saddle,
He took along his taut and supple bow.
The good youth rode to the open field
To hunt like a young man,
Like a young man and bogatyr.
15   And he rode onto Marinka's street.
At the home of the beauty, of Marinka, of
        Ignaty's daughter,
Two gray doves were sitting
In her window, in her window with a wooden frame.
Dear Dobrynya Nikitich
20   Drew his taut and supple bow,
And he lay a tempered arrow on it,
He released the arrow at the gray doves.
The tempered arrow didn't fly,
It didn't fly toward the gray doves,
25   But the tempered arrow flew straight
Toward the beauty, toward Marinka, into her high palace.
    Dear Dobrynya Nikitich
Quickly dismounted his good steed,
He quickly walked along the passageways
30   And even more quickly along the new vestibule.
When he reached the white-stone palace,

Dobrynya didn't cross his white face,
And Dobrynya didn't pray to the miraculous image,
He took back his tempered arrow.*
35   The beauty Marinka, Ignaty's daughter,
Spoke these words herself:
"Hail to you, Dobrynya Nikitich!
Why didn't you pray to God
And why didn't you bow to me?"
40   Dobrynya, the son of Nikita, spoke:
"Oh you bitch and whore, Marinka, Ignaty's daughter!
You've been a viper in the city,
You've been a bloodsucker in the city,
You've ruined many innocent people,
45   You want to ruin me, Dobrynya,
But I'm not your morsel and I'm not your food.
If you eat me, then you'll strangle,
If you swallow me, then you'll choke."
He took back his tempered arrow,
50   He left the white-stone palace.
The beauty Marinka, Ignaty's daughter,
Took a knife, a dagger,
She cut out Dobrynya's footprints.
Dear Dobrynya Nikitich
55   Was riding through the distant open field,
He rode to the city, to Kiev,
Then the pangs of love began to affect Dobrynya,
He rode into Marinka's street,
He quickly dismounted his good steed,
60   Even more quickly he went along the passageways.
When he entered the white-stone palace,
He crossed himself as was instructed,
He made his bows as was prescribed,
Dobrynya prayed and bowed
65   In four directions, in all directions,
And to the beauty Marinka in particular.
The beauty Marinka, Ignaty's daughter,

---

*Dobrynya does not observe the entrance ritual and acts in an insulting way toward Marinka.

Rudely kept sitting and didn't get up from her seat,
Didn't get up from her seat and didn't bow.

70   She spoke these words herself:
"Well, Dobrynya, you were roaming at liberty,
But now, Dobrynya, you're in my hands.
If I want, I'll turn Dobrynya,
I'll turn Dobrynya into a magpie,

75   I'll turn Dobrynya into a raven,
I'll turn Dobrynya into a pig,
I'll turn Dobrynya into a bay-colored aurochs."
        She set about turning Dobrynya,
She turned Dobrynya into a magpie,

80   She turned Dobrynya into a raven,
She turned Dobrynya into a pig,
She turned Dobrynya into a bay-colored aurochs.
She had twenty-seven aurochs in the field,
He happened to be the thirtieth aurochs in the field.*

85   The aurochs' horns were made of gold,
The aurochs' feet were made of silver,
The aurochs' hair was made of patterned velvet.
        Dobrynya's own dear sister
Was waiting for her dear brother,

90   She spoke these words herself:
"This seems to be a serious matter."
The sister turned herself into a magpie,
She flew to Marinka's street,
To the beauty Marinka, Ignaty's daughter,

95   She sat in the window with a wooden frame,
She spoke these words herself:
"Oh you bitch and whore, Marinka, Ignaty's daughter!
You've been a viper in the city,
You've been a bloodsucker in the city,

100   You've ruined many innocent people,
You want to ruin my brother.
But he's not your morsel and he's not your food,
If you eat him, then you'll strangle,

---

*The singer, who counts in multiples of three, uses the number twenty-seven (nine times three) to indicate something far, far away.

If you swallow him, then you'll choke.
105   If I want, I'll turn Marinka,
I'll turn Marinka into a magpie,
I'll turn Marinka into a raven,
I'll turn Marinka into a pig,
I'll let Marinka loose to roam around Kiev."
110   The beauty Marinka, Ignaty's daughter,
Took a solemn vow
To turn Dobrynya back the way he was,
Back the way he was and as he was before.
Marinka turned into a magpie,
115   She flew to the distant open field.
When she came to the distant open field,
To the shepherds, to the shepherds of the aurochs,
She perched on Dobrynya Nikitich,
She perched on his shoulder, on his right one,
120   She spoke these words:
"My dear, Dobrynya Nikitich!
Make me a solemn vow,
You take me, Marinka, in marriage,
I'll turn Dobrynya back the way he was,
125   Back the way he was and as he was before."
Dear Dobrynya Nikitich
Made a solemn vow
To take Marinka in marriage.
She set about turning Dobrynya,
130   She turned Dobrynya back into a magpie,
She turned Dobrynya back into a raven,
She turned Dobrynya back into a pig,
She turned Dobrynya back the way he'd been,
The way he'd been and as he'd been before.
135   They walked to the city, to Kiev.
They held a banquet and celebrated a feast.*
Dear Dobrynya Nikitich
Took Marinka in marriage.
They went to the warm bedroom to sleep.

---

*The dinner and celebration following a wedding ceremony.

140 Dear Dobrynya Nikitich
  Took his sharp saber with him,
  He cut off Marinka's reckless head.
    Dear Dobrynya Nikitich
  Got up very early in the morning,
145 He washed himself very thoroughly,
  He dressed himself very handsomely,
  He gathered all the priests and archpriests,
  He spoke these words himself:
  "Yesterday Dobrynya was married and wasn't a bachelor,
150 Today Dobrynya is a bachelor and isn't married—
  He cut off Marinka's reckless head."
    All the priests and archpriests gathered,
  They made a blazing fire,
  They threw Marinka's white body
155 On this fire, on this blazing fire.
  In the beauty, in Marinka, Ignaty's daughter,
  In every joint there was a baby snake,
  A baby snake and a baby reptile.

❧ 9 ❧

Dobrynya Nikitich and Vasily Kazimirovich

*L*ike many Russian epics, the one called "Dobrynya Nikitich and Vasily Kazimirovich" opens with a feast at Prince Vladimir's court. This scene is revealing because it shows how Vladimir consults with the members of his court and how important affairs of state are decided at such gatherings. In this instance, Vladimir asks for someone to take the "taxes and tribute" due for the past twelve years to Tsar Batur Batvyesov. In the translated variant, this name replaces the historical name Khan Batu (died 1255), who was the leader of the Tatar forces during the conquest of Kievan Rus and the early period of Tatar rule. Like Kalin Tsar in the bylina "Ilya Muromets and Kalin Tsar," Tsar Batur is addressed as "Dog," perhaps because the dog was a totem for some Tatar clans. The phrase "Polenyetsian land" (line 21), as is the case with many geographical names in Russian epics, is fictitious and merely suggests something foreign. In response to Prince Vladimir's request for a volunteer to deliver the tribute, all the people, or "ranks," at the feast fall silent except Vasily Kazimirovich. He "boasts" that he can transport a huge tribute consisting of various items in multiples of the epic number forty. Afterward Vasily has second thoughts about his "bragging" at the feast, perhaps because he has accepted a task that is beneath the dignity of a bogatyr. It should be pointed out that this is the only bylina in which Vladimir is presented as paying tribute for a long time to another ruler. After meeting and becoming sworn brothers, Vasily Kazimirovich and Dobrynya Nikitich persuade Prince Vladimir to renounce paying tribute and instead to demand payment from Tsar Batur. During his meeting with the Russian envoy Vasily, Tsar Batur several times repeats the menacing words "You'll never leave here alive." Tsar Batur then proposes three competitions that involve playing chess, cards, or dice, shooting an enormous bow and arrow, or wrestling. Vasily replies that he places his trust in the Mother of God (the Virgin Mary) and in his sworn brother Dobrynya. For his part, Dobrynya each time realizes that the unexplained but assumed conditions are a matter of life or death, and he skillfully manages to overcome all challenges. The third competition turns into an epic battle scene that ends when Tsar Batur promises to send tribute to Prince Vladimir.

While the epic "Ilya Muromets and Kalin Tsar" may concern the invasion of Kievan Rus by the Tatars from 1238 to 1242, the song "Dobrynya Nikitich and Vasily Kazimirovich" appears to involve the period of Tatar rule (Propp 1958b: 355–68). Some folklorists consider that this bylina, which has been recorded twenty-seven times, reflects Tatar domination in the fourteenth and fifteenth centuries, when Russian princes were required to collect tribute from their people and to take it to the Tatar Khan. This was a dangerous mission for Russian envoys because they ran the risk of being put to death. Within such a context the ending of the bylina is historically incorrect but may instead be based on earlier songs describing how a Russian hero, such as Dobrynya, traveled to collect tribute from peoples subservient to Kievan Rus before the Tatar conquest. Although Russian princes themselves delivered tribute to the Tatar Khans, in the bylina Prince Vladimir himself does not make payment but instead sends his representatives.

Other scholars connect the epic about Dobrynya and Vasily with events in 1480 (Smolitskii 1963). At that time Khan Akhmat demanded that Muscovite Prince Ivan III pay tribute and appear in person, but the Prince refused to give such obeisance. As a result, Khan Akhmat sent an invading army, which stopped opposite Russian forces across the Ugra River near the southern Russian city of Kaluga. After a "standoff" lasting about a month, Khan Akhmat withdrew his forces without a decisive battle. After this event Muscovite Rus stopped paying tribute to the Golden Horde. The adherents of the Historical School see a prototype of Vasily Kazimirovich, who appears only in this song, in the historical figure Vasily Kazimir whose name is mentioned numerous times in Russian chronicles from 1456 to 1481 (Vs. F. Miller 1897–1924, 2: 186–210).

Although Vasily Kazimirovich acts as Prince Vladimir's official emissary in this epic, Dobrynya intercedes for Vasily at critical moments and resolves all the "difficult tasks" imposed by Tsar Batur, much as the magical helper assists the main character in a magic tale. Dobrynya emerges as a many-sided figure who is restrained in his actions, is endowed with "courtesy" (that is, knowledge), is entrusted with difficult diplomatic missions, and is a brave bogatyr who always looks out for the interests of the Kievan state.

S.I. Guliaev collected the variant chosen for this anthology from the talented blind singer L.G. Tupitsyn in 1871 near the city of Barnaul in the Altai Region of southwestern Siberia.

Dobrynya Nikitich and ~ Vasily Kazimirovich ~

Source: S.I. Guliaev, *Bylinas and Songs of the Altai* (Barnaul, 1988), no. 10.

> At the palace of gracious Prince Vladimir,
> Of our Sun, Vladimir Vseslavyevich,
> There was a banquet, a feast of honor,
> For many princes and boyars,
5   And for all the rich polyanitsas,
> And for all the brave druzhina.
> Vladimir treated them all and honored them all,
> He, the Prince, greeted them all.
>   Halfway through the feast the boyars had drunk their fill,
10   And halfway through the meal they'd eaten their fill.
> The Prince was walking around the hall,
> He was waving his white hands,
> And he was shrugging his powerful shoulders,
> And he spoke these words himself:
15   "Hail to you, my princes and my boyars!
> Hail to you, all my rich polyanitsas

And all my brave druzhina!
Who would serve me, the Prince, with loyalty and truth,
With devoted loyalty and truth?
20 Who would ride to the distant land,
To the distant Polenyetsian land,
To Tsar Batur Batvyesov?
Who would deliver the taxes and tribute to him
For the years, for the past years,
25 For the period of twelve years?
Who would deliver forty wagons of pure silver?
Who would deliver forty wagons of red gold?
Who would deliver forty wagons of fine pearls?
Who would deliver forty times forty bright falcons?
30 Who would deliver forty times forty black sable furs?
Who would deliver forty times forty black hounds?
Who would deliver forty gray stallions?"
      Then the highest rank hid behind the lowest,
Neither the highest nor the lowest rank responded.
35 From a seat, from a middle seat
And from a white-oak bench,
A daring good youth stepped forward
On his feet, on his nimble feet,
In his green morocco leather boots,
40 With their heels, with their silver heels,
With their nails, with their gilded nails,
By name Vasily, Kazimir's son.
      Having moved away from the table, Vasily bowed,
And he spoke these words:
45 "Hail to you, our father, Vladimir the Prince!
I'll serve you with devoted loyalty and truth,
Devoted in and out of sight.
I'll ride to the distant land,
To the distant Polenyetsian land,
50 To Tsar Batur Batvyesov.
I'll deliver your taxes and tribute
For the years, for the past years,
For the period of twelve years.
I'll deliver your gold and silver,
55 I'll deliver your fine pearls,

I'll deliver forty times forty bright falcons,
I'll deliver forty times forty black sable furs,
I'll deliver forty times forty black hounds,
I'll deliver your forty gray stallions."
60   Then Vasily became despondent
And hung his reckless head,
And Vasily lowered his bright eyes
Toward the father,* toward the brick floor.
He put on his black hat and went away
65   From the palace, from the high palace.
        He went out on the wide street,
He walked along the wide street.
Toward him came a daring good youth,
By name the young Dobrynya Nikitich.
70   Dobrynya took off his down hat and bowed very low:
"Greetings, daring good youth,
By name Vasily, Kazimir's son!
Why are you coming so cheerless from the feast?
Didn't you get a good place from the Prince?
75   Didn't you get a goblet of green wine?
Or did someone dishonor you, Vasily?
Or did you brag too much about riding somewhere?"
And then Vasily passed by as sullen as a bull.
        Dobrynya ran ahead a second time,
80   He took off his down hat and bowed very low:
"Greetings, daring good youth,
By name Vasily, Kazimir's son!
Why are you coming so cheerless from the feast?
Why are you coming so cheerless and so joyless?
85   Vasily, didn't you get a good place?
Didn't you get a goblet of green wine from the Prince?
Or did you brag too much, Vasily, about riding
                somewhere?"
And then Vasily passed by sullen as a bull.
        And Dobrynya ran ahead a third time,
90   He took off his down hat and bowed very low:

---

* Here the word "father" is merely a noun of address.

"Greetings, daring good youth,
By name Vasily, Kazimir's son!
Why are you coming so cheerless from the feast?
Why are you coming so cheerless and so joyless
       from the feast?
95   Vasily, didn't you get a good place?
Didn't you get a goblet of green wine?
Or did someone dishonor you, Vasily?
Or did you brag too much about riding somewhere?
I won't betray you during battle
100   Or during a time of quick death."
      And then Vasily was overjoyed,
He took Dobrynya in his embrace,
He pressed Dobrynya to his heart,
And he spoke these words himself:
105   "Hail to you, my daring good youth,
By name the young Dobrynya Nikitich!
Dobrynya, be a big brother to me
And I, Vasily, will be a little brother to you.
I was at gracious Prince Vladimir's
110   At a gathering of honor,
At a gathering of honor, at a big feast.
I bragged too much about riding from the Prince
To that land, to that distant land,
To Tsar Batur Batvyesov,
115   To deliver taxes and tribute to him,
For the years, for the twelve years.
To deliver there gold and silver,
To deliver there fine pearls,
To deliver forty times forty bright falcons,
120   To deliver forty times forty black sable furs,
To deliver forty times forty black hounds,
To deliver forty gray stallions."
     And the young Dobrynya Nikitich spoke:
"We won't deliver anything from Prince Vladimir,
125   We won't deliver taxes and tribute from him,
We'll demand from the Dog Batur Batvyesov,
We'll demand taxes and tribute from him."
     And then the youths swore brotherhood,

They returned back to Prince Vladimir.
130   They entered the white-stone palace,
They crossed themselves as was prescribed,
They made bows as was instructed,
They bowed in all directions,
To the princes and the boyars in particular.
135   "Greetings to you, Vladimir the Prince,
And to the darling Princess!"
        And gracious Vladimir the Prince then spoke:
"You're welcome, daring good youths,
Vasily, Kazimir's son,
140   And Dobrynya Nikitich,
To sit down at our table and to share a meal!"
        The Prince poured goblets of green wine,
Not small goblets but a bucket and a half,
He served the daring good youths.
145   The youths took the goblets with one hand,
They drank the goblets in one draught,
And they sat down on the oaken benches.
They spoke these words themselves:
"Hail to you, our gracious Vladimir the Prince!
150   We don't wish to deliver taxes and tribute from you,
We wish to take them from Batur Batvyesov
And to bring taxes and tribute from him
To our gracious Prince Vladimir.
Sit down, our gracious Vladimir the Prince,
155   Sit down at the oaken table
And quickly write letters in cursive:
'Give me, Dog, the taxes and tribute
For the years, for the past years,
And for the period of twelve years.
160   And you give us some gold and silver,
And you give us some fine pearls,
And you give us some bright falcons,
And you give us some black sable furs,
And you give us some black hounds,
165   And you give us some gray stallions.' "
        Gracious Vladimir the Prince
Gave the daring youths the letters in cursive,

And Vasily Kazimirovich took the letters
And put them in his pocket.
170 The youths stood up on their nimble legs,
They spoke these words themselves:
"Bless us, gracious Vladimir the Prince,
To ride to the Polenyetsian land."
  And the youths went out on the main porch,
175 The youths whistled like a nightingale,
The youths roared like a wild animal.
  From the far, far away open field
Two steeds came running, two powerful ones,
With all a bogatyr's equipment.
180 The youths took their steeds by their silk reins,
And they stepped into their sturdy stirrups,
And they climbed in their Circassian saddles.
Only at the Prince's did people see
The daring youths mounting their steeds,
185 They didn't see where the youths had ridden away.
They found the first set of hoofprints three versts away,
They found the second set of hoofprints twelve
    versts away,
But they couldn't find the third set of hoofprints.
  The good youths came to the distant land,
190 To the distant Polenyetsian land,
To Tsar Batur Batvyesov,
To his palace, to his high palace.
They stopped on the wide street,
They quickly dismounted their good steeds,
195 They didn't tie their steeds to anything,
They didn't leave their steeds to be tended,
They didn't ask permission from the gatekeepers at
    the gates,
They didn't ask permission from the doorkeepers at
    the doors,
They threw the doors wide open,
200 They entered the white-stone palace,
The youths didn't pray to God,
They didn't bow to the Dog Batur,
They spoke these words themselves:

"Greetings, Dog Tsar Batur!
205   We've brought you taxes and tribute
From gracious Prince Vladimir."
     And Vasily Kazimirovich took out,
He took out the letters in cursive
From his silken pocket
210   And laid them on the oaken table:
"Dog, accept the taxes and tribute
From gracious Prince Vladimir."
     The Dog Batur Batvyesov unsealed them,
He unsealed the letters in cursive,
215   And he spoke these words himself:
"Hail to you, Vasily, Kazimir's son!
You'll never leave here alive!"
     Vasily, Kazimir's son, then answered:
"I put my trust in the Miraculous Mother, the
          Most Holy Mother of God,
220   And I put my trust in my dear brother,
In my own sworn brother,
In Dobrynya Nikitich."
     The Dog Batur spoke these words:
"Good youths, let's play some dice and cards!"
225   Vasily, Kazimir's son, then spoke:
"I didn't expect to have that kind of game with you here,
And I didn't bring along the proper people from Kiev."
     And Batur started playing dice and cards
With the young Dobrynya Nikitich.
230   The first time the Dog couldn't beat him,
The young Dobrynya Nikitich beat him.
And the second time the Dog couldn't beat him,
The young Dobrynya Nikitich beat him.
And the third time the Dog couldn't beat him,
235   The young Dobrynya Nikitich beat him.
     Then the Dog was offended,
Batur the Dog spoke these words:
"Vasily, you'll never leave here alive!"
     Vasily, Kazimir's son, then spoke:
240   "I put my trust in the Mother, the Most Holy
          Mother of God,

And I put my trust in my dear brother,
In my own sworn brother,
In Dobrynya Nikitich."
    The Dog spoke these words:
245 "Hail to you, Vasily, Kazimir's son!
Let's shoot at a distance of three versts,
At a distance of three and a half versts,
To hit a damp and twisted oak
And to hit a golden ring."
250   And Vasily, Kazimir's son, then spoke:
"I didn't expect to have that kind of shooting with
        you here,
And I didn't bring along the proper people from Kiev."
    The Dog went out on the main porch,
He screamed and yelled in a shrill voice:
255 "Hail to you, my faithful servants!
Please bring me my taut bow
And bring me a tempered arrow."
    Nine Tatars brought him his taut bow,
Six Tatars brought him a tempered arrow.
260 The Dog took his taut bow
And took his tempered arrow,
The Dog tightened his taut bow
And put an arrow on the string,
And he shot at a distance of three versts,
265 At a distance of three and a half versts.
The first time he shot—he undershot,
The second time he shot—he overshot,
The third time he shot—he missed.
    And he gave his taut bow to Dobrynya,
270 To Dobrynya Nikitich,
And he gave him a tempered arrow.
Dobrynya tightened the taut bow,
And the taut bow roared like a wild animal,
And Dobrynya broke the taut bow in two,
275 And he threw the taut bow on the damp earth.
He aimed the tempered arrow point forward,
And he threw the arrow a distance of three versts,
A distance of three and a half versts,

And he hit the damp and twisted oak,
280   He hit the golden ring—
The damp oak shattered into splinters.
        And then the Dog was offended,
He took it for a great insult.
The Dog spoke these words:
285   "Hail to you, Vasily, Kazimir's son!
You'll never leave here alive!"
        Vasily, Kazimir's son, then spoke:
"I put my trust in the Most Pure Mother of God,
And I put my trust in my dear brother,
290   In my own sworn brother,
In Dobrynya Nikitich."
        The Dog Tsar Batur then spoke:
"Youths, can we wrestle a little with you?"
        Vasily, Kazimir's son, then spoke:
295   "Dog, I didn't expect to have that kind of wrestling,
I didn't bring along the proper people from Kiev."
        And then the Dog was offended.
He screamed and yelled, the Dog, in a shrill voice.
The Tatars came running—you couldn't count
                their number.
300   And Dobrynya went out on the wide street,
And he walked up and down the street.
Three Tatars grabbed Dobrynya.
He took the first Tatar and tore him to pieces,
He took the second Tatar and trampled him,
305   And he took the third Tatar by his feet,
He walked through the Tatar force,
He waved his white arms,
He thrashed the Tatars with this Tatar.
When he went in one direction—he cleared a street,
310   When he turned to the side—he cleared a lane.
        Vasily was standing on the main porch,
Vasily didn't chance to have a battle mace,
Vasily didn't chance to have a sharp saber,
He didn't chance to have a Tatar spear,
315   But he chanced to have a white-oak axle,
A white-oak axle seven sazhens long.

He grabbed the white-oak axle,
He swung it with all his might,
And he thrashed the Tatars with it.
320   Then the Dog grew frightened,
He tried to hide under the benches.
The Dog ran out on the main porch,
He screamed and yelled in a shrill voice:
"Hail to you, my daring good youths!
325 Leave me at least some Tatars to have offspring,
Leave me at least some Tatars to have descendants."
Then the youths didn't listen to him.
      The Dog screamed and yelled in a shrill voice:
"I'll give the taxes and tribute,
I'll give them to gracious Prince Vladimir
330 For the years, for the past years,
For the period of twelve years.
I'll give him forty wagons of red gold,
I'll give him forty wagons of fine pearls,
335 I'll give him forty wagons of pure silver,
I'll give him forty times forty bright falcons,
I'll give him forty times forty black sable furs,
I'll give him forty times forty black hounds,
I'll give him forty gray stallions."
340   The youths then listened to him,
They threw their weapons down on the damp earth,
They went to the high new palace,
The Dog paid them the taxes and tribute.
He filled wagons decorated with gold,
345 He sent them to the capital city of Kiev,
To gracious Prince Vladimir,
To our Sun, Vladimir Vseslavyevich.
      Then the good youths mounted their good steeds,
They stepped into their sturdy stirrups,
350 And they climbed in their Circassian saddles,
And the youths rode to their country,
To gracious Prince Vladimir.
They came to the high new palace,
They stopped on the wide street,
355 They entered the white-stone palace,

They crossed themselves as was prescribed,
They bowed as was instructed:
"Greetings, gracious Vladimir the Prince!"
    "Welcome, daring good youths!"
360   He seated them on oaken benches,
He poured out goblets of green wine,
Not small goblets but a bucket and a half,
He served the wine to the daring good youths.
The youths took it with one hand,
365   The youths drank it in one draught,
They stood up on their nimble feet and bowed very low:
"Hail to you, our gracious Vladimir the Prince!
We've brought you the taxes and tribute
From the Dog Batur Batvyesov."
370   Gracious Vladimir the Prince then bowed to them,
He bowed to the damp earth:
"Thanks to you, my daring good youths!
You've served me with loyalty and truth,
With devoted loyalty and truth."

Epics About
Alyosha Popovich

10

Alyosha Popovich, His Squire Yekim, and Tugarin

lyosha Popovich is the youngest of the three main Russian bogatyrs, the others being Ilya Muromets and Dobrynya Nikitich. Alyosha appears as the central hero in three epics: "Alyosha and Tugarin," "Dobrynya and Alyosha Popovich," and "Alyosha and the Sister of the Petroviches-Zbrodoviches." In them Alyosha emerges as a complex and contradictory figure, who might best be regarded as the "trickster" in the Russian epic tradition. He is noted for his slyness, agility, and craftiness, may be fun loving, is sometimes depicted as a "mocker of women," and may occasionally be a liar and cheat. Because his patronymic (Popovich) indicates that Alyosha is the son of a priest (*pop*), some singers emphasize this as a part of their negative treatment of him (Smirnov and Smolitskii 1974: 343–60, 396–406).

The bylina about "Alyosha Popovich and Tugarin" has been collected in forty recordings, many being fragmentary or in prose, and exists in two main versions. According to the first, Alyosha and his squire (or arms bearer) Yekim (or Torop) set out riding from Rostov, a city east of Moscow. When they come to a crossing of three roads, they choose the one to Kiev rather than those to the cities of Suzdal or Chernigov. Along the way they run into a religious pilgrim, with whom Alyosha exchanges his clothing. The two companions then come across the giant Tugarin, who asks questions about Alyosha, knowing that they are destined to fight. Through his disguise as a pilgrim, Alyosha tricks Tugarin, kills him, and takes his head to Prince Vladimir in Kiev. In the second version, Alyosha and his servant also set out from Rostov for Kiev, but they arrive there without any adventures along the way. At a feast in Prince Vladimir's palace, Alyosha, who has not yet been recognized as a bogatyr, takes the lowest place in the social hierarchy by sitting next to the stove. At the feast, Tugarin not only acts arrogantly toward Vladimir but gorges himself and behaves openly as Princess Apraxia's lover. In some variants she responds freely, much to the disgust of Alyosha who, in a tense but somewhat comic scene, insults Tugarin with stories about the deaths of a dog and a cow. Finally provoked, Tugarin hurls a dagger at Alyosha and then accepts a challenge to fight. In some variants the fight takes place in the "open field," where Tugarin flies with "paper wings," falls to earth after Alyosha's prayer for rain is answered, and is killed by Alyosha. Such "divine intervention," which may also occur in the bylina "Dobrynya and the Dragon," is probably derived from "religious verses." While the first version of this epic concerns the theme of a hero encountering and defeating a monster on a journey, the second shows Tugarin to be an aggressor who has seized Kiev and dominates Prince Vladimir's court.

The depiction of Tugarin is inconsistent and contradictory, since zoomorphic and anthropomorphic features are combined in him (Propp 1958b: 206–24; Putilov 1971b: 54–62). During the battle with Alyosha, a serpentine essence may clearly emerge in Tugarin, and he may be called "the Serpent Tugarin" (Zmei) or "Tugarin the Serpent's Son" (Zmeyevich). Like the dragon that Dobrynya fights, Tugarin has wings and can fly under the clouds, but his wings are made of paper and seem to be artificial. Although he may be a giant, glutton, and kidnapper of women, features that are often associated with a dragon in Russian epics and magic tales, in the scene at Vladimir's feast Tugarin has a predominantly human appearance. In some recordings Tugarin acquires specific historical characteristics, a process that reveals how a mythological monster may be transformed into a traditional Tatar enemy of Kiev. In this respect, Tugarin resembles a potentate whom twelve bogatyrs carry into the feast at Prince Vladimir's palace on a "platter of red gold."

As in many other epics, several different historical layers may be reflected in "Alyosha Popovich and Tugarin." For example, members of the Historical School have attempted to discern several historical personages in this bylina. The figure of the Polovetsian Khan Tugor-kan, who lived in the last part of the eleventh century, has been regarded as overlaying the mythological dragon motif. Since Tugor-kan's daughter married Prince Sviatopolk Iziaslavich of Kiev, during periods of peace between the Russians and the Polovetsians Tugor-kan was received with honor in Kiev. However, despite his kindred relations with Kievan Rus, in 1096 he besieged Pereiaslavl (a city near Kiev), where he was killed in battle. The similarity of the names "Tugarin" and "Tugor-kan" (Khan) seems obvious, but for linguistic reasons it appears more likely that the name was derived from the Slavic root *tug,* meaning grief, insult, or coercion.

According to the adherents of the Historical School, events of the thirteenth century are also reflected in this song. In particular, Alyosha Popovich is connected with the hero Alexander Popovich, who is mentioned many times in Old Russian chronicles. He served the Principality of Rostov and died in 1223 during the battle on the River Kalka, the first shattering encounter of the Russians with the Tatars. However, the medievalist D.S. Likhachev (1949) believes that the name Alexander Popovich was entered in the chronicles in the fifteenth century under the influence of epic songs, thus reflecting oral poetry rather than history. Since a majority of the variants connect Alyosha Popovich with Rostov, a city northeast of Moscow, the epic "Alyosha and Tugarin" and its main bogatyr may have originated in the Principality of Rostov. Other tokens of Rostov involve the name of Alyosha's father, who is called the "cathedral priest" Leonty or Fyodor. In Rostov a certain Bishop Leonty was killed in 1071 by rebellious pagans, and another esteemed prelate had the name Fyodor.

Since they share the same plot and contain similar motifs, interactions have taken place between the songs "Alyosha and Tugarin" and "Ilya Muromets and Idolishche." As a means of explaining these similarities, some scholars consider that Alyosha Popovich gradually became a less heroic figure and that Ilya Muromets came to occupy a central position in the epic consciousness of the singers. According to this interpretation, Alyosha's victory over a monster began to be attributed instead to Ilya Muromets. Other investigators regard the two songs as separate realizations of the same subject.

In the translated variant, which belongs to the second version of the song, the singer, just as in the epic "Ilya Muromets and Kalin Tsar," addresses Tugarin with the epithet "Dog." The performer also inserts the episode about the exchange of clothing with a pilgrim (described as Alyosha's sworn brother Guryushko) from the first version but neglects to develop this motif further as an element of Alyosha's trickery during his encounter with Tugarin. Also it is Tugarin's horse that actually sports the strange paper wings. After the horse's wings are soaked by rain and it falls to earth, Tugarin becomes a horseman whom Alyosha outwits by hiding under the horse's mane and by suddenly reappearing to cut off Tugarin's huge head.

N.E. Onchukov took down the translated bylina in 1902 on the Pechora River in Pustozersk District of Archangel Province from the singer P.G. Markov.

Alyosha Popovich, His Squire Yekim, and Tugarin

Source: N.E. Onchukov, *Pechora Bylinas* (St. Petersburg, 1904), no. 85.

> From the far, far away open field,
> Two daring youths were riding,
> They were riding steed to steed, saddle to saddle,
> And braided bridle to bridle.
> 5   They were talking to each other:
> "Where should we ride then, brother?
> Should we ride or shouldn't we ride to Suzdal?
> In Suzdal there's much to drink,
> If we good youths would spend our money drinking,
> 10   A bad rumor would be spread about us.
> Should we ride or shouldn't we ride to Chernigov?
> In Chernigov the girls are pretty,
> We could get to know the pretty girls,
> But a bad rumor would be spread about us.
> 15   Should we ride or shouldn't we ride to Kiev?
> If we go to the defense of Kiev,
> We good youths would have something to brag about."
>   They arrived in the city of Kiev,
> They went to the Prince, to Vladimir,
> 20   To the hall, to the bright hall.

The youths dismounted their good steeds,
They left their steeds untied,
There was no one to leave the steeds with,
There was no one to tend their steeds.
25   They entered the hall, the bright hall,
They crossed themselves as was prescribed,
They bowed as was instructed,
They said a prayer to Jesus,
They bowed in all four directions,
30   But to the Prince and Princess in particular.
        "Greetings to you, Vladimir of capital Kiev!
Greetings to you, our mother, Princess Apraxia!"
        Vladimir of capital Kiev spoke:
"Greetings to you, my daring good youths!
35   What land are you from, what city?
Who's your father and who's your mother?
What name do they call you youths by?"
        Then one daring good youth spoke:
"My name is Alyosha Popovich,
40   I'm the son of the Rostov priest Levonty,
And the other is Yekim, my squire."
        Then Vladimir of capital Kiev spoke:
"The news has long ago been spreading about you,
Now I chance to see Alyosha face to face.
45   The first place for you is next to me,
The second place for you is opposite me,
The third place for you is where you want to sit."
        Alyosha Popovich spoke:
"I won't sit in the place beside you,
50   I won't sit in the place opposite you,
I'll sit in the place where I want to sit,
I'll sit on the stove, on the tiled stove,
Under the fine chimney damper."
        A little time went past,
55   The door of the hall was opened wide,
The infidel monster came in,
The Dog Tugarin Zmeyevich.
The Dog didn't pray to God,
He didn't greet the Prince and Princess,

60   He didn't bow to the princes and boyars.*
                The height of the Dog was three sazhens,
                The breadth of the Dog was two girths,
                A tempered arrow would fit between his eyes,
                A span would fit between his ears.
65   The Dog sat down at the oaken table,
                At the right hand of Prince Vladimir,
                At the left hand of Princess Apraxia.
                     Alyosha couldn't restrain himself behind the stove:
                "Hail to you, Vladimir of capital Kiev!
70   Don't you and the Princess live in love?
                The infidel monster is sitting between you,
                The Dog Tugarin Zmeyevich."
                     They brought a white swan to the table,
                The Dog took out his steel knife,
75   The Dog snagged the white swan,
                The Dog tossed it in his mouth,
                He moved it from cheek to cheek,
                He spit out the swan bones.
                     Alyosha couldn't restrain himself behind the stove:
80   "At my father's home, at my dear father's home,
                At the home of the Rostov priest Levonty,
                There was an old watchdog.
                The dog dragged itself around under the table,
                And it choked on a swan bone.
85   The Dog Tugarin won't escape that fate,
                He'll lie in the field, in the distant open field."
                     They brought a large pie to the table,
                The Dog took out his steel knife,
                He snagged the pie on his steel knife,
90   The Dog tossed the pie in his mouth.
                     Alyosha couldn't restrain himself behind the stove:
                "At my father's home, at my dear father's home,
                At the home of the Rostov priest Levonty,
                There was an old cow in the yard,
95   The cow dragged itself around the yard,

---

*Tugarin does not observe this Russian entrance ritual because he is a foreigner and enemy who deliberately shows his scorn for Vladimir and his court.

The cow choked on some dregs,
The Dog Tugarin won't escape that fate,
He'll lie in the distant open field."
    Then the Dog Tugarin spoke:
100   "Is that a serf sitting on your stove?
Is that a serf and a lout sitting there?"
    Vladimir of capital Kiev spoke:
"That's neither a serf nor a lout sitting there,
That's a mighty Russian bogatyr,
105   By name Alyosha Popovich."
    The Dog took out his steel knife,
The Dog threw the knife behind the stove,
He threw it at Alyosha Popovich.
Alyosha's Yekim was nimble,
110   He grabbed the knife by the handle,
The knife had silver inlays,
The inlays weighed twelve poods.
    Alyosha and Yekim started boasting:
"Since we're not from here,
115   And since the bread is not from here,
Let's drink up everything, let's eat the last kalach."*
    The Dog came out from behind the table,
He spoke these words himself:
"Alyosha, go with me to the field."
120   Alyosha Popovich spoke:
"Dog, I'm ready to go with you now."
    The squire Yekim then spoke:
"Hail to you, Alyosha, my sworn brother!
Will you go yourself or will you send me?"
125   Alyosha Popovich then spoke:
"I'll go myself and I won't send you—
Your strength is twice as great as mine."
Alyosha set out along the road on foot.
His sworn brother was approaching him,
130   His sworn brother Guryushko was approaching,
On his feet he was wearing shoes of wild boar skin,

---

*The meaning of the passage is unclear, but Alyosha and Yekim seem to be making ironic remarks about the voracious glutton and outsider Tugarin.

On his head he was wearing a hat from the Greek land,
In his hands he was carrying a walking staff,
The staff weighed ninety poods,
135   But he supported himself with that staff.
       Alyosha Popovich spoke:
"Greetings to you, my sworn brother,
My sworn brother Guryushko!
Give me your shoes of wild boar skin,
140   Give me your hat from the Greek land,
Give me your walking staff."
Alyosha put on the shoes of wild boar skin,
Alyosha put on the hat from the Greek land,
He took the walking staff in his hands,
145   Alyosha set out along the road on foot,
He supported himself with this staff.
He saw the Dog in the open field,
The Dog was flying through the skies,
The wings of his steed were made of paper.
150   Then Alyosha, the son Popovich,
Prayed to the Savior, to the Almighty,
To the Miraculous Mother, to God's Mother:
"Hail to you, our Savior, the Almighty!
Miraculous Mother, Mother of God!
155   Let the Lord send heavy rain from the sky,
Let the Lord soak the paper wings,
Let the Lord drop Tugarin to the damp earth."
       Alyosha's prayer was pleasing to God,
The Lord sent heavy rain from the sky,
160   Tugarin's paper wings were soaked,
The Lord dropped the Dog on the damp earth.
       Tugarin was riding through the open field,
He was shouting and yelling at the top of his lungs:
"Should I trample Alyosha with my steed?
165   Should I kill Alyosha with my spear?
Should I swallow Alyosha alive?"
       Alyosha was agile,
He hid below the steed's mane,
The Dog was looking through the open field
170   To see where Alyosha now lay trampled.

Then Alyosha Popovich
Jumped up from below the steed's mane,
With his walking stick
He struck Tugarin on his reckless head,
175   His head rolled off his shoulders like an onion,
His body fell on the damp earth.
    Then Alyosha, the son Popovich,
Caught Tugarin's good steed,
With his left hand he held the steed,
180   With his right hand he cut up Tugarin's body,
He cut the body into small pieces,
He scattered the body through the open field,
He stuck Tugarin's reckless head,
Alyosha stuck it on his sharp spear,
185   He took the head to the Prince, to Vladimir,
He brought it in the hall, in the bright hall,
He spoke these words himself:
"Hail to you, Vladimir of capital Kiev!
If you don't have a big cauldron,
190   Then here is Tugarin's reckless head.
If you don't have any big drinking cups,
Then here are Tugarin's bright eyes.
If you don't have any big platters,
Then here are Tugarin's big ears."

11

Dobrynya and Alyosha Popovich

*T*he central theme of the song "Dobrynya and Alyosha Popovich" concerns the return of a husband to his wife's wedding, a subject that appears in *The Odyssey* and in the magic tales, epics, ballads, and legends as well as in the works of the written literature of many peoples (Sumtsov 1893). According to the features common to the story, the husband, for explained or unexplained reasons, leaves home for seven, nine, or twelve years and asks his wife to wait for him. A friend returns, falsely says that the husband has died, and plans to marry the wife. Far away from home, the husband miraculously hears about the impending wedding and just as miraculously returns home before the ceremony is completed. He may appear at the wedding feast disguised as a minstrel, beggar, pilgrim, or monk; he may perform as a musician; and he may be recognized by his wife through his ring in a glass of wine, a birth mark or scar, or through the music. The wife has usually been faithful and is happily reunited with her husband, but he may take retribution against the friend. This song is the most popular in the Russian epic tradition, having been recorded over 300 times.

The Russian version of this ancient story has been adapted to the Kievan cycle and has included, as active figures, Dobrynya Nikitich, his mother, his wife Nastasia, Alyosha Popovich, Prince Vladimir, and Princess Apraxia (Propp 1958b: 277–86; Smirnov and Smolitskii 1974: 413–18). The complex nature of this epic and its numerous personages give singers ample opportunities to develop the psychology of the participants, their emotions, and their motivations. In the translated variant, Dobrynya tells his wife to wait for him six years, after which she may marry anyone but his sworn brother Alyosha Popovich. Nastasia fulfills her vow, but, after Alyosha returns with the false news that Dobrynya is lying dead in the "open field," she parries the efforts of Prince Vladimir and Princess Apraxia to match her with Alyosha by extending her vow six more years. Only after twelve years have passed does Nastasia finally consent to marry Alyosha. While Dobrynya is far away from home, his prophetic horse tells him about the wedding and then rapidly takes him to Kiev, where even his mother does not recognize him. In passing, it should be mentioned that the overall wedding activities before the church ceremony could last as long as several weeks. Dobrynya disguises himself as a skomorokh and goes to the wedding feast, where Nastasia eventually recognizes him from the golden ring that he places in her wine glass. Dobrynya punishes Alyosha by thrashing him. In this bylina Alyosha appears as a dishonest person because he twice violates accepted moral code in Kievan Rus. First, Alyosha proposes marriage to Dobrynya's wife despite the fact that he cannot marry his "sworn brother's" wife according to the traditional prohibition against such a marriage among eastern Slavs (Gromyko 1984). Second, Alyosha spreads the rumor that Dobrynya has died and greatly grieves his mother. Although in some recordings Prince Vladimir sends Dobrynya on a mission, here no explanation is given about why he leaves home, where he goes, or what he does during his long absence. Prince Vladimir also plays an unseemly role by trying to arrange Alyosha's marriage to Dobrynya's wife. In some variants Vladimir forces Nastasia to agree to the marriage by threatening to make her a washer woman or to exile her from Kiev. In the ending, which varies considerably from song to song, Dobrynya may ridicule Alyosha and at times Ilya Muromets may intercede for Alyosha.

A.F. Gilferding collected the variant chosen for translation from the fine singer Abram Chukov in 1871 in Kizhi District of Olonets Province. Chukov omits an introduction and opens the song with Dobrynya's elaborate lament to his mother about his fate as a bogatyr. As the ever-wise epic mother, she replies that no one is born with all talents and that his is "courtesy," that is, "knowledge." Chukov also presents a detailed description of Dobrynya disguised as a colorfully dressed but "lowly" skomorokh at the wedding feast. There Dobrynya astounds and charms all present with his playing on the gusli and with the songs that he has learned in Jerusalem and in Tsargrad, the Old Russian name for Constantinople. This scene recalls those with the gusli player Sadko in the epic by that name. The middle part of the song focuses on Nastasia, who remains faithful to Dobrynya and manages to postpone the wedding for six more years despite the coercion of Alyosha and Prince Vladimir. Dobrynya's mother is also deeply saddened by the false news that Alyosha spreads about Dobrynya's death. In the end, Dobrynya makes Vladimir feel ashamed of his conduct and forgives Alyosha for attempting to marry Nastasia but will not forgive him for making his mother suffer in vain. The belief among fishermen in North Russia that the performance of a bylina could have a magical calming effect on the sea is expressed in the concluding lines.

Dobrynya and Alyosha Popovich

Source: A.F. Gilferding, *Onega Bylinas,*
4th ed., vol. 2 (Moscow, 1950), no. 149.

> Dobrynya was speaking to his mother,
> Dobrynya Nikitich was talking to his mother:
> "My darling lady, my dear mother,
> The honorable widow Ofimya Alexandrovna!
> 5   Why did you bear me, unhappy Dobrynya?
> My lady, my dear mother, you should have born me
> As a white grieving stone,
> My lady, my dear mother, you should have wrapped me
> In a white sleeve, in a sleeve of fine linen,
> 10   And my lady, my dear mother, you should have lifted me
> Up on the high mountain, up on the Saracen Mountain,
> And my lady, my dear mother, you should have lowered me
> Into the Black Sea, into the Turkish Sea.
> I, Dobrynya, would have lain there in the sea forever,
> 15   I would have lain there forever,
> I, Dobrynya, wouldn't have ridden through the open field,
> I, Dobrynya, wouldn't have killed innocent souls,
> I wouldn't have spilled blood in vain,

I, Dobrynya, wouldn't have made fathers and mothers cry,
20   I, Dobrynya, wouldn't have made young wives widows,
I wouldn't have made young children orphans."
     His lady and dear mother gave an answer,
The honorable widow Ofimya Alexandrovna:
"I would have gladly born you, child,
25   With the luck and fate of Ilya Muromets,
With the strength of Svyatogor the bogatyr,
With the boldness of bold Alyosha Popovich,
I would have born you with the stylish walk
Of Churila Plyonkovich,
30   But I bore you with the courtesy of Dobrynya Nikitich.
There are only so many qualities, God hasn't given others,
God hasn't given others and hasn't granted others."
     Dobrynya very quickly saddled his steed,
He quickly mounted his good steed,
35   He laid saddlecloths on saddlecloths,
And on the saddlecloths he laid felt blankets,
On the felt blankets he put a Circassian saddle,
He tightened all the twelve taut girths,
He put the thirteenth on for strength,
40   So that the good steed wouldn't slip out from under the saddle
And wouldn't throw the good youth in the open field.
The saddle girths were made of silk,
The clasps of the girths were made of steel,
And the buckles on the saddle were made of red gold.
45   Just as silk won't tear and steel won't wear,
And just as red gold won't tarnish,
So the youth sat on his horse and didn't grow old.
     His dear mother saw Dobrynya off,
She said goodbye and then returned,
50   She went home and started weeping.
     By his stirrup, by his right stirrup,
Dobrynya's beloved wife then saw him off,
The young Nastasia, Vikula's daughter,
(She had been taken in marriage from the Lithuanian land),*

---

* This may be an inserted remark by the singer.

55 She spoke these words herself:
    "My darling, Dobrynya Nikitich!
    Dobrynya, when will you return home?
    When can Dobrynya be expected to return from
                    the open field?"
        Dobrynya Nikitich gave an answer:
60 "Since you've started asking me,
    Then I'll tell you now.
    Expect me, Dobrynya, in three years.
    If I don't return in three years, then wait another three,
    And when six years have passed,
65 If I, Dobrynya, don't return from the open field,
    Pray for me, Dobrynya, as one who's dead.
    And you, Nastasia, will have your full freedom.
    Live as a widow or get married,
    Get married to a prince or to a boyar,
70 Or to a mighty Russian bogatyr,
    But don't get married to my sworn brother,
    To the bold Alyosha Popovich."
        His lady, his dear mother,
    Started walking around her chamber,
75 She started raising her voice,
    And she spoke these words herself:
    "Just as the one and only bright sun
    Now has set behind the dark forests
    And only the young shining moon has remained,
80 So my one and only dear child,
    Young Dobrynya, Nikita's son,
    Is far, far away in the open field.
    Will God grant that I'll see him alive once more?
    Only his beloved wife has remained,
85 The young Nastasia, Vikula's daughter,
    As consolation for the widow's anguish and great sorrow."
        They waited for Dobrynya to return from the open field
                    for three years,
    For three years and also for three days,
    Three whole years of time had passed,
90 But Dobrynya hadn't returned from the open field.
    They waited for Dobrynya three more years,

Day after day sped by as fast as rain may fall,
Week after week sped by as fast as grass may grow,
Year after year sped by as fast as a river may run.
95   Three more years of time had passed,
Six whole years of time had passed,
But Dobrynya hadn't returned from the open field.
    At that hour and at that time
Alyosha arrived from the open field,
100   He brought them the unhappy news
That Dobrynya Nikitich wasn't alive—
He was lying dead in the open field.
His reckless head had been smashed,
His powerful shoulders had been riddled with arrows,
105   He lay with his head in a dense willow bush.
Then his lady, his dear mother, wept,
Her bright eyes were filled with tears,
Her white face was stricken with grief
Over her child, over her dear child,
110   Over the young Dobrynya, over Dobrynya Nikitich.
        Then our Sun, Vladimir, started pacing,
He started arranging a marriage for Nastasia Vikulichna,
Arranging a marriage and urging her on:
"Why should you live as a young widow
115   And while away your young life?
You should get married to a prince, or to a boyar,
Or to a mighty Russian bogatyr,
Or to the bold Alyosha Popovich."
        Nastasia, Vikula's daughter, spoke:
120   "Hail to you, our Sun, Vladimir of capital Kiev!
I've fulfilled my vow to my husband—
I've waited for Dobrynya six whole years,
I'll fulfill my wifely vow,
I'll wait for Dobrynya six more years.
125   When twelve years of time have passed,
Then I'll be ready to get married.
        Again day after day sped by as fast as rain may fall,
Week after week sped by as fast as grass may grow,
Year after year sped by as fast as a river may run,
130   Twelve years of time had passed,

Dobrynya hadn't returned from the open field.
Then our Sun, Vladimir, started pacing,
He started arranging a marriage for Nastasia Vikulichna,
Arranging a marriage and urging her on:
135 "Hail to you, my young Nastasia, Vikula's daughter!
How can you live as a young widow
And while away your young life?
You should get married to a prince, or to a boyar,
Or to a mighty Russian bogatyr,
140 Or to the bold Alyosha Popovich."
      She didn't marry a prince, or a boyar,
Or a mighty Russian bogatyr,
But she decided to marry the bold Alyosha Popovich.
Their feast had been going on for the third day,
145 And that day they were to go to God's church,
She and Alyosha were to accept the golden crowns.
      At that hour and at that time
Dobrynya happened to be near Tsargrad,
Dobrynya's steed then stumbled.
150 Dobrynya, Nikita's son, then spoke:
"You rotten wolf's food and coarse bear's fur!
Why are you stumbling today?"
      Then his good steed proclaimed to him
In a human voice:
155 "Hail to you, my beloved master!
You don't know the trouble hanging over you,
Your Nastasia, the Princess,
She, the Princess, is going to marry
The bold Alyosha Popovich.
160 Their feast is going on for the third day,
Today they are to go to God's church,
She and Alyosha are to accept the golden crowns."
      Then young Dobrynya, Nikita's son,
Struck his Burushko between the ears,
165 Between the ears and between the legs,
His Burushko started leaping
From mountain to mountain and from hill to hill,
It leaped across rivers and lakes,
And it passed wide plains between its feet.

170   Dobrynya had to be in the city of Kiev.
           A bright falcon wasn't flying by,
           A good youth was driving his horse by.
           He didn't ride through the gates but went over the wall,
           Over the city wall,
175   Past the corner tower,
           To the courtyard, to the widow's courtyard.
           He rode into the courtyard without warning,
           He entered the chambers without a word,
           At the gates he didn't ask permission from the gatekeepers,
180   At the doors he didn't ask permission from the doorkeepers,
           He shoved them all away,
           He boldly entered the widow's palace,
           He crossed himself as was prescribed,
           He made a bow as was instructed,
185   First in three directions, then in a fourth,
           To the honorable widow Ofimya Alexandrovna in particular:
           "Greetings, honorable widow Ofimya Alexandrovna!"
               The doorkeepers and the gatekeepers came after him,
           They came after him and all complained,
190   They spoke these words themselves:
           "Hail to you, Ofimya Alexandrovna!
           This daring good youth
           Came riding from the field like a fast courier,
           He rode into the courtyard without warning,
195   He entered the palace without a word,
           He didn't ask permission from the gatekeepers at the gate,
           He didn't ask permission from the doorkeepers at the doors,
           He shoved us all away,
           He boldly entered the widow's palace."
200   Ofimya Alexandrovna then spoke:
           "Hail to you, my daring good youth!
           Why did you ride into the orphan's courtyard without
                   warning?
           Why did you enter her palace without a word?
           Why didn't you ask permission from the gatekeepers at
                   the gates?
205   Why didn't you ask permission from the doorkeepers at
                   the doors?

Why did you shove them all away?
If my dear child were alive,
The young Dobrynya, Nikita's son,
He would have cut off your reckless head
210   For your nasty actions."
         The daring good youth then spoke:
"Yesterday I parted from Dobrynya,
Dobrynya set out riding for Tsargrad
And I set out riding for Kiev."
215   The honorable widow Ofimya Alexandrovna
                  then spoke:
"After the first six years had passed,
Alyosha arrived from the open field,
He brought us the unhappy news
That Dobrnynya Nikitich wasn't alive,
220   He was lying dead in the open field.
His reckless head had been smashed,
His mighty shoulders had been riddled with arrows,
He lay with his head in a dense willow bush.
Then I wept over him in sorrow,
225   My bright eyes were filled with tears,
My white face was stricken with grief
Over my child, over my dear child,
Over my young Dobrynya, over Dobrynya Nikitich."
         The daring good youth then spoke:
230   "My sworn brother charged me,
The young Dobrynya, Nikita's son,
To ask for him about his beloved wife,
About the young Nastasia, about Nastasia Vikulichna."
         Ofimya Alexandrovna then spoke:
235   "Dobrynya's beloved wife is getting married
To the bold Alyosha, to Alyosha Popovich.
Their feast is going on for the third day,
And today they are to go to God's church,
She and Alyosha are to accept the golden crowns."
240   The daring good youth then spoke:
"And my sworn brother, the young Dobrynya, Nikita's son,
Charged me further to say:
'If God allows you to be for a time in Kiev,

Then take my skomorokh attire,
245   And take my maple gusli
That's always hanging on a peg in the new hall.' "
      Then Ofimya Alexandrovna came running,
She handed him the skomorokh attire
And also the maple gusli.
250   The youth dressed up like a skomorokh,
He went to the fine feast of honor,
He went to the prince's courtyard,
He didn't ask permission from the gatekeepers at the gates,
He didn't ask permission from the doorkeepers at the doors,
255   He shoved them all away,
He boldly entered the prince's palace,
Then he crossed himself as was prescribed,
And he bowed as was instructed,
First in three directions, then in a fourth,
260   To our Sun Vladimir in particular.
"Greetings to you, our Sun, Vladimir of capital Kiev
And to you, young Princess Apraxia!"
      The doorkeepers and gatekeepers came after him,
They came after him and all complained,
265   They spoke these words themselves:
"Greetings to you, our Sun, Vladimir of capital Kiev!
This daring skomorokh
Came from the open field like a fast courier,
And now he's come here as a skomorokh,
270   He didn't ask permission from us gatekeepers at the gates,
He didn't ask permission from us doorkeepers at the doors,
And he shoved us all away,
He boldly entered the prince's palace.
      Vladimir of capital Kiev spoke:
275   "Hail to you, my daring skomorokh!
Why did you enter the prince's courtyard without
        warning?
Why did you enter his palace without a word?
Why didn't you ask permission from the gatekeepers at
        the gates?
Why didn't you ask permission from the doorkeepers at
        the doors?

280   Why did you shove them all away?"
     The skomorokh didn't heed his words,
    The skomorokh didn't pay attention to his words,
    The daring skomorokh then spoke:
    "Our Sun, Vladimir of capital Kiev!
285   Tell me, where's the place for us skomorokhs?"
     Vladimir of capital Kiev spoke:
    "The place for you skomorokhs
    Is on that stove, on that glazed stove,
    On that stove, on that glazed stove by the wall."
290   The skomorokh quickly leaped on the indicated place,
    On that stove, on that glazed stove.
    He tightened the silken strings,
    The gilded strings of his gusli,
    He ran his fingers over the strings
295   And he raised his voice.
    Although he was playing in Kiev,
    He had learned his tune in Tsargrad.
    He performed his tune in the city of Kiev,
    He mentioned everyone by name in Kiev,
300   He mentioned everyone from young to old.
    All at the feast listened carefully to his playing,
    And all at the feast fell silent,
    They spoke these words themselves:
     "Our Sun, Vladimir of capital Kiev!
305   A daring skomorokh can't play that way!
    Only a Russian can play that way,
    Only a daring good youth can do it."
     Vladimir of capital Kiev spoke:
    "Hail to you, my daring skomorokh!
310   For your playing, for your joyful playing,
    Come down from the stove by the wall
    And sit with us at the oaken table,
    At the oaken table to share our meal.
    Now I'll offer you three favorite places:
315   As the first place sit down beside me,
    As the second place sit opposite me,
    As the third place sit wherever you want,
    Wherever you want or like.

The skomorokh came down from the stove, from the
glazed stove,
320 The skomorokh didn't sit beside the Prince
And the skomorokh didn't sit opposite the Prince,
But he sat down on a bench
That was opposite the betrothed Princess,
Opposite the young Nastasia Vikulichna.
325 The daring skomorokh then spoke:
"Hail to you, our Sun, Vladimir of capital Kiev!
Please bless the pouring of a goblet of green wine
And the offering of this goblet to someone I know,
To someone I know and will reward."
330 Vladimir of capital Kiev spoke:
"Hail to you, my daring skomorokh!
You've been granted a great privilege,
Whatever you want, then do it,
Whatever you think of, then do it also."
335 When this daring skomorokh
Was pouring the goblet of green wine,
He dropped his gold ring into the goblet,
He offered it to the betrothed Princess,
And he spoke these words himself:
340 "Hail to you, my young Nastasia, Vikula's daughter!
Please take this goblet with one hand,
Please drink this whole goblet in one draught.
If you drink it to the bottom, you'll see something good,
But if you don't drink it to the bottom, you won't see
something good."
345 She took the goblet with one hand,
She drank the whole goblet in one draught,
And in the goblet she saw the gold ring
With which she and Dobrynya had been betrothed,
She spoke these words herself:
350 "Hail to you, my princes and boyars,
All you princes and all you nobles!
The one sitting beside me isn't my husband,
The one sitting opposite me is my husband,
My husband is sitting on the bench,
355 He offered me a goblet of green wine."

She jumped up from the table, from the oaken table,
And fell at Dobrynya's nimble feet,
She spoke these words herself:
"Hail to you, my young Dobrynya, Nikita's son!
360 Forgive me, forgive me, Dobrynya Nikitich,
For not following your instructions
And for getting married to the bold Alyosha.
Our hair is long but our wit is short,*
We go wherever they lead us,
365 We ride wherever they take us."
Dobrynya, Nikita's son, then spoke:
"I'm not surprised by a woman's reasoning.
The husband leaves for the forest and the wife marries,
Their hair is long but their wit is short,
370 But I'm surprised by our Sun Vladimir
And by his Princess Apraxia,
Our Sun Vladimir acted as a matchmaker
And his Princess Apraxia also acted as a matchmaker,
They arranged a marriage for the wife of a living husband."
375 Then our Sun Vladimir became ashamed,
He hung his reckless head,
He lowered his bright eyes toward the damp earth.
Alyosha Levontyevich then spoke:
"Forgive me, forgive me, my sworn brother,
380 Young Dobrynya, Nikita's son!
Forgive me for my stupid offense,
I sat beside your beloved wife,
Beside the young Nastasia Vikulichna."
Dobrynya, the son of Nikita, spoke:
385 "God will forgive you for one offense,
You sat beside my beloved wife,
Beside the young Nastasia Vikulichna.
But I'll not forgive you, brother, for your other offense.
When you came from the open field after the first six years,
390 You brought the unhappy news
That Dobrynya Nikitich wasn't alive,

---

*A paraphrase of a misogynous Russian proverb.

He was lying dead in the open field.
And then my lady, my dear mother,
Wept in sorrow over me.
395   Her bright eyes were filled with tears
And her white face was stricken with grief,
I won't forgive you, brother, for this offense."
     Then he grabbed Alyosha by his yellow curls,
And he jerked Alyosha across the oaken table,
400   Then he threw Alyosha against the brick floor,
And he pulled out his traveling whip,
And he thrashed him with the whip.
During the beating no screaming was heard.
     Just as long as Alyosha had been married,
405   Just so long Alyosha had slept with his wife.
Everyone, brothers, gets married during his life,
And marriage comes about for everyone,
But God forbid such a marriage as Alyosha's.
     Then Dobrynya took his beloved wife,
410   The young Nastasia Vikulichna,
And went to his lady, his dear mother,
And he wished her good health.
     Since then they've been singing this old song about Dobrynya
To the blue sea for ensuring calm weather
415   And to you good people for listening.

Epics About
Other Kievan Heroes

12

Mikhailo Potyk

*M*ikhailo Potyk appears as the main hero only in the epic bearing his name. Interpretations of this song have varied widely, perhaps because it contains numerous archaic beliefs and blends features originating among the eastern Slavs before, during, and after Kievan Rus (Froianov and Iudin 1993; Novichkova 1982). Furthermore, this bylina has been considered to be either a conglomeration of random elements that do not form a unified story, or a flexible cycle that consists of motifs from diverse sources and genres (Iarkho 1910). However it may be regarded, this work often becomes one of the longest Russian epics, sometimes amounting to over a thousand lines. About sixty variants have been recorded.

In the most extensive versions of this song, Prince Vladimir, at an opening feast, sends the bogatyrs Ilya Muromets, Dobrynya Nikitich, and Mikhailo Potyk to collect tribute from three different lands subject to Kiev. On the way home near a backwater, Potyk sees a white swan and wants to shoot it, but "she" declares that she is actually a maiden, Marya the White Swan. She offers herself in marriage to Potyk if he will take a vow that the surviving spouse for a certain time has to enter the tomb of the spouse that dies first. The bogatyr agrees to Marya's condition, takes her to Kiev, and marries her. Prince Vladimir soon sends Potyk on another mission, this time instead to take tribute from Kiev to a foreign ruler. Potyk gambles at checkers with the ruler and in the end wins both the tribute and the kingdom, an action that resembles an episode in the bylina "Dobrynya and Vasily Kazimirovich." When Potyk learns that Marya has died, without hesitation he returns home, prepares three metal rods, enters the tomb, and is sealed in with his wife. During the night, when a serpent comes to devour her body, Potyk beats the serpent with the rods and forces it to bring him "living water," with which he revives his wife. (Living water is a common motif in Russian magic tales.) After hearing Potyk's shouts, the people of Kiev open the tomb, releasing him and his wife. Marya the White Swan then becomes famous for her immortality. As a consequence, suitors may come seeking her, including the king of Lithuania, who may respond to her wish to be taken away or may abduct her. Potyk, who may have been absent on another mission for Prince Vladimir, pursues the pair and confronts his wife, who gives him a sleeping potion to drink, pronounces a spell over him, and turns him into a stone. Potyk's sworn brothers, Ilya Muromets and Dobrynya Nikitich, come looking for him disguised as wandering pilgrims. On their way, they meet an old pilgrim, who actually is Saint Nicholas, has been sent by the Mother of God (the Virgin Mary), and shatters the stone, thus freeing Potyk. (Saint Nicholas performs a similar role as a magical helper in the epic "Sadko.") Still loving his wife, Potyk for a second time drinks her magical potion, after which she nails him to a door. Nastasia, as Marya's sister or as the king's daughter, sets him free on the condition that he marry her, and then she nails a dead Tatar to the door in place of Potyk. For a third time, the ever-trusting Potyk is ready to drink his wife's enticing potion, but, warned by Nastasia, he instead kills Marya, returns to Kiev with Nastasia, and marries her. The translated song belongs to the expanded version of this Russian epic.

According to Georg Polívka (1903), the plot of "Potyk" consists of three main episodes, which can be connected or can form separate tales in several European traditions: (1) taking a bride who demands a wedding agreement about being buried together with her husband; (2) confrontation in the tomb with a dragon and the revival of the wife; (3) her abduction and pursuit by her husband, who may return her or execute her. Thus the epic theme of bride taking may be joined to that of the unfaithful spouse. In the Russian realizations of this multifaceted story (Propp 1958b: 109–26), songs consisting only of the first episode may have a happy ending after Potyk marries Marya. Songs containing the first two episodes may conclude happily after Marya's "resurrection" in the tomb, or, in those instances when she herself changes into a serpent, they may end when Potyk kills her. Songs comprising all three episodes finish with Potyk's execution of Marya. The variants of this bylina differ further depending on the way that various elements are included. For instance, the song may begin with Potyk going on a hunt during which he meets and wants to shoot a white swan near water, features that are associated with Russian wedding songs. In some cases, in the evening on the way to Kiev, Marya may turn her future husband into various animals, just as the sorceress Marinka transforms Dobrynya in the song about them; Ilya Muromets or Dobrynya may subdue the bride, much as Siegfried subdues Brunhild in place of Gunther in the *Nibelungenlied.* In some variants, forty princes with their armies may come to Kiev and demand the surrender of Marya after her revival; Potyk may defeat them only to have her disappear with one suitor. Within the Russian tradition, the bylina "Potyk" shares features with magic tales as well as with the songs "Ivan Godinovich" and "Solomon and Vasily Okulovich," which involve an unfaithful wife. In addition, "Potyk" has several correspondences with the story about a swan maiden.

Especially in variants where Marya transforms herself into a serpent, the episode in the tomb exposes her true nature and shows that she is a sorceress and enchantress, that she comes from the world of the dead, and that she may be regarded as belonging to the "living dead" or as being a vampire. Her intention from the very beginning is to lure Potyk into the otherworld and explains why she seeks such an unusual wedding agreement. By killing Marya, Potyk not only frees himself from her charms and his love for her but also rids the world of the living from an unclean supernatural being. Potyk himself has a many-sided and contradictory character: he is a true bogatyr who defeats enemy forces in battle, he acts as a trickster when he outwits Tsar Bukhar, he deliberately prepares himself for the encounter with the serpent in the tomb, and he tests living water on a baby serpent before he sprinkles it on Marya. At the same time, Potyk is so passionately in love with Marya the White Swan that he trusts her despite the warnings of Prince Vladimir, Ilya Muromets, and Dobrynya. Potyk's eagerness to drink the magic potion three times prompts some singers to motivate his conduct by turning him into a drunkard who receives special dispensation from Prince Vladimir to drink without paying in Kiev.

As T.A. Novichkova (1982) has pointed out, the basic plot as well as many elements of this bylina are related to the hero's struggle with death. Marya the White Swan embodies the idea of death: in Russian folk beliefs the color white is the color of death; the swan is a bird that may be connected with the otherworld; and the bogatyr meets Marya near water—a river may symbolize the boundary between the world of the living and the world of the dead. The serpent does not represent a dragon such as that appearing in the song "Dobrynya and the Dragon" but is an underground creature that devours dead bodies, a feature perhaps reflecting an ancient belief. According to one type of ancient burial custom, wives were buried together with their husbands. The motif of the sleeping potion corresponds to a folk belief that death was a form of sleep; the transformation of Potyk into a stone is also connected with a group of ideas about death. Curiously, Potyk is saved from the sorceress Marya by two other women: the Mother of God, who sends Saint Nicholas to rescue him; and Nastasia, who becomes his second wife. These elements recall how Dobrynya is saved from the sorceress Marinka by his mother or sister, and they also reveal how this epic consists of both pagan and Christian elements. And finally, the scene about Potyk being nailed to the door resembles a crucifixion.

Even though this highly diverse bylina contains numerous archaic ethnographic details, it, just as other songs involving traditional epic themes, has been outwardly adapted to the Kievan cycle, particularly in regard to the setting and to Prince Vladimir's court. Several assorted historical references from various periods are also made. Tsar Bukhar, to whom Potyk takes tribute, appears to have a Tatar name. Podolia, an area in west-central Ukraine, from the fourteenth to the eighteenth centuries formed part of Lithuania and in epics is sometimes regarded as a foreign or "overseas" land. Lithuania, which in the sixteenth century was joined to the Kingdom of Poland, often represents a foreign country in general in the Russian epic world.

Folklorists have explained the origin of the hero's name in several ways, none of which has proven entirely satisfactory. For example, some investigators believe that the hero's name is derived from the thirteenth-century Bulgarian Saint Mikhail, who was from the city of Potuk and was known as a dragon slayer.

A.F. Gilferding recorded the translated variant in 1871 in Olonets Province from the singer P.L. Kalinin.

⌇ Mikhailo Potyk ⌇

Source: A.F. Gilferding, *Onega Bylinas,* 4th ed., vol. 1
(Moscow and Leningrad, 1949), no. 6.

At our Sun's, at Vladimir's,
A banquet was going on for the third day.
The sun was inclining toward evening,
The feast of honor was in full swing,
5   Everyone at the feast had drunk his fill,
Everyone at the feast of honor had eaten his fill,
Everyone at the feast burst out bragging.
  Our Sun, Vladimir of capital Kiev, spoke:
"There's nothing for me, your Sun, Vladimir, to brag about.
10   The taxes and arrears haven't been collected
For twelve years, for thirteen years,
For thirteen and a half years."
  Three mighty Russian bogatyrs were sitting there:
The old Cossack Ilya Muromets,
15   The young Dobrynya, Nikita's son,
And Mikhailo Potyk, Ivan's son.
  Vladimir of capital Kiev spoke:
"Hail to you, three mighty Russian bogatyrs!
Our old Cossack Ilya Muromets!
20   Please ride to the Stone Horde,*
To the Stone Horde, to the big land.
Please collect the taxes and arrears
For twelve years, for thirteen years,
For thirteen and a half years.
25   Our young Dobrynya, Nikita's son!
Please don't ride to the big land,
To the big land, but to the Golden Horde.
Please collect the taxes and arrears there
For twelve years, for thirteen years,

---

* A rare name in Russian epics, where the Tatar "Golden Horde" is usually mentioned.

30   For thirteen and a half years.
     Our third mighty bogatyr, Mikhailo Potyk, Ivan's son!
     Please ride to the land, to the Podolian land,
     Please collect the taxes and arrears there
     For twelve years, for thirteen years,
35   For thirteen and a half years."
          The bogatyrs became thoughtful,
     They hung their reckless heads,
     They lowered their bright eyes
     Toward the floor, toward the brick floor.
40   Mikhailo Potyk, Ivan's son, spoke:
     "Why have you bogatyrs become thoughtful?
     You bogatyrs should give an answer now."
          The Cossack Ilya Muromets spoke:
     "Hail to you, our Sun, Vladimir of capital Kiev!
45   Please send me to the big land,
     To the big land, to the Stone Horde.
     I'll collect the taxes and arrears there
     For twelve years, for thirteen years,
     For thirteen and a half years."
50   Dobrynya, Nikita's son, then spoke:
     "Hail to you, our Sun, Vladimir of capital Kiev!
     Please don't send me to the big land,
     To the big land, but to the Golden Horde.
     I'll collect the taxes and arrears there
55   For twelve years, for thirteen years,
     For thirteen and a half years."
          Mikhailo Potyk, Ivan's son,
     Spoke to Vladimir:
     "Hail to you, our Sun, Vladimir of capital Kiev!
60   Please send me to the land, to the Podolian land.
     I'll collect the taxes and arrears
     For twelve years, for thirteen years,
     For thirteen and a half years."
          The first mighty Russian bogatyr,
65   The old Cossack Ilya Muromets,
     Got up very early in the morning,
     He washed himself very cleanly,
     He prepared himself very thoroughly.

He saddled his good steed,
70   He laid saddlecloths on saddlecloths,
He laid felt blankets on the saddlecloths,
He put a Circassian saddle on the felt blankets,
He tightened the twelve taut girths,
He put on the thirteenth for the sake of strength,
75   So that in the open field his good steed wouldn't
        slip from under the saddle
And wouldn't throw the good youth in the open field.
People saw the good youth mounting his steed,
But they didn't see the daring youth riding away.
He didn't ride by the roads or by the gates,
80   He went over the city wall,
He went past the corner tower,
He set off riding toward the cross of Lebanon,
Then the bogatyr took his repose.
        The second mighty Russian bogatyr,
85   The young Dobrynya Nikitich,
Got up very early in the morning,
He washed himself very cleanly,
He prepared himself very thoroughly.
He saddled his good steed,
90   He laid saddlecloths on saddlecloths,
He laid felt blankets on the saddlecloths,
He put a Circassian saddle on the felt blankets,
He tightened the twelve taut girths,
He put on the thirteenth for the sake of strength,
95   So that in the open field his good steed wouldn't
        slip from under the saddle
And wouldn't throw the good youth in the open field.
People saw the good youth mounting his steed,
But they didn't see the daring youth riding away.
He didn't ride by the roads or by the gates,
100   He went over the city wall,
He went past the corner tower,
He set off riding toward the cross of Lebanon,
Then the bogatyr took his repose.
        The third mighty Russian bogatyr,
105   Mikhailo Potyk, Ivan's son,

Got up very early in the morning,
He washed himself very cleanly,
He prepared himself very thoroughly.
He saddled his good steed,
110   He laid saddlecloths on saddlecloths,
He laid felt blankets on the saddlecloths,
He put a Circassian saddle on the felt blankets.
He tightened the twelve taut girths,
He put on the thirteenth for the sake of strength,
115   So that in the open field his good steed wouldn't slip
           from under the saddle
And wouldn't throw the good youth in the open field.
People saw the good youth mounting his steed,
But they didn't see the daring youth riding away.
He didn't ride by the roads or by the gates,
120   He went over the city wall,
He went past the corner tower,
He set off riding toward the cross of Lebanon,
Then the bogatyr took his repose.
       Then the bogatyrs became sworn brothers,
125   They called each other sworn brothers.
       The Cossack Ilya Muromets spoke:
"Whichever of us collects things first,
Let them hurry to the other brother."
Then the brothers said goodbye.
130   The old Cossack Ilya Muromets
Rode to the big land,
To the big land, to the Stone Horde,
To collect the taxes and arrears
For twelve years, for thirteen years,
135   For thirteen and a half years.
Suddenly all the men got ready to leave,
They refused to pay their taxes and arrears
For twelve years, for thirteen years,
For thirteen and a half years.
140   Then the old Cossack Ilya Muromets
Dealt with these men in his own way,
Then the men became frightened,
They tried to hide from him behind each other,

They paid their taxes and arrears
145   For twelve years, for thirteen years,
For thirteen and a half years.
     The young Dobrynya, Nikita's son,
Didn't ride to the big land,
To the big land, but to the Golden Horde,
150   He started collecting the taxes and arrears,
For twelve years, for thirteen years,
For thirteen and a half years.
Suddenly all the men got ready to leave,
They refused to pay their taxes and arrears
155   For twelve years, for thirteen years,
For thirteen and a half years.
The young Dobrynya Nikitich
Dealt with these men in his own way.
Then the men became frightened,
160   They tried to hide from him behind each other,
They paid their taxes and arrears
For twelve years, for thirteen years,
For thirteen and a half years.
     Mikhailo Potyk, Ivan's son,
165   Went to the land, to the Podolian land,
He started collecting the taxes and arrears,
For twelve years, for thirteen years,
For thirteen and a half years.
Suddenly all the men got ready to leave,
170   They refused to pay their taxes and arrears
For twelve years, for thirteen years,
For thirteen and a half years.
Then Mikhailo Potyk, Ivan's son,
Dealt with these men as a bogatyr would.
175   Then the men became frightened,
They tried to hide from him behind each other,
They paid their taxes and arrears
For twelve years, for thirteen years,
For thirteen and a half years.
180   He collected the taxes and arrears
For twelve years, for thirteen years,
For thirteen and a half years.

Then Mikhailo Potyk, Ivan's son,
Went to walk and roam through the backwaters,
185   He wanted to shoot white swans.
He walked and roamed through the backwaters,
He wanted to shoot some white swans,
He found one white swan,
The swan was swimming in the backwater.
190   He tightened his taut bow,
He placed a tempered arrow on it,
He wanted to shoot the white swan.
The white swan then spoke to him:
"Hail to you, Mikhailo Potyk, Ivan's son!
195   Please don't shoot the white swan.
I'm not just a white swan,
I'm a beautiful girl,
I'm Marya the White Swan Princess,
I'm a Princess and a Podolian.
200   Please don't kill me, the Podolian,
Take me now in marriage,
Please take me now to the city of Kiev,
Please bring me into the Christian faith,
Let's accept the golden crowns together,
205   Let's spend our lives together."
Then Mikhailo Potyk, Ivan's son, made up his mind.
He accepted Marya the White Swan,
The White Swan Princess,
The Princess and a Podolian,
210   He made a solemn pledge with Marya.
Then he received the taxes and arrears
From the king, from the Podolian king,*
For twelve years, for thirteen years,
For thirteen and a half years.
215   He departed for the city of Kiev,
To our Sun, to Vladimir,
To the Prince of capital Kiev.
Then Mikhailo Potyk, Ivan's son,

---

* The singer could have developed this passage more. The word "king" in Russian (*korol*) always denotes a foreign ruler.

Came to the capital, to the city of Kiev,
220   To the gracious Prince, to Vladimir.
Mikhailo brought the taxes and arrears
From the land, from the Podolian land,
From the king, from the Podolian king,
He gave them to Vladimir, Prince of capital Kiev,
225   Then the Prince was overjoyed.
From Mikhailo Potyk, Ivan's son,
He received the taxes and arrears
For twelve years, for thirteen years,
For thirteen and a half years.
230   Vladimir of capital Kiev thanked Mikhailo
For collecting the taxes and arrears
For twelve years, for thirteen years,
For thirteen and a half years,
From the land, from the Podolian land.
235   Mikhailo brought Marya the White Swan Princess,
The Princess and Podolian,
Into the Christian faith.
He took a solemn vow with her:
"Whichever of us dies first
240   And goes into the damp earth,
The other also has to go there for three months,
Has to go into the damp earth."
        Vladimir of capital Kiev spoke:
"Mikhailo Potyk, Ivan's son!
245   Why are you making this solemn vow,
This unequal vow,
To go for a long time into the damp earth?"
        Then Mikhailo Potyk, Ivan's son,
Mikhailo spoke himself:
250   "Obviously I had to make a solemn vow
With Marya the White Swan,
Because I took a liking to her."
He accepted the golden crowns with her,
He started spending his life with her.
255   At that hour and at that time
The overseas Tsar Bukhar suddenly appeared,
Tsar Bukhar suddenly appeared with his envoy,

He wanted to collect the taxes and arrears
From our Sun, Vladimir,
260   From the Prince of capital Kiev.
"Hail to you, our Sun, Vladimir of capital Kiev!
Please submit your taxes and arrears to me
For twelve years, for thirteen years,
For thirteen and a half years."
265   Our Sun, Vladimir of capital Kiev,
Summoned Mikhailo Potyk, Ivan's son:
"Mikhailo Potyk, Ivan's son!
The overseas Tsar Bukhar has come to us,
He wants to collect taxes and arrears from us,
270   For twelve years, for thirteen years,
For thirteen and a half years."
Mikhailo Potyk, Ivan's son, spoke:
"Hail to you, our Sun, Vladimir of capital Kiev!
Please sit down, Vladimir, on the chair with leather straps,
275   Please write some letters in cursive:
'The taxes and arrears have been dispatched
With Mikhailo Potyk, Ivan's son,
For twelve years, for thirteen years,
For thirteen and a half years.'
280   I'll start riding now without the taxes and arrears."
Mikhailo Potyk, Ivan's son,
Started riding to the overseas Tsar Bukhar,
He was carrying the letters in cursive
To Tsar Bukhar, to the overseas Tsar:
285   "The taxes and arrears have been dispatched
With Mikhailo Potyk, Ivan's son,
For twelve years, for thirteen years,
For thirteen and a half years."
Mikhailo came to Tsar Bukhar, the overseas Tsar,
290   He gave the letters in cursive
To the overseas Tsar Bukhar.
The overseas Tsar Bukhar
Accepted the letters in cursive,
He unsealed the letters very quickly,
295   He read them even more quickly.
Then Tsar Bukhar himself was overjoyed:

"Mikhailo Potyk, Ivan's son!
Where did you leave the arrears?"
        "The axles on our wagons have broken
300   And our wagons have broken down.
The repairmen have stayed awhile there in the field
To repair the wagons in the open field."
        The overseas Tsar Bukhar spoke:
"Mikhailo Potyk, Ivan's son!
305   What do people amuse themselves with in your Russia?"
        "In our Russia people amuse themselves—
They play with oaken checkers,
They put them on maple boards."
        Then they got a maple board,
310   Then they put the oaken checkers
On the board, on the maple board.
Then they played with oaken checkers
On the maple board.
And on the board, on the maple board
315   Mikhailo Potyk, Ivan's son,
Staked his own good steed,
He staked his reckless head.
The overseas Tsar Bukhar
Made a stake on the maple board,
320   He staked the taxes and arrears
For twelve years, for thirteen years,
For thirteen and a half years.
Then they played with oaken checkers
On the maple board.
325   Mikhailo Potyk, Ivan's son, lost,
He lost his own good steed,
He lost his reckless head
On the board, on the maple board,
To the overseas Tsar Bukhar.
330   Then the overseas Tsar Bukhar,
Then the Tsar was overjoyed.
He set up the board for a second time,
He set up the oaken checkers
On the board, on the maple board.
335   Then Mikhailo Potyk, Ivan's son,

Staked on the board, on the maple board,
His Marya the White Swan,
The White Swan Princess,
The Princess and Podolian.
340   Second, he staked his parent and mother
On the board, on the maple board.
The overseas Tsar Bukhar
Made a stake on the board, on the maple board,
He staked Mikhailo's good steed,
345   He staked Mikhailo's reckless head,
He staked the taxes and arrears
For twelve years, for thirteen years,
For thirteen and a half years.
    Then they played a game for a second time,
350   They finished a game for a second time.
Mikhailo Potyk, Ivan's son, won,
He won his own good steed,
He won his reckless head,
And he won the taxes and arrears
355   For twelve years, for thirteen years,
For thirteen and a half years.
    They set up the board for a third time.
Mikhailo Potyk, Ivan's son,
Staked the taxes and arrears
360   For twelve years, for thirteen years,
For thirteen and a half years.
On the board, on the maple board,
He staked his own good steed,
He staked his reckless head.
365   The overseas Tsar Bukhar
Made a stake on the board, on the maple board,
He staked half the overseas kingdom and half its
        possessions.
Then they started playing a game for a third time,
Then they played a game for a third time.
370   Then Mikhailo Potyk, Ivan's son,
Won the game for a third time,
He won half the overseas kingdom and half its possessions
From Tsar Bukhar, from the overseas Tsar.

The overseas Tsar Bukhar grew angry—
375   He set up the board for a fourth time.
He staked all the overseas kingdom of Bukhara.
Mikhailo Potyk, Ivan's son,
Staked half the overseas kingdom and half its possessions,
He staked the taxes and arrears
380   For twelve years, for thirteen years,
For thirteen and a half years.
Then they played a game for a fourth time.
Mikhailo Potyk, Ivan's son,
Won the game for a fourth time
385   From Tsar Bukhar, from the overseas Tsar,
He won the whole overseas kingdom of Bukhara.
      They set up the board for a fifth time.
The overseas Tsar Bukhar
Staked his reckless head.
390   Mikhailo Potyk, Ivan's son,
Then staked the overseas kingdom of Bukhara
On the game, on the fifth game.
Then they started playing with checkers,
Then the door was opened wide,
395   Mikhailo's sworn brother shoved his way in,
Dobrynya, Nikita's son, had arrived.
      "My young Potyk, Ivan's son!
You're playing with oaken checkers
On the board, on the maple board,
400   You don't know the trouble hanging over you.
Your Marya the White Swan,
The White Swan Princess,
The Princess and Podolian,
Has just now died."
405   Mikhailo Potyk, Ivan's son,
Jumped up on his nimble feet,
He grabbed the maple board
With the checkers, with the oaken checkers,
He struck the door and its frame,
410   He knocked out the door and its jambs.
      The overseas Tsar Bukhar became frightened,
He implored Mikhailo Potyk, Ivan's son:

"Mikhailo Potyk, Ivan's son!
Leave me, the tsar, among the living—
415   Take all the overseas kingdom of Bukhara!"
        Mikhailo Potyk, Ivan's son,
Then spoke to his brothers himself:
"Hail to you, sworn brothers!
Please take from Tsar Bukhar, from the overseas Tsar,
420   All the overseas kingdom of Bukhara,
Leave the tsar as a caretaker,
Now I don't have time to fool with him.
Now I'll ride to the city of Kiev
To the gracious Prince, to Vladimir."
425   Then Mikhailo Potyk, Ivan's son, rode away.
        The mighty Russian bogatyrs
Then received the taxes and arrears from the tsar,
Then they received all the overseas kingdom of Bukhara,
They left the tsar as a caretaker.
430   Mikhailo Potyk, Ivan's son,
Came to the city of Kiev
To the gracious Prince, to Vladimir.
The Prince then asked him:
"Mikhailo Potyk, Ivan's son!
435   How did you manage to leave from there?"
        Mikhailo Potyk, Ivan's son, then spoke:
"Hail to you, our Sun, Vladimir of capital Kiev!
Our taxes and arrears have been won
For twelve years, for thirteen years,
440   For thirteen and a half years,
From Tsar Bukhar, from the overseas Tsar,
And all the overseas kingdom of Bukhara has been won
From Tsar Bukhar, from the overseas Tsar,
All the kingdom of Bukhara and all its possessions.
445   Several bogatyrs stayed there to receive everything,
My sworn brothers,
The old Cossack Ilya Muromets
And the young Dobrynya, Nikita's son."
        "And what can I reward you with right now?
450   Should I give you cities and their suburbs,
Or should I give you towns and their settlements?

Do you want any golden treasure?"
　　　　"I don't want anything,
I don't want cities and their suburbs,
455　　I don't want towns and their settlements,
I don't want any golden treasure.
Please give me for the taverns, for the tsar's taverns,*
Please give me the great privilege
To drink wine without ever paying,
460　　In some places by the mug or half mug,
In other places by a quarter or half bucket,
And at times in other places by a whole bucket."
　　　　Our Sun, Vladimir of capital Kiev,
Granted him the great privilege
465　　In the taverns, in the tsar's taverns,
To drink wine without ever paying,
In some places by the mug or half mug,
In other places by a quarter or half bucket,
And at times in other places by a whole bucket.
470　　　　Vladimir of capital Kiev spoke:
"Mikhailo Potyk, Ivan's son!
You've made a solemn vow in vain."
　　　　Mikhailo Potyk, Ivan's son, spoke:
"Hail to you, our Sun, Vladimir of capital Kiev!
475　　That has already been decided—
Now I have to go into the damp earth,
To go into the damp earth for three months."
　　　　Mikhailo Potyk, Ivan's son,
Then ordered a coffin to be made
480　　So that it would be possible for him to stand up in it,
To stand up and to sit down in it,
And at times to lie down in it.
He took many provisions there,
He took candles and incense there,
485　　He took enough bread for three months,
He took enough water for three months.
He went then to the blacksmiths,

---

*In some later periods in Russia, all alcohol was sold through establishments
controlled by the state.

He ordered them to forge some iron tongs.
He took three rods along:
490   The first was made of lead,
The second was made of iron,
The third he took there was made of copper.
        He departed then for the damp earth,
He departed for three months.
495   Mikhailo Potyk, Ivan's son, lived there,
He lived in the mother damp earth for one day,
He started living there for a second day.
An accursed serpent came swimming toward him,
The serpent had twelve trunks,*
500   It crawled into his iron coffin.
        Mikhailo Potyk, Ivan's son,
Grabbed the accursed serpent
With the iron tongs,
First he beat the serpent with the lead rod,
505   Second he beat it with the iron rod,
Third he beat it with the copper rod.
        Then the serpent implored him:
"Mikhailo Potyk, Ivan's son!
Don't kill me, the accursed serpent!
510   I'll give you a solemn vow
To revive Marya the Swan for you,
The White Swan Princess,
The Princess and Podolian.
I'll get some living water for you."
515   Mikhailo Potyk, Ivan's son, spoke:
"Hail to you, accursed serpent!
Cunning serpent,
Please give me a baby serpent as a solemn pledge."
Then the cunning serpent
520   Gave him a baby serpent as a solemn pledge.
Mikhailo chopped the baby serpent into fine pieces.
The accursed serpent departed,

---

*Since the singer uses the feminine word for snake (*zmeia*) instead of the masculine word for dragon (*zmei*), it is not clear what is being described. The serpent/dragon has twelve heads.

Then it obtained the living water.
Mikhailo put the pieces of the baby serpent back together,
525   He soaked the little baby serpent—
The little baby serpent started coiling.
Mikhailo splashed Marya the White Swan,
He splashed her then three times:
The first time she trembled,
530   The second time she moved,
The third time she pronounced the words:
"Fie! Fie! Fie! I've slept a long time!"
      Mikhailo Potyk, Ivan's son, then spoke:
"If it weren't for me you would have slept forever."
535   Then Mikhailo Potyk, Ivan's son, shouted
With his bogatyr's voice.
The palaces were shaken,
Their windows all fell out,
Everyone in the city was frightened.
540   Then everyone in the city said:
"Our freak didn't live long in the damp earth.
He went into the damp earth for three months—
Now only the third day has come upon us
And the freak wants out of the damp earth."
545   Then they lifted him out of the damp earth,
Out of the damp earth into the wide world.
      Then Mikhail Potyk, Ivan's son,
Went roaming around the taverns, around the tsar's taverns,
To drink wine without ever paying,
550   In some places by the mug or half mug,
In other places by a quarter or half bucket,
And at times by a whole bucket.
      Marya the White Swan,
The Princess and Podolian,
555   Sent a message to the Lithuanian king
That the Lithuanian king should come,
He should take away Marya the White Swan,
The White Swan Podolian,
The Podolian and Princess,
560   To the land, to the Lithuanian land.
      Then the Lithuanian king arrived,

Then the king arrived on the sly,
He took away Marya the White Swan,
The White Swan and the Princess,
565   The Princess and Podolian.
     Mikhailo Potyk, Ivan's son,
Didn't know the trouble hanging over him,
That the Lithuanian king
Had taken away his Marya the White Swan,
570   The White Swan Princess,
The Princess and Podolian.
Someone came galloping with unhappy news
To Mikhailo Potyk, Ivan's son:
"Mikhailo Potyk, Ivan's son!
575   You're drinking and enjoying yourself,
You don't know the trouble hanging over you,
Your Marya the White Swan,
The White Swan Princess,
The Princess and Podolian,
580   Has gone away with the Lithuanian king
To the motherland, to the land of Lithuania."
     Mikhailo Potyk, Ivan's son,
Put on a woman's clothing,
He dressed himself as a woman
585   And he started riding in pursuit
Of the Lithuanian king.
The Lithuanian king wouldn't find out,
He wouldn't find out about the pursuit.
     Then Mikhailo Potyk, Ivan's son,
590   Left in his pursuit
Of the Lithuanian king.
Marya the White Swan saw him,
The White Swan Princess,
The Princess and Podolian.
595   She spoke to the king herself:
"Hail to you, my Lithuanian king!
Someone is riding after us in pursuit,
A woman is riding after us—
Although dressed like a woman,
600   A woman's not riding in pursuit of us,

But Mikhailo Potyk, Ivan's son.
Send me quickly to meet him
And give me some sleeping potions,
He has a great weakness for wine.
605   If I offer him a goblet of green wine,
He'll drink it and then he'll fall asleep."
      Then she rode up to meet Mikhailo,
She was weeping very bitterly:
"Mikhailo Potyk, Ivan's son!
610   The Lithuanian king carried me away,
He carried me away from Kiev by force."
      She offered Mikhailo a goblet of green wine:
"Drink a goblet of green wine."
He drank it, and right then he fell asleep.
615   Then she mounted the bogatyr's steed,
She threw Mikhailo on one shoulder, on one magic shoulder,
Then she lowered him across one shoulder,
Then she recited a charm over Mikhailo:
"There where the young Mikhailo Potyk, Ivan's son, was standing,
620   Let a grieving white stone stand there,
Let Mikhailo be inside the stone."
      She departed with the Lithuanian king
For the land of Lithuania,
And she rode away to the land of Lithuania
625   To the Lithuanian king.
She lived there with the Lithuanian king,
She lived with him for a long time.
      Mikhailo's sworn brothers missed him,
The old Cossack Ilya Muromets
630   And the young Dobrynya Nikitich.
They dressed themselves as pilgrims,
They put on shoes made from the bark of a lime tree,
They put on colorless clothing,
They started walking there as pilgrims
635   From our Sun Vladimir, from the Prince of capital Kiev,
To the king, to the Lithuanian king,
To seek Mikhailo Potyk, Ivan's son,
Their own sworn brother.
During the day they were guided by the sun,

640   And during the night they were guided by a shining
     little stone.*
   They came to the stone, to the white stone.
   From a crossroads, from another crossroads,
   Then there came an old pilgrim,
   An old and graying pilgrim,
645   A graying and balding pilgrim.
    "Greetings to you, my wandering pilgrims!"
    "Greetings to you, old pilgrim,
   Old and savvy pilgrim,
   Savvy and graying pilgrim,
650   Graying and balding pilgrim!"
    "Where are you pilgrims headed?"
   Then the mighty Russian bogatyrs spoke:
   "Hail to you, old pilgrim!
   Even though we're dressed as pilgrims,
655   We're not wandering pilgrims,
   We're mighty Russian bogatyrs:
   The old Cossack Ilya Muromets
   And the young Dobrynya Nikitich.
   We've come looking for Mikhailo Potyk, Ivan's son,
660   Our own sworn brother,
   A Holy Russian bogatyr."
    The mighty Russian bogatyrs then spoke:
   "Where are you from, old pilgrim?"
    "I'm an old pilgrim from a long way off,
665   A long way off and not from here."
   He went along to look for Mikhailo Potyk, Ivan's son.
    Then the wandering pilgrims
   Came to the Lithuanian king,
   The pilgrims stood in the middle of the city,
670   Opposite the royal courtyard,
   Then the wandering pilgrims screamed—
   The palaces there were shaken,
   All the windows there fell out,
   Everyone in the city was frightened:

---

 * The passage is unclear but it may refer to precious or semiprecious stones sewn
into the clothing of wandering pilgrims, a motif that appears in other variants.

675   "What kind of miracle has happened,
What kind of pilgrims have come to us?"
      The Lithuanian king then spoke:
"That makes three miracles that have turned up."
      Marya the White Swan spoke,
680   The White Swan Princess,
The Princess and Podolian:
"That's no miracle that's turned up now,
Two bogatyrs have come to us now:
The old Cossack Ilya Muromets
685   And the young Dobrynya Nikitich.
The third pilgrim is unknown,
An unknown and graying pilgrim,
A graying and balding pilgrim,
This pilgrim is a stranger.
690   King, please invite to a feast
These wandering pilgrims.
If they don't come to our feast,
The two mighty Russian bogatyrs
Will ravage our land of Lithuania."
695   Then the Lithuanian king
Hastily went out into the wide courtyard
With Marya the White Swan,
With the White Swan Podolian,
With the Podolian and Princess.
700   She went up to the sworn brothers
Of her own sworn husband,
Then she invited them to a feast,
She was weeping very bitterly over her husband.
      The mighty Russian bogatyrs then asked her,
705   The old Cossack Ilya Muromets
And the young Dobrynya Nikitich:
"Have you seen Mikhailo Potyk, Ivan's son?"
"I haven't seen Mikhailo Potyk, Ivan's son.
I've been weeping bitterly over him,
710   I remember him every day."
      And she invited them to a feast
To see the Lithuanian king.
The Lithuanian king then came

And invited the bogatyrs as guests.
715   Then the wandering pilgrims
Came to the king, to the Lithuanian king.
They were received as guests of the Lithuanian king.
Then he gave them honorable gifts,
He gave them gold and silver,
720   And he gave them some small pearls,
And he gave them precious stones.
          Then the wandering pilgrims took their leave,
The pilgrims departed from the feast,
The pilgrims didn't learn anything there
725   About the mighty Russian bogatyr,
About Mikhailo Potyk, Ivan's son.
They departed along the path, along the road,
During the day they were guided by the sun,
During the night they were guided by a shining little stone.
730   Then they came to the stone, to the white grieving stone.
          The old pilgrim spoke,
The old and savvy pilgrim:
"Now, my wandering pilgrims,
Now you have to go in one direction,
735   And I have to go in another.
As a farewell, let's divide our possessions.*
          The mighty Russian bogatyrs then spoke:
"Hail to you, old pilgrim,
Old and savvy pilgrim,
740   Savvy and graying pilgrim,
Graying and balding pilgrim!
Please divide the gifts now."
          The old pilgrim divided them,
The old and savvy pilgrim
745   Then divided the great gifts,
He divided them into four shares.
          The mighty Russian bogatyrs then spoke:
"Why then, our old pilgrim,
Our old and savvy pilgrim,

*The gifts from the Lithuanian king.

750   Why are you dividing the gifts,
        Why are you dividing them into four shares?
        There are three of us here now,
        Who will the fourth share fall to?"
                The old pilgrim spoke to them:
755   "Hail to you, my wandering pilgrims!
        Please let's try lifting this stone—
        The fourth share will fall to the one
        Who lifts this stone above his shoulders."
                The mighty Russian bogatyrs thought this over
760   In their bogatyrs' minds:
        "Can we really lift this stone?
        If we do, this share will fall to us."
                The old pilgrim spoke to them,
        The old and savvy pilgrim:
765   "Hail to you, my mighty Russian bogatyrs!
        Please lift the grieving white stone!"
        Dobrynya, Nikita's son,
        Tried to lift the grieving white stone,
        To lift the stone above his shoulders.
770   Dobrynya lifted it to his waist—
        Dobrynya sank in the earth up to his knees,
        He couldn't lift the stone
        Above his bogatyr's shoulders.
                Then the old Cossack Ilya Muromets tried,
775   He lifted the white grieving stone,
        He lifted the stone to his chest—
        Ilya Muromets sank in the earth up to his thighs.
                Then the old pilgrim came up,
        The old and graying pilgrim,
780   The graying and balding pilgrim.
        He laid his hands on the white grieving stone
        And lifted the stone above his shoulders,
        He lowered the stone over his shoulders,
        He lowered the stone against the damp earth.
785   He recited a charm over the stone:
        "Let this stone split in two,
        Let Mikhailo Potyk, Ivan's son,
        Come out of the stone, out of the white grieving stone!"

The stone then broke in two,
790   Mikhailo Potyk, Ivan's son, came out,
He saw his own sworn brothers:
"Greetings to you, my own sworn brothers!"
      "Greetings to you, Mikhailo Potyk, Ivan's son!
How did you get into this grieving white stone?"
795   "My Marya the White Swan did this,
The White Swan Podolian,
The Podolian and the Princess.
She offered me a sleeping potion,
She offered it with green wine—
800   When I drank it right then I fell asleep,
And now I don't remember what happened."
      Then the old pilgrim spoke to him,
The old and savvy pilgrim:
"Mikhail Potyk, Ivan's son!
805   If you're in the city of Kiev
At the gracious Prince's, at Vladimir's,
Please build two churches, two cathedral churches.
Build one church for the Savior
And a second church for the Mother, the Most Holy
            Mother of God,
810   And in it a chapel for Saint Nicholas.
The Mother, the Most Holy Mother of God, entreated me
To descend for your sake to the damp earth,
To save you from death, from a vain death,
From a vain death, from a magic death."
815   The old pilgrim said goodbye,
The old and savvy pilgrim,
The pilgrim departed in his direction.
      The mighty Russian bogatyrs then spoke:
"Hail to you, sworn brother,
820   Mikhailo Potyk, Ivan's son!
Come with us in our direction,
To the city of Kiev,
To the gracious Prince, to Vladimir."
      Mikhailo Potyk, Ivan's son, spoke:
825   "Hail to you, sworn brothers!
I have to go to the land of Lithuania

To the king, to the Lithuanian king.
He drove away my good steed
And he carried away Marya the White Swan,
830   The White Swan Princess,
The Princess and Podolian."
    Then the sworn brothers spoke:
"Hail to you, sworn brother,
Mikhailo Potyk, Ivan's son!
835   She's no wife to you—she's a sorceress,
She'll finish off your bogatyr's head,
You'll suffer a vain death from her."
    Then Mikhailo Potyk, Ivan's son,
Didn't listen to his sworn brothers,
840   He ordered them to take the gifts
And to depart for the city of Kiev.
He set off walking to the Lithuanian king,
To the Lithuanian and Polish king,
He set off walking to the land of Lithuania.
845   He arrived as a wandering pilgrim,
Then he stood in the middle of the city,
Opposite the royal courtyard,
He shouted at the top of his lungs.
The palaces there were shaken,
850   All the windows fell out,
Everyone was frightened by the freak.
    Then they spoke themselves:
"Several miracles have recently occurred,
Now a miracle has happened again."
855   Marya the White Swan spoke,
The White Swan Princess,
The Princess and Podolian:
"That's not a wandering pilgrim
But Mikhailo Potyk, Ivan's son."
860   She hastily poured a goblet of a sleeping potion,
She hastily ran out into the wide courtyard,
There she met Mikhailo Potyk
With the goblet of green wine.
He drank the goblet of green wine—
865   When he'd drunk the goblet of green wine,

When he'd drunk it, right then he fell asleep.
Then she dragged him to the servants' rooms.
Then Nastasia the Princess saw
That the bogatyr was being dragged to the servants' rooms,
870   She felt sorry for him.
Marya the White Swan,
The White Swan Princess,
Came to the servants' vestibule,
She nailed the bogatyr to the wall there,
875   She drove nails into his hands and feet,
But she lacked a fifth nail,
A fifth nail for his heart,
A middle nail for his heart.
She ran out of the servants' rooms,
880   She ran after the fifth nail.
    The young Nastasia, the Princess,
Pulled the nails off the wall,
She nailed a Tatar to that place,
She nailed a dead Tatar there,
885   A dead and frozen Tatar.
Then Nastasia the Princess
Led the bogatyr out of the servants' rooms.
    Marya the White Swan came running,
The White Swan Princess,
890   The Princess and Podolian.
She didn't look there at the wall,
She nailed the Tatar there instead of the bogatyr.
She departed for the Lithuanian king,
Then she bragged to him herself:
895   "Now I've destroyed the person who hated me,
Mikhailo Potyk, Ivan's son."
    Mikhailo secretly lived three days with Nastasia,
He asked for a bogatyr's steed
From Nastasia the Princess:
900   "Hail to you, my young Nastasia, the Princess!
Please ask your parent, your father,
If he has a bogatyr's steed
To ride to the open field and to look for a fight."
    The young Nastasia, the Princess,

905 Then went to the Lithuanian king,
 To her parent, to her father:
 "Hail to you, old Lithuanian king!
 Hail to you, my parent and father!
 Please give me a bogatyr's steed
910 To ride to the open field and to look for a fight,
 To refresh my woman's face."
  The Lithuanian king then spoke:
 "Please go to the stalls in the stables,
 Please pick a suitable steed."
915 She went to the stalls in the stables,
 Then she picked the bogatyr's steed
 Of Mikhailo Potyk, Ivan's son,
 Then she drove the bogatyr's steed
 Of Mikhailo Potyk, Ivan's son,
920 To her royal porch.
 The bogatyr dressed like a woman,
 The bogatyr rode away like a woman,
 Then the bogatyr rode away to the open field.
 From the open field he rode back as a bogatyr,
925 He stood in the middle of the courtyard
 Of the Lithuanian king,
 Then he demanded a great army.*
  Marya the White Swan recognized him,
 The White Swan Princess,
930 The Princess and Podolian.
 Hastily she ran out into the wide courtyard,
 She filled a goblet with green wine
 And offered him a sleeping potion.
  The young Nastasia, the Princess,
935 Leaned out of the window up to her waist:
 "Mikhailo Potyk, Ivan's son!
 If you drink the goblet of green wine,
 If you drink it, right then you'll fall asleep.
 She'll cut off your reckless head
940 With your own sharp saber."

---

*As a bogatyr looking for a fight, Potyk wants to challenge the king's whole army.

Mikhailo Potyk, Ivan's son,
Didn't drink the goblet of green wine.
He swung his own sharp saber,
He took off her reckless head
945   For her nasty actions.
Then the Holy Russian bogatyr grew angry:
"I'll ravage all the Lithuanian land,
I'll take off the king's reckless head!"
Then Nastasia the Princess entreated him:
950   "Mikhailo Potyk, Ivan's son!
Please don't chop off my parent's reckless head
For his nasty actions,
Please don't ravage the land of Lithuania."
He subdued his bogatyr's anger;
955   He took Nastasia the Princess
From the Lithuanian king,
He took the young Nastasia honorably,
He carried her away to the city of Kiev,
To the gracious Prince, to Vladimir,
960   And he brought Nastasia into the Christian faith.
Then he and Nastasia accepted the golden crowns,
They began to spend their lives together.
He built two churches, two cathedral churches,
The first cathedral church
965   He built for the Savior,
He built the second cathedral church
For the Mother, the Most Holy Mother of God,
And for Saint Nicholas.
A song of praise has been sung to Mikhailo Potyk,
Ivan's son,
970   And to the blue sea for calm weather,
And to all good people for listening.

13

Ivan Godinovich

*T*he main events in the bylina "Ivan Godinovich," which has been collected sixty times, can be summarized as follows. At an opening feast, Prince Vladimir reproaches Ivan Godinovich because he alone is still not married. Ivan Godinovich replies that he has a prospective bride (Nastasia or Avdotya Likhodeyevna) in a distant land—in Lithuania, in India, in the Golden Horde, or, as in the translated song, in Chernigov, which is north of Kiev and is treated as a foreign city. After he asks for and receives help from Prince Vladimir, Ivan Godinovich and several bogatyrs set out to obtain the bride. When her father refuses to give Nastasia in marriage to Ivan Godinovich because she has already been promised to someone else (Koshcherishche, Afromey Afromeyevich, or Koshchei Tripetov), the Russian heroes abduct Nastasia by force. On the way back to Kiev, Ivan Godinovich is overtaken by Koshcherishche, and they start fighting. Ivan overcomes his opponent, sits on him to rip open his heart and liver, and asks Nastasia to give him a knife. However, she, tempted by Koshcherishche's promise that she will become a tsaritsa if she marries him, grabs Ivan Godinovich by his "yellow curls," throws him on the ground, and gives the knife instead to Koshcherishche, who ties Ivan Godinovich to an oak tree and amuses himself with Nastasia in the white tent. When some "prophetic" birds perch on a tree and talk among themselves about the ominous situation, Koshcherishche, angry at the implication of their words for him, wants to kill them with a bow and arrow. Ivan, much as Ilya Muromets in "Ilya Muromets and Kalin Tsar," recites an incantation that causes the arrow instead to hit Koshcherishche and to kill him. Nastasia begs forgiveness from Ivan, asks him for a promise that he will not "beat and torment her," and, after receiving a vague answer, attacks him with a saber. Ivan suddenly frees himself by shattering the oak tree and cruelly executes Nastasia in a scene that resembles the ending of "Dobrynya and Marinka."

Although the singer in the translated song suggests that Ivan Godinovich and Nastasia are married in "God's church" (line 96), the essential theme nevertheless involves bride taking and a competition between two suitors (Propp 1958b: 126–34; Putilov 1971a: 128–37, 186–89). The contrast that is implied between the world of Kiev and the world of the "heathen tsar" echoes the opposition between the land of the living and the land of the dead in Russian magic tales, where the hero may have to defeat a monster before returning home with his bride. The occasionally mentioned alternate names Koshchei or Koshcherishche indicate singers' associations with Koshchei the Immortal, who in Russian magic tales represents a "dragon-like" villain and abducts women. In this regard, a comparison of recordings of "Ivan Godinovich" and of the related song "Potyk" reveals how they have acted upon each other and also shows how they express the same prohibition in Russian epics—a bogatyr should not take a bride from the otherworld. While the bride in "Potyk" (Marya the White Swan) obviously belongs to the world of myth and magic, the prospective bride of Ivan Godinovich is an ordinary human being who, at the turning point in the plot, makes her own calculated decision to help Koshcherishche and thus gambles with her own fate. Nastasia's latent connection with the otherworld becomes apparent only in some variants where those celebrating a feast with Prince Vladimir try to dissuade the hero from marrying Nastasia with comments such as "she won't be a wife to you but a poisonous snake." Despite its general lack of fantastic elements inherent to magic tales, this bylina nevertheless contains a few echoes of the supernatural: the enchanted arrow that veers and kills Koshcherishche, the talking birds that presage future events, and the miraculous way that Ivan is suddenly able to shatter the oak and set himself free. Against the background of such ancient features, the song is set in Kievan Rus, begins at a feast in Prince Vladimir's palace, and transforms the monster Koshchei of magic tales into a heathen tsar who is an enemy of Kiev and may be called a Tatar.

The bylina "Ivan Godinovich" contains references to the traditional wedding ceremony (Loboda 1904: 203–31), which consisted of several parts and could last several weeks. Ivan and his companions form a wedding party or wedding train and, on their way to the bride's home, encounter the tracks of several animals, which represent the allegorical motif of a hunter searching for game during the preliminary stages of matchmaking. The idealized portrait of the bride (lines 21–27) resembles similar descriptions in wedding songs, and birds symbolize the couple and their families. Until the church ceremony, the two families are depicted as being hostile and as being separated by a great distance from each other.

Although Nastasia is treated as a nefarious woman and a traitor to her fiancé, she has little choice but to accept her abduction by Ivan and his companions. Even though she betrays Ivan, originally she was engaged to marry Koshcherishche, who wants to preserve their prior agreement. Despite this, as Marinka in "Dobrynya and Marinka" and Solomonida in "Tsar Solomon and Vasily Okulovich," Nastasia is depicted as betraying her fiancé or husband and is executed because of the choice she makes. She represents yet another type of woman and shows that a considerable variety of female figures exists in the world of the Russian epic.

A.F. Gilferding took down the selected text in 1871 from A.B. Batov in Vygozero in Olonets Province.

❧ Ivan Godinovich ❧

Source: A.F. Gilferding, Onega Bylinas, 4th ed., vol. 2 (Moscow, Leningrad, 1950), no. 188.

> In the city, in Kiev,
> At gracious Prince Vladimir's,
> There was held, there was held a feast of honor.
> All at the feast ate their fill,
> 5   All at the feast drank their fill,
> All at the feast burst out bragging.
> One bragged about his father and mother,
> Another bragged about his young wife.
> Vladimir, Prince of capital Kiev, spoke:
> 10   "All the good youths have been married,

All the girls have been given in marriage,
Only one, one good youth,
Walks around a bachelor and strolls unmarried,
Ivan Godinovich."

15   Ivan Godinovich then spoke:
"My dear lord and uncle!
I have a chosen bride,
I have a chosen bride in Kiev,
A bride in Kiev and in Chernigov,*
20   The daughter of Dmitry, the rich Prince.
In everything Nastasia is the best of the best:
Nastasia has a body as white as snow,
She has the gait of a peacock,
She has the speech of a swan,
25   She has the brows of a black sable,
She has the eyes of a bright falcon,
And she has a face the color of poppies."
          Vladimir, Prince of capital Kiev, spoke:
"Hail to you, Ivan Godinovich!
30   Then what is it you want?
Do you want cities and their suburbs,
Or do you want countless golden treasure,
Or do you want a great force and army?"
          Ivan Godinovich then spoke:
35   "Vladimir, Prince of capital Kiev,
My dear lord and uncle!
I don't want anything.
I don't want cities and their suburbs,
I don't want a great force and army,
40   I don't want countless golden treasure.
Just give me three of the very best youths,
The very best and most select:
First, the old Cossack Ilya Muromets,
Second, Isak Petrovich,†
45   Third, Alyosha Popovich."

---

*The combination of names implies that the bride comes from an important and wealthy city.

†A rarely met bogatyr in Russian epics.

People saw the good youths mounting their steeds,
But they didn't see the daring youths riding away.
Smoke was rising in the open field,
Smoke was rising and dust was swirling in a column.
50   They didn't ride by a path or by a road,
They rode past a three-cornered tower,
Their steeds jumped over the city wall.
They came to the city of Chernigov,
To Dmitry, the rich Prince,
55   To the palace, to the white-stone palace,
To the porch, to the smoothly finished porch.
There they tied their good steeds
To the rings, to the gilded rings,
And they entered the white-stone palace,
60   They crossed themselves as was prescribed,
They made a bow as was instructed.
        "Greetings to you, all merchants, all boyars,
All strong and mighty bogatyrs!"
In particular they bowed low
65   To Dmitry the Prince and to the Princess.
        Dmitry, the rich Prince, then spoke:
"Why have you come, new guests,
New and unfamiliar guests?
Please sit down to share a meal
70   And to carve white swans."
        Then the good youths spoke:
"Dmitry, the rich Prince!
We didn't come to share a meal
Or to carve white swans,
75   We've come and entered on an old matter, on
                matchmaking,
To make a proposal to Nastasia Dmitriyevna,
For Ivan, for Ivan Godinovich."
        Dmitry, the rich Prince, then spoke:
"Hail to you, good youths!
80   Nastasia was promised three years ago
To that land, to that heathen land,
To that Tsar, to Koshcherishche."
        Then the good youths spoke:

"Dmitry, the rich Prince!
85   If you don't give her freely, we'll take her with a fight."
　　　Nastasia Dmitriyevna spoke:
"My dear lord and father,
Dmitry, the rich Prince!
I won't go to that land, to that heathen land,
90   I won't marry that Tsar, that Koshcherishche,
But I'll marry Ivan Godinovich."
　　　The good youths took Nastasia.
Ivan Godinovich
Took her by her white hands,
95   By her white hands and by her gilded rings,
And led her to the church, to God's church,
They got in the gilded carriage.*
People saw the good youths mounting their steeds,
But they didn't see them riding away,
100   Dust alone was rising in the open field.
　　　On the way the good youths came across three tracks:
The first track was that of a wild lion,
The second track was that of a white deer,
The third track was that of a black sable.
105   　　　Ivan Godinovich then spoke:
"Old Cossack, Ilya Muromets!
Please go after the wild lion,
Please go get the wild lion,
That will be a present for my grandfather.
110   Hail to you, Isak Petrovich!
Please go after the deer, after the white deer,
Please go get the white deer,
That will be a present for my grandfather.
Alyosha Popovich!
115   Please go after the sable, after the black sable,
Please go get the black sable,
That will be a present for my grandfather."
　　　One good youth remained,
Ivan Godinovich,

---

* An unclear passage where the singer includes an anachronism ("the gilded carriage") and may compress the usual sequence of events.

120 He set up a white tent himself,
  He amused himself with Nastasia.
    A little time passed by,
  Tsar Koshcherishche was approaching,
  He was shouting a bogatyr's shout,
125 He was whistling a nightingale's whistle.
  He pronounced these words himself:
  "Hail to you, Ivan Godinovich!
  If you eat my meat, you'll choke on it."*
    Ivan saw that trouble had come,
130 Inescapable trouble had come.
  He rushed out of the white tent
  Into the clearing in the green oak grove,
  He glanced and looked in a southerly direction,
  Tsar Koshcherishche was approaching.
135 Wherever his horse's hooves struck,
  Wells of spring water were left.†
  Ivan Godinovich
  Mounted his good steed,
  He took all his bogatyr's gear along.
140   Two mountains didn't collide together,
  Two bogatyrs came together.
  They clashed with their steel maces,
  The maces were bent at the handles,
  They were bent and broken,
145 But the bogatyrs didn't bloody each other.
  They clashed with their sharp sabers,
  Their sharp sabers were nicked,
  They were nicked and broken in half,
  But the bogatyrs didn't bloody each other.
150 They clashed with their sharp spears,
  Their sharp spears were blunted,
  But the bogatyrs didn't bloody each other.
  They dismounted their good steeds
  And entered the clearing in the green oak grove,

---

*An English equivalent would be "You've bitten off more than you can chew."

†An example of epic hyperbole—the hoofprints were so deep that they turned into wells with water in them.

155   They came together in hand-to-hand combat.
            Ivan Godinovich
       Took the Tatar by the collar,
       And he put his right leg
       Along the Tatar's left leg,
160   And he threw the Tatar on the damp earth,
       And he sat on the Tatar's chest, on his white chest,
       On his white chest, on his regal chest,
       On his regal Tatar chest.
       Ivan spoke these words himself:
165   "Hail to you, Nastasia Dmitriyevna!
       Give me a knife or dagger
       To rip out the Tatar's heart and liver,
       The Tatar's regal heart,
       For the viewing of good people,
170   For the trampling of aged old women,
       For the cawing of black ravens,
       For the howling of gray wolves."
          Then Tsar Koshcherishche spoke:
       "Hail to you, Nastasia Dmitriyevna!
175   Don't give him a knife or dagger.
       If you live with him,
       You'll be known as a simple washerwoman,
       You'll bow to the young and old.
       But if you live with me,
180   You'll be known forever as a tsaritsa,
       The young and old will bow to you."
          A woman's hair is long but her wit is short.
       Nastasia rushed out of the white tent,
       And she grabbed Ivan Godinovich by his yellow curls,
185   And she knocked Ivan Godinovich against the damp earth,
       And she tied Ivan Godinovich
       To an oak, to a damp oak,
       With grass, with feather grass,
       And she and Koshcherishche entered the white tent.
190   Then a little time passed by,
       Three gray doves, three little doves flew up,
       They spoke among each other:
       "What's this person tied for,

What's this person tied and bound for?
195   For a wench, for a whore, for a panderer,
For a panderer and a murderer."
        The Tatar didn't like these words,
The Tatar rushed out of the white tent,
He pulled out a taut bow
200   From the quiver of Ivan Godinovich,
And he took one of his tempered arrows,
And he stretched the taut bow,
He aimed the tempered arrow,
He wanted to shoot the little gray doves.
205   Ivan Godinovich
Recited a charm beside the damp oak:
"Hail to you, my father, my taut bow,
Hail to you, my mother, my tempered arrow!
Arrow, don't fall on water,
210   Arrow, don't fall on a mountain,
Arrow, don't fall on a damp oak,
Don't strike the little gray doves.
Arrow, turn toward the Tatar's chest,
Toward the Tatar's chest, toward his regal chest,
215   And rip out his heart and liver,
For the viewing of good people,
For the trampling of aged old women,
For the cawing of black ravens,
And for the howling of gray wolves."
220   And the arrow didn't fall on water,
And the arrow didn't fall on a mountain,
And the arrow didn't fall on a damp oak,
It didn't hit the little gray doves.
The arrow turned toward the Tatar's chest,
225   Toward the Tatar's chest, toward his regal chest,
And ripped out his heart and liver,
For the viewing of good people,
For the grumbling of aged old women,
For the cawing of black ravens,
230   And for the howling of gray wolves."
        Then Nastasia started crying:
"I swung away from one shore,

But I didn't reach the other shore."*
Ivan Godinovich spoke:
235   "Please untie me, Nastasia Dmitriyevna,
Untie me from the oak, from the damp oak."
Nastasia spoke these words:
"Hail to you, Ivan Godinovich!
If I untie you from the damp oak,
240   Will you beat and torment me?"
Ivan Godinovich then spoke:
"Hail to you, Nastasia Dmitriyevna!
I won't beat and torment you,
I'll just give you three lessons from a young man,
245   Lessons from a young man and prince."
Nastasia didn't like these words,
And she rushed out of the white tent,
And she entered the clearing in the green oak grove,
And she took a sharp saber in her hands,
250   And she brandished it at Ivan Godinovich,
And she wanted to cut off his reckless head.
The bogatyr's anger flared up,
Ivan became enraged beside the damp oak,
The damp oak was bent to the ground,
255   It was shattered into jagged pieces.
Ivan Godinovich walked away
In freedom from the damp oak,
He grabbed Nastasia by her yellow braid,
He knocked Nastasia against the damp earth,
260   He cut off her lips and nose:
"I don't need these things any more,
She kissed with these unhappy things."
He dug out her eyes and temples:
"I don't need these things any more,
265   She looked with these unhappy things."
He cut away her arms up to the elbows:
"I don't need these things any more,
She embraced with these unhappy things."

---

*A proverb indicating that Nastasia gave up one possible husband but did not get the other one.

He cut away her legs up to the knees:
270   "I don't need these things any more,
She stumbled with these unhappy things."
    That's how Ivan was married,
He was married and slept with his wife,
He was married briefly but now has no one to sleep with.*

---

* The conclusion is intended to be ironic.

14

Dunai

*D*unai is the main figure in four Russian songs: "Dunai and Nastasia," "Dunai's Fight with Dobrynya," "Dunai the Matchmaker," and "The Death of Dunai and Nastasia." The last two themes almost always form a single, closely connected story that is called simply "Dunai" and that, as one of the most popular Russian epics, has been collected in over a hundred variants (Propp 1958b: 134–54). Briefly stated, the content of the song is as follows. At a feast attended by all social groups at court in Kiev, Prince Vladimir announces that he would like to get married. When Dunai suggests Apraxia, the younger daughter of the Lithuanian king, Vladimir agrees and sends Dunai along with Dobrynya to make a marriage proposal. After the king refuses, they take Apraxia by force and leave for Kiev. On the way, Dunai decides instead to track down and fight a Tatar bogatyr who, after being defeated, turns out to be Nastasia, a bogatyrka and the older sister of Apraxia. Dunai and Nastasia, who apparently knew each other when Dunai served her father several years before in Lithuania, agree to marry in Kiev. At the wedding feast, Dunai brags about himself, only to be challenged by his wife, who says she can shoot an arrow better than he can. After she proves this, he kills her and then commits suicide when he finds out that she was pregnant.

The texts of "Dunai" often contain allusions to the other two songs, which singers probably created later to expand and to motivate the epic's implied "prehistory" (Putilov 1971b: 79–83). In "Dunai and Nastasia," Dunai serves at the court of the Lithuanian king, has a love affair with the king's older daughter Nastasia, and brags about the relationship publicly. The king discovers the affair and orders Dunai to be executed, but Nastasia manages to save him at the last minute. This is a typical ballad subject, which more often ends with the death of one or both lovers. (In the translated song, the king does not seem to know about the affair.) In "Dunai's Fight with Dobrynya," presumably sometime after the events in Lithuania, Dunai sets up a "black" tent in the open field, hangs a sign threatening anyone who touches the sumptuous food and drink, and leaves. Dobrynya happens to pass by, accepts the challenge, razes the tent, and, when Dunai returns, fights with him until Ilya Muromets stops them and takes them to Kiev. There Prince Vladimir resolves the dispute in Dobrynya's favor and puts Dunai in prison. This explains why some variants of the song "Dunai" open with him in prison. Thus the expected outcome of a fight between two Russian heroes is not realized since Dobrynya and Dunai are not reconciled and do not become "sworn brothers."

The bylina "Dunai" is devoted to a common theme in epics—bride taking or matchmaking. The basic motifs of this subject occur in the oral traditions of various peoples, both in epics and in magic tales (B.M. Sokolov 1923). Bride taking is described as a heroic undertaking that is dangerous for the future groom. The matchmaker, as a magical helper, may overcome the trials or obstacles that the groom faces; the bride is presented as a warrior maiden and often as a sorceress; and on the wedding night the groom is expected to subdue the bride, thereby destroying her magic power. While Brunhild in *The Nibelungenlied* represents a bride who is both a warrior maiden and a sorceress, in the Russian song Nastasia has lost one side of these characteristics—she is a bogatyrka or polyanitsa but not a sorceress. At the same time, she has acquired features that make her resemble a Tatar invader. This is another example of how a traditional folklore element has been modified under the influence of historical events, in this instance the effect of the Tatar domination over Kievan Rus. In "Dunai," Apraxia forms a contrast to her sister Nastasia and reflects the idealized portrait of a bride in medieval times. In some traditions, a suitor has to undergo trials in which he, for instance, must win contests at shooting arrows, wrestling, and riding a horse to prove himself worthy of the bride, who may be his opponent. Although the arrow-shooting episode in "Dunai" comes after his marriage to Nastasia, it recalls, for instance, the test with bow and arrow in Odysseus's competition with the suitors in *The Odyssey*. Another motif in "Dunai" connects the song with a magic tale—the description of the unborn child of Dunai and Nastasia beginning with line 296: "Silver covers its legs up to the knees. . . ." Such an idealized depiction occurs in Russian magic tales and indicates that the child will become a bogatyr.

The translated variant of "Dunai" contains several other cultural and historical references. Like the matchmaker in a traditional Russian wedding, Dunai pronounces the expression "I've come about a good cause, about arranging a marriage for your daughter, for Apraxia." The Lithuanian king rejects the proposal because Apraxia is his younger daughter and because the older daughter Nastasia has still not married. In traditional Russian life, people observed a strict order in the marriage of their daughters. Toward the end of the song, when Nastasia pleads for her life, she describes punishments that might have been inflicted on an unfaithful wife. Until the sixteenth century, Russian nobility had the right to join the service of another prince without first obtaining permission. This might include rulers in foreign countries, such as Lithuania, where Dunai is mentioned as having served the king. Although it is true that Tatar mercenaries served in Lithuania in the fifteenth and sixteenth centuries, their appearance in this bylina may also demonstrate how singers tend to convert all enemies of Kievan Rus into Tatars. Several followers of the Historical School have attempted to connect the bylina about Dunai with specific historical events. In particular, they see in the song a reflection of the story in Russian chronicles about the marriage of Vladimir I to Rogneda, a princess from the city of Polotsk. Rogneda rejected his marriage proposal, calling him the son of a slave and refusing to pay symbolic obedience by taking off his boots, actions that prompted him to besiege Polotsk and to abduct and marry her. During the time of Kievan Rus, princely families frequently arranged marriages with royal families in countries as close as Byzantium and Lithuania or as distant as France and Germany.

Even though "Dunai" existed as a masculine first name in Kievan Rus, its use in an epic is suggestive since it also is the Russian name for the Danube River, which, according to some scholars, was the region where the Slavic ethnos was formed, approximately in the sixth century. The word "Dunai" is also encountered as a refrain in East Slavic lyric songs and in a formulaic phrase at the end of Russian epics, a feature that may reveal the "ethnic memory" of the Slavs (Machinskii 1981). The bylina concludes with a mythological motif about the origin of toponyms: the existing Danube and the imaginary Nastasia Rivers flow from the spot where the two main characters die.

Dunai is one of the rare tragic figures in the Russian epic tradition. He does not die at the hand of an enemy but as a result of his own quick-tempered character. Like other bogatyrs, he is generous and is willing to defend Vladimir's honor in a foreign country, but he is equally quick to act rashly without thinking about the consequences, a character flaw that leads to his death. Dunai cannot endure the fact that his wife is more skillful at shooting an arrow and kills her, but he is capable of repentance and immediately commits suicide when he realizes what he has done.

A.F. Gilferding recorded the selected variant of "Dunai" in 1871 from the singer K.I. Romanov in Olonets Province.

✍ Dunai ✎

Source: A.F. Gilferding, *Onega Bylinas,* 4th ed., vol. 2 (Moscow, 1950), no. 94.

In the capital city, in Kiev,
At the gracious Prince's, at Vladimir's,
There was a banquet, a feast of honor,
For many princes, for the boyars,
5   For the bogatyrs, for the mighty bogatyrs,
For all the merchants, for the trading merchants,
For all the village men.
The bright sun was going down,
The feast of honor was in full swing.
10   Vladimir of capital Kiev spoke:
"Hail to you, all princes and boyars,
All mighty bogatyrs,
All trading merchants,
All village men!
15   All at the feast are married,
I, the Prince, alone am not married.
Do you know a worthy princess for me?
She should be tall in stature,
She should be shapely in figure,

20   And she should be beautiful in face,
    Her step should be quick and her speech should be
        pleasant.
    I, the Prince, should have someone to live with and
        to be with,
    To consult with and to spend my life with.
    And for all you princes and for all you boyars,
25   For all you mighty bogatyrs,
    For all you trading merchants,
    For all you village men,
    And for all the beautiful city of Kiev
    Should there be someone to honor?"
30   Everyone at the feast fell silent,
    And no one had an answer to this question.
    One daring good youth,
    By name Dunai Ivanovich,
    Came out from behind an oaken table.
35   He was very drunk but didn't stagger,
    He spoke words but didn't get confused,
    He bowed and paid his respects:
    "Prince Vladimir of capital Kiev!
    I know and I'm acquainted
40   With a worthy princess for you.
    In that land, in brave Lithuania,
    His royal majesty
    Has two grown daughters,
    Both daughters are ready for marriage.
45   The older daughter is Nastasia the Princess,
    This daughter is always roaming and looking for a fight,
    But the younger daughter always lives at home,
    This is Apraxia the Princess.
    She's tall in stature,
50   She's shapely in figure,
    And she's beautiful in face,
    Her step is quick, and her speech is pleasant.
    For you, Prince, she'll be someone to live with and
        to be with,
    To consult with and to spend your life with.
55   And for all the princes and all the boyars,

For all the mighty bogatyrs,
For all the trading merchants,
For all the village men,
And for all the beautiful city of Kiev
60   She'll be someone to honor."
        These words were pleasing.
Prince Vladimir of capital Kiev spoke:
"Hail to you, Dunai Ivanovich!
Take from me an army of forty thousand,
65   Take a treasure of ten thousand,
And go to this land, to brave Lithuania,
And arrange a marriage in good faith.
If they don't give her to you honorably, take her by force,
But just bring back Apraxia the Princess."
70   Dunai Ivanovich then spoke:
"Our Sun, Vladimir of capital Kiev!
I don't need an army of forty thousand,
I don't need a treasure of ten thousand.
Give me my favorite comrade,
75   My favorite comrade, Dobrynya Nikitich."
        Prince Vladimir of capital Kiev spoke:
"Hail to you, Dobrynya Nikitich!
Please go and be a comrade to Dunai."
Dobrynya quickly agreed,
80   And quickly they departed from the city of Kiev,
Quickly they mounted their good steeds.
People saw the good youths mounting their steeds,
But they didn't see the good youths riding.
Just as bright falcons take flight,
85   So the good youths set off riding.
And quickly they were in that land, in brave Lithuania,
With his royal majesty,
At the court, at the royal court,
Opposite its very windows,
90   And quickly they dismounted their good steeds.
        Dunai Ivanovich spoke:
"Hail to you, Dobrynya Nikitich!
Stay by the steeds and tend the steeds,
And keep an eye on the royal bodyguard,

95   And on the Prince's palace.
            When I need you, then I'll call you,
            So that we can leave at the right time."
                 And he came to his royal majesty,
            He knew the royal customs,
100   You don't have to cross yourself or pray.*
            He bowed and paid his respects:
            "Greetings father,† King of brave Lithuania!"
                 The King of brave Lithuania looked at him closely:
            "You're a former servant, a faithful servant!
105   You lived three years with me,
            The first year you served as a groom,
            And the second year you served as a cupbearer,
            And the third year you served as a steward,
            You served with loyalty, with loyalty and truth.
110   For your young man's service
            I'll seat you at the main table,
            At the main table, in a place of honor.
            Eat your fill, young man,
            And drink all you want, young man."
115   And he seated him at the main table in a place of honor.
                 The King started questioning him:
            "Tell me, tell me, Dunai, keep nothing back,
            Where are you going, where are you heading?
            To visit us or to make yourself well known,
120   To live awhile with us or to serve awhile again?"
                 "Father, King of brave Lithuania!
            I've come about a good cause,
            About arranging a marriage for your daughter, for Apraxia."
                 The king wasn't pleased by these words:
125   "Hail to you, Dunai, the son of Ivan!
            You haven't come for a good cause but for a bad one.
            If you're arranging marriage for my younger daughter,
            Why do you spurn my older daughter?

_____

*Dunai does not observe this Russian entrance ritual because he is in a foreign country.

†The word "father" here is only a sign of respect for an older person or one of a higher rank.

Hail to you, my mighty Tatars!
130   Take Dunai by his white hands,
And lead Dunai to the deep dungeon,
[Lock it with iron bars,]*
Seal it with oaken boards,
And cover it with reddish yellow sand,
135   And let Dunai stay awhile in Lithuania,
Stay awhile in Lithuania and sit awhile in the dungeon,
And perhaps Dunai will figure things out."
        Dunai stood up on his nimble feet,
He raised his hands above his reckless head,
140   And he leaned with his hands against the oaken table.
The oaken table was shoved aside,
The drinks on the table were spilled,
All the dishes were scattered,
[All the Tatars were frightened].
145   And quickly the faithful servants came running
From the courtyard, from the royal courtyard:
"Hail to you, our father, King of brave Lithuania!
You eat, you drink, and you amuse yourself,
You don't know the trouble hanging over you.
150   A strange husky fellow's in the courtyard,
He holds the reins of two good steeds in his left hand
And a Saracen club in his right hand.
Just as a bright falcon takes flight,
So this fine young man jumped up,
155   He swung his club in all directions
And killed the Tatars to the last.
He'll leave no Tatars for posterity."
        Then the King figured things out.
The King of brave Lithuania spoke:
160   "Hail to you, Dunai Ivanovich!
Remember our former hospitality,
Leave at least some Tatars for posterity.
I'll give my daughter, the Princess,
In marriage to your Prince, to Vladimir."

---

*Lines in square brackets were added by the editor of the 1873 edition of
Gilferding's collection.

165   Quickly they mounted their good steeds,
Quickly they rode off from the royal court
With the young Apraxia the Princess.
And on the way, on the road,
The dark night overtook them.
170   They pitched a linen tent,
And then the good youths lay down to sleep.
They put their good steeds at their feet,
And their sharp spears at their heads,
And their sharp sabers by their right hands,
175   And their steel daggers by their left hands,
And the good youths slept, slept soundly,
Passing away the dark night.
        The good youths didn't see anything,
They didn't see so much as they heard
180   A Tatar riding to the open field.
They got up early in the morning
And departed on the path, on the road.
A Tatar was riding in pursuit,
His good steed was sinking up to its fetlocks
        in the muddy road,
185   It was kicking stones off the road,
It was hurling them two arrow shots away.
        Dobrynya Nikitich rode off
With Apraxia the Princess to the city of Kiev.
Dunai Ivanovich rode off
190   Along the horse's hoofprints,
In pursuit of this Tatar.
There where he could overtake the Tatar,
There where he could jab the Tatar with his spear,
There he spoke with the Tatar:
195   "Tatar, stop in the open field,
Tatar, roar like a wild animal,
Tatar, hiss like a snake!"
        The Tatar roared like a wild animal,
The Tatar hissed like a snake,
200   The dark forests collapsed into pieces,
The stones were scattered in the open field,
The grasses were withered in the open field,

Flowers were strewn on the ground,
Dunai fell off his good steed.*
205   Dunai quickly stood on his nimble feet
And knocked the Tatar off his good steed:
"Speak, Tatar, keep nothing back.
Tatar, what clan are you from, what tribe?"
          The Tatar spoke these words:
210   "Hail to you, Dunai, son of Ivan!
If I were on your chest,
I wouldn't ask about your homeland or your ancestry
But would rip open your white chest."
          Dunai sat on the Tatar's white chest.
215   When he spread out the Tatar's cloak,
He wanted to rip open the Tatar's white chest,
But he saw by the breasts that this was a female.
He was horrified at heart,
And he stopped his arm at the shoulder.
220   "Dunai, why didn't you recognize me?
Didn't we ride together on more than one road,
Didn't we sit together at more than one gathering,
Didn't we drink together from more than one goblet?
You lived with us exactly three years:
225   The first year you served as a groom,
And the second year you served as a cupbearer,
And the third year you served as a steward."
          "Hail to you, Nastasia the Princess!
Let's ride quickly to the city of Kiev,
230   And let's accept the wondrous crosses and the golden
                    crowns."
          They came to the city of Kiev,
To the church, to the cathedral church.
The younger sister was getting married,
The older sister came to the altar.
235   Their feast went on exactly for three days.
          At the feast Dunai burst out bragging:
"In all the city of Kiev,

---

*Such passages usually describe the actions of a monster. For an example, see
lines 41 to 48 in "Ilya Muromets and Nightingale the Robber."

No youth can compare with Dunai Ivanovich—
He gave himself in marriage and presented a friend
      with a wife."
240   Nastasia the Princess gave an answer:
"Hail to you, Dunai Ivanovich!
Dunai, haven't you bragged about nothing?
I haven't been long in the city,
But I've come to know much in the city.
245   No youth can compare in fancy clothing,
In fancy clothing with Dobrynya Nikitich,*
And none can compare with the boldness of
      Alyosha Popovich,
And none can compare in shooting with Nastasia
      the Princess.
I've shot a tempered arrow,
250   With the arrow I've hit the edge of a knife,
I've cleaved the arrow into two halves,
Both halves have come out equal,
Equal to the eye and even in weight."
      And then Dunai became ashamed,
255   Dunai Ivanovich then spoke:
"Hail to you, Nastasia the Princess!
Let's ride, Nastasia, to the open field,
To shoot some tempered arrows."
And they rode out to the open field.
260   And she shot a tempered arrow
And with the arrow she hit the edge of a knife,
She cleaved the arrow into two halves,
Both halves came out equal,
Equal to the eye and even in weight.
265   And Dunai Ivanovich shot,
He shot a first time and overshot,
He shot a second time and undershot,
He shot a third time and missed.
Then Dunai Ivanovich grew angry,
270   He aimed a tempered arrow

---

*Churila Plyonkovich is usually portrayed as the "dresser" in Russian epics.

At Nastasia's white chest.
            Then Nastasia begged him:
"Hail to you, Dunai Ivanovich!
You'd do better to inflict three punishments on me
275   And not to shoot me with a tempered arrow.
Inflict a first punishment on me:
Take a silken whip,
Soak the whip in hot pitch,
And beat me on my naked body.
280   And inflict a second punishment on me:
Take me by my woman's hair,
Tie me to a saddle stirrup,
And drive the steed through the open field.
And inflict a third punishment on me:
285   Lead me to a crossroads,
And bury me up to my breasts in the damp earth,
And beat me with sharp oaken sticks,
And cover me with reddish yellow sand.
Starve me and feed me with oats,
290   But keep me exactly three months,
And let my womb bring forth,
Let me give birth to an infant,
Let me leave posterity in the world.
I have an infant in my womb,
295   There's no such infant in the city:
Silver covers its legs up to the knees,
Gold covers its arms up to the elbows,
Dense stars are spread along its temples,
And a bright sun shines in the top of its head!"
300   Despite these words
He released the tempered arrow
At Nastasia's white chest.
Nastasia fell on her head.
He ripped open her white chest,
305   Took out her heart and liver.
There was an infant in her womb,
There was no such infant in the city:
Silver covered its legs up to the knees,
Gold covered its arms up to the elbows,

310   Dense stars were spread along its temples,
             And a bright sun shown in the top of its head.
             Then he laid hands upon himself.
                  There where Dunai's head fell
             The stream Dunai River set off flowing,
315   And there where Nastasia's head fell
             The stream Nastasia River started flowing.

15

Solovei Budimirovich

he bylina "Solovei Budimirovich" belongs to a group of Russian epics about bride taking (Loboda 1904: 127–68; Propp 1958b: 167–79). Some variants open with a lyrical introduction about the expanse and beauty of the Russian land—its forests, mountains, rivers, and fields. A number of cities, both from Kievan and from later Muscovite times, may be mentioned: Smolensk, Pskov, Byelo-ozero, Kazan, Ryazan, and Astrakhan. Intriguing attempts have been made to use these actual place names, as well as obscure references to the Island of Kodol and the land of Vedenyets, to attribute the homeland of Solovei Budimirovich to the Baltic region, the Black Sea, and even Venice, but no single explanation has proved entirely satisfactory. The basic function of the geographic allusions is to show that Solovei has come from a distant place and is not from Kiev. The prelude also sets an optimistic mood and may be regarded as a hymn to the Russian land. Only twenty-eight recordings have been made of this imaginative and colorful epic.

After the introduction, a vivid and detailed description follows of the vessels that bring Solovei and his druzhina to Kiev. In some recordings the ships look like a wild animal and in others they resemble a serpent; the bow is depicted as a real or fantastic animal (dragon or aurochs) and the stern is shaped like a tail. This is a fairly accurate picture of merchant ships that existed in Kievan Rus and that resembled Scandinavian vessels of the time (Kotliarevskii 1889). Such ships formed one of the main means of transportation and trade, especially along the route from the Baltic Sea in the north, along the Dnieper River past Kiev, and to the Black Sea in the south. In the translated variant, the sails are made of the finest silk and are decorated with furs. Furthermore, the ship is like a living being, something that is characteristic of the Russian folk tradition, where various objects are named after parts of the human body. Similar descriptions of ships appear in the epics "Sadko," "Vasily Buslayevich Travels to Jerusalem," and "Ilya Muromets and the Falcon Ship."

Many actions, customs, and symbols from the traditional Russian wedding ceremony appear in this bylina. Solovei's arrival in Kiev as a suitor from a distant overseas land mirrors wedding lyrics in which the groom is portrayed as a "foreigner" from a "distant-alien land," even though he may live in the same village as the bride. Although Solovei's mother comes to Kiev with him but plays no further role in the epic, in the preliminaries to a real wedding the mother ensures that the matchmaking observes traditional family customs. Matchmakers coming to the home of the future bride at first do not reveal the purpose of their visit; similarly Solovei does not immediately tell Prince Vladimir that he has come to make a marriage proposal. The prospective groom may also be portrayed as a "merchant" who is seeking "goods," that is, the bride. Furthermore, Solovei gives Prince Vladimir and his family presents, an action that plays an important role in the wedding ritual. The decorative description of the ships, suggestions that Solovei is a wealthy merchant, and the numerous expensive gifts represent a poetic idealization of the suitor. Overnight Solovei builds "three gold-topped palaces" in the garden of the prince's niece, Lyubava (she also may be called Zabava). This motif occurs in wedding poetry, where the groom cuts down the trees in the bride's garden and builds her a palace. Although the name "Solovei" means "nightingale" and was used in Kievan Rus, in wedding songs a nightingale may be a symbol of the groom; "Budimir" was a common Slavic name that suggests the verb "to build"; and the name "Lyubava" is derived from the noun for "love." Despite its numerous connections with the wedding ceremony, this song has not been derived from the wedding ritual but represents the theme of bride taking or matchmaking that is a widespread subject in the epics of many peoples.

This bylina is also connected with Russian magic tales, although no direct genetic link exists between them. Before a marriage may take place in a magic tale, the groom is often expected to undergo "tests" or to perform difficult tasks, one of which may involve building a palace overnight. Although the reference to one episode in the song about Solovei is obvious, in the epic the members of Solovei's druzhina construct the palace, while in the tales magical helpers carry out the task for the hero.

In contrast to the songs about "Potyk," "Ivan Godinovich," and "Dunai," which involve marriage to a woman from a distant land or from the otherworld and have a tragic outcome, the song "Solovei Budimirovich" concerns a suitor who comes to Kiev from "beyond the sea" and concludes with an idyllic marriage to Prince Vladimir's niece. His niece is not a sorceress, bogatyrka, or foreigner, as is often the case in other Russian songs about bride taking, but an ordinary Russian woman. Although Solovei may reproach Lyubava because she violates accepted norms of conduct by proposing herself in marriage, she actually is responding to his symbolic advances. In some variants, Lyubava's forwardness becomes an excuse for Solovei to leave without marrying her. The feast at the end of the song celebrates an engagement, after which Solovei takes Lyubava home, where the marriage will take place.

A.I. Liashchenko (1922) has attempted to relate the song about Solovei to a specific historical figure, the future Norwegian king Harold III, who journeyed to Kiev, served Prince Yaroslav the Wise (ruled Kiev from 1019 to 1054), and proposed marriage to his daughter Elizabeth but was rejected. Harold then served in the Varangian contingent at the Byzantine court in Constantinople, eventually returned to Kiev in 1042, married Yaroslav's daughter, and went back to Norway, where he became king. He died in England at the battle of Stamford Bridge in 1066 shortly before the Norman conquest.

An assistant of P.N. Rybnikov collected the translated song in 1860 in Kizhi District of Olonets Province from the singer A.N. Sorokin.

৶ Solovei Budimirovich ৵

Source: P.N. Rybnikov, Songs, vol. 2 (Petrozavodsk, 1990), no. 133.

The dark forests, the forests came close to the city
of Smolensk,
The high Saracen Mountains came close to it,
The open fields came close to the city of Pskov,
The mosses and swamps came close to Byelo-ozero,
5   The rivers and lakes came close to the blue sea.
The mother river Volga was right there,
It was wide and long,
It passed by Kazan, Ryazan, and Astrakhan,*
Its mouth opened into the blue sea,
10   Into the blue sea, into the Turkish Sea.†
From beyond the sea, from beyond the Turkish Sea,
From under an oak, a damp oak,
From under an elm, a red elm,
From under a curly birch,
15   From under the cross of Lebanon,
From beyond the Island of Kodol,
From the land of Vedenyets,
Came sailing, came sailing out three ships,
Three ships, three scarlet ones.
20   The ships were covered with decorations:
The bow and stern resembled a wild animal,
And the sides resembled an aurochs;
All the anchors and chains were made of silver,
The thin sails were made of expensive silk,
25   Of expensive patterned silk.
Also on the scarlet ships
Instead of hands there was hung something white—

---

*Kazan and Astrakhan are cities on the Volga River, but Ryazan is located
southeast of Moscow on the Oka River and not on the Volga as the singer assumes.
    †The Volga flows into the Caspian Sea and not into the "Turkish Sea," which
today is called the Black Sea.

Expensive overseas rabbit furs;
Instead of a face there was hung
30   An expensive overseas fox fur;
Instead of eyes there were inserted
Expensive overseas migratory falcons;
Instead of brows there were hung
Expensive overseas sable furs;
35   Instead of a forehead there was inserted
An expensive semiprecious stone;
Instead of curls there was hung
An expensive overseas beaver fur.
        Also on the scarlet ship
40   The cabins were lined with tiles,
In the cabins were benches with seats,
They were covered with overseas fox and marten furs
And with overseas black sable furs.
On one of these benches with seats
45   Was sitting the young Solovei,
The young Solovei, Budimir's son.
At his right hand was sitting
His darling lady and mother,
The honorable widow Ulyana Grigoryevna,
50   And at his left hand was sitting
His brave druzhina,
Thirty youths and one,
Each youth better than the other,
All the youths were hand-picked.
55   All the brave druzhina
Wore boots of green morocco leather,
The silver buckles were fastened with gilded nails,
A sparrow could fly under the high heels,
And an egg could be rolled off the tips.*
60   They all wore clothing made of colorful cloth,
On their heads they wore black hats from Murman.†
        These ships were going and running
To the capital city of Kiev,

---

*These boots had very high heels and sharply curled tips.
†The name for the coast of the Kola Peninsula bordering the Arctic Ocean.

To our Sun, our Prince Vladimir.
65   The daring young Solovei then spoke
To his brave druzhina:
"Hail to you, my brave druzhina!
Carry out the orders that I've given you,
Obey your senior ataman.
70   Take your iron bars,
Take your long iron bars,
Probe in the famous sea, in the blue sea,
In the sea, in the Turkish Sea,
To see if any gold or silver,
75   Or any small fine pearls are there."
Then his brave druzhina jumped up,
Jumped up on its nimble feet.
They took the iron bars,
The long iron bars,
80   They probed in the famous sea, in the blue sea,
In the sea, in the Turkish Sea.
They couldn't find any gold or silver,
Or any small fine pearls.
The young Solovei then spoke again
85   To his brave druzhina:
"Hail to you, my brave druzhina!
Carry out the orders that I've given you,
Obey your senior ataman.
Pick up your spyglasses,
90   Climb up to the upper yardarms,
Look for the famous city of Kiev—
Is the famous city of Kiev far away?"
Then his brave druzhina
Picked up their spyglasses,
95   They climbed up to the upper yardarms,
They looked for the famous capital city of Kiev,
They spoke these words themselves:
"Hail to you, young Solovei, Budimir's son!
The famous city of Kiev isn't far away."
100   When they arrived in the city of Kiev
They stopped their scarlet ships

At the landing, at the merchant's landing.
The young Solovei then spoke
To his brave druzhina:
105 "Hail to you, my brave druzhina!
Carry out the orders that I've given you,
Obey your senior ataman.
Take the golden keys,
Open the bound chests,
110 Fill the first basin with red gold,
Fill the second with pure silver,
Fill the third with small and large
Fine pearls.
Take forty times forty—forty black sable furs,
115 Take countless marten and fox furs,
Take numberless geese and swans.
Cast three gangplanks on the steep shore.
The first gangplank is made of red gold,
The second gangplank is made of pure silver,
120 The third gangplank is made of copper."
Out along the gangplank of red gold
Came the young and daring Solovei,
The daring Solovei, Budimir's son.
Out along the gangplank of pure silver
125 Came his darling lady and mother,
The honorable widow Ulyana Grigoryevna.
Out along the gangplank of copper
Came all his brave druzhina.
They started walking through the famous city of Kiev.
130 They were going to our Sun, to Prince Vladimir, to his
wide courtyard,
To the prince's wide courtyard.
Solovei left half his druzhina in the prince's courtyard,
With the other half he went to the white-stone palace.
He entered the white-stone palace,
135 He crossed himself correctly as was prescribed,
He made a bow as was instructed,
He bowed in all four directions
To our Sun, the Prince, and to the Princess Apraxia
in particular,

To the young Lyubava Putyatichna in particular,
140   And to all the other princes in particular.
He presented our Sun, the Prince, a basin filled with red gold,
He presented the Princess Apraxia a basin filled with
            pure silver,
He presented the young Lyubava Putyatichna
Some small and large fine pearls,
145   He also presented her some patterned silk.
Silk woven with red gold doesn't crease,
And that woven with pure silver doesn't break.
The silk woven with red gold or with pure silver is
            not as expensive
As the overseas patterns are:
150   No such patterns can be found in Kiev.
Solovei presented the other princes and boyars
With overseas fox and marten furs,
With overseas black sable furs,
And with overseas geese and swans.
155   Our Sun, Vladimir the Prince, then spoke:
"Hail to you, my daring good youth!
I'd like to know what land and horde you're from,
Who your father and your mother are,
And how you're called by name?
160   I'd like to know what I can reward you with
In exchange for your expensive gifts?"
The young Solovei then spoke these words:
"Hail to you, our Sun, Vladimir the Prince,
Vladimir the Prince of capital Kiev!
165   I come from that land, from that rich horde,
I come from beyond the famous blue sea,
From the Island of Kodol,
From the land of Vedenyets,
I'm the young Solovei, Budimir's son.
170   I've come to your city of Kiev.
Hail to you, our Sun, Vladimir the Prince!
Please give me a small place
To build three gold-topped palaces!"
Our Sun, Vladimir the Prince, then spoke:
175   "Hail to you, young Solovei, Budimir's son!

In exchange for your expensive gifts
Choose a place behind me,
Choose a second place in front of me,
Choose a third place beside me,
180 And choose a fourth place where you would like.
Build just what you have in mind."*
     Then the young Solovei, Budimir's son,
Left the white-stone palace.
He went to the wide courtyard,
185 Then he went to his ships, to his scarlet ships,
He spoke these words himself
To his brave druzhina:
"Hail to you, my brave druzhina!
Carry out the orders that I've given you,
190 Obey your senior ataman.
Take off your boots of green morocco leather,
Put on your working boots,
Take off your clothing of colorful cloth,
Put on your elk-skin clothing,
195 Take off your black hats from Murman,
Put on your working hats,
Take your fine steel axes,
Run to the Hill, to Horse's Hill,
To the garden, to Putyatichna's garden,
200 Where pies are baked and pancakes are sold,
Where little kids are hucksters.
Chop out the logs and stumps,
Throw them out in all directions,
By morning, by daybreak,
205 Make three gold-topped palaces,
Build them with fancy vestibules.
The first vestibule must be latticed,
The second vestibule must be glassed in,
The third vestibule must be gilded with red gold.
210 Around them make a steel stockade,
In the middle make a merchant's arcade.

---

* Solovei receives permission to build a palace anywhere near Vladimir's palace.

We have to move to live there by morning, by daybreak."
    Then they took off their boots of green
        morocco leather,
    They put on their working boots,
215   They took off their clothing of colorful cloth,
    They put on their elk-skin clothing,
    They took off their black hats from Murman,
    They put on their working hats,
    They took their fine steel axes,
220   They ran to the Hill, to Horse's Hill,
    To the garden, to Putyatichna's garden,
    Where pies are baked and pancakes are sold,
    Where little kids are hucksters.
    They chopped out the logs and stumps,
225   They threw them out in all directions.
    By morning, by daybreak, they had made the
        three gold-topped palaces,
    They had built them with fancy vestibules.
    The first vestibule was latticed,
    The second vestibule was glassed in,
230   The third vestibule was gilded with red gold.
    Around them they had made a steel stockade,
    In the middle they had made a merchant's arcade.
        Early in the morning, the young Putyatichna got up,
    She glanced out of her window with a wooden frame
235   At her Hill, at Horse's Hill,
    She was astonished at this miracle:
    "Yesterday the hill was completely empty,
    Today the hill is completely full!"
    She put on thin stockings without shoes,
240   She put on an expensive cloak,
    She tied a silken kerchief on her head,
    She took along her dear trusted servant woman,
    She ran to the Hill, to Horse's Hill,
    To her garden, to her dear garden.
245   She listened at the first palace,
    By the latticed vestibule—
    People there were speaking in a whisper and were
        praying to God,

Solovei's mother was praying to God.
She listened by the second palace,
250   By the glassed-in vestibule—
People there were jingling gold treasure,
They were counting Solovei's gold treasure.
She listened by the third palace,
By the gilded vestibule—
255   There great games and fun were going on.
She entered the gold-topped palace—
There in one corner people were talking, in another
             they were making noise,
In the middle great fun and games were going on.
Thus she didn't think about praying to the Lord God
260   And about bowing in all directions.*
Her asshole loosened and her boot tops were filled.
     The young Solovei, Budimir's son, looked up,
He saw Lyubava Putyatichna,
He pulled up a golden chair for her:
265   "Please sit down, my young Lyubava Putyatichna,
Please sit down on the golden chair!"
     She sat down on the golden chair,
She spoke these words herself:
"Hail to you, young Solovei, Budimir's son!
270   Are you married or are you a bachelor?
Take me in marriage!"
     The young Solovei then spoke these words:
"Hail to you, my young Lyubava Putyatichna!
I would take you in marriage, Lyubava,
275   You have pleased me in everything, Lyubava,
But in one thing you haven't pleased me, Lyubava,
You're arranging your marriage yourself, Lyubava!"
     Then Lyubava became ashamed,
She stood up on her nimble legs,
280   She didn't pray to the Lord God,
She didn't bow to the youths,
She went back home from the palace,

---

*Lyubava forgets to perform the entrance ritual of crossing oneself and bowing to the icons and people present.

She went to her white-stone chambers.
　　　Then the young Solovei, Budimir's son,
285　Went to our Sun, to Prince Vladimir,
He came to Prince Vladimir,
He crossed himself as was prescribed,
He made his bows as was instructed,
He bowed in all four directions
290　To the Prince and to the Princess Apraxia in particular,
And to the young Lyubava Putyatichna in particular.
He sat down on a chair with leather straps,
He spoke these words himself:
"Hail to you, our Sun, Vladimir the Prince!
295　I've come to you for a good cause—for making a match
With your young Lyubava Putyatichna."
　　　Our Sun, Vladimir the Prince, then spoke:
"Hail to you, young Solovei, Budimir's son!
Has Lyubava pleased you in everything?"
300　　The young Solovei, Budimir's son, then spoke:
"Lyubava has pleased me in everything,
But in one thing Lyubava hasn't pleased me,
Lyubava has arranged her marriage herself."
　　　That's how much matchmaking took place
　　　　　between them.
305　　Then a small feast of honor for a wedding began,
A banquet and a feast of honor began.
Our Sun, Vladimir the Prince,
For the sake of his dear niece,
The young Lyubava Putyatichna,
310　Held a banquet and a feast of honor
For many princes and for council boyars,
For rich dignitaries and for merchants, for
　　　　　daring polyanitsas,
For mighty Russian bogatyrs,
He gathered them for the feast of honor.
315　 . The banquet and the feast of honor began,
Everyone at the feast drank their fill,
Everyone at the feast of honor ate their fill,
Everyone boasted with their boasts.

Some bragged of one thing, others boasted of
something else:

320 One bragged about his countless gold treasure,
Another bragged about his young man's strength and luck,
Another bragged about his good steed,
Another bragged about his famous family,
Another bragged about his youthful bravery,

325 A clever and wise one bragged about his old father,
About his old father and old mother,
A silly fool then bragged about his young wife.
    The young Solovei, Budimir's son,
Didn't get married then in the famous city of Kiev,

330 He set out for his land of Vedenyets,
On those ships, on those scarlet ships.
Our Sun, Vladimir the Prince, then saw him off,
He presented Solovei with red gold, with pure silver,
And with small fine pearls.
    Dunai, Dunai,
    I know nothing more about this story.*

---

* A rhymed stock phrase that singers sometimes use to signal the end of a song.

16

Vasily Ignatyev

*T*he bylina "Vasily Ignatyev" has probably been derived from the song "Ilya Muromets and Kalin Tsar" (Propp 1958b: 343–54). Both epics have the same basic scheme: the Tatars attack Kiev, all bogatyrs have left the city, and Prince Vladimir searches for and finds a defender who defeats the enemy force. However, the rescuing hero turns out to be the unknown Vasily Ignatyev, who has wasted all his belongings on drink. Instead of a majestic and idealized Holy Russian bogatyr such as Ilya Muromets, Vasily, an "unheroic" drunkard from the urban poor, becomes the savior of Kiev. However, it is possible that Vasily may have been a member of a druzhina who has squandered his equipment, arms, and horse on drink. The bylina understandably is sometimes called "Vasily the Drunkard."

This song, which has been recorded seventy-five times, exists in two versions. One is heroic and is concerned with fighting, but the other involves a social conflict between the upper and the lower classes. In the first version, Vasily recovers enough from his drinking to stand on the city wall and shoot three arrows into the besieging Tatar force. His arrows kill three people, including the son of the Tatar commander Batu, who demands that the city of Kiev hand over the guilty person to him. Vasily gives himself up to Batu, with whom he comes to an agreement about fighting with the Tatars against the Russians. In reality, Vasily tricks Batu and destroys his army, after which Batu flees, vowing never again to come to Kiev.

The second version, one example of which has been translated here, in several ways more closely resembles the epic "Ilya Muromets and Kalin Tsar" but nevertheless has several distinctive features of its own. Some variants open with an extraordinary passage about aurochs, the European wild bull, which was a dangerous animal to hunt and which became extinct in the seventeenth century. In the beginning of the song, young aurochs relate to their mother how they saw a beautiful maid reading the Gospels and weeping by a "gray grieving stone," a mysterious symbol usually associated with misfortune and death in Russian folklore. In some recordings the maid laments on the city wall of Kiev. The mother aurochs interprets this figure as the Mother of God (The Virgin Mary), who is lamenting the impending destruction of Kiev (V.F. Miller 1897–1924, 1: 305–27). According to R.S. Lipets (1972), the ancient Slavs had a cult of aurochs, to which they attributed magical powers, talent for prophesy, and connections with the supernatural, qualities symbolized by the aurochs' "golden horns." The large curved horns of the aurochs made fine drinking vessels, which may have served a sacral function and may have involved mead as a ritual drink. Echoes of these features appear in the tavern scene, where Prince Vladimir three times "treats" Vasily's hangover by giving him "sweet mead" in an aurochs's horn (lines 170–72). This may represent a purifying rite that prepares Vasily to confront a hostile army all alone. Aurochs appear from time to time in other Russian epics, especially in "Dobrynya and Marinka." Christian elements, in this instance the Mother of God, who was regarded as the Protectress of Kiev, have been superimposed on a pagan mythological base. The dirge-like introduction undoubtedly was composed after the events of 1240, when the army of Batu Khan destroyed Kiev. The opening, which conveys a medieval religious interpretation of the Tatar invasion as punishment for the sins of Kievan Rus, may have been a separate work that later was added to the epic about Vasily Ignatyev. In some respects, the beginning section is related to "religious verses." In the bylina as a whole, a discrepancy results because the prophesy about the doom of Kiev is not fulfilled and the city is saved by Vasily.

While an external struggle takes place between Kiev and the Tatars, an internal clash occurs between the aristocratic boyars and the lower-class Vasily. In the translated variant, Vasily, after his single-handed victory over the enemy army, comes to Prince Vladimir's palace, where, instead of being recognized as a hero and being rewarded, he is met with scorn by the "fat-bellied" boyars. They reject him because they no longer need him now that the danger has passed and because he belongs to what today would be called "street people." In some recordings, such derision so angers Vasily that he takes revenge by killing all the boyars. This bylina, just as the one about Ilya Muromets's quarrel with Vladimir, may reflect social conflicts in Muscovite Russia toward the end of the six-teenth and in the beginning of the seventeenth centuries.

As frequently happens in Russian epics, several different chronological layers coexist in the bylina "Vasily Ignatyev." In the selected song, a propensity toward historical amalgamation is partly revealed by various allusions. The geographical names Shakhovo, Lyakhovo, and Saracen Field (lines 9–11) are fictitious but suggest foreign lands; Kulikovo Field (line 12) is the site where a Russian army first defeated the Tatars in 1380; and the Puchai, or Pochaina, River (line 20) is where the people of Kiev, according to legend, were converted to Christianity and were baptized in 988. The names Korshak, Konshak, and Kirshak (lines 39–41) may al-lude to the Polovetsian Khan Konchak, who lived in the second half of the twelfth century. The Polovetsians were major opponents of Kievan Rus in the eleventh and twelfth centuries before the Tatar invasion. A *yarlyk* (line 51) was a written document by which Tatar khans granted privileges to some specific person or group from the thirteenth through the fifteenth centuries. As in the bylina "Ilya Muromets and Kalin Tsar," the com-mander of the Tatar army instructs his messenger to violate Russian customs as provocatively as possible when he delivers the letter. Although Skurlata is called the tsar of the Tatar forces (line 37), his name is un-doubtedly derived from that of a member of Ivan the Terrible's *op-richnina,* Malyuta Skurlatov, who died in 1573. The *oprichnina* functioned as a special kind of "secret police" for several years during the reign of Ivan the Terrible (see the introduction to the song "Ivan the Terrible and His Sons"). Skurlata's patronymic, Smorodovich, comes from the name "Smoroda," the mythological river of death in Russian folklore. The description of the tavern where Prince Vladimir finds Vasily also suggests the atmosphere of Muscovite Russia at the end of the six-teenth century and during the seventeenth century, when "sovereign tav-erns" were established as a means of increasing taxes for the state treasury. The reference to Vladimir walking through Kiev and dropping into the "tsar's big taverns" represents another anachronism, since the first tsar, Ivan IV, was crowned in 1547, long after the demise of Kievan Rus.

N.E. Onchukov collected the song selected for translation on the Pechora River in Archangel Province in 1902 from the woman per-former Anna D. Ostasheva.

⮦ Vasily Ignatyev ⮧

Source: N.E. Onchukov, *Pechora Bylinas* (St. Petersburg, 1904), no. 18.

It wasn't along the mother Neva River—
Two bay aurochs were swimming,
    Their dear mother came to meet them:
"Greetings to you, my aurochs, my little children!"
5   "Greetings to you, dear mother,
Our aurochs with golden horns!"
    "Where have you been and stayed, my aurochs?
What did you aurochs see?"
    "Mother, we were in Shakhovo,
10   Our lady, we were in Lyakhovo,
We crossed the famous Saracen Field,
Kulikovo Field from corner to corner,
And the capital city of Kiev from end to end.
We didn't see any wonders,
15   The only wonder we saw wasn't small,
It wasn't a small wonder but a big one.
A young and beautiful maid appeared,
She wore only a smock without a belt,
She wore only stockings without shoes,
20   She came to the Puchai River,
And she carried a book, the Gospels.
She came to the Puchai River,
She waded into the water up to her knees,
And more deeply above her waist,
25   And more deeply up to her white breasts.
She went up to a gray stone,
She lay the book on the gray grieving stone,
She stood there from dawn to dusk,
She read the book from cover to cover,
30   The more she read, the more she wept."
    "Oh, you stupid aurochs, little children!
You stupid and foolish aurochs!

That wasn't a young and beautiful maid who appeared,
That was the Most Holy Lady, Our Mother of God.
35   She sensed a misfortune hanging over the city,
She sensed a great misfortune hanging over Kiev."

Skurlata the Tsar rose up,
Skurlata the Tsar, Smoroda's son,
With his beloved son-in-law's father, Korshak,
40   With his beloved son-in-law, Konshak,
With his beloved nephew, Kirshak.
He assembled, the dog, a huge army,
In front of him, the dog, were forty thousand,
On his right, the dog, were forty thousand,
45   On his left, the dog, were forty thousand,
Behind him, the dog, the number was endless.
He left, the dog, for the open field,
He, the dog, arranged his tents very well,
He, the dog, adorned the tops most beautifully,
50   He, the dog, set out tables in the tents,
He wrote a yarlyk, an urgent letter,
He chose the very best Tatar,
The best, the biggest, and the most agile of all.
He himself instructed the Tatar:
55   "Please ride, my daring good youth,
Ride past the sentry outposts,
Ride past the city walls,
At the gates don't stop to ask permission from
        the gatekeepers,
At the doors don't stop to ask permission from
        the doorkeepers,
60   Leave your steed in the middle of the street,
Leave your steed untended and untied,
Go to Prince Vladimir,
Enter the dining hall,
Lay down the yarlyk on the oaken table,
65   Lay down the yarlyk and quickly go away."
Our Sun, Vladimir the Prince, then looked,
He saw the yarlyk, the urgent letter,
Our Sun, Vladimir the Prince, then spoke:

"Hail to you, Dobrynya, Nikita's son!
70   Please read the yarlyk, the urgent letter."
          When Dobrynya read it, he grinned:
        "If you give up the city voluntarily, I'll take it voluntarily,
        If you don't give up the city voluntarily, I'll take it by force,
        I'll take it by force and with bloodshed,
75   I'll make the Prince himself bow beneath my sword,
        I'll take Apraxia the Princess for myself,
        I'll send all your cathedral churches up in smoke."
          The Prince was offended by this,
        He took this for a great insult.
80   Then our Sun Vladimir started getting ready,
        He put his marten coat on one shoulder,
        He put his down cap on one ear,
        He set off walking through the city of Kiev.
          He met a senior drunkard:*
85   "Greetings to you, my senior drunkard!"
          "Greetings to you, our Sun, Vladimir the Prince!
        Why aren't you walking as you used to?
        Why do you hang your reckless head?
        And why do you lower your bright eyes?"
90   "Hail to you, my senior drunkard!
        A misfortune is hanging over my city,
        A great misfortune is hanging over my Kiev.
        Do you know of any visiting bogatyrs?"†
          "Father, our Sun, Vladimir the Prince!
95   Don't consult with us but with the boyars,
        They might be able to assist you."
          Our Sun Vladimir went on from there.
        He met a middle drunkard:
        "Greetings to you, my middle drunkard!"
100   Greetings to you, our Sun, Vladimir the Prince!
        Why aren't you walking as you used to?
        Why do you hang your reckless head?

---

*The Russian word indicates a person who is thin, a beggar, and a drunkard. The singer expands this episode by "ranking" these people from the lower classes and by creating a threefold repetition.

†This implies that none of the bogatyrs are in the city.

Why do you lower your bright eyes?"
      "Hail to you, my middle drunkard!

105   A misfortune is hanging over my city,
A great misfortune is hanging over my Kiev,
Do you know of any visiting bogatyrs?"
      "Our Sun, our father, Vladimir the Prince!
Don't consult with us but with the boyars,

110   They might be able to assist you."
      Our Sun Vladimir went on from there.
He met a junior drunkard:
"Greetings to you, my junior drunkard!"
      "Greetings to you, our Sun, Vladimir the Prince!

115   Why aren't you walking as you used to?
You're walking with your reckless head hanging,
You're walking with your bright eyes lowered."
      "Hail to you, my junior drunkard!
A misfortune is hanging over my city,

120   A great misfortune is hanging over my Kiev.
Do you know of any visiting bogatyrs?"
      "Our Sun, our father Vladimir the Prince!
Walk through the city of Kiev,
Drop in the tsar's big taverns,

125   Drop in the sovereign's bars.
In one a daring good youth
Is lying on a stove, on a glazed stove.
He doesn't have a cross or belt,
He's not wearing a linen shirt,

130   He's lying only under a bast mat,
He's squandered everything on wine,
He's pawned everything in the tsar's tavern,
He's been sleeping there for three whole days."
      Our Sun Vladimir went on from there,

135   He walked through the city of Kiev,
He dropped in the tsar's big taverns,
He dropped in the sovereign's bars,
In one he looked at the stove, at the glazed stove,
He saw the daring good youth:

140   "Hail to you, my daring good youth,
      Young Vasily, Ignaty's son!

You've slept enough and now it's time to get up,
It's time to rouse yourself from your big binge,
Get up, Vasily, Ignaty's son,
145 Please serve me with loyalty and truth,
With devoted loyalty and truth."
  Vasily didn't react to this,
Our Sun Vladimir shouted a second time:
"Hail to you, my daring good youth,
150 Young Vasily, Ignaty's son!
You've slept enough and now it's time to get up,
It's time to rouse yourself from your big binge,
Please get up, Vasily, Ignaty's son,
Please serve me with loyalty and truth,
155 With devoted loyalty and truth."
  Vasily didn't react to this,
Our Sun Vladimir shouted a third time:
"Hail to you, my daring good youth,
Young Vasily, Ignaty's son!
160 You've slept enough and now it's time to get up,
It's time to rouse yourself from your big binge,
Please get up, Vasily, Ignaty's son,
Please serve me with loyalty and truth,
With devoted loyalty and truth."
165 And now Vasily woke up,
He roused himself from his big binge,
Vasily Ignatyevich spoke:
"I'd be glad to serve you, even to lay down my life,
But my reckless head still aches."
170 The Prince filled a goblet with green wine,
Not a large or a small goblet but a bucket and a half,
An aurochs's horn filled with sweet mead,
For snacks he added a kalach baked from the finest flour.
Our Sun Vladimir served the goblet with both hands,
175 And Vasily took it with one hand,
Vasily drank it in one draught,
And after drinking the goblet Vasily spoke:
  "Vasily's ardent heart hasn't been refreshed,
My reckless head hasn't been cheered up."
180 Our Sun Vladimir took the goblet for a second time,

He filled the goblet with green wine,
Not a large or a small goblet but a bucket and a half,
An aurochs's horn filled with sweet mead,
For snacks he added a kalach baked from the finest flour.
185   And Vasily took the goblet with one hand,
Vasily drank it in one draught,
And after drinking the whole goblet Vasily spoke:
"Vasily's ardent heart hasn't been refreshed,
Vasily's reckless head hasn't been cheered up."
190   Our Sun Vladimir filled a goblet for a third time,
Our Sun Vladimir served it with both hands,
And Vasily took it with one hand,
Vasily drank it in one draught,
And after drinking the goblet Vasily spoke:
195   "Vasily's ardent heart has been refreshed,
My reckless head has been cheered up,
Now I can serve you with loyalty and truth.
But I don't have a cross or belt,
I don't have a linen shirt,
200   I don't have a good steed,
I don't have a harness for a horse,
I don't have a young man's weapons,
I don't have a taut bow,
I don't have any tempered arrows,
205   I don't have a battle mace,
I don't have a Tatar spear.
Everything's been squandered on wine,
Everything's been pawned in the tsar's tavern."
          Then our Sun, Vladimir the Prince, started walking,
210   He went to the bartenders and tavern keepers:
"Hail to you, my bartenders and tavern keepers!
Return everything to Vasily without payment."
They returned everything to Vasily without payment,
          Vasily started equipping himself,
215   Vasily started getting ready,
Then he saddled and bridled his good steed,
Then Vasily mounted his good steed,
Then he drew his taut bow,
He aimed his tempered arrow,

220 He recited a charm over his arrow:
"You fly, my tempered arrow,
Higher than the tallest tree,
But lower than the moving clouds,
You fly, my arrow, into the open field,
225 You fly into Skurlata's right eye,
You come out, my arrow, of his left ear."
Vasily mounted his good steed,
Vasily urged it into the open field.
Its gray mane was spread straight out,
230 Its tail was curled straight up,
Flames blazed from the steed's mouth,
Sparks showered from the steed's nostrils,
Clouds of smoke poured out of the steed's ears.
Vasily urged his steed into the open field,
235 When he came to a Tatar outpost,
He picked the very best Tatar,
The best, the biggest, and the stoutest of all,
He grabbed the Tatar by his nimble feet,
He started swinging the Tatar,
240 He swung to his right and cleared a whole street,
He swung to his left and cleared the lanes:
"Although your tendons are thin, you won't break off,
Although your bones are brittle, you won't break apart."
Then he smashed the entire army,
245 He trampled everyone with his good steed.
Then he started riding to Prince Vladimir,
He came to Prince Vladimir's palace,
He entered the dining hall,
Our Sun Vladimir seated him at the oaken table,
250 Vladimir gave him some green wine to drink,
He served him drinks for three whole days.
All the fat-bellied boyars gathered,
They gathered to meet with Prince Vladimir,
Our Sun Vladimir was pacing the floor,
255 He spoke quiet and gentle words:
"Hail to you, my daring good youth,
Young Vasily, Ignaty's son!
What would you like to receive from me now?

Please accept some cities and their suburbs,
260   Please accept some towns and villages."*
      Vasily, Ignaty's son, then spoke:
"I don't want any cities or their suburbs,
I don't want any towns or villages,
Please grant me what I would like:
265   Wherever I walk, wherever I ride,
Everywhere let me drink wine without paying."
      The fat-bellied boyars replied to this:
"Vasily isn't needed by us anymore,
Vasily's request is now rejected."
270   Vasily spoke these words:
"Hail to you, our Sun, our father Vladimir the Prince!
Will I, Vasily, ever be needed by you again?"
      The boyars replied a second time:
"Vasily isn't needed by us anymore,
275   Vasily's request is now rejected."
      Vasily spoke these words:
"Will I, Vasily, ever be needed by you again?"
      The boyars replied a third time:
"Vasily isn't needed by us anymore,
280   Vasily's request is now rejected."
      Vasily jumped to his nimble feet,
He grabbed some cedar boards from the table,
He killed all the fat-bellied boyars.

---

*These are the things that a prince would usually award to a bogatyr or boyar but not to Vasily, who comes from the lowest urban class.

❧ 17 ❧

Churila Plyonkovich

*I*n addition to being the main character in the songs "Churila and Prince Vladimir" and "Churila and Katerina," Churila also appears in the song "Dyuk" as a competitor and foil to Dyuk. The bylina "Churila and Prince Vladimir" is relatively rare, appearing in about ten recordings, while "Churila and Katerina" exists in more than eighty variants.

In the song "Churila and Prince Vladimir," fishermen, hunters, and shepherds come to Prince Vladimir and complain that Churila and his druzhina have seized their fishing holes, hunting spots, and pastures and have also abused their women. Prince Vladimir does not know who Churila is, finds out where he lives, and, with members of his court, goes there intending to punish him. Churila and his father, Plyonko, receive Prince Vladimir and his druzhina with great respect and give him expensive presents. As a result, the Prince forgives Churila and invites him to serve at court in Kiev. Not only do the women in Kiev lose their heads over Churila's handsomeness, but Princess Apraxia also asks the Prince to name Churila as her personal chamberlain. Sensing future trouble, Prince Vladimir relieves Churila of all duties and allows him to leave Kiev. The song "Churila and Katerina" begins when she invites him to visit her while her husband, Bermyata, is attending church services. While Churila is with her, Chernava, a female servant, reports the unexpected guest to the husband. He returns home; asks his wife questions, to which she gives clever answers; finds Churila sleeping in bed, and kills him. The two versions of the second song differ according to the way Katerina's character is presented (Propp 1958b: 484–86). In one version, where she is portrayed as a cunning woman and unfaithful wife, her husband, Bermyata, may kill both her and Churila. In the other version, Katerina becomes a tragic figure who sacrifices everything for love and commits suicide after Bermyata kills Churila. The second part of the translated variant most closely follows the second version. Russian folklorists consider the first subject about Churila to be a bylina novella and the second to be a ballad based on the triad of an old husband, his young wife, and her lover.

Churila represents a "dude" or "dandy" who is a Don Juan, boasts of his expensive clothing, and shows off his good looks. He, as Dyuk, is wealthier than Vladimir, possesses a luxurious estate, and is completely independent of Prince Vladimir, who has never heard of Churila and does not know where his estate is located. The numerous members of Churila's druzhina are dressed in the same extravagant fashion, their physical features are identical, and their horses have the same equipment. I.Ia. Froianov and Iu.I. Iudin (1995) explain these puzzling features as reflecting a stage in the history of the East Slavs when tribal organization still predominated and the power of the princes had not yet been fully established. Perceived in such a context, Prince Vladimir has no authority over Churila, who is a member of a different tribe. The fishermen, hunters, and shepherds belong to the "prince's tribe," and they are intruded upon by another tribe, which Vladimir is forced to challenge. Viewed in this vein, the presents Prince Vladimir receives from Churila and his father may be regarded as tribute. Later singers no longer understood such relations and consequently have treated Prince Vladimir satirically. He takes no resolute action against Churila, he accepts a bribe as a corrupt official, and he is scared to death of Churila's druzhina, which he mistakes for a Tatar force about to attack Kiev. Furthermore, Froianov and Iudin believe that Churila and his druzhina may form a male fraternity of neophytes who have passed their initiatory rites, are eligible to marry, and in the meantime are allowed to do most anything without retribution. The term "free people" may also hint that Churila's druzhina is a band of robbers.

Despite his ability to hurl a mace high in the air and catch it as a bogatyr does and despite his skill at leaping from one running horse to another, Churila has no heroic features and accomplishes no exploits typical for a bogatyr, such as defending Kiev from an enemy attack or slaying a monster. In the Russian epic tradition, he most closely resembles Dyuk, who comes from a distant rich city and disdains Kiev as a "poor relative." Although singers may present Churila as a lively "swashbuckling Hollywood type," as a rule they treat him ironically. Several hypotheses have been proposed to connect the songs about

Churila with a specific region and historical period, but none has proved well founded. According to one derivation, the name "Churila" comes from the given name "Cyril"; according to another derivation, "Churila" comes from the form "Dzhurilo," which is popular in Ukrainian oral poetry and indicates a "lady's man" in lyric songs. Some folklorists assume that the songs about Churila originated in the western Ukrainian areas of Galich and Volynia, since an aristocratic family by the name of Churilov lived in these regions from the fourteenth through the seventeenth centuries. And finally, yet others believe that the songs about Churila depict the mores, clothing, and residences of the boyars in Muscovite Russia in the sixteenth and seventeenth centuries (Vs.F. Miller 1897–1924, 1: 187–200).

The variant selected for translation was recorded in 1939 by G.N. Parilova and A.D. Soimonov in Pudoga Region of Karelia from A.M. Pashkova. The song is representative of the last phase in the Russian epic tradition. Since Pashkova was literate, she sometimes includes elements from written literature (the description of Plyonko's estate as a West European medieval castle), and in places she may use anachronisms from contemporary life. Pashkova nevertheless has skillfully created a composite bylina that combines both subjects about Churila. She presents a chess game as a symbol of lovemaking; she provides social commentary, especially in her asides; and she inserts a passage about how one of Churila's loves marries someone else. Pashkova also emphasizes the immorality of Churila's conduct by having his affair with Katerina take place on Annunciation Day, a main religious holiday on March 25. Several motifs are analogous to those in other songs. For instance, the intricate buttons depicting embracing lovers recall similar buttons in the epic about Dyuk. The passage about how Apraxia cuts her finger while carving a swan in Churila's presence resembles a passage in the bylina about Alyosha and Tugarin where Apraxia is so taken by Tugarin at a feast that she cuts her finger.

☙   Churila Plyonkovich   ☙

Source: G.N. Parilova and A.D. Soimonov,
Bylinas of the Pudoga Region (Petrozavodsk, 1941), no. 1.

In the city, in Kiev,
At the gracious Prince's, at Vladimir's,
(This Vladimir did nothing but hold feasts.)*
There was a banquet and a feast of honor.
Long tables were set up,

5   And surrounding benches were set up,
And the benches were covered with Persian rugs.
On the tables, on the long tables,
There was placed a great number
Of tasty dishes
10   And drinks of mead.
At those tables, at those oaken tables,
On the surrounding benches,
Were sitting princes and boyars,
Mighty Russian bogatyrs,
15   And daring polyanitsas.
Day was inclining toward evening
And the feast of honor was in full swing.
     Our Sun, Prince Vladimir of capital Kiev,
Had enjoyed himself and had become drunk,
20   He went out on the porch with a railing,
He leaned against the smoothly finished railing,
He looked and glanced in the open field.
From the far, far away field, from the open field,
A great crowd was coming,
25   Village men were coming,
Kiev tradesmen were coming.
Their caftans were all torn,

---

*This is one of several personal remarks that the singer makes in passing about the song.

Their boots were all worn down,
Their felt hats were hanging on their ears.
30 They were coming toward the prince's courtyard,
Toward the porch with a railing,
They bowed low and paid their respects:
    "Hail to you, our Sun, Vladimir of capital Kiev!
Please accept our complaint,
35 Please give us an honest judgment.
We're peasants from the River Saroga,
Year-round fisherman from the River Saroga.
You're eating, drinking, and enjoying yourself,
You don't know our trouble.
40 At home on the River Saroga
Some strange people have appeared,
They've tossed out all our nets,
They've ripped out all our snagging lines,
And they've cast their own nets.
45 They have nets made of fine thread,
The strings in them are made of seven kinds of silks,
Their nets have silver floats,
And their sinkers are gilded.
They've caught all the Saroga fish,
50 They've pulled out all the white fish and salmon,
And now there's nothing left for us poor people to catch,
There's no fresh morsel for the prince's table,
There's no profit for us poor people.
They've revealed and named themselves,
55 They belong to the druzhina of Churila,
Of Churila, Plyonko's son."
    Vladimir of capital Kiev spoke:
"Hail to you, my village men,
My Kiev tradesmen!
60 How can I make an honest judgment?
I haven't heard or seen Churila Plyonkovich,
I don't know where Churila's estate is,
I don't know where Churila resides,
I don't know where Churila lives."
65   The men stood awhile and walked away.
The crowd then moved on past,

And another crowd appeared from the open field.
Village men were coming,
Kiev tradesmen were coming,
70 Tradesmen and workers were coming.
Their caftans were all torn,
Their bast shoes were all worn down,
And their felt hats were hanging on their ears.
They came straight to the white-stone palace,
75 To the porch with a railing,
To the gracious Prince, to Vladimir.
They bowed to him and bent low
With their heads to the very mother damp earth.
Then they spoke these words:
80 "Hail to you, our Sun, Vladimir of capital Kiev!
Please accept a complaint from us,
Please give us an honest judgment.
You're eating, drinking, and enjoying yourself,
But you don't know the trouble hanging over us.
85 We're peasants from the dark forest,
And we're hunters from the dark forest,
In the dark forests where we live
Some strange people have appeared,
They've pulled out all our traps,
90 And they've thrown out all our snares,
And they've set out their own traps,
And they've made up their own snares,
And they've caught all the martens and foxes,
And they've shot all the gray hares.
95 Now there's nothing left for us poor people to catch,
And there's no income for the prince's court,
And there's no profit for us peasants.
They've revealed and named themselves,
They all are wonderful hunters,
100 They belong to the druzhina of Churila."
    Vladimir of capital Kiev spoke:
"Hail to you, my village men,
And to you, my Kiev tradesmen!
I accept your complaint,
105 But I can't give you a just judgment,

I haven't seen or heard Churila,
I don't know where Churila lives,
I don't know where Churila resides."
     This crowd passed from the courtyard,
110   And another appeared from the open field,
It drew near to the prince's palace,
To the porch with a railing,
To the gracious Prince, to Vladimir.
They bowed to him and bent low
115   With their heads to the damp earth:
"Hail to you, our Sun, Vladimir of capital Kiev!
Please accept our complaint,
And please give us an honest judgment.
We're mowers from the green meadows,
120   You're eating, drinking, and enjoying yourself,
But you don't know the trouble hanging over us.
On the meadows, on the green meadows,
Some strange people have appeared,
They've driven up their herds of bay steeds,
125   They've trampled our grass and meadow,
They've scattered all our shocks and ricks,
And they've driven us mowers away.
There's no more work for us peasants,
There's no income for the prince's court,
130   And there's no profit for us peasants.
They've revealed and named themselves,
They belong to the druzhina of Churila."
     Vladimir of capital Kiev spoke:
"Hail to you, my village men,
135   And to you, my Kiev tradesmen!
I accept your complaint,
But I can't give you a just judgment.
I haven't seen or heard Churila,
I don't know where Churila lives,
140   And I don't know where Churila resides."
     This crowd also disappeared,
And a fourth appeared from the field.
Village men were coming
Kiev tradesmen were coming,

145 All considered themselves gardeners.
   Their caftans were all torn,
   Their bast shoes were all worn down,
   And their felt hats were hanging on their ears.
   They came straight to the prince's courtyard,
150 To the porch with a railing,
   And to our Sun, Prince Vladimir.
   Then they spoke these words:
   "Our Sun, Vladimir of capital Kiev!
   You're eating, drinking, and enjoying yourself,
155 But you don't know the trouble hanging over us.
   At home in our field, in our open field,
   In the gardens, in the peasants' gardens,
   Some strange people have appeared.
   They've pulled out all the turnips and cabbages,
160 They've trampled all the onions and garlic,
   They've harmed the very old women,
   They've dishonored the young married women,
   And they've insulted the young girls,
   They've insulted and they've mocked them.
165 Now there's no more income for us peasants,
   And there's no peace for our wives and daughters.
   They've revealed and named themselves,
   They belong to the druzhina of Churila."
    Vladimir of capital Kiev spoke:
170 "Hail to you, my village men!
   I accept your complaint,
   But I can't give you an honest judgment,
   I haven't seen Churila with my eyes,
   I haven't heard Churila with my ears,
175 I don't know where Churila's estate is,
   I don't know where Churila lives,
   I don't know where Churila resides."
    The peasants stood awhile and wept,
   They wept and walked away.
180 Our Sun, Vladimir of capital Kiev
   Went back into his high palace,
   Into the hall, into the dining hall.
   He questioned and he asked

The princes, the boyars, and all his subordinates:
185 "Please tell me and report to me
About that robber,
About Churila, about the young Churila.
He's done a lot of mischief in our parts,
There's no life for the peasants and workers."
190   Then the princes and boyars exchanged some glances,
They didn't dare say anything about Churila.
A young fellow volunteered on the side,
A cook, Ivan Ivanovich:
"I know where Churila resides,
195 And I know where Churila lives.
Churila's home is on the Pochai River,
On the Pochai River in an open field.
His courtyard covers seven versts,
A high palace stands in the courtyard,
200 High towers stand at the corners,
Deep moats have been dug all around,
And false bridges have been made
For passing walkers and for passing riders,
So that they can't reach Churila unannounced.*
205 The gate to the courtyard is made of planks,
Exactly seventy icons hang above the gate,
The threshold under the gate is made of walrus tusk,
Churila has seven palaces in the courtyard,
The tops on the palaces are gilded."
210   Vladimir of capital Kiev spoke:
"Hail to you, my cook, Ivan Ivanovich!
If you're telling the truth, then I'll reward you,
But if you're not telling the truth, then I'll chop off
        your head."
The cook then spoke and swore an oath:
215 "Hail to you, our Sun, Vladimir of capital Kiev!
A cook's head is not very dear,
My prince's honor is dear to me."
    Then our Sun, Vladimir of capital Kiev,

---

* The false bridges are part of the defenses and are intended to trick an outsider.

Selected his best comrades,
220   He took princes and boyars and Russian bogatyrs,
He gathered a party of seventy people.
He said goodbye to the young princess,
He set out on the path, on the road,
He was searching for Churila's estate.
(Such was the geography that the prince didn't know
in his own princedom.)
225   The daring good youths started riding,
The princes and boyars, and with them the mighty
          Russian bogatyrs,
And our Sun, Vladimir of capital Kiev.
They rode to the open field,
In the open field they thought things over:
230   "Where is the Pochai River?
What direction should we ride in?"
       They stood there and thought for a long time:
"Whatever direction a black raven comes flying from,
Dark forests are probably in that direction,
235   And whatever direction a free bird comes flying from,
A free bird, a gray gull,
The Pochai River probably flows in that direction."
       And they guided their good steeds and started riding,
They rode and rode all day until evening,
240   The whole dark night until first light,
And then they came to the Pochai River.
Troops were near the Pochai River,
They were surprised by this,
And they were frightened by these troops.
245   Vladimir of capital Kiev spoke:
"Hail to you, my princes and my boyars,
And my mighty Russian bogatyrs!
Let's start riding on a path back home,
A heathen army is there,
250   Infidel Tatars are probably there,
And they want to attack Holy Russia.
And while we're riding and roaming,
They'll fall on the city of Kiev,
They won't leave us even one estate."

255   The young Batyk then spoke:
  "Hail to you, Vladimir of capital Kiev!
  That isn't a host or great army there,
  Those aren't infidel Tatars standing there.
  A breeze is moving through the air,
260 And I don't catch a Tatar scent.
  This is what my young man's eye can see—
  Free people are standing there,
  They're having fun and amusing themselves
  In the field, in the open field.
265 My sharp ear can hear
  The crowing of a rooster
  And the sound of people's voices—
  That's probably a residence."
    And they started riding in that direction,
270 They rode all day until evening,
  The whole dark night until first light,
  They rode up to a high mansion.
  The courtyard covered seven versts,
  A high stockade stood around the courtyard,
275 Four towers stood at the corners,
  And the tops on the towers were gilded.
  They rode up to the plank gate,
  Exactly seventy icons were hanging over the gate,
  The threshold under the gate was made of walrus tusk.
280   Vladimir of capital Kiev spoke:
  "The cook didn't lie, he told the truth,
  I'll reward the cook for this."
    Suddenly the plank gate was opened,
  And then a savvy old man came out,
285   He bowed low to our Sun, to the Prince:
  "Hail to you, our Sun, Vladimir of capital Kiev!
  Please ride into our wide courtyard
  With your comrades, with all your comrades,
  With your princes and with your boyars.
290 Tie up your good steeds
  To that post, to that smoothly finished post,
  To that gilded ring.
  Stalls for horses have been built there,

And the finest grain's been poured there.

295   Would you please come in,
Into my white-stone palace
To share a meal,
To carve up a white swan."
       Then Vladimir of capital Kiev spoke:
300   "Please tell me, savvy old man,
Who am I having a conversation with,
How are you called by your first name,
And how are you honored by your patronymic?"
       The savvy old man then spoke to him:
305   "I'm Plyonko Stanislavovich,
And I'm the dear father of Churila."
       Vladimir of capital Kiev spoke:
"I'm trying to reach Churila."
       Plyonko Stanislavovich then spoke:
310   "I apologize for Churila,
Churila doesn't happen to be home,
We didn't anticipate such guests,
We didn't expect any guests today.
My son, Churila Plyonkovich,
315   Isn't far away in the open field,
He's having fun with his druzhina,
In the open field by the Pochai River,
(And they thought it was an army.)
We're expecting him home for dinner soon."
       Then Vladimir of capital Kiev
320   Entered the white-stone palace.
Here were porches with railings,
And the handrails were smoothly finished,
The tops on them were gilded.
They passed through three latticed vestibules,
325   Three glassed-in vestibules,
Three marble vestibules,
They entered the white-stone palace,
They entered the hall, the dining hall.
In the palace everything was like the sky:
330   A sun was in the sky and a sun was in the palace,
A moon was in the sky and a moon was in the palace,

Stars were in the sky and stars were in the palace.
Just as a star may fall in the sky,
So the sparks of a falling star were strewn in the palace.
335   Long tables were standing there,
Surrounding benches had been put there,
Persian rugs had been spread out there.
        Vladimir of capital Kiev sat down
With his princes and his boyars,
340   With his mighty Russian bogatyrs.
They had starved on the road,
They ate their fill at Plyonko's.
The dishes there were appropriate,
Geese and swans had been roasted,
345   Gray ducks had been well steamed,
And overseas wines were standing there.
They ate their fill and drank their fill.
        Dear Vladimir of capital Kiev
Looked out the window with a wooden frame:
350   From the river, from the Pochai River,
Was riding a party of good youths,
Their steeds were flying like eagles,
And the good youths were sitting like falcons.
All the horses were the same color,
355   The youths were wearing the same clothing,
Shoulder for shoulder the good youths were alike,
Face for face the good youths were alike.
The steeds had Circassian saddles,
The steeds had gilded bridles,
360   The steeds had silken reins.
The youths' caftans were made of patterned velvet,
On their heads were Turkish hats,
On their feet were boots of green morocco leather,
And of expensive foreign leather,
365   And of sturdy Yaroslavl embroidery.
Their boot tips were like an awl and their heels were high:
You could roll an egg off the tips,
And a nightingale could fly under their heels.*

---

*The boots had tips ending in a large upward curl and had high heels.

They were riding and enjoying themselves,
370   They were throwing their steel maces,
They were tossing them from hand to hand.
Then Vladimir the Prince became frightened:
"Hail to you, my princes and my boyars,
And my mighty Russian bogatyrs!
375   Please start riding to the capital city of Kiev,
A heathen army is probably coming,
Infidel Tatars are coming."
Plyonko Stanislavovich then spoke:
"Don't be afraid, my Prince, and don't be frightened,
380   It's Churila's jokesters who are coming."
The crowd passed by the courtyard,
A second appeared from the field.
Two hundred youths were coming,
Their steeds had white coats,
385   Their harnesses were better than those before,
Their clothing was the best to be had.
Face for face the youths were alike,
Shoulder for shoulder these youths were alike,
They were riding and were having fun,
390   They were throwing their steel maces,
They were throwing them from hand to hand.
This party passed by the courtyard.
A third party then appeared,
Three hundred daring youths.
395   They had dark-bay steeds,
They had silver bridles,
And they had Circassian saddles,
And they had silken reins.
They were divided into three parties,
400   In the middle was a daring good youth,
That very Churila Plyonkovich.
He was leaping from steed to steed
Across two steeds to a third,
He leaped straight on the Circassian saddle,
405   He put his feet in the stirrups,
And he had fun with his mace.
He threw the heavy mace

Higher than the forest but under the clouds,
And he caught the mace with one hand.
410   Vladimir of capital Kiev spoke:
"My princes and my boyars, my mighty Russian
            bogatyrs!
A heathen army has swooped down upon us,
A heathen Turkish army,
The sultan himself is in the middle of this army,
415   I recognize him by his manner,
I can tell him by his walk."
        Plyonko Stanislavovich then spoke:
"Hail to you, Vladimir of capital Kiev!
Don't be frightened and don't be scared.
420   That isn't the Turkish sultan coming,
That's my beloved son who's coming,
Churila, Plyonko's son.
He's a prankster and a mischief maker."
        And Churila rode into the wide courtyard,
425   He dismounted his good steed,
He wanted to enter the white-stone palace.
Then Plyonko Stanislavovich came out,
He said these words to Churila:
"Hail to you, my dear little child,
430   Churila, Plyonko's son!
In my hall, in my dining hall,
Are sitting long-expected guests,
Long-expected but also uninvited.
Churila, you know how to play a lot of pranks,
435   So, Churila, you should know how to give an answer
Before our Sun, Prince Vladimir."
        Then Churila dismounted his good steed,
He threw off his sable coat,
He took off his bogatyr's armor,
440   He didn't enter the dining hall,
He took the golden keys,
He went straight to the storehouses,
He took marten, fox, and black sable furs,
He didn't take many or a few—he took forty times forty.
445   He took several bound chests,

He filled them with silver and gold,
He also took a sable coat,
A fur coat covered with patterned velvet.
Then he entered the white-stone palace,
450   He entered the hall, the dining hall,
Where a joyful feast was going on,
He bowed low and paid his respects
To all the princes, to the Kiev boyars,
And to our Sun, Prince Vladimir in particular:
455   "Hail to you, our Sun, Vladimir of capital Kiev!
Please grant me your forgiveness
For my great guilt and for my stupidity.
Please accept these little gifts:
Marten, fox, and black sable furs for the princes and
          the boyars."
460   To our Sun, Prince Vladimir,
He presented a sable coat,
He presented chests of gold and silver.
          Vladimir spoke these words:
"Thank you, my daring good youth!
465   For your gifts, for your honorable gifts,
I won't remain in debt to you.
There have been many petitioners against Churila,
But now Churila has more well-wishers,
All the princes and boyars will plead for you,
470   And I'll give you an honest judgment.
God will forgive you for what you've done.
*(He made a judgment. These were scoundrels;
          the judgment was for the coat.)*
Hail to you, my daring good youth,
Churila, Plyonko's son!
Please listen to Prince Vladimir,
475   Let's ride together to the capital city of Kiev.
Serve me with loyalty and truth,
I'll give you appropriate work."
          Churila Plyonkovich then spoke:
"Hail to you, Vladimir of capital Kiev!
480   I'd go very willingly
If my dear father would release me."

Plyonko Stanislavovich then spoke:
"Hail to you, my dear little child!
Prince Vladimir is doing you a great honor,
485 I release you willingly."
Then Churila Plyonkovich
Saddled his good steed,
He loaded chests of colorful clothing,
He tied the chests to the saddle,
490 He bound the chests to the saddle straps,
He prayed to the icon of the Savior,
He said goodbye to his dear father,
He departed on the path, on the road.
In the open field he overtook
495 Prince Vladimir and his druzhina,
He went past the Prince and rode ahead.
He arrived in the city of Kiev,
Without reporting he rode into the wide courtyard,
Without asking he entered the white-stone palace.
500 The prince's servants spoke:
"Hail to you, you village lout!
Without asking you ride into the wide courtyard,
Without reporting you enter the white-stone palace!"
Churila didn't have time to give an answer,
505 Prince Vladimir was returning from the road,
He was giving orders to his servants:
"Take the guest by his arm,
Take the guest to his chambers,
Set aside some special rooms.
510 This is Churila Plyonkovich,
He's come to us to stay as a guest,
And he's come to us to serve the court."
The prince's servants took
Churila Plyonkovich
515 To the rooms, to the special rooms.
He set out his belongings,
He dressed in colorful clothing,
He put on a suit of patterned felt,
On his feet he put boots of green morocco leather,
520 Of expensive Turkish leather,

In a fashionable foreign cut,
And with sturdy Yaroslavl embroidery.
His boot tips were like an awl and his heels were high,
You could roll an egg off the tips,
525   And a nightingale could fly under his heels.
He combed his yellow curls,
He buttoned his bright buttons.
These buttons were made of diamonds,
The buttonholes were made of seven kinds of silks,
530   And on each button was depicted
A stout good youth,
And on each buttonhole was depicted
A darling girl, a beautiful girl.
When unbuttoned—they embraced,
535   And when buttoned—they kissed.
Churila, the good youth, had finished dressing.
He looked in the crystal mirror,
And he went into the dining hall.
He spoke to Prince Vladimir:
540   "This good youth didn't come to be a guest
But to serve the prince's court."
        Vladimir of capital Kiev spoke:
"I'll give you work as a steward,
As a steward and as a cupbearer.
545   Youth, please arrange the oaken tables,
Please put out all the gilded goblets,
Please set out all the sweet dishes
And all the drinks of mead,
Please set out all the overseas wines."
550   Then Churila grinned,
He was surprised at this kind of work.
And Churila started working,
He arranged the oaken tables,
He arranged the gilded goblets.
555   Then the invited guests sat down.
The young Churila, Plyonko's son,
Walked around the oaken tables,
He shook his yellow curls,
He jingled his gilded rings.

560 The women of the court admired him,
They admired Churila's beauty.
The young Princess Apraxia
Was eating a white swan
With the table knife.
565 She cut her white hand,
Her white hand, her left hand.
She spoke these words:
"Don't be surprised, women of the court,
By my feminine reasoning.
570 Glancing at the young steward,
At Churila Plyonkovich,
At his face, at his white face,
At his curls, at his yellow curls,
At his fingers, at his gilded rings,
575 Something happened to me, a young woman.
My bright eyes became dim,
My head started spinning,
I couldn't see the wide world,
And I cut my left hand a little,
580 I spilled my scarlet blood
On the tables, on the oaken tables,
On the napkins, on the linen napkins.
I can't share the meal,
I can't carve the white swan,
585 And the goblet of green wine
Has stuck in my mouth."
      She stood up from the oaken table,
She bowed to Vladimir the Sun:
"Hail to you, our Sun, Vladimir of capital Kiev!
590 Wasn't this deliberate on your part?
Didn't you choose a poor kind of service
For the young Churila Plyonkovich?
Please listen to your young wife,
Change Churila's work.
595 He shouldn't be a steward or a cupbearer,
But he should be a chamberlain,
So that in our bright bedroom
He would tidy up the wooden beds,

He would spread the down comforters,

600 He would cover the sable blankets."
  Vladimir of capital Kiev spoke:
"My young Princess Apraxia!
Pray to the Lord and to the Savior
That I love you, Princess,

605 Because I'd cut off your reckless head
If you would shame and would dishonor me
Before all the table at court."
  The Princess Apraxia then spoke:
"Prince, my daring master,

610 You are my betrothed husband.
If you won't take Churila as a chamberlain
To tidy up the wooden beds
And to spread out the down comforters,
Then take Churila as a basin holder.

615 I'll get up very early in the morning,
So that Churila, Plyonko's son,
Can pour water for me in the basin,
And can give me a linen towel."
  Then Vladimir saw that trouble had come,

620 Vladimir spoke these words:
"Yes, Churila Plyonkovich,
I'll remove you from the post of steward,
I'll give you work as a summoner.
You'll ride around the city of Kiev

625 To summon guests to a feast of honor,
Princes and boyars with their wives,
And single bogatyrs,
All the merchants and the trading people."
  Some people always buy off trouble,

630 But Churila looks for trouble.
He got up very early in the morning,
He dressed and readied himself,
He mounted his good steed,
He started riding through the city of Kiev,

635 Through the streets, through the straight streets,
Through the round-about lanes.
When good people saw him,

They ran after him and chased each other
To look at Churila Plyonkovich.
640   The fences cracked where girls were looking,
The windows rang when young married women glanced,
Very old women gnawed their crutches,
All glancing at the young Churila,
At his heavenly beauty,
645   At his curls, at his yellow curls,
At his rings, at his gilded rings.
       Then those invited and those uninvited
Came in throngs to the prince's courtyard.
Our Sun, Vladimir of capital Kiev,
650   Then saw that trouble had come,
One couldn't walk through the courtyard because of
                the people there.
The young Princess Apraxia
Began to yearn very much for Churila,
She yearned very much and fell very ill.
655   Then the Prince saw that trouble had come,
He spoke these words to Churila:
"Hail to you, my daring good youth!
Thank you for your honor and your kindness,
You've served the city of Kiev,
660   And the Grand Prince Vladimir,
And all of the prince's court.
I don't need your service now,
You can live wherever you please,
And you can work, Churila, wherever you like."
665   Churila was very glad,
He said goodbye to Prince Vladimir,
But he didn't go to Princess Apraxia.
Churila went into the wide courtyard,
He prayed to the icon of the Savior
670   For being freed from this work.
He lost his head, became preoccupied,
And left his good steed in Kiev.
He went out into the straight street,
Into the postal road,
675   He hired himself a coachman,

He rode away from Kiev.
He came to his Galich City,
To his provider and father.
Then both of them were overjoyed
680   That he was rid of such trouble.
Churila went into the high palace,
Into his white-stone chamber,
Into his hall, into his dining hall.
He sat down at the oaken tables.
685   The faithful servants were overjoyed,
They served him tasty foods,
And many drinks of mead,
And overseas sweet meads.
Churila ate his fill,
690   Churila drank his fill,
And he went to his bedroom, to his warm bedroom,
He lay down on the bed, on the wooden bed,
On the comforter, on the down comforter.
He started sleeping, resting, and taking repose.
695   He didn't wake up for three whole days,
He lounged around on the bed.
On the fourth day
The good youth woke up,
He got up very early in the morning,
700   He washed himself very clean,
He went out on the porch with a railing,
He ordered his bay steed to be saddled,
And he mounted his good steed,
His steed, his bogatyr's steed.
705   Suddenly a stern messenger appeared,
He handed Churila a letter,
Churila read the letter,
In the letter this was written:
"A beautiful girl, his love,
710   Has waited long for him and has expected him,
Has despaired about waiting for him,
She's getting married to another,
They'll be betrothed today,
And they'll be married tomorrow."

715   Then the youth's feelings were aroused:
             "I won't go and try to reason with her."
             He tightened his taut bow,
             He placed a tempered arrow on it,
             He recited a charm over the arrow:
720   "Fly, fly, tempered arrow,
             To the lake, to the round lake,
             Kill, kill, tempered arrow,
             The gray duck on the quiet water,
             The good youth on the bay steed,   ·
725   And my love in the high palace."
             He released the tempered arrow,
             Higher than the towering forest
             And lower than the moving clouds.
             The tempered arrow fell
730   In the round lake on the very bottom.
             The tempered arrow didn't kill,
             It didn't kill or wound anyone.*
             Then Churila dismounted his good steed,
             He went to the cathedral church,
735   He stood through Sunday vespers,
             He had a prayer said to the icon of the Savior,
             He went home to the high palace.
             Then the youth's feelings were aroused,
             The youth went for a walk around the estate.
740   He walked along a street and a lane,
             He saw a high palace standing there,
             A woman was sitting in the palace.
             She opened the window with a wooden frame,
             She summoned Churila Plyonkovich.
745   "Come in, my daring good youth!
             My husband doesn't happen to be at home,
             No one has turned out to be in the house."
             Churila, Plyonko's son, then spoke:
             "I don't know what your name is,

---

*Since an arrow can be a courtship symbol in love songs and the arrow here sinks in the lake, this poetic passage parallels the end of Churila's relationship with the "beautiful girl."

750   I don't know what your patronymic is."
              "My name is Nastasia Mikulichna."
              These words pleased Churila,
          The youth's feelings were aroused,
          He entered the porch with a railing.
755   And Nastasia, the darling Mikulichna,
          Opened the plank door
          That was hung on silken loops
          And was hung on round-headed nails.
          She let in Churila Plyonkovich,
760   She took him by his white hands,
          By his rings, by his gilded rings,
          She led him to the dining hall,
          She spoke these words to him:
          "Churila, what will you and I amuse ourselves with?
765   Would you like to share a meal,
          Or would you like to carve a white swan?"
              "Thank you, Nastasia Mikulichna!
          At my parent's, at my father's,
          I was very full and wasn't hungry."
770   And Nastasia, the darling Mikulichna,
          Picked up her crystal board,
          Her crystal chessboard,
          She picked up her silver chessmen,
          And she said these words:
775   "We'll amuse ourselves awhile with this game,
          If you win, I'll bet one hundred rubles,
          If I win, God will forgive you."
              And they sat down at the chessboard,
          They played the first round—Churila won,
780   And she paid him one hundred rubles.
          They played the second round—Churila won,
          And Nastasia paid him one hundred rubles.
          And they played the third round—Churila won,
          Nastasia paid him three hundred rubles.
785   She looked in Churila's bright eyes,
          She said sweet words to Churila:
          "Hail to you, Churila, Plyonko's son!
          I can't play checkers and chess."

She took him firmly by the hand,
790 She kissed him on his sweet lips,
She asked him and persuaded him:
"Come, my daring good youth,
To my bedroom, to my warm bedroom,
You and I will amuse ourselves awhile there."
795 Then the youth's feelings were aroused,
He obeyed Nastasia.
They went to her warm bedroom,
They lay down on the wooden bed,
They lay down on the down comforter.
800 And then the girl Chernava, her servant,
Walked around the rooms, murmuring and grumbling:
"Nastasia, you're not sticking to your business,
You've locked yourself up with a youth in your bedroom."
But Nastasia didn't hear these words,
805 She had closed herself up in her warm bedroom.
Then the girl Chernava, her servant,
Knocked on the bedroom door,
But Nastasia didn't answer her,
She was amusing herself with Churila.
810 Then the girl, her servant, spoke:
"I'll go to the cathedral church,
I'll tell your husband everything and upset him."
Nastasia didn't respond.
The girl went to the cathedral church,
815 She prayed to the Lord God,
She bowed to the holy icons.
The girl then spoke these words:
"Hail to you, my beloved master,
Old Bermyata, Vasily's son!
820 You're standing in church and praying to God,
You don't know the trouble hanging over you.
There's disorder in your home,
There's a traitor in your palace,
There's an uninvited guest in your home,
825 An uninvited and an unexpected guest.
He's a prankster and deceiver,
The young Churila, Plyonko's son."

Bermyata kept on standing and praying to God,
He didn't pay any attention to Chernava.
830   Chernava spoke a second time:
"My dear master,
Old Bermyata, Vasily's son!
There's disorder in our home,
There's an uninvited guest in our palace,
835   He's uninvited and he's unrequested,
Churila Plyonkovich,
And in your bedroom he's amusing himself
With Nastasia, your darling Mikulichna."
Bermyata spoke these words:
840   "Hail to you, my girl Chernava, my servant!
If you're telling the truth, then I'll reward you,
If you're not telling the truth, I'll cut off your head."
And he kept on standing and praying to God,
But the girl Chernava was impatient,
845   She spoke to him for a third time:
"My beloved master!
If you don't believe me, go look yourself."
Bermyata, Vasily's son,
Went to his white-stone palace,
850   He didn't enter the wide courtyard—
Behind the smoothly finished post,
At the gilded ring,
Stood Churila's bogatyr steed,
It was standing by the stall for horses,
855   The finest wheat had been poured for it.
Bermyata's nimble legs gave way,
Bermyata's old eyes became dim,
He entered the porch with a railing,
The door was tightly locked.
860   He knocked with the gilded ring—
There was no answer from Nastasia,
She was busy with Churila,
She was lying on the wooden bed.
Then Bermyata knocked a second time—
865   There was no answer from Nastasia.
Bermyata, Vasily's son, knocked

With all his bogatyr's strength.
Then Nastasia, his darling Mikulichna,
Opened the plank gates,
870 She was clad in stockings without shoes
And in a nightgown without a belt.
    Bermyata, Vasily's son, then spoke:
"Nastasia, my darling Mikulichna!
Why aren't you dressed up today?
875 We have a main holiday today,
The Annunciation of Christ."
    And Nastasia, his darling Mikulichna,
Knew how to give an answer:
"My dear beloved husband!
880 Today I don't feel well,
My head hurts from the fumes."
    Bermyata, Vasily's son, then spoke:
"Why is Churila's bogatyr steed
Standing in my courtyard
885 And eating my finest grain?"
    Nastasia Mikulichna then spoke:
"My beloved brother
Exchanged steeds with Churila,
He brought the steed to show it to you
890 And left his steed in your courtyard.
Please look at it and be happy."
    Then Bermyata entered his bright hall,
On wooden pegs, on smoothly finished pegs,
Were hanging Churila's bright clothes,
895 And on the shelf, on the oaken shelf,
Was lying Churila's hat.
Bermyata, Vasily's son, then spoke:
"How did Churila's clothes
Get in my bright hall?"
900 Nastasia knew how to give an answer:
"Today my kind nephew
And Churila were fraternizing,
They exchanged their colorful clothes."
    Bermyata went to the warm bedroom—
905 The young Churila, Plyonko's son,

Was lying in his underwear
On the bed, on the wooden bed,
On the comforter, on the down comforter,
He was sleeping soundly and didn't wake up,
910   He didn't sense the trouble hanging over him.
          Then Bermyata, Vasily's son,
Took his sharp saber,
He cut off Churila's good head.
Pearls didn't scatter around the chamber,
915   Churila's head rolled around,
His yellow curls were scattered
Along the brick floor.
          And Nastasia, darling Mikulichna,
Ran into the wide courtyard,
920   She took a steel knife with her,
She put it with the blunt end in the ground,
And she fell on the sharp end
With her white breast.
And she cut her flowing arteries,
925   Her scarlet blood started pouring out.
          Thus suddenly two heads had fallen,
Two of the very best heads.
Then they sang a song of praise to Churila.*
          And Bermyata, dear Vasilyevich,
930   Waited for Christ's Resurrection,
He let Easter week go past,
Waiting for Holy Radunitsa.†
He took the girl Chernava, his servant,
He led her to the cathedral church,
935   They accepted the gilded crowns
And the wedding rings.
They started living and spending their lives together.
          On this the bylina has come to an end.

---

*Singers often end an epic with "praise" to the main character, something that seems out of place for Churila.

†On Tuesday of the week after Easter, a day called *radunitsa*, people commemorate their ancestors by visiting the cemetery.

∽ 18 ∾

Dyuk Stepanovich

*T*he song "Dyuk Stepanovich" is an example of a bylina novella. It is an engaging story about an outsider who comes to Kiev and makes himself an unwelcome visitor because he finds fault with everything and says that things are much better at home. Dyuk fights and wins a "duel of snobs" with Churila and then returns home. The main elements in the variants of this bylina may be presented as follows. Despite the warnings of his mother about a dangerous road and about boasting, Dyuk, who is usually called a boyar's son, departs from Galich (Volynia, Korela, or wealthy India) for Kiev. Although in some recordings he may initially hunt swans and geese, along the way Dyuk encounters menacing obstacles such as mountains that may suddenly clash together, pecking birds, or the dragon Zmei Gorynishche, all of which his horse easily carries him past. After quickly arriving in Kiev, in some instances on Easter Sunday, Dyuk meets Prince Vladimir in church, may have his first encounter with his future rival Churila, and is invited to a feast. While walking on the way there with Prince Vladimir, Dyuk speaks disparagingly about the muddy streets that dirty his boots, and later at the feast he rejects the bread and wine because of their inferior quality. After Dyuk brags about the superiority of his native city, Prince Vladimir puts him in prison and sends Ilya Muromets and Dobrynya Nikitich to Galich to inventory Dyuk's possessions and to find out whether he is making empty boasts. In Galich the appraisers are struck by the splendor of the city and by the fact that even the servants are dressed better than Princess Apraxia. Dyuk's mother greets the two heroes with respect and allows them to evaluate her wealth, but they soon realize that they will not have enough ink and paper to complete the inventory. The appraisers return to Kiev and announce the results to Prince Vladimir, who releases Dyuk from prison. The Kievan

253

"dandy" and lady's man Churila, stung by Dyuk's elegance and jealous of his wealth, challenges him to a competition that in some instances lasts three years. They are to change clothing and steeds every day with the ultimate test of proving who has the most luxuriant clothing and the best steed. Dyuk triumphs in these "duels," shames Churilo, Vladimir, and Kiev, and returns to Galich. As one of the more popular Russian epics, the song has been recorded more than one hundred times.

Investigators have devoted much attention to the place names in this bylina in an effort to determine precisely what city Dyuk may have come from (Vs.F. Miller 1897–1924, 1: 97–122). The image of "wealthy India" may have been derived from an assumed twelfth-century Byzantine work called the "Epistle of Presbyter John" and translated into Old Russian as the "Legend about the Realm of India." In the Russian version, Presbyter John invites the Byzantine emperor Manuil to India but tells him in advance that all the riches of Byzantium are too meager to pay even for the parchment necessary to inventory the possessions of India. The name "Korela" may refer to an ancient Karelian city on Lake Ladoga and may reflect contacts between the North Russian bearers of the epic tradition near Lake Onega and Karelians in the same area. Other scholars believe that the numerous descriptions of buildings, customs, and clothing are indicative of Muscovite Russia in the sixteenth and seventeenth centuries. V.Ia. Propp (1958b: 477–507) regards the bylina as being a satire on Muscovite life at that time.

Most students of Russian epics believe that the city of Galich in southwestern Rus was the place where this bylina originated (Froianov and Iudin 1990). After the death of Prince Vladimir Monomakh in 1125, the Kievan principality gradually declined and ceased to be the center of the Russian Land. During the twelfth and thirteenth centuries the Galich-Volyn principality reached its height; princes from the region twice seized the Kievan throne and joined Kiev to their lands. Viewed in this light, the bylina "Dyuk Stepanovich" can be regarded as a regional work that was composed by local singers. This supports the idea that the Russian epic tradition was created both in Kiev and in other areas such as Chernigov, Rostov, Novgorod, or Ryazan. Prompted by regional loyalties, the creators of "Dyuk Stepanovich" glorified their native city Galich and denied Kiev the prestige of the grand prince's capital. In their wealth, splendor, and elegance, Galich and its boyar Dyuk Stepanovich surpass the once-powerful Kiev and Prince Vladimir.

The names "Dyuk" and "Stepanovich" have also prompted speculation as to their possible historical sources. Some folklorists consider the name "Dyuk" to be connected with the Byzantine noble family Dukas, which was related to the Byzantine emperors. Several members of the Hungarian royal house bore the name "Stefan" and in the twelfth and thirteen centuries were well known in southwestern Rus, which then had close contacts with Hungary and Byzantium. Although the introduction of western or Greek names into an epic song created in the Galich-Volyn principality is plausible, the name "Dyuk" may actually be derived from a Ukrainian word (*duk*) meaning "rich person."

Whatever the origin of the song and the name of its hero may be, Dyuk Stepanovich is not an alien enemy. He comes to and is accepted in Kiev as a Russian from another city, he observes Russian customs, and he is an orthodox Christian. However, unlike other Russian heroes, such as Ilya Muromets, Dobrynya Nikitich, and Alyosha Popovich, who come from other cities, are recognized as Kievan bogatyrs, and stay in Kiev, Dyuk leaves and returns home. Dyuk also differs because he is not a "militant" hero who fights monsters or the enemies of Kiev; he is an outsider who brags about the higher civilization of his homeland in comparison with that of Kiev. Nevertheless, he takes part in a "duel" to the death with the envious Kievan "dude" Churila, who attempts to defend the honor of Kiev and Prince Vladimir against an intruder.

Despite its apparent abundance of specific details, this bylina nevertheless contains supernatural elements (Korobka 1910). The arrows that Dyuk hunts with in the beginning of some recordings are radiant and may return by themselves to his quiver. The three barriers that Dyuk passes on the way to Kiev occur in epics and magic tales, where they may represent the guarded gate to the other world. Dyuk's horse can change its coat every day and in some variants has wings; horses called Burushko (bay horse) or Kosmatushko (shaggy horse) often possess magical powers and serve as helpers to their masters in Russian epics. The birds and wild animals depicted on Dyuk's buttons utter shrieks that terrify people, just as the monster Nightingale the Robber does. The description of Galich from a distance as being on fire and having a golden glow conveys a sense of the other world as it may appear in magic tales.

As often happens when a bogatyr leaves home on his first journey, Dyuk departs for no apparent reason. As usually is the case in Russian epics, no father is mentioned, but the always-present epic mother has foresight about future events in her son's life. The fact that Dyuk sometimes hunts swans and geese on his trip to Kiev suggests that he may be searching for a bride since such hunting symbolism occurs in the wedding ceremony. Thus this song, which contains numerous material references, may be interpreted as consisting of several historical, cultural, and mythological layers, all of which enrich an entertaining tale and give singers an opportunity to enliven the story with epic hyperbole.

N.P. Kolpakova recorded this bylina in 1956 on the Pechora River in Archangel District from T.S. Kuzmin. The song, which represents an example of a work collected near the end of the Russian epic tradition, begins with four lines that paraphrase the opening of the poem "Song about the Merchant Kalashnikov" written by the Russian poet M.Iu. Lermontov in a folklore style in 1837.

✍ Dyuk Stepanovich ☙

Source: A.M. Astakhova et al., *Bylinas of Pechora and the Winter Shore* (Moscow and Leningrad, 1961), no. 84.

Who would tell us, brothers, an old song,
Who would tell us an old song in an old style,
Who would sing, brothers, an ancient song,
Who would sing this song to the sound of a gusli?
5   It happened that in Little Galich,
It happened that in very wealthy Korela,
There lived the young boyar Dyuk Stepanovich
With his own dear mother,
With Amelfa Alexandrovna.
10   Dyuk Stepanovich then spoke to her:
"Hail to you, my beloved mother,
Darling Amelfa Alexandrovna!
Please give me your dear blessing
To go to the capital city of Kiev,
15   To pay my respects to Prince Vladimir
And to Princess Apraxia."

His mother, Amelfa Alexandrovna, then spoke:
"Hail to you, my beloved child,
Young boyar, Dyuk Stepanovich!
20   Clashing mountains are on the path to that place,
Pecking birds are on the path to that place."
Dyuk Stepanovich then spoke to her:
"I have my Burushko-Kosmatushko,
I'm not afraid of the clashing mountains,
25   I'm not afraid of the pecking birds."
Then his mother gave him her blessing,
And he set out for the capital city of Kiev.
Dyuk Stepanovich approached,
He approached the clashing mountains,
30   The mountains barely parted—
Dyuk's Burushko galloped through them.
Dyuk approached the pecking birds,
The pecking birds barely spread their wings—
Dyuk's Burushko galloped past them.
35   Dyuk Stepanovich arrived,
He arrived in the capital city of Kiev,
He entered God's church,
He stood by the right choir.*
The mass of Our Lord then ended,
40   Dyuk Stepanovich went outside,
He was invited to a feast at Prince Vladimir's.
Dyuk Stepanovich was walking along the pavement,
He glanced at his own boots,
Dyuk Stepanovich then spoke:
45   "Everything here isn't like it is at home,
The pavements are all made of wood,
And they haven't been sprinkled with sand,
I'll dirty my morocco leather boots."
He was invited to a feast of honor at Prince Vladimir's.
50   The young boyar Churila Plyonkovich
Was also then in capital Kiev.
Churila was walking through Kiev,

*The raised area in front of the iconostasis in a Russian Orthodox church.

Churila was shading himself with a parasol.
Girls were watching him—all the fences were cracking,
55   Young married women were watching him—the windows
            were ringing,
Very old women were gnawing their crutches.
They seated Dyuk at oaken tables,
The tables were covered with embroidered tablecloths.
They offered Dyuk Stepanovich,
60   They offered him a goblet of green wine,
He drank half the goblet and poured the rest
            under the table.
He took a kalach and bit off part of it,
He ate the upper crust and threw the lower part under
            the table.
Prince Vladimir spoke to him:
65   "Hail to you, young boyar,
Young boyar, Dyuk Stepanovich!
Why did you empty the goblet under the table?
Why did you throw the kalach under the table?"
Dyuk Stepanovich spoke to him:
70   "Everything with you in Kiev isn't like it is at home.
Your ovens in Kiev are made out of clay,
And your brushes are made out of pine needles,
The kalaches smell of pine.
With us in Little Galich,
75   In very wealthy Korela,
All our ovens are made out of tiles,
All our brushes are made out of silk.
Your vodka has become a little musty,
We soak our brushes in honey water,
80   Our vodka is kept in cellars,
It rocks in barrels on silver chains,
Our vodka never gets musty."
Then the young boyar Churila, Plyonko junior, spoke:
"Hail to you, Vladimir of capital Kiev!
85   The young boyar has boasted a little too much,
I advise you to put him in prison
And to send some scouts to Galich."
Then they took Dyuk Stepanovich,

And they put him in prison.
90 Then the scouts were chosen,
Ilya Muromets was sent,
And Dobrynya Nikitich was also sent.
Our boyars got ready very quickly,
They started riding to Little Galich.
95   Dobrynya Nikitich set out riding
With the old Ilya Muromets.
They came out on Saracen Mountain,
And they looked through their silver spyglass.
The young Dobrynya Nikitich spoke:
100 "Hail to you, Ilya Ivanovich!
Little Galich is on fire."
     Ilya Muromets then spoke:
"What should we say, young Dobrynya Nikitich,
Did Dyuk Stepanovich really send orders
105 That Little Galich should be set afire?"
     They rode down from Saracen Mountain,
They rode up to Little Galich.
Everywhere the roofs on the houses were golden,
The golden roofs burned like fire.
110 They dismounted their good steeds
And tied their steeds to oaken posts.
Ilya and Dobrynya entered,
They entered the white-stone palace.
They passed through the first hall,
115 An old woman was sitting there,
She was all dressed in silks from overseas.
     Ilya Muromets then spoke to her:
"Greetings to you, Dyuk's mother."
     The old woman spoke to him:
120 "I'm really not Dyuk's mother,
I'm really just Dyuk's kalach baker."
They entered a second hall,
An old woman was sitting there,
The woman was all dressed in silver.
125 Ilya Muromets then spoke to her:
"Greetings to you, Dyuk's mother."
     The old woman spoke to him:

"I'm really not Dyuk's mother,
I'm really just Dyuk's nurse."

130   Dear Ilya Ivanovich then spoke to her:
"Please tell us then, Dyuk's nurse,
Where can we see Dyuk's mother?"
        The old woman spoke to them:
"Dyuk's mother is still at mass."

135   After a little time had passed
Dyuk's mother then came home.
Three people led her under her arms,
She was all dressed in the finest pearls.
Along the pavement made of guelder rose

140   Carpets were spread before her,
The carpets were picked up after her.
When Dyuk's mother arrived,
Ilya Muromets paid his respects to her:
"Greetings to you, Dyuk's mother!

145   We've come to you to clear up something.
Your son boasted a little too much,
He boasted a little too much and now is sitting in prison."
        Dyuk's mother spoke to him:
"Hail to you, my daring good youths!

150   Please come into my chambers."
She led them into the new dining hall,
In the dining hall the floor was made of crystal,
Live fish were swimming under the floor.
Dyuk's mother then poured them each

155   A goblet of overseas green wine,
When you drink one goblet, you want a second,
When you drink a second, you want a third.
Then Dyuk's mother took them
To show them her possessions.

160   Young Dobrynya Nikitich wrote,
Dobrynya wrote on a piece of paper,
Wrote in cursive on a piece of paper,
He wrote and counted harnesses for steeds,
He couldn't note down all the harnesses,

165   Dobrynya didn't have enough paper.
        Then Dyuk's mother spoke to them:

"Hail to you, my daring good youths!
Please tell this to your Prince Vladimir:
Let him sell the city of Chernigov for ink,
170   Let him sell the famous city of Kiev for paper,
And then let him send them to me to make an inventory."
        Ilya and Dobrynya took their leave
From Dyuk's mother, from his mother,
And they set out for home to the capital city of Kiev.
175   They came to Prince Vladimir,
The bogatyrs told him what they had seen.
Then Dyuk Stepanovich was released,
They regaled him with green wine.
        Churila, Plyonko junior,
180   Was quick-tempered and envious,
Churila spoke these words:
"Then let's make a great wager,
Not for one hundred rubles, not for a thousand,
But for our reckless heads.
185   Let's ride on our good steeds,
On our good steeds for twelve whole days,
Each day we'll change our steeds,
We'll change and vary our steeds."
        Dyuk Stepanovich spoke,
190   He then spoke these words:
"My Burushko is the only steed I brought with me."
But Dyuk didn't refuse the wager.
He got up very early in the morning,
He went out in the cold dew
195   And led out his Burushko-Kosmatushko.
Burushko could change its coat.
Thus they rode for twelve whole days.
On the twelfth day they were supposed to jump
Across the deep Puchai River,
200   To jump across and back with one's steed.
Then Churila, Plyonko junior, jumped first—
Churila fell into the middle of the river.
Dyuk Stepanovich jumped second—
He jumped across and back—
205   He dragged Churila out by the hair.

Dyuk Stepanovich then spoke,
Then he spoke these words:
"Prince Vladimir of capital Kiev!
Will you order someone to chop off Churila's head?"
210 Then Prince Vladimir of capital Kiev spoke:
"Leave us Churila at least for memory's sake,
Don't chop off his reckless head."
But Churila was envious,
Then he spoke these words:
215 "Then let's go to God's churches,
Let's go there for twelve whole days,
And each day we'll change our clothing,
We'll change and vary our clothing."
Dyuk Stepanovich then spoke:
220 "Churila, I have only the clothes I brought with me."
But he didn't turn down the wager.
He sat down on a chair with leather straps,
Dyuk quickly wrote letters in cursive
To his dear own mother,
225 He sewed them up in saddle bags,
He dispatched his shaggy Burushko.
Burushko ran to Little Galich.
Then Amelfa Alexandrovna saw the horse,
Her dear son Dyuk Stepanovich wasn't there,
230 And then she started weeping bitterly.
She looked in the saddle bags,
She saw the letters in cursive,
She read the letters in cursive,
She packed some colorful clothing for Dyuk,
235 Changes of colorful clothing,
Changes of clothing for twelve whole days.
Then Dyuk Stepanovich and Churila
Set off for God's church.
Churila stood by the right choir,
240 Dyuk Stepanovich stood by the left choir.
The time for the twelfth day had come,
A multitude of people gathered.
When Churila, Plyonko junior, would fasten his buttons—
A youth would embrace a pretty maid,

245   When Churila would unfasten his buttons—they would kiss.
Then Churila glanced at Dyuk Stepanovich,
Then he thought that Dyuk had lost his reckless head.
Then the church service ended,
Dyuk Stepanovich took out his silken whip,
250   When Dyuk Stepanovich struck his buttons—
They roared like fierce wild animals,
They hissed like creeping snakes.
Then all the people were knocked off their feet,
Prince Vladimir and Princess Apraxia barely left alive.
255   Then Prince Vladimir of capital Kiev spoke:
"Hail to you, young boyar, Dyuk Stepanovich!
You've outdone our Churila Plyonkovich."
Dyuk Stepanovich then spoke:
"Hail to you, Prince Vladimir of capital Kiev!
260   Will you order someone to chop off Churila's reckless
     head?"
Vladimir of capital Kiev spoke:
"Leave us Churila at least for memory's sake."
Dyuk Stepanovich then spoke:
"Hey, Churila, you young boyar's son!
265   Churila, you shouldn't associate with bogatyrs,
You should spend your time with Kievan women."
Dyuk said farewell to Prince Vladimir
And set off riding on his shaggy Burushko
To his mother Amelfa Alexandrovna.

❧ 19 ❧

Stavr Godinovich

*T*he bylina "Stavr Godinovich" combines two stories that exist in many traditions and appear in several genres: a wife who saves her husband from prison, and a woman who disguises herself as a man and is tested various ways to learn her sex. The Russian epic combining these subjects has been collected in fifty variants that appear in heroic or novelistic versions (Vs.F. Miller, 1897–1924, 1: 263–82; Selivanov 1986). According to the heroic version, the boyar Stavr visits Kiev and, during a boasting bout at a feast for Prince Vladimir's court, brags about his wealth and his young wife. Stavr foolishly adds that she can outwit both Prince Vladimir and the members of his court. Prince Vladimir responds to this "challenge" by putting Stavr in prison. When Stavr's wife, Vasilisa Nikulichna, learns about this at home, she disguises herself as a man, assumes the masculine form of her name (Vasily Nikulich), and, in some instances accompanied by a druzhina, goes to Kiev to rescue her husband. Much as the hostile Tatar emissary in the song "Ilya Muromets and Kalin Tsar," Vasilisa presents herself as a threatening envoy and demands tribute for twelve years from Vladimir, who is frightened even though his daughter Apraxia perceives a woman in the envoy. Stavr's wife passes a series of tests (bathhouse, leaving the correct imprint in a bed, shooting arrows, wrestling, or playing chess) whose purpose is to verify whether she is a man or a woman. In the end, the wily envoy agrees to accept Stavr in place of tribute, thereby freeing him from prison. Prince Vladimir is tricked by Stavr's wife and is compelled to accept the truth of Stavr's boast about her.

In the translated variant, which belongs to the novelistic version, the singer uses the form "Stavyór" for the first name instead of Stavr. This version also opens with a boasting scene at court, but Stavr's wife comes to rescue her husband as a suitor for Prince Vladimir's daugh-

264

ter, with the result that the motif of exacting tribute is replaced by the motif of bride taking. The suitor comes from another city (usually Chernigov) or from a foreign country; as in the song "Solovei Budimirovich," he sets up a tent or suitor's quarters outside Kiev; he comes as an envoy or matchmaker who speaks for himself; and he has to submit to several trials for a prospective groom. In some traditions, such trials may involve archery, wrestling, and horse racing, often in competition with the sought-after bride. Prince Vladimir hesitates to give his daughter in marriage to the visitor, but she, sensing a woman in the pretender, insists on testing his sex. She demands two "feminine" tests (undressing in the bathhouse and sleeping in a bed so as to leave the imprint of a man's broad shoulders) while Prince Vladimir demands two "masculine" tests (shooting an arrow and wrestling). At the feast before the church wedding, Vasilisa feigns a bad mood and asks to be entertained by gusli players, who fail to cheer her up. She then asks for Stavr, whom she knows to be a fine gusli player but who has been imprisoned by Prince Vladimir. In a scene that alludes to the skomorokhs and resembles an episode in the epic "Dobrynya and Alyosha," Stavr fails to recognize his wife, even after she mentions games that they played together as children and that had erotic overtones. Only after Vladimir allows them to leave for the tent outside Kiev and after Vasilisa puts on woman's clothing does the slow-witted Stavr finally recognize his wife. They return to Kiev, where Vasilisa proves her husband's reckless boast and humiliates Prince Vladimir, much as Dobrynya humiliates him in the song "Dobrynya and Alyosha." In some variants, Prince Vladimir makes amends by granting Stavr tax-free trade in Kiev, as though he were a wealthy merchant. The selected song concludes with lines reflecting a belief that the performance of a bylina would ensure calm weather on the ocean.

Some scholars regard the heroic version of this bylina as being the original, while others insist on the primacy of the novelistic version. Since the same subject has been developed in Russian tales in an amusing rather than in a heroic manner (Veselovskii 1885–90, XV: 26–55), it seems more plausible to accept the second interpretation. Be that as it may, consideration of the interactions between the two versions offers an insight into the process of change that can take place in the composition of epic songs. On the one hand, depending on how closely this story is adapted to a heroic epic, the heroic elements may be intensified and Vasilisa may become a bogatyrka. On the other hand, the novelistic version may not culminate in a duel between a hero and his opponent, but it nevertheless involves a confrontation of wits and exhibits many of the characteristics of a Russian epic, that is, the same language and stylistic devices, pattern scenes, types of repetition and elaboration, and slow pace. The result is an entertaining tale that brings together several traditional motifs and that is clearly set at court in Kievan Rus. The "heroine" also is related to the "wise maid" who overcomes all obstacles in magic tales, except that Vasilisa relies on her intelligence, wits, and feminine intuition rather than on magic to save her husband and hence to preserve her family. In these respects, she presents a contrast to some other women who appear in Russian epics, such as Apraxia (feminine ideal in a medieval society), Marinka (bewitching courtesan), and Nastasia (bogatyrka). Despite the fact that the song bears Stavr's name, which means "cross" in Greek, he is not a bogatyr—his wife actually is the main figure, who in good humor makes fun of male conventions.

Members of the Historical School have assumed that an actual historical event was imposed on a "migratory subject" about sexual disguise in the bylina. Such an interpretation is based on an entry in Old Russian chronicles stating that in 1118 a Novgorod commander by the name of Stavr angered Prince Vladimir Monomakh, who had him seized and imprisoned in Kiev. Thus the treatment of a distinguished citizen of Novgorod by a Kievan prince has been regarded as providing the impetus for the creation of an epic song.

A.F. Gilferding took down this song from the singer A.E. Chukov in 1871 in Kizhi District of Olonets Province.

❧ Stavyor Godinovich ❧

Source: A.F. Gilferding, *Onega Bylinas,* 4th ed., vol. 2 (Moscow, 1950), no. 151.

In the capital city, in Kiev,
At gracious Prince Vladimir's,
There was a banquet, a feast of honor,
For many princes and for many boyars,
5   For all invited and respected guests,
For those invited and respected guests who came.
    All at the feast of honor ate their fill,
All at the feast of honor drank their fill,
All at the feast then burst out bragging.
10   One youth boasted about his good steed,
One bragged about his silken clothing,
One boasted about his towns and settlements,
One boasted about his cities and their suburbs.
The rich one bragged about his golden treasure,
15   The smart one bragged about his own dear mother,
But the foolish one boasted about his own young wife.
    Vladimir of capital Kiev spoke:
"Hail to you, Stavyor Godinovich!
You've come from the Lithuanian land,
20   You're sitting here but you aren't bragging.
Don't you have any golden treasure?
Don't you have any good steeds?
Don't you have any towns and settlements?
Don't you have any cities and their suburbs?
25   Isn't your dear mother wonderful?
Isn't your young wife pretty?"
    Stavyor Godinovich then spoke:
"Although I have golden treasure,
The golden treasure of a youth is never exhausted,
30   That's nothing for me, a youth, to boast about.
Although I have good steeds,

The good steeds just stand and are not ridden,
That's nothing for me, a youth, to boast about.
Although I have cities and their suburbs,
35   That's nothing for me, a youth, to boast about.
Although I have towns and settlements,
That's nothing for me, a youth, to boast about.
Although my dear mother is wonderful,
That's nothing for me, a youth, to boast about.
40   Although my young wife is pretty,
That's nothing for me, a youth, to boast about.
She can outwit all you princes and boyars,
She can charm you, our Sun, Vladimir, out of your mind."
        Then everyone at the feast fell silent.
45   Vladimir of capital Kiev spoke:
"We'll put Stavyor in a deep dungeon,
Let Stavyor's young wife come,
Let her rescue Stavyor from the dungeon,
Let her outwit all you princes and boyars,
50   Let her charm me, Vladimir, out of my mind."
He put Stavyor in a deep dungeon.
        Stavyor had his own servant there,
The servant mounted Stavyor's good steed,
He rode away to the Lithuanian land
55   To the young Vasilisa Nikulichna.
"Hail to you, Vasilisa, Nikula's daughter!
You're sitting, drinking, and amusing yourself,
You don't know the misfortune hanging over you.
Your young Stavyor Godinovich
60   Has been put in a deep dungeon.
He bragged about you, his young wife,
That you can outwit all the princes and boyars,
That you can charm our Sun, Vladimir, out of his mind."
        Vasilisa, Nikula's daughter, spoke:
65   "I can try to ransom Stavyor with money—I won't succeed,
If I try to rescue Stavyor by force—I won't succeed,
No, I can rescue Stavyor
Only by my feminine intuition."
        She quickly ran to the barbers,
70   She trimmed her hair like a youth's,

She dressed herself like Vasily Nikulich,*
She took along a brave druzhina,
Forty youths who were daring archers,
Forty youths who were also daring wrestlers,
75 She set off riding to the city of Kiev,
To the gracious Prince Vladimir.
Coming close to the city of Kiev,
She pitched her fine white tent,
She left her druzhina by the white tent,
80 She rode to the city of Kiev,
To the gracious Prince Vladimir.
She came to the white-stone palace,
She crossed herself as was prescribed,
She bowed as was instructed,
85 She bowed low and paid her respects
First in three directions, then in a fourth,
To our Sun, Vladimir, in particular.
"Greetings to you, our Sun, Vladimir of capital Kiev!
And to the young Princess Apraxia!"
90 "Where are you from, my daring good youth,
What land are you from, what country are you from?
What given name do they call you by,
What patronymic do they name you by?"
The daring good youth then spoke:
95 "I'm from the Lithuanian land,
The son of the Lithuanian king,
The young Vasily Nikulich.
I've come to you about matchmaking, about
            proposing marriage
To your daughter, to your favorite daughter.
100 What do you intend to do with me?"
Vladimir of capital Kiev spoke:
"I'll go and consult with my daughter."
He went to his beloved daughter,
He spoke these words himself:
105 "Hail to you, my beloved daughter!

*Vasilisa Nikulichna assumes the masculine equivalent of her name.

An envoy of the Lithuanian land has come,
The son of the Lithuanian king,
Young Vasily Nikulich.
He's come about matchmaking, about proposing marriage
110   To you, my favorite daughter.
What am I going to do with the envoy?"
    His beloved daughter spoke to him:
"Hail to you, my lord and my dear father!
Just what do you have in mind now?
115   You're giving a girl in marriage to a woman!
Her speech and words are like a woman's,
Her soft breasts are like a woman's,
Her thin fingers are like a woman's,
You can tell the places where she wore her rings."
120   Vladimir of capital Kiev spoke:
"I'll go and test the envoy."
    He went to the envoy of the Lithuanian land,
He spoke these words himself:
"Hail to you, my envoy of the Lithuanian land,
125   Young Vasily Nikulich!
After the trip and after the road, wouldn't you like
To go to the steaming bathhouse?"
    Vasily Nikulich spoke:
"After the road this wouldn't be bad."
130   They heated the steaming bathhouse for him,
They asked him to enter the steaming bathhouse,
He entered the steaming bathhouse,
But while Vladimir was getting ready,
The envoy in the meantime steamed himself
        in the bathhouse,
135   He came out of the bathhouse and paid Vladimir
        his respects:
"I'm very thankful for the steaming bathhouse!"
    Vladimir of capital Kiev spoke:
"You didn't wait for me in the bathhouse.
I would have come to the bathhouse and would have
        added steam for you,
140   I would have added steam and would have doused you."
    Vasily Nikulich spoke:

"That's your personal business,
Your princely personal business,
But our business is that of an envoy,
145   We don't have time to boast a lot
Or to steam ourselves a lot in the bathhouse.
I've come about matchmaking, about proposing marriage
To your daughter, to your favorite daughter.
What do you intend to do with me?"
150   Vladimir of capital Kiev spoke:
"I'll go and consult with my daughter."
He went to his beloved daughter,
He spoke these words himself:
"Hail to you, my beloved daughter!
155   An envoy of the Lithuanian land has come,
The son of the Lithuanian king,
The young Vasily Nikulich.
He's come about matchmaking, about proposing marriage
To you, my favorite daughter.
160   What am I going to do with the envoy?"
          His beloved daughter spoke to him:
"Hail to you, my lord and my dear father!
Just what do you have in mind now?
You're giving a girl in marriage to a woman!
165   Her speech and words are like a woman's,
Her soft breasts are like a woman's,
Her thin fingers are like a woman's,
You can tell the places where she wore her rings."
          Vladimir of capital Kiev spoke:
170   "I'll go and test the envoy."
          He went to the envoy of the Lithuanian land,
He spoke these words himself:
"Hail to you, my envoy of the Lithuanian land,
Young Vasily Nikulich!
175   After the steaming bathhouse wouldn't you like
To rest in a warm bedroom?"
          Vasily Nikulich spoke:
"That wouldn't be bad after the bathhouse."
He went to the warm bedroom,
180   He lay with his head where his feet should be,

And he lay with his feet on the pillow.
When he came out of the warm bedroom,
Vladimir of capital Kiev went there.
He looked around the warm bedroom,
185   And he spoke these words himself:
"He has the wide shoulders of a bogatyr."
     Vasily Nikulich spoke:
"Our Sun, Vladimir of capital Kiev!
I've come about matchmaking, about proposing marriage
190   To your daughter, to your favorite daughter.
What do you intend to do with me?"
     Vladimir of capital Kiev spoke:
"I'll go and consult with my daughter."
He went to his beloved daughter,
195   He spoke these words himself:
"Hail to you, my beloved daughter!
An envoy of the Lithuanian land has come,
The son of the Lithuanian king,
Young Vasily Nikulich.
200   He's come about matchmaking, about proposing marriage
To you, my favorite daughter.
What am I going to do with the envoy?"
     His beloved daughter spoke to him:
"Hail to you, my lord and my dear father!
205   Just what do you have in mind now?
You're giving a girl in marriage to a woman!
Her speech and words are like a woman's,
Her soft breasts are like a woman's,
Her thin fingers are like a woman's,
210   You can tell the places where she wore her rings."
     Vladimir of capital Kiev spoke:
"I'll go and test the envoy."
He went to the envoy of the Lithuanian land,
He spoke these words himself:
215   "Hail to you, my envoy of the Lithuanian land,
Young Vasily Nikulich!
Wouldn't you like to have some fun with my courtiers,
To go with them to the wide courtyard,
To shoot at a golden ring,

220 At the sharp edge of a knife,
And to split an arrow in two
So that the halves would be equal in size and
even in weight?"
Vasily Nikulich spoke:
"My archers stayed in the open field,
225 In the open field by my white tent.
Should I really try by myself?"
He went out into the wide courtyard,
The Prince's archer started shooting first,
The first time he shot and undershot,
230 The second time he shot and overshot,
The third time he shot and missed.
"You shoot, Vasily Nikulich!"
Then Vasily Nikulich
Quickly stretched his taut bow,
235 He laid a tempered arrow on it,
He shot at the golden ring,
At the sharp edge of the knife,
He split the arrow in two,
The halves were equal in size and even in weight.
240 He spoke these words himself:
"I've come about matchmaking, about
proposing marriage
To your daughter, to your favorite daughter.
What do you intend to do with me?"
Vladimir of capital Kiev spoke:
245 "I'll go again to consult with my daughter."
He went to his beloved daughter,
He spoke these words himself:
"Hail to you, my beloved daughter!
An envoy of the Lithuanian land has come,
250 The son of the Lithuanian king,
Young Vasily Nikulich.
He's come about matchmaking, about
proposing marriage
To you, my favorite daughter.
What am I going to do with the envoy?"
255 His beloved daughter spoke to him:

"Hail to you, my lord and my dear father!
What do you have in mind now?
You're giving a girl in marriage to a woman.
Her words and speech are like a woman's,
260   Her soft breasts are like a woman's,
Her thin fingers are like a woman's,
You can tell the places where her rings were."
      Vladimir of capital Kiev spoke:
"I'll go and test the envoy."
265   He came to the envoy of the Lithuanian land,
He spoke these words himself:
"Hail to you, my envoy of the Lithuanian land,
Young Vasily Nikulich!
Wouldn't you like to have some fun with my courtiers,
270   Wouldn't you like to wrestle in the wide courtyard?"
      Vasily Nikulich spoke:
"My wrestlers stayed in the open field,
In the open field by my white tent.
Should I really try by myself?"
275   He went out into the wide courtyard,
Then Vasily started wrestling,
He took one wrestler in one hand and another
        in the other hand,
He smashed them against a third wrestler in the middle,
He lay all three together on the ground,
280   Those he took down didn't get up from the spot.
      Vladimir of capital Kiev spoke:
"Young Vasily Nikulich!
Restrain your bogatyr's rage,
Leave me some people for posterity!"
285   Vasily Nikulich spoke:
"Our Sun, Vladimir of capital Kiev!
I've come about matchmaking, about proposing marriage
To your daughter, to your favorite daughter.
What are you doing to do with me?
290   If you don't give her to me with honor, I'll take her
        without honor,
I'll take her without honor and I'll give you a beating."
      Vladimir didn't go to ask his daughter anymore,

He started arranging a match for his daughter.
    Their feast's been going on for three days,

295   They're to go today to God's church,
She and Vasily are to accept the golden crowns.
Vasily became despondent and became sad,
He hung his reckless head,
He lowered his bright eyes toward the damp earth.

300   Vladimir of capital Kiev approached him:
"Hail to you, Vasily Nikulich!
Why aren't you cheerful today?"
    Vasily Nikulich spoke:
"For some reason I'm not in a cheerful mood.

305   Either my father has died,
Or my mother has died.
Do you have some young gusli players
Who can play awhile on the maple gusli?"
They brought some young gusli players,

310   They played but not very cheerfully.
    Vasily Nikulich spoke:
"Our Sun, Vladimir of capital Kiev!
Do you have some young prisoners
Who can play awhile on the maple gusli?"

315   They released some young prisoners,
They played but not very cheerfully.
    Vasily Nikulich spoke:
"Our Sun, Vladimir of capital Kiev!
I heard from my parent, from my father,

320   That our Stavyor Godinovich had been imprisoned
In your deep dungeon—
He's good at playing the maple gusli."
    Vladimir of capital Kiev spoke:
"If I release Stavyor, then I won't see Stavyor again,

325   But if I don't release Stavyor, then I'll anger the envoy."
He didn't dare to anger the envoy,
He released Stavyor from the dungeon,
Stavyor then played the maple gusli.
    Then Vasily Nikulich cheered up,

330   He spoke these words himself:
"Do you remember, Stavyor, do you recall,

When we were little how we went outside
And you and I played svayechka?*
The silver nail was yours,
335 And the gilded ring was mine,
I hit the mark from time to time,
But you hit the mark every time."
    Stavyor didn't heed the words,
Godinovich didn't listen to the words:
340 "I didn't play svayechka with you."
    Vasily Nikulich spoke:
"Do you remember, Stavyor, do you recall,
That we studied reading and writing together?
My inkwell was silver,
345 And your pen was gilded.
I dipped my pen from time to time,
But you dipped your pen every time."
    But Stavyor didn't heed these words,
Godinovich didn't listen to these words:
350 "You and I didn't study reading and writing together."
    Vasily Nikulich spoke:
"Our Sun, Vladimir of capital Kiev!
Let Stavyor go to the white tent
To see my brave druzhina."
355   Vladimir of capital Kiev spoke:
"If I release Stavyor, then I won't see Stavyor again,
But if I don't release Stavyor, then I'll anger the envoy."
He didn't dare to anger the envoy.
He released Stavyor to go to the white tent,
360 To see his brave druzhina.
    They came to the white tent,
They dismounted their good steeds.
Then the young Vasily Nikulich
Quickly entered the fine white tent,
365 He took off his young man's clothing,
He put on woman's clothing,
He went out on the wide street,

---

*A children's game in which a nail is thrown into a ring on the ground (Vladimir Dal).

He spoke these words himself:
"Now, Stavyor, do you recognize me?"
370   Stavyor Godinovich then spoke:
"Hail to you, young Vasilisa, Nikula's daughter!
Let's not go anymore to the city of Kiev
To the gracious Prince Vladimir,
Let's leave for the Lithuanian land."
375   Vasilisa, Nikula's daughter, spoke:
"That does you no honor or praise, good youth,
To leave Kiev like a thief!
Let's go to Prince Vladimir,
We'll finish performing the wedding."
380   They came to our Sun, Vladimir,
Vasily Nikulich spoke:*
"Our Sun, Vladimir of capital Kiev!
Why did you imprison our Stavyor Godinovich
In your deep dungeon?"
385   Vladimir of capital Kiev spoke:
"He bragged about his young wife,
That she could outwit all the princes and boyars,
That she could charm me, your Sun, Vladimir,
        out of my mind."
Vasilisa, Nikula's daughter, spoke:
390   "What do you have in mind now?
You're giving a girl in marriage to a woman,
To me, to Vasilisa Nikulichna!"
Then our Sun, Vladimir, became ashamed.
He hung his reckless head,
395   He lowered his bright eyes toward the damp earth,
He spoke these words himself:
"Hail to you, Stavyor Godinovich!
For your great boasting
Trade in our city, in Kiev,
400   In our city, in Kiev, forever without duty."
        Then Stavyor Godinovich
Rode to the Lithuanian land

---

*The singer again uses the masculine gender for Vasilisa.

With the young Vasilisa Nikulichna.
Since then they've been singing this old song
about Stavyor
405   To the blue sea for calm weather
And to you good people for listening.

～ 20 ～

Khoten Bludovich

*K*hoten Bludovich does not belong among the central heroes in the Russian epic tradition and appears only in the song bearing his name. The bylina "Khoten Bludovich," which essentially concerns bride taking, has been recorded thirty-five times. At a feast in Prince Vladimir's palace, Bludov's widow proposes to marry her son Khoten to Chaina, the daughter of the widow Chasov, who rejects the proposal in an insulting and abusive manner. (In Kievan Rus, a woman was often called by her husband's name.) After returning home, Bludov's widow tells her son Khoten about how she has been publicly offended. Seeking revenge for an affront to his family honor, he goes to the home of Chasov's widow and wreaks such havoc that she in turn is insulted and appeals to Prince Vladimir for satisfaction. After receiving his permission, she hires an army of mercenaries, puts her nine sons at their head, and sends them against Khoten, who fights the army alone and kills or captures all the sons. Chasov's widow is forced to submit and begs Khoten to take Chaina as his wife. At first, he threatens to take her as a washerwoman or to marry her to one of his servants, but then, often at the insistence of Prince Vladimir, he agrees to marry Chaina.

Unlike the songs "Potyk," "Ivan Godinovich," or "Dunai," where the heroes leave home and find brides somewhere far away from Kievan Rus, in "Khoten Bludovich" the action takes place entirely within a Russian city. Chaina is not a sorceress-enchantress (such as Marya the White Swan in "Potyk" or Marinka in "Dobrynya and Marinka"), nor is she a bogatyrka (such as Nastasia in "Dunai"); she is an ordinary young woman from a well-off family. The apparent "realism" of the quarrel between families, the urban setting in "Khoten Bludovich," and the comparative absence of magical elements suggest a comparatively late origin for this bylina.

In most variants, the events occur in Kiev, Prince Vladimir represents one of the chief figures, and Chasov's widow may be related to
him. However, many scholars presume that this song reflects the life
and customs of Novgorod, and they believe that the location in Kiev is a
later adaptation (Vs.F. Miller 1897–1924, 1: 220–32; Smirnov and
Smolitskii 1978: 426–33). Many folklorists also emphasize the role of
social differences in the family conflict. In some recordings, Chasov's
widow may be well-to-do and aristocratic while Bludov's widow may
be poor and may belong to the lower classes. There also are indications
that Khoten himself is far from being a respectable match. However, the
precise social positions of the two families are not always clear and
vary from song to song. In the translated variant, both widows are
invited to a feast at Prince Vladimir's palace and are addressed as
"ladies," suggesting that they are social equals or nearly so. Singers
reveal their sympathies for Bludov's widow and her son when they
depict Chasov's widow and her daughter Chaina as haughty and arrogant, and when they portray her sons as cowards who are afraid to fight
Khoten even with an army. Khoten, on the contrary, has been transformed into a Kievan-like bogatyr who fights alone and wins against
overwhelming odds. In the song included in this anthology, Khoten is
described as having saved Kiev from the Tatars when they besieged the
city earlier. At the same time, Khoten is also presented ambiguously as
a hero because he displays the same reckless and unrestrained character
as Vasily Buslayev, one of the main personages in the Novgorod cycle
of epics. Just as Buslayev, Khoten rides around the city and "raises
hell," he picks quarrels with the inhabitants, and he engages in petty
conflicts with them. Thus the "Kievization" of what is essentially a
conflict between two families remains incomplete. No bogatyrs are at
the opening feast at Prince Vladimir's, and, even though he grants
Chasov's widow permission to raise an army, he does not help her with
his courtly druzhina.

   Although the names of the characters in this bylina vary, they usually
convey suggestive overtones. "Khoten" is derived from a verb meaning
"to want" or "to desire" so that he may be regarded as a "desired son."
However, "Bludov" is related to a verb implying "to roam," "to lose one's
way," or "to commit lechery," thus suggesting that Khoten, just as his
"lecher father," spends his time running around town and that the given
name "Khoten" may also connote "lust." The name "Chasov" may indicate an honorable or respected person, and the name "Chaina" may be

derived from a verb suggesting a "desired" or "expected daughter." Whatever their implications may be in today's Russian, the names "Khoten" and "Blud" were used during the time of Kievan Rus.

Several other features involving bride taking appear in the song about Khoten. Although both mothers are widows, they rule their respective families and make all decisions about whom their children will marry without consulting them. However, these two mothers differ considerably from those depicted in songs about Dobrynya or Vasily Buslayev, where the mothers have prophetic insights into the future fate of their sons. Chaina, as an unmarried woman, is probably sitting shut up in her "tower" and waiting for a suitable young man to come. Many motifs and symbols that occur in the peasant wedding ritual up to the church ceremony may appear in the song (Loboda 1904: 169–202), in particular the conventional hostility depicted between families, the haughty and reluctant bride, and the negative portrayal of the groom. Just as the arrow that Dobrynya shoots at Marinka's palace in "Dobrynya and Marinka" may be a courtship symbol, so Khoten's lance may have sexual associations during his "assault" on Chaina's palace.

A.D. Grigorev recorded the variant chosen for translation in 1901 on the Mezen River in Archangel Province from Anna P. Chupova.

⋙ Khoten Bludovich ⋘

Source: A.D. Grigorev, *Archangel Bylinas and Historical Songs,* vol. 3
(St. Petersburg, 1910), no. 373.

    In the capital city, in Kiev,
At the gracious Prince's, at Vladimir's,
There was a banquet, there was a feast of honor.
At the feast there were two widows—
5   One was Afimya, Chasov's wife,
And the other was Avdotya, Bludov's wife.
    Then Avdotya, Bludov's wife,
Poured a goblet of green wine,

She offered it to Afimya, Chasov's wife,
10   And she spoke these words herself:
"Hail to you, Afimya, Chasov's wife!
Accept a goblet of green wine from me
And drink the goblet till it's dry.
I have Khotenushko, Bludov's son,
15   You have Chaina the beautiful.
Would you or wouldn't you give her in marriage,
              or would you refuse?"
        Then Afimya, Chasov' wife,
Accepted the goblet of green wine from her,
She poured it out on Avdotya's white breasts,
20   She poured it over her clothing worth five hundred rubles,
And she spoke these words herself:
"Hail to you, Avdotya, Bludov's wife!
Your husband was a lecher,
And your son was born a freak,
25   He's a freak and a near-sighted chicken.
On the day it scratches, it will find some seeds—
On that day the chicken will be full.
On the day it doesn't scratch, it won't find any seeds—
On that day the chicken will be hungry."*
30   Then Avdotya was offended,
She took this for a great insult.
Avdotya left the feast of honor,
The princely feast, the feast of honor.
She walked and hung her reckless head,
35   She walked and lowered her bright eyes
Toward the earth, toward the mother damp earth.
        Khotenushko, Bludov's son, came to meet her,
He spoke these words himself:
"Hail to you, my mother, mother and lady!
40   Why are you returning so unhappy from the feast of honor,
From the princely feast of honor?
Why are you walking and hanging your reckless head?
Why are you walking and lowering your bright eyes

---

*The meaning of this passage is unclear, but the comparison with a chicken is
obviously intended to be insulting and degrading.

Toward the earth, toward the mother damp earth?
45   Didn't you receive a place from the prince according
                to your family?
Or weren't the stewards gracious to you?
Or weren't the cupbearers pleasant to you?
Or did they pass you by with a drinking glass?
Or didn't the goblets of green wine reach you?
50   Or did a drunkard make fun of you?
Did a foolish person abuse you?
Did an impolite person offend you with a crude word?"
        Avdotya, Bludov's wife, then spoke to him:
"Hail to you, Khotenushko, Bludov's son!
55   I received a place from the prince according to my family,
They didn't pass me by with a drinking glass,
And the goblets of green wine reached me,
No drunkard made fun of me,
No foolish person abused me,
60   No impolite person offended me with a crude word.
There were only two widows at the feast.
I, Avdotya, Bludov's wife, was one,
And Afimya, Chasov's wife, was the other.
I poured a goblet of green wine,
65   I offered it to Afimya, Chasov's wife,
I spoke these words myself:
'Hail to you, Afimya, Chasov's wife!
Accept a goblet of green wine from me
And drink the goblet till it's dry.
70   I have Khotenushko, Bludov's son,
You have Chaina the beautiful.
Would you or wouldn't you give her in marriage,
                or would you refuse?'
Then Afimya, Chasov's wife,
Accepted the goblet of green wine from me,
75   She herself poured it out on my white breasts,
And she poured it over my clothing worth five
                hundred rubles,
And she spoke these words herself:
'Hail to you, Avdotya, Bludov's wife!
Your husband was a lecher

80   And your son was born a freak,
        He's a freak and a near-sighted chicken.
        On the day it scratches, it will find some seeds—
        On that day the chicken will be full.
        On the day it doesn't scratch, it won't find any seeds—
85   On that day the chicken will be hungry.'
            Then Khotenushko, Bludov's son,
        Turned his good steed around,
        He started riding through the city, through the capital city.
        He rode up to Chasova's palace,
90   He jabbed his lance in the wide gate,
        On his lance he carried the gate into the courtyard—
        The posts had been made crooked,
        The many small railings had been scattered.
            Then Chaina the beautiful looked out,
95   She looked out of a window,
        And she spoke these words herself:
        "Hail to you, Khotenushko, Bludov's son!
        Your father was a lecher,
        And you were born a freak,
100   You're a freak and a near-sighted chicken.
        You ride around the city, around the capital city,
        You ride around the city and ruin everything,
        You ruin widows' houses.
        On the day you scratch, you'll find some seeds—
105   On that day you, the chicken, will be full.
        On the day you don't scratch, you won't find any seeds—
        On that day you, the chicken, will be hungry."
            He smashed the high chamber with his mace,
        He smashed the chamber from its roof down to its windows.
110   Chaina the beautiful almost fell behind a bench.
            Then Afimya, Chasov's wife,
        Came from the feast of honor,
        From the princely feast of honor.
        She spoke these words herself:
115   "It seems there hasn't been a storm or a bad wind,
        But my little house has been wrecked."
            When Chaina the beautiful met her,
        She spoke these words herself:

"Hail to you, my mother, mother and lady!
120   Khotenushko, Bludov's son, came riding,
He jabbed his lance in the wide gate,
On his lance he carried the gate into the courtyard—
The posts had been made crooked,
The many small railings had been scattered.
125   I looked out of the window,
And I spoke these words myself:
'Hail to you, Khotenushko, Bludov's son!
Your father was a lecher,
And you were born a freak,
130   You're a freak and a near-sighted chicken.
You ride around the city, around the capital city,
You ride around the city and ruin everything,
You ruin widows' homes.'
He smashed the high chamber with his mace,
135   He smashed the chamber from its roof down to its windows,
I almost fell behind a bench."
       Then Afimya was offended,
She took this for a great insult.
Afimya left to see the Prince, to see Vladimir,
140   She spoke these words herself:
"Lord, Prince Vladimir of capital Kiev!
Grant me satisfaction against Khotenushko,
Against Khotenushko, Bludov's son."
       Prince Vladimir of capital Kiev spoke:
145   "Hail to you, Afimya, Chasov's wife!
If you wish, take a thousand, if you wish, take two,
But beyond that only what's necessary.
If you strike off Khotenushko's reckless head,
There will be no reprisal for Khotenushko."
150   Then Afimya, Chasov's wife,
Went and hired an army of three thousand,
She sent three sons as voyevodas.
When her sons were leaving, they cried,
And they spoke these words themselves:
155   "Hail to you, our mother, mother and lady!
We can't beat Khotenushko in the open field,
We'll lose our reckless heads.

When capital city Kiev was besieged
By that great force,
160   By the evil infidel Tatars,
He ransomed and he rescued the city
From that force, from that great force,
From the evil Tatars, from the infidel Tatars."
Then Chasova's army set out,
165   Her army set out for the open field.
When her sons were leaving, they cried.
Then Khotenushko, Bludov's son,
Caught sight of the army in the open field,
He rode up to the army and asked:
170   "Hail to you, Chasova's army!
Are you a voluntary or indentured army?"*
Then Chasova's army answered:
"We're a voluntary and a hired army."*
Then Khotenushko started riding through this army,
175   Wherever he turned he cleared a street,
Whenever he waved his arms he cleared a whole square.
Then he smashed the whole army to the last man.
He took those three brothers alive,
He took them alive and bound them by their hair,
180   He bound them by their hair and threw them across his steed,
He threw them across his steed and took them to his tent.
Afimya was expecting her army back from
the open field,
She couldn't wait for the army any longer.
Again she went and hired an army of three thousand,
185   She sent three more sons as voyevodas.
When her sons were leaving, they cried:
"Hail to you, our mother, mother and lady!
We can't beat Khotenushko in the open field,
We'll lose our reckless heads."
190   Afimya, Chasov's wife, then spoke:
"Hail to you, my children, my dearest children!
I would have done better to bear nine stones than you,

_____

*Khoten asks whether the army consists of "free" men who are fighting by choice
or "indentured" men who have been ordered to fight.

I would have taken the stones to the swift river,
Then there wouldn't have been any passage for
      small vessels,
195   Big vessels would have been smashed."*
Her sons set out for the open field.
      Khotenushko, Bludov's son, caught sight of them,
He rode up to Chasova's army,
He asked the army himself:
200   "Are you a voluntary or indentured army?"
      Then Chasova's army answered:
"We're a voluntary and a hired army."
      Then Khotenushko started riding through this army,
Wherever he turned he cleared a street,
205   Whenever he waved his arms he cleared a whole square.
Then he smashed the whole army to the last man.
He took the three brothers alive,
He took them alive and bound them by their hair,
He bound them by their hair and threw them across his steed,
210   He threw them across his steed and took them to his tent.
      Afimya was expecting her army back from the
      open field,
Again she couldn't wait for the army any longer,
Again she went and hired an army of three thousand,
She sent three more sons as voyevodas.
215   When her sons were leaving, they cried:
"Hail to you, our mother, mother and lady!
We can't beat Khotenushko in the open field,
We'll lose our reckless heads."
When the capital city of Kiev was besieged
220   By that great force
And by the evil infidel Tatars,
He ransomed and rescued the city
From that force, from that great force,
From the evil Tatars, from the infidel Tatars."
225   "Hail to you, my children, my dearest children!
I would have done better to bear nine stones than you,

*Afimya in effect "curses" her sons, wishing that they had been stones to cause harm in the world.

I would have taken the stones to the swift river,
Then there wouldn't have been any passage for
    small vessels,
Big vessels would have been smashed."
230   Then Chasova's army started riding,
When the sons were leaving, they cried.
    Then Khotenushko, Bludov's son,
Caught sight of the army in the open field,
He rode up to Chasova's army,
235   He asked the army himself:
"Are you a voluntary or indentured army?"
    Then Chasova's army spoke:
"We're a voluntary and a hired army."
    Then Khotenushko started riding through this army,
240   Wherever he turned he cleared a street,
Whenever he waved his arms he cleared a whole square.
Then he smashed the whole army to the last man.
He took those three brothers alive,
He took them alive and bound them by their hair,
245   He bound them by their hair and threw them across
    his steed,
He threw them across his steed and took them to his tent.
    Afimya was expecting her army back from the
    open field,
She couldn't wait for her army any longer,
She went to Khotenushko, Bludov's son,
250   And she spoke these words herself:
"Hail to you, Khotenushko, Bludov's son!
Take my Chaina the beautiful,
Return all my nine sons for a ransom."
    Khotenushko, Bludov's son, then spoke:
255   "Hail to you, Afimya, Chasov's wife!
I don't want your Chaina the beautiful!
Cover my sharp lance,
Take and cover with gold and silver
My lance's shaft that's seven sazhens long
260   From the joint of the tip to the base.
Take and cover the lance with gold and silver,
With gold and silver, and with fine pearls,

Then I'll return all nine sons for a ransom."*
Then Afimya, Chasov's wife,
265   Rolled up wagons filled with pure silver,
Ordyn wagons filled with red gold,
She covered his sharp lance,
She covered it with gold and silver,
With gold and silver, and with fine pearls,
270   But she was one-fourth short.
Afimya, Chasov's wife, then spoke:
"Hail to you, Khotenushko, Bludov's son!
Take my Chaina the beautiful,
Return all my nine sons for a ransom."
275   Then Khotenushko, the son of Bludov, spoke:
"I don't want your Chaina the beautiful!
You cover my sharp lance with gold and silver,
With gold and silver, and with fine pearls,
Then I'll return all nine sons for a ransom."
280   Prince Vladimir of capital Kiev spoke:†
"Hail to you, Khotenushko, Bludov's son!
Take Chaina the beautiful from her."
Khotenushko, Bludov's son, then spoke:
"I'll take Chaina the beautiful from her,
285   I won't take her for myself in marriage,
But I'll take her for my faithful servant,
For my squire, for Mishka."
Prince Vladimir of capital Kiev spoke:
"Hail to you, Khotenushko, Bludov's son!
290   Take her for yourself in marriage,
Really, she doesn't come from a low family,
She comes from a royal family."
Then Khotenushko took her for himself in marriage,
He returned all nine sons for a ransom.
295   Since then praises have been sung to Khotenushko,
Praises have been sung and this old song has been recited.

---

*Since the lance is about fifty feet long and presumably will be stuck upright in the ground, only a huge ransom will cover the weapon from top to bottom.
†The singer has omitted a transitional passage bringing everyone before Prince Vladimir.

III

Novgorod Cycle

~ 21 ~

Sadko

*T*he songs about Sadko, like those about Vasily Buslayev, in many ways are closely connected with the life, history, and culture of Novgorod (Smirnov and Smolitskii 1978: 314–35). This city, which was often addressed as "Lord Great Novgorod," was one of the principal urban centers in Kievan Rus, was located in the northwest, was primarily a merchant city, and had a democratic assembly called the *veche*. Novgorod was situated on the Volkhov River near the northern side of Lake Ilmen, carried on trade through river passages with the Baltic area in the west and with the Caspian region in the east, was associated with the Hanseatic League, and colonized much of the Russian North and Western Siberia. The city was known especially for its merchants, craftsmen, fishermen, sailors, and minstrels (skomorokhs). Novgorod belonged to a different cultural zone than the southern city of Kiev and shared many ethnographic features with nearby Scandinavia or with Finnish groups living in the same area. While much of the Russian land was devastated by the Tatar invasion in the middle of the thirteenth century, the northwestern part of the country, including Novgorod, remained largely untouched.

The three songs about Sadko are remarkable because they represent the only Russian epic in which the main character makes a journey to the otherworld (Propp 1958b: 87–109). They also combine elements of everyday life, customs, and institutions in Novgorod from the twelfth through the fifteenth centuries with folk beliefs and with motifs from magic tales. The epics about Sadko consist of three episodes alternating between the fantastic and the real: (1) the *gusli* player Sadko becomes a rich merchant (lines 1–92 in the translated variant); (2) Sadko the merchant wagers that he can buy all the goods in Novgorod (93–167); and (3) Sadko goes on a trading trip, descends to the undersea kingdom of the Sea Tsar, and returns home (168–387). It should be pointed out that in Old Russian the word "guest" meant "merchant." Some fifty variants of the songs about Sadko have been collected, but most are incomplete or fragmentary. Although the second episode and the more frequently collected third episode were performed separately or together, the first episode appears only in a variant recorded from the singer A.P. Sorokin, who lived near Lake Onega in northwestern Russia.

The feasts in the first and second episodes refer to a fraternal institution called *bratchina,* which, according to A.A. Popov (1854), had ancient pagan origins, over time became associated with parish churches, and held ritual feasts on certain religious holidays for the ostensible purpose of collecting donations for the church. The members of these fraternities zealously protected their right to exclude uninvited people even if they were from the upper classes or were high officials. The epic boasting in the more realistic second episode, where Sadko brags that he is rich enough to buy all the goods in Novgorod, reveals a different side of these feasts, which sometimes ended in brawls. In many, but not all, variants, Sadko loses his bet and is forced to admit that Novgorod is greater than he is. In the third episode, the journey, which Sadko makes with the epic number of thirty ships, passes along an accurately described route leading not to the Golden Horde on the Volga River in the east but to the Baltic Sea in the west. This route ran north along the Volkhov River to Lake Ladoga, from there turned west along the Neva River to the Gulf of Finland, and from there passed into the Baltic Sea. Sadko and his crew engage in another Novgorod institution, the *artel,* or cooperative, in which all members swear to observe strict rules of conduct while on a trading trip and at the end share any profits. The singer has replaced the word *artel* with the term druzhina, which refers to a prince's retinue.

As Iu.I. Smirnov and V.G. Smolitskii (1978: 388–96) have described in detail, many elements in the songs about Sadko are connected with ancient beliefs, magic tales, or memorates about encounters with supernatural beings. In the first episode, which includes threefold repetition typical for magic tales and also represents an apology for the skomorokhs, Sadko, excluded from the feasts of the bratchina, three times plays his gusli alone on the shore of Lake Ilmen. Much as a magical helper assists the main character in a magic tale, the Sea Tsar, the ruler of the rivers, lakes, and streams in East Slavic mythology, rewards Sadko. The "golden fish" that the Sea Tsar tells Sadko about in themselves are symbolic of the other world. Sadko's enchanting playing, which reappears in the parallel third episode in the underwater kingdom of the Sea Tsar, recalls Orpheus's ability to charm nature with his music or the magical powers of the singer Väinämöinen in The Kalevala. In the third episode, after the ships miraculously stand still during a storm, the drawing of lots involves beliefs about making a human sacrifice to assuage the sea, the most well known association being the biblical story about Jonah and the whale. According to yet another belief, bad storms are caused by the dancing of the Sea Tsar. The patron saint of sailors, Saint Nicholas, or Mikola Mozhaisky, as he is called in Sorokin's variant, comes to ask Sadko to stop playing so that the sea will calm down from the interminable dancing of the Sea Tsar. Similarly again to a magical helper in magic tales, the saint advises Sadko to pick the servant girl Chernava as a bride instead of one of the three times three hundred daughters of the Sea Tsar, another epic exaggeration for the more usual number of twelve in tales where the hero is given the difficult task of picking the correct bride. In passing it should be pointed out that Chernava, as a servant girl, appear in several epics, usually at a critical moment for the hero. Saint Nicholas also warns Sadko that if he consummates the marriage he will never return home to Novgorod. Although this is contrary to the usual outcome of a magic tale, where the hero comes home with a bride from the other world, Sadko heeds the advice of the saint, picks Chernava, and wakes up standing by the river "Chernava" back in Novgorod, where Sadko's wife and his returning druzhina greet him.

The bylina "Sadko" emerges as a varied and colorful mixture of realistic and fantastic characteristics that portray the life and beliefs of Novgorod. The version created by the singer Sorokin is unusual for the Russian epic tradition because it represents a composite of all songs about one hero. Although Sorokin's text includes imaginative details and offers a fine illustration of repetition and parallelism in oral poetry, nevertheless the song has several unclear passages. No explanation is given of why Sadko the gusli player is not invited to the feasts, why the Sea Tsar wants Sadko so badly, why Sadko takes his gusli with him into the undersea kingdom, and why he agrees to marry one of the Sea Tsar's daughters in the otherworld when he is already married.

P.N. Rybnikov collected this epic from A.P. Sorokin in Olonets Province in 1860.

❧ Sadko ❧

Source: P.N. Rybnikov, *Songs,* vol. 2 (Petrozavodsk, 1990), no. 135.

In Novgorod, in famous Novgorod,
There lived Sadko the merchant, the rich guest.
But formerly Sadko had no property,
He only had his maple gusli.
5   Sadko used to go and play at feasts.
The first day they didn't invite Sadko to a feast of honor,
The second they didn't invite him to a feast of honor,
And the third they didn't invite him to a feast of honor.
Because of this Sadko grew sick at heart.
10   Sadko went to Ilmen Lake,
He sat down on a white grieving stone
And played his maple gusli.
The water in the lake grew rough,
Sadko was frightened,
15   He went away from the lake to his city, to Novgorod.
    The first day they didn't invite Sadko to a feast
        of honor,
The second they didn't invite him to a feast of honor,
And the third they didn't invite him to a feast of honor.
Because of this Sadko grew sick at heart.
20   Sadko went to Ilmen Lake,
He sat down on a white grieving stone
And played his maple gusli.
The water in the lake grew rough,

Sadko was frightened,
25 He left the lake and went to his city, to Novgorod.
        The first day they didn't invite Sadko to a feast
            of honor,
    The second they didn't invite him to a feast of honor,
    And the third they didn't invite him to a feast of honor.
    Because of this Sadko grew sick at heart.
30 Sadko went to Ilmen Lake,
    He sat down on a white grieving stone
    And played his maple gusli.
        The water in the lake grew rough,
    The Sea Tsar appeared,
35 He came out of Ilmen, out of the Lake,
    He spoke these words himself:
    "Hail to you, Sadko of Novgorod!
    I don't know what I can reward you with
    For my pleasure, for my great pleasure,
40 For your tender playing.
    Perhaps with countless golden treasure?
    Otherwise then go to Novgorod
    And strike a great wager,
    Bet your reckless head,
45 And demand from the other merchants
    Shops of beautiful cloth,
    And argue that in Ilmen Lake
    There's a fish with golden fins.
    When you strike your great wager,
50 Go and tie a silken net
    And come fish in Ilmen Lake.
    I'll give you three fish with golden fins.
    Then, Sadko, you'll be happy."
        Sadko went away from Ilmen, from the lake.
55 When Sadko came to his city, to Novgorod,
    Sadko was invited to a feast of honor.
    Then Sadko of Novgorod
    Played his maple gusli,
    Then they gave Sadko something to drink,
60 They regaled Sadko.
        Then Sadko started bragging:

"Hail to you, my merchants of Novgorod!
I know a wondrous wonder in Ilmen Lake.
There's a fish with golden fins in Ilmen Lake."
65   Then the merchants of Novgorod
Spoke these words to him:
"You don't know any wondrous wonder,
There can't be any fish with golden fins in Ilmen Lake."
        "Hail to you, my merchants of Novgorod!
70   Will you make a great wager with me?
Let's strike a great wager.
I'll bet my reckless head,
And you bet your shops of the finest goods."
        Three merchants rushed forward,
75   Each bet three shops of the finest goods.
Then they tied a silken net
And went to fish in Ilmen Lake.
They cast a net in Ilmen Lake,
They caught a fish with golden fins.
80   They cast a second net in Ilmen Lake,
They caught a second fish with golden fins.
They cast a third net in Ilmen Lake,
They caught a third fish with golden fins.
Then each of the Novgorod merchants
85   Handed over three shops of the finest goods.
        Sadko began to trade,
He began to receive great profits.
In his white-stone palace
Sadko arranged everything as in the heavens:
90   In the heavens there was a sun and in the palace a sun,
In the heavens there was a moon and in the palace a moon,
In the heavens there were stars and in the palace stars.
        Then Sadko the merchant, the rich guest,
Invited to his home to a feast of honor
95   The men of Novgorod
And the elders of Novgorod,
Foma Nazaryev and Luka Zinovyev.
All ate their fill at the feast,
All drank their fill at the feast,
100   All boasted with their boastings.

One bragged about his countless golden treasure,
Another bragged about his daring strength and luck,
Another bragged about his good steed,
Another bragged about his famous family,

105 About his famous family and his youthful daring,
The smart one bragged about his old father,
The foolish one bragged about his young wife.
        The elders of Novgorod spoke:
"We all have eaten our fill at the feast of honor,

110 We all have drunk our fill at the feast of honor,
We all have boasted with our boastings.
Why doesn't Sadko brag about something,
Why doesn't Sadko boast about something?"
        Sadko the merchant, the rich guest, then spoke:

115 "And what should I, Sadko, brag about,
What should I, Sadko, boast about?
My golden treasure doesn't run out,
My colorful clothing doesn't wear out,
My brave druzhina doesn't betray me.

120 Should I brag or shouldn't I brag about my countless
                golden treasure?
With my countless golden treasure
I'll buy out the wares of Novgorod,
The bad wares and the good!"
        He had scarcely uttered these words

125 When the elders of Novgorod
Struck a great wager with him
For countless golden treasure,
For thirty thousand coins.
Sadko had to buy out the wares of Novgorod,

130 The bad wares and the good,
So that no more wares would be for sale in Novgorod.
        Sadko got up very early the next day,
He woke up his brave druzhina,
Without counting he gave them some golden treasure,

135 And he dispersed his druzhina along the trading streets,
And he himself went straight to the merchant stalls,
He bought out the wares of Novgorod,
The bad wares and the good

With his countless golden treasure.
140   The next day Sadko got up very early,
He woke up his brave druzhina,
Without counting he gave them some golden treasure,
And he dispersed his druzhina along the trading streets,
And he himself went straight to the merchant stalls.
145   Double the wares had been brought,
Double the wares had been piled up,
For the glory, for the great glory of Novgorod.
Again he bought out the wares of Novgorod,
The bad wares and the good
150   With his countless golden treasure.
      On the third day Sadko got up very early,
He woke up his brave druzhina,
Without counting he gave them some golden treasure,
And he dispersed his druzhina along the trading streets,
155   And he himself went straight to the merchant stalls.
Triple the wares had been brought,
Triple the wares had been piled up,
Moscow wares had been delivered in time
For the glory, for the great glory of Novgorod.
160   Then Sadko started thinking:
"It's impossible to buy wares from the whole wide world.
If I buy out the Moscow wares,
Overseas wares will be delivered in time.
It seems I'm not a rich Novgorod merchant,
165   Famous Novgorod is richer than me."
He gave up the thirty thousand coins
To the elders of Novgorod.
      With his countless golden treasure
Sadko built thirty ships,
170   Thirty ships, thirty scarlet ones.
On these ships, on these scarlet ships,
He piled the wares of Novgorod.
Sadko set out along the Volkhov,
From the Volkhov to Lake Ladoga,
175   And from Ladoga to the Neva River,
And from the Neva River to the blue sea.
He set out along the blue sea,

He turned to the Golden Horde.
He sold the wares of Novgorod,
180   He received great profits,
He filled forty-bucket barrels with red gold and pure silver.
    He started back to Novgorod,
He set out along the blue sea.
On the blue sea bad weather arose,
185   The scarlet ships stood still on the blue sea,
The wind drove the waves and tore the sails
And smashed at the scarlet ships,
But the ships didn't move from their place on the blue sea.
    Sadko the merchant, the rich guest, then spoke
190   To his druzhina, to his brave druzhina:
"Hail to you, my brave druzhina!
For a long time we've traveled through the sea,
But we haven't paid tribute to the Sea Tsar.
It seems the Sea Tsar is demanding tribute from us,
195   Demanding tribute to the blue sea.
Hail to you, my brothers and brave druzhina!
Pick up a forty-bucket barrel of pure silver
And lower the barrel into the blue sea."
His brave druzhina
200   Picked up the barrel of pure silver
And lowered the barrel into the blue sea.
The wind drove the waves and tore the sails
And smashed at the scarlet ships,
But the ships didn't move from their place on the blue sea.
205   Then his brave druzhina
Took a forty-bucket barrel of red gold
And lowered the barrel into the blue sea.
The wind drove the waves and tore the sails
And smashed at the scarlet ships,
210   The scarlet ships still didn't move from their place
        on the blue sea.
    Sadko the merchant, the rich guest, then spoke:
"It seems the Sea Tsar is demanding
A living person as a tribute to the blue sea.
Brothers, make some wooden lots,
215   I myself will make one on gold, on red gold,

All of you sign your names,
Cast the lots on the blue sea.
If someone's lot goes to the bottom,
That person must go into the blue sea."
220   They made some wooden lots,
And Sadko made his on gold, on red gold,
All of them signed their names,
They cast their lots on the blue sea.
The lots of all the brave druzhina
225   Floated like ducks on water,
But Sadko the merchant's sank to the bottom like a rock.
     Sadko the merchant, the rich guest, then spoke:
"Hail to you, my brothers and brave druzhina!
Those lots weren't made correctly.
230   Make your lots on gold, on red gold,
And I'll make a wooden lot."
They made some lots on gold, on red gold,
And Sadko made himself a wooden lot,
All of them signed their names,
235   They cast their lots on the blue sea.
The lots of all the brave druzhina
Floated like ducks on water,
But Sadko the merchant's sank to the bottom like a rock.*

. . .

240   Sadko the merchant, the rich guest, then spoke:
"Hail to you, my brothers and brave druzhina!
It seems the Sea Tsar is demanding
The rich Sadko himself as a tribute to the blue sea.
Bring me my finely molded inkwell,
245   A swan quill, and a sheet of official paper."†
They brought him the finely molded inkwell,

*At this point Rybnikov omits a passage and adds the following remarks. "The trial does not end with this. Sadko suggests that the druzhina should make its lots out of oak, while he makes his out of a lime tree; then the druzhina makes its lots out of lime, and he makes his out of oak."

†An anachronism since legal paper with a state seal on it appeared only in the beginning of the eighteenth century.

A swan quill, and a sheet of official paper.
He began bequeathing his property.
Some property he willed to God's churches,
250   Other property to poor religious beggars,
Other property to his young wife,
The remaining property to his brave druzhina.
        Sadko the merchant, the rich guest, then spoke:
"Hail to you, my brothers and brave druzhina!
255   Give me my maple gusli,
I have to play for the last time,
I'm not to play the gusli any more.
Should I take my gusli with me into the blue sea?"
        He picked up his maple gusli,
260   He spoke these words himself:
"Throw an oaken plank on the water.
I'll lie down on the oaken plank,
It won't be so terrible for me to accept death on the blue sea."
They threw the oaken plank on the water,
265   Then the ships started off through the blue sea,
They started flying like black ravens.
Sadko stayed on the blue sea.
From this fear, from this great fear,
He fell asleep on the plank, on the oaken plank.
270   Sadko woke up in the blue sea,
In the blue sea, on the very bottom.
He saw the bright sun shining through the water,
The evening twilight and the morning dawn.
Sadko saw a white-stone palace
275   Standing in the blue sea,
Sadko entered the white-stone palace.
The Sea Tsar was sitting in the palace,
The Tsar's head looked like a haystack.*
        The Tsar then spoke these words:
280   "Hail to you, Sadko the merchant, the rich guest!
Sadko, you've sailed upon the sea for a long time,
You haven't paid me, the Tsar, any tribute,

---

*The Sea Tsar looks shaggy from the water plants that are covering him.

But today you've come to me yourself as a gift.
They say you're a master at playing the maple gusli.
285   Play your maple gusli awhile for me."
      Then Sadko played his maple gusli,
Then the Sea Tsar danced in the blue sea,
Then the Sea Tsar was carried away with dancing.
Sadko played a day, then played a second,
290   And Sadko also played a third.
The Sea Tsar kept on dancing in the blue sea.
In the blue sea the water grew rough,
The water was clouded with yellow sand,
Many ships were being smashed on the blue sea,
295   Much property was being destroyed,
Many pious people were being drowned.
      Then people prayed to Mikola Mozhaisky.
Then someone touched Sadko on the right shoulder:
"Hail to you, Sadko of Novgorod!
300   That's enough playing on your maple gusli!"
Sadko of Novgorod turned around and looked.
Behold, there stood a gray old man.
      Sadko of Novgorod spoke:
"I don't have a will of my own in the blue sea,
305   I was ordered to play the maple gusli."
      The old man spoke these words:
"Rip out the strings
And break out the pegs.
Say: 'There don't seem to be any strings,
310   And there aren't any suitable pegs,
There's nothing to play on any more,
The maple gusli's been broken.'
      The Sea Tsar will say to you:
'Would you like to marry in the blue sea
315   A darling, a beautiful girl?'
      Say these words to him:
'I don't have a will of my own in the blue sea.'
      Again the Sea Tsar will say:
'Well, Sadko, then get up very early in the morning,
320   Choose yourself a maid, a beauty.'
      When you're choosing a maid, a beauty,

Then let the first three hundred maids pass by,
And let the second three hundred maids pass by,
And let the third three hundred maids pass by.
325   Behind them will walk a maid, a beauty,
A beauty, a maid—Chernava.
Take this Chernava for yourself in marriage.
When you lie down to sleep the first night,
Don't commit sin with your wife in the blue sea,
330   You'll stay forever in the blue sea.
But if you don't sin with her in the blue sea
And just lie down to sleep by the maid, the beauty,
Sadko, you'll turn out to be in Novgorod.
And with your countless golden treasure
335   Build a cathedral church to Mikola Mozhaisky."
         Sadko ripped out the strings on his maple gusli
And broke out the pegs on his gusli.
         The Sea Tsar spoke to him:
"Hail to you, Sadko of Novgorod!
340   Why aren't you playing your maple gusli?"
         "The strings on my gusli have been ripped out,
And the pegs on my maple gusli have been broken out,
And there don't happen to be any extra strings,
And there aren't any suitable pegs."
345   The Tsar spoke these words:
"Would you like to marry in the blue sea
A darling, a beautiful girl?"
         Sadko of Novgorod then spoke to him:
"I don't have a will of my own in the blue sea."
350   Again the Sea Tsar spoke:
"Well, Sadko, then get up early in the morning
And choose yourself a maid, a beauty."
         Sadko got up early in the morning,
He looked—three hundred beautiful girls were coming.
355   He let the first three hundred maids pass,
And let the second three hundred maids pass,
And let the third three hundred maids pass.
Behind was walking a maid, a beauty,
A beauty, a maid—Chernava.
360   He took Chernava for himself in marriage.

When their banquet, the feast of honor was over,
When Sadko lay down to sleep the first night,
He didn't commit sin with his wife in the blue sea.
    Sadko woke up in Novgorod,
365   Next to the Chernava River on its steep bank.
He looked—behold, his scarlet ships
Were sailing along the Volkhov.
    Sadko's wife was mourning both for him and for
        his druzhina in the blue sea:
"Sadko wasn't meant to return from the blue sea!"
370   But the druzhina was mourning only for Sadko:
"Sadko remained in the blue sea!"
But Sadko was standing on the steep bank,
He met his druzhina from the bank of the Volkhov.
    Then his druzhina was amazed:
375   "Sadko remained in the blue sea,
Yet he's turned up before us in Novgorod
And is greeting his druzhina from the bank of the Volkhov."
    Sadko met his brave druzhina
And led it into his white-stone palace.
380   Then his wife was overjoyed,
She took Sadko by his white hands,
She kissed him on his lips, on his sweet lips.
From the scarlet ships, Sadko started unloading
His property—the countless golden treasure.
385   He unloaded his scarlet ships,
He built a cathedral church to Mikola Mozhaisky.
Sadko no longer traveled to the blue sea,
Sadko started living his life in Novgorod.

☙ 22 ☙

Vasily Buslayev

Vasily Buslayev (sometimes Buslavyevich) appears in two epics, the first being his rebellion against his native city, Novgorod, and the second being his pilgrimage to Jerusalem. Some seventy-five variants have been recorded and may be devoted to the rebellion, may concern the pilgrimage, or may be composite songs of both subjects (Smirnov and Smolitskii 1978: 362–73). Most variants of the first song open with remarks about how Vasily's father belonged to the upper classes, never contended with Novgorod or Moscow, lived to the age of nine hundred years, and died leaving his son to be raised by his mother. Motifs about the birth and growth of a future epic hero may be included in the description of Vasily's childhood. He grows rapidly, has extraordinary strength, may be taught forms of magic such as shape-shifting, and causes trouble because he rips off the arms and legs of his playmates. These actions provoke the anger of the men of Novgorod, who threaten to kill him. In response, Vasily collects his own druzhina, which consists of lower-class tradesmen, and together they go to a feast, or *bratchina,* uninvited, conduct that violates the code of such fraternities and antagonizes their members (see the introduction to "Sadko"). There during a boasting bout, he challenges all of Novgorod to a fight the next morning on the bridge over the Volkhov River, which divides the city into cathedral and trade sections. The bridge was the place where traditional fights with fists or sticks took place between opposing groups in the city. Vasily's mother tries to make peace with the men of Novgorod, but when they refuse her offer she may give her son a sleeping potion and lock him up at home. The next day his druzhina fights poorly without him but is helped by the servant girl Chernava, who swings her yoke with devastating effect. She returns home and releases Vasily, who joins the fray with bad consequences for the men of Novgorod. In desperation, they

307

send a peacemaker, who may be Vasily's godfather, sworn brother, former mentor, religious pilgrim, or perhaps the bishop of Novgorod. The fantastically huge "bell" that this person sometimes wears represents a misunderstanding on the part of those singers who have forgotten an older meaning of the same word (*kolokol*) as a hat worn by pilgrims. Vasily becomes so enraged at the peacemaker that in many instances he kills him. The men of Novgorod then ask Vasily's mother to intercede and stop his rampage against his fellow citizens. She is the only person who has any influence on her young son and understands how to control his aggressive anger. As T.A. Novichkova (1987) demonstrates, many aspects of Novgorod culture, institutions, beliefs, and customs from the twelfth through the fifteenth centuries have been absorbed into this epic.

Several details in the translated variant of the first song about Vasily Buslayev need to be mentioned. He and his druzhina go to a "prince's feast," even though the people of Novgorod at an early date expelled the princes from the city and established an oligarchy. Vasily and his men are probably going to a feast organized by the bratchina. Although the servant girl who fights with Vasily's druzhina and releases him is not named, in most recordings she is called Chernava. Two peacemakers appear, the first being Vasily's sworn brother, whom he kills with the justification that the brother came armed. The second person is Vasily's godfather, who appears with a gigantic bell and its clapper. The concluding scene, in which Vasily's mother warily approaches him during the battle knowing full well that he might kill even her during his fighting frenzy, has been shortened.

Most interpretations of the first song about Vasily Buslayev emphasize that he is a rebel against Novgorod, its institutions, and its ruling classes (Propp 1958b: 442–65). Some treat him as a symbol of Novgorod rebelliousness and compare him to the Viking-like brigands called *ushkuiniks,* who raided towns and villages along waterways, especially in the fourteenth century. However, several elements inherent to Novgorod life—a rebellious youth, traditional fights with fists or sticks, social conflicts, the bratchina, and the mediating role of the church—to varying degrees have been converted by singers into a Kievan heroic epic. Through analogy, singers draw upon motifs and scenes in a Kievan martial epic to describe similar situations in Vasily's conflict with Novgorod. Thus a fight arouses associations with a heroic epic and leads to a traditional battle scene, in which a

Russian hero mows down overwhelming opponents. The meeting between Vasily and the peacemaker may become a climatic duel between an epic hero and his adversary. Furthermore, Vasily displays characteristics common to epic heroes: he has the verve, the fighting spirit, and the eagerness to challenge everyone and everything. In addition, Vàsily and his druzhina may be described as going to a "prince's feast," just as a bylina set in Kiev may open with a feast given by Prince Vladimir.

Although there are outward resemblances between the first song about Vasily Buslayev and a heroic epic, there also are differences. Vasily's opponent is not an external enemy but someone from the same community. Unlike most encounters between a bogatyr and a foreign enemy in Russian epics, this song does not clearly resolve the confrontation between Vasily and Novgorod. On the one hand, Vasily resembles a typical bogatyr, but on the other hand he is a rebel or troublemaker who upsets life in Novgorod. Vasily may be associated with the heroes of Kievan epics, but he is out-of-date in the trading city of Novgorod, where life from the twelfth through the fifteenth centuries was no longer heroic. Viewed within the Russian epic tradition, Vasily belongs to an earlier epoch and, unlike the bogatyrs in Kiev, has no real place in Novgorod. Singers have created a story that is striking in its sharp contrasts, and in Vasily they have also depicted a figure whose character is more contradictory and complex than that of most other Russian heroes.

Although singers admire Vasily's energy, daring, and strength, they also depict negative sides of his character, something that departs from the ordinarily positive presentation of a bogatyr. Vasily's rebellion against Novgorod is meaningless and brings no benefits to him or to anyone else. While epic heroes usually serve their communities in some useful way, Vasily is "a rebel without a cause." Thus he antagonizes his own society, carries out no unselfish acts to help others, and has no heroic ideals. He forms his own druzhina but deliberately chooses tradesmen from the lower-class urban population, a social combination that contrasts with that in the epic "Volkh Vseslav-yevich," where Volkh picks his retinue from among his social equals. When singers intensify social differences by changing the members of Vasily's retinue into tavern "riff-raff," their variants parallel the epic "Ilya Muromets Quarrels with Prince Vladimir," in which Ilya allies himself with similar people in his rebellion against Prince Vladimir. Curiously, Vasily's character in this song shares several features with a

Viking berserker in Scandinavian sagas: uncontrolled and ecstatic rage during battle, a position as an outsider or outlaw to one's own community, a group of similar companions, attacks on one's own people, and immense but destructive strength. In some respects, this Russian epic may allude to contacts that had long existed between the Novgorod region and Scandinavia.

P.N. Rybnikov took down this song from "an old man" in Kolodozero in Olonets Province during the early 1860s.

❧ Vasily Buslayev ❧

Source: P.N. Rybnikov, *Songs,* vol. 2 (Petrozavodsk, 1990), no. 169.

	Buslav lived and didn't grow old,
	Having lived, Buslav passed away.
	Buslav's dear child remained,
	His dear beloved child,
5	The young Vasily Buslavyevich.
	Vasily started going out on the street,
	His jokes were no laughing matter:
	He'd grab someone's arm—the arm would come off,
	He'd grab someone's leg—the leg would come off,
10	And whoever he struck on the back,
	That one would stoop when he walked.
	And the men of Novgorod spoke:
	"Hail to you, Vasily Buslavyevich!
	With your young man's boldness
15	You'll make the Volkhov River turn sour."*
	Vasily went out into the wide streets,
	He came home cheerless and joyless,
	And his devoted mother met him,
	The honorable widow, Avdotya Vasilyevna:

---

* This is a hint that they might throw Vasily in the river and drown him.

20   "Hail to you, my dear child,
                  My dear beloved child,
                  Young Vasily Buslavyevich!
                  Why are you coming home so cheerless and so joyless?
                  Did someone on the street insult you?"

25   "No one on the street insulted me.
                  When I grab someone by the arm—the arm comes off,
                  When I grab someone by the leg—the leg comes off,
                  And whoever I strike on the back,
                  That one will stoop when he walks.

30   And the men of Novgorod said
                  That with my young man's boldness
                  I'd make the Volkhov River turn sour."
                     And the mother spoke these words:
                  "Hail to you, Vasily Buslavyevich!

35   Choose a brave druzhina for yourself,
                  So that no one in Novgorod will insult you."
                     And Vasily filled a chalice with green wine,
                  A chalice measuring a bucket and a half.
                  He put the chalice in the middle of the courtyard,

40   And he uttered these words over the chalice:
                  "Whoever takes this chalice with one hand
                  And drinks this chalice in one draught
                  Will belong to my brave druzhina!"
                     And he sat on a chair with leather thongs

45   And quickly wrote letters in cursive.
                  In the letters Vasily wrote these words:
                  "Vasily is calling and inviting you to a feast of honor."
                  He tied the letters to arrows,
                  And he shot the arrows around Novgorod.

50   The men of Novgorod came out
                  Of the church, of the cathedral church,
                  They found the arrows,
                  The gentlemen looked at the arrows:
                  "Vasily is calling and inviting you to a feast of honor."

55   And the men of Novgorod gathered in bunches,
                  They gathered in bunches and in crowds,
                  And they went to Vasily's feast of honor.
                  And they were in Vasily's wide courtyard,

And they spoke these words themselves:
60   "Hail to you, Vasily Buslavyevich!
Now that we've come to your courtyard,
We'll eat up all your food,
And we'll drink up all your drinks,
We'll take away your colorful clothing,
65   We'll drag away your red gold."
        He didn't like these words.
Vasily rushed to the wide courtyard,
Vasily grabbed his scarlet club,
And Vasily walked around the courtyard,
70   And he swung his club.
Wherever he swung—a street would appear,
Wherever he swung again—a lane would appear.
The men of Novgorod were lying in bunches,
They were lying in bunches and in crowds,
75   As though bad weather had struck the men down.
        And Vasily entered his gold-topped palace,
Soon someone came, a new one came
To Vasily in his wide courtyard.
Kostya Novotorzhanin approached
80   The goblet of green wine,
And he took the goblet with one hand,
He drank the goblet in one draught.
Vasily rushed from the new vestibule,
Vasily grabbed his scarlet club.
85   He struck Kostya on the back,
Kostya stood without flinching,
The curls on his reckless head hadn't budged.
"Hail to you, Kostya Novotorzhanin!
Be my brave friend,
90   Enter my white-stone palace."
        Soon someone came, a new one came.
Potanyushka the Lame then came
To Vasily in his wide courtyard,
He approached the goblet of green wine,
95   He took the goblet with one hand
And he drank the goblet in one draught.
        When Vasily rushed from the new vestibule,

Vasily grabbed his scarlet club,
He struck Potanyushka on his crippled legs,
100   Potanyushka stood without flinching,
The curls on his reckless head hadn't budged.
"Hail to you, Potanyushka the Lame!
Be my brave friend,
Enter my white-stone palace."
105   Soon someone came, a new one came.
Fomushka the Hunchbacked approached
The goblet of green wine,
He took the goblet with one hand,
And he drank the goblet in one draught.
110   Vasily didn't come from the new vestibule to strike him.
"Go to my white-stone palace
And drink our sweet drinks,
And eat our tasty foods.
We have no one to fear in Novgorod!"
115   Thus Vasily chose three comrades in Novgorod.
       And a feast of honor was held by the Prince of Novgorod
For many princes, for the boyars,
And for the strong and mighty bogatyrs,
But the young Vasily wasn't honored.
120   He spoke these words to his mother:
"Hail to you, my lady and mother,
The honorable widow, Avdotya Vasilyevna!
I'll go to the princes at their feast of honor."
       Avdotya Vasilyevna then spoke:
125   "Hail to you, my dear child,
My dear beloved child!
There's a place for an invited guest,
But there's no place for an uninvited guest."
       Vasily didn't listen to his mother,
130   He took his brave druzhina
And went to the prince at his feast of honor.
At the gate he didn't ask permission from the gatekeepers,
At the door he didn't ask permission from the doorkeepers,
He went straight to the dining hall.
135   He stepped with his left leg into the dining hall
And with his right leg behind the oaken table,

Behind the oaken table, into the icon corner,
And he moved toward the bench near the stove,
And Vasily shoved with his right hand,
140   With his right hand and with his right foot—
All the guests then stood near the stove.
And Vasily moved toward the bench near the door,
He shoved with his left hand and with his left foot—
Some guests then stood in the new vestibule.*
145   Other guests were frightened,
In fear they scattered to their homes.
And Vasily sat down behind the oaken table
With his brave druzhina.
        Everyone gathered again for the feast,
150   Everyone at the feast ate his fill,
Everyone at the feast of honor drank his fill,
And everyone at the feast burst out boasting.
        Kostya Novotorzhanin then spoke:
"There's nothing for me, Kostya, to boast about.
155   I was left very young by my father,
I was left very young and green.
Is that what I, Kostya, should brag about?
I'll strike a great wager with you—
My reckless head against all Novgorod,
160   Except for three monasteries:†
The Transfiguration of the Saviour,
The Mother, the Most Holy Mother of God,
And also the Smolensk Monastery."
        They struck a great wager,
165   And they wrote agreements,
And they put their hands to them,
And they bowed their heads over them.
"In the morning Vasily has to cross the Volkhov Bridge.
If Vasily is brought down before he reaches the bridge,
170   Then he can be executed,
His reckless head can be cut off.
If Vasily is brought down beside the bridge,

---

*Vasily pushes everyone out of the main hall into the vestibule.
†The singer should have had Vasily make this wager instead of Kostya.

Then he can be executed,
His reckless head can be cut off.
175 If Vasily is brought down in the middle of the bridge,
Then he can be executed,
His reckless head can be cut off.
But if Vasily passes through the third barrier,*
Then nothing more can be done to him."
180 And Vasily went home from the feast,
He came home cheerless and joyless.
And his devoted mother met him,
The honorable widow, Avdotya Vasilyevna:
"Hail to you, my dear child,
185 My dear beloved child!
Why are you coming home so cheerless and so joyless?"
Vasily Buslavyevich then spoke:
"I made a great wager with the men of Novgorod
To go in the morning to the Volkhov Bridge.
190 If I'm brought down before I reach the bridge,
If I'm brought down beside the bridge,
If I'm brought down in the middle of the bridge,
Then I can be executed,
My reckless head can be cut off.
195 But if I pass through the third barrier,
Then nothing more can be done to me."
When Avdotya Vasilyevna heard this,
She locked him up in an iron cage,
She propped up the iron doors
200 With his scarlet club.
And she filled a chalice with red gold,
A second chalice with pure silver,
A third chalice with fine pearls,
And she took them as gifts to the Prince of Novgorod
205 So that he would forgive her beloved son.
The Prince of Novgorod spoke:
"I'll forgive him when I cut off his head!"
Avdotya Vasilyevna went home,

---

*That is, if he crosses the whole bridge.

Sorrowful and sad she went,
210   She scattered the red gold and the pure silver
And the fine pearls through the open field.
She spoke these words herself:
"Neither the gold, nor the silver, nor the fine pearls
      are dear to me,
Dear to me is the reckless head
215   Of my beloved son,
The young Vasily Buslayev."
And Vasily was sleeping and couldn't wake up.
    When the men of Novgorod gathered in bunches,
They gathered in bunches and in crowds,
220   With their walking sticks,
They shouted at the tops of their lungs:
"Vasily, come across the Volkhov Bridge,
Keep our solemn agreements!"
    And Fomushka the Hunchbacked rushed forward,
225   He killed a force of a whole hundred,
And he killed a force of a second hundred,
And he killed a force of a third hundred,
He killed a force of almost five hundred.
In relief Potanyushka the Lame rushed forward,
230   And Kostya Novotorzhanin rushed forward.
    A servant, Vasily's washerwoman,
Was washing clothing on the Volkhov River,
And the yoke of the girl started jumping,
Then the yoke started swinging,
235   It killed a force of a whole hundred,
It killed a force of a second hundred,
It killed a force of a third hundred,
It killed a force of almost five hundred.
    And the servant rushed to the iron cage,
240   And she spoke these words herself:
"Hail to you, Vasily Buslavyevich!
You're sleeping, Vasily, and won't wake up,
But your brave druzhina
Is walking and roaming in blood up to its knees."
245   Vasily woke up from his sleep,
He spoke these words himself:

"Hail to you, my kind servant!
Please unlock the iron doors."
     When she unlocked the iron doors for him,
250   Vasily grabbed his scarlet club
And he went to the Volkhov Bridge,
He spoke these words himself:
"Hail to you, my kind and brave druzhina!
Now go and take a rest,
255   And now I'll play a little with these kids."
And Vasily started walking along the bridge,
And he started swinging his club.
Wherever he swung—a street would appear,
Wherever he swung again—a lane would appear.
260   And the men of Novgorod were lying in bunches,
They were lying in bunches and in crowds,
As though bad weather had struck the men down.
     And Vasily's sworn brother came to meet him,
In his hands he was carrying a stick of nine hundred poods,
265   And he spoke these words himself:
"Hail to you, my sworn brother!
Young rooster, don't flare up,
Don't attack your sworn brother!
Do you remember how we studied reading together?
270   At that time I was your big brother,
And now again I'll be your big brother."
     Vasily spoke these words:
"Hail to you, my sworn brother!
Did the devil bring you to meet me now?
275   We have something serious going on here.
Brother, we're playing for our heads."
     And his sworn brother got set
To strike Vasily's reckless head with a stick.
Vasily grabbed the stick with his right hand,
280   And he struck his brother with his left hand,
And he kicked him with his left foot.
The brother's soul was long departed.
And Vasily spoke these words himself:
"Not as to an old friend,
285   And not as to a sworn brother—

My brother came with a weapon on his shoulder."
And Vasily walked on along the bridge with the stick.
    And toward Vasily Buslayev
Came his godfather, the Elder Pilgrim.

290   A bell that weighed a thousand poods
                was on his reckless head,
A clapper that weighed five hundred poods
                was in his right hand.
The Elder Pilgrim spoke:
"Hail to you, my godchild!
Young rooster, don't flare up,

295   Don't attack your godfather!"
    And Vasily Buslavyevich then spoke:
"Hail to you, my godfather!
Did the devil bring you at this time
To confront your beloved godson?

300   We have something serious going on here.
Father, we're playing for our heads."
And he raised his stick that weighed nine hundred poods,
And he lashed his father's reckless head
So that the bell was shattered to pieces.

305   His godfather stood without flinching,
His yellow curls hadn't budged.
Vasily struck his godfather right between his eyes,
And he lashed his godfather
On his reckless head between his bright eyes.

310   And his bright eyes popped out like beer mugs.
And then Vasily attacked the stone houses.
    And the Mother, the Most Holy Mother of God,
Came from the Smolensk Monastery:
"Hail to you, Avdotya Vasilyevna!

315   Summon your dear child,
Your dear beloved child,
The young Vasily Buslayev.
At least he should leave some people for posterity."
    Avdotya Vasilyevna came out of her new vestibule,

320   She summoned her dear child.

23

Vasily Buslayev Travels to Jerusalem

*I*n the second bylina about Vasily Buslayev, a song that may be performed separately or as a shortened second episode in a composite work, he makes a trip to visit sacred places in the Holy Land. The epic may be called "Vasily Goes to Pray," "The Death of Vasily Buslayev," or "Vasily Buslayev Travels to Jerusalem" (Propp 1958b: 466–77). A certain amount of time has undoubtedly passed between the two episodes. Vasily tells his mother that he wants to travel to Jerusalem because the time has come for him to repent his earlier misdeeds, possibly an allusion to a life of fighting, killing, and robbery as a Viking-like *ushkuinik*. In this sense, the song hints at the theme of a repentant sinner. However, when Vasily asks his mother for her blessing, an obligatory request for a hero wanting to make a trip away from home, she either hesitates or refuses. In the translated variant, the mother reluctantly agrees but has a presage that Vasily will never return home alive. She knows her son's character well, realizes that he has not changed since childhood, and has doubts about his sincerity. Vasily sets out on a ship with his druzhina, and along the way he stops at the Saracen Mountain (also Mount Zion, Mount Favor, or Mount of Olives). There he comes across a skull that he abuses and that predicts his death. Going on to the Holy Land, Vasily performs the duties expected of a pilgrim, but he also bathes naked in the Jordan River, despite the warning of an old woman who also predicts his death. On the way home, Vasily stops at the same mountain but this time finds an enormous gravestone which he dares his druzhina to jump across. When he himself tries to jump lengthwise, he falls and dies.

The epic about Vasily Buslayev reflects pilgrimages that people of all classes in Kievan Rus made to Greece or to Palestine from the eleventh to the fourteenth centuries. Such pilgrims appear from time to time in Russian epics and in particular form the subject of the song entitled "Forty Pilgrims and One" (see the introduction to this last work). They wore simple but distinctive clothing, carried a staff, had no weapons, traveled in groups insofar as possible on foot, and took an oath to observe strict rules of conduct during the journey. Vasily does not travel as a pious pilgrim who lives simply and observes strict vows but, on the contrary, travels with his druzhina as though on a military expedition. The splendid description of Vasily's ship is more suitable to the song "Solovei Budimirovich," in which a rich suitor comes to Kiev in search of a bride. Particularly effective in the selected recording is the presentation of the ship returning with signs of mourning in a passage that is reminiscent of Theseus's return home to Athens after killing the Minotaur in Crete.

Despite the fact that Vasily performs the prescribed duties of a pilgrim in Jerusalem, he continues his youthful rebellious ways, and his character has changed little, if any, from the first song. Equally combative in the second song, Vasily may be regarded as committing three blasphemous acts, each of which represents a test. Vasily kicks the skull that he finds on Saracen Mountain and scoffs at it. The skull tells him that it used to be a better bogatyr than he is, that it was killed by the two-eyed Saracen-Chud, and that Vasily will die and lie in the grave beside the skull. The Saracen-Chud is always hostile to Russian heroes, the Chud being a Finno-Ugric people whose descendants still live today in northern Russia. Despite the warning of an old woman, Vasily bathes naked in the sacred River Jordan where John the Baptist baptized Jesus. At such accidental meetings in Russian epics, women may prophesy a hero's fate, one example of which occurs in the bylina "Dobrynya and the Dragon." And Vasily profanes a gravestone by trying to leap backward across its length. In regard to these three acts, his death may be considered punishment for his sacrilegious behavior and for his lack of faith in anything but himself.

However, as T.A. Novichkova (1989) points out, Vasily may also be confronting supernatural forces of which he is not only aware, but also tries to counteract. The "miraculous cross" that is visible from a distance but disappears when approached suggests something magical about the "world" he has entered. Dreams are usually prophetic in Russian epics, but when the skull on Saracen Mountain and the woman on the Jordan River relate their dreams and predict Vasily's death, he mocks them. In each case he also utters a charm, believing that in such a way he can ward away the "evil eye." And finally Vasily defies the ancient superstition that one should never disturb a grave. In effect Vasily challenges supernatural forces, especially the skull that symbolizes death, but he learns, just as the earlier bogatyr did, that he cannot escape death.

The second epic about Vasily Buslayev may be regarded as a logical continuation of the first, something that singers reveal by the way that they frequently combine the two subjects. The epic joins together medieval pilgrimages and Christianity in Kievan Rus with ancient pagan beliefs, which were to survive among Russian peasants into the twentieth century. The song contains a mixture of Christian and pagan elements, Vasily may make a trip to the other world or the world of the dead, and he undergoes three tests, each of which he fails before succumbing to a mysterious and perhaps supernatural death. Thus this song contains a number of obscure features, beliefs, and superstitions that do not lend themselves to a precise explanation.

N.E. Onchukov collected this variant of the song in 1902 from the singer P.G. Markov in a far northern area near the Pechora River.

✍ Vasily Buslayev Travels to Jerusalem ✍

Source: N.E. Onchukov, *Pechora Bylinas* (St. Petersburg, 1904), no. 89.

A white birch wasn't bending to the ground,
Pale leaves weren't spreading out,
Vasily was bowing to his mother,
He was bowing to her nimble feet,
5   He spoke these words himself:
"My darling lady and my mother,
The honorable widow, Amelfa Timofeyevna!
Please give me your solemn blessing,
Your solemn and eternal blessing,

10   From my reckless head to the damp earth.*
          I, Vasily, have to go to the city of Jerusalem
          To take a large offering,
          A large offering—forty thousand rubles."
                His lady and mother spoke,
15   The honorable widow, Amelfa Timofeyevna:
          "My darling, my dear child,
          Young Vasily, Buslav's son!
          The road to the city of Jerusalem isn't short,
          By indirect route you have to travel exactly three years,
20   By direct route you have to travel three months,
          On the straight-traveled path there's a swift whirlpool,
          There's a swift whirlpool and much piracy."
                His lady and his mother spoke,
          The honorable widow, Amelfa Timofeyevna:
25   "Whoever thinks of saving himself can save himself here,
          Many good youths have already gone there,
          The youths didn't return back home."
                Vasily bowed to her a second time:
          "My darling lady and my mother,
30   The honorable widow, Amelfa Timofeyevna!
          Give me your solemn blessing,
          Your solemn and eternal blessing,
          From my reckless head to the damp earth.
          I, Vasily, have to go to the city of Jerusalem,
35   To pray at the Holy of Holies,
          To kiss the Sepulcher of our Lord.
          In my youth I killed and robbed many people,
          Toward old age one has to save one's soul.
          There are thirty of us daring good youths,
40   We'll outrow the swift whirlpool,
          If there's much piracy, we'll pay our respects to it."
          Vasily's mother spoke,
          The honorable widow, Amelfa Timofeyevna:
          "Whoever thinks of saving himself can save himself here."
45   Vasily bowed a third time:

---

* The meaning of this line is not clear but may mean "from head to toe."

"My darling lady and my mother,
The honorable widow, Amelfa Timofeyevna!
If you give your blessing I'll go and if you don't I'll go,
I can't give up my brave druzhina,
50   I have thirty daring good youths."
      His lady and mother spoke,
The honorable widow, Amelfa Timofeyevna:
"Let there be a solemn blessing
For the young child, for Vasily,
55   For you, Vasily, to go to the city of Jerusalem,
To pray at the Holy of Holies,
To kiss the Sepulcher of our Lord,
Not to take a small offering,
Not a small offering, but forty thousand rubles."
60   Vasily started preparing himself,
Buslav's son started getting ready.
Vasily built a new scarlet ship,
The bow and stern were painted like wild animals,
The ship was decorated with the coils of a serpent,
65   The masts of the ship were made of cypress,
The rigging of the ship was made of white silk,
Not local silk, but Shemakhan silk,
The sails of the ship were made of white canvas,
The pennant on the ship was gilded,
70   The pennant had a value of fifty rubles.
The anchors of the ship were steel,
In place of eyes the ship was fitted
With stones, with precious stones.
In place of brows the ship was fitted
75   With sable furs, with black sable furs,
Not with local but with Siberian sable furs.
In place of the eyelashes the ship was fitted
With beaver pelts, with gray beaver pelts,
Not with local but with trans-Uralian pelts.
80   Vasily went to the scarlet ship
With all his brave druzhina,
They pulled up the oaken gangplank,
They stowed the gangplank along the deck of the ship,
They weighed the steel anchors,

85   They raised the thin canvas sails.
   Foma the Fat stood on the stern,
   And Kostya Nikitich stood on the bow,
   And Potanya the Little was handling the sails,
   Potanya was handling the sails,
90   Potanya was good at climbing the rigging.
    Whether they sailed for a long or a short time,
   They approached the Saracen Mountain,
   Vasily came on deck of the scarlet ship,
   Vasily glanced and looked at the steep mountain,
95   Vasily saw a miraculous cross,
   Vasily, Buslav's son, then spoke,
   Vasily spoke these words:
   "Hail to you, my brave druzhina,
   Thirty daring good youths!
100   Lower the canvas sails,
   Cast the steel anchors,
   Lay the gangplank with its end on shore.
   Brothers, let's disembark for the steep mountain,
   Let's pray to the miraculous cross and to God."
105   His druzhina didn't disobey him,
   They lowered the canvas sails,
   They cast the steel anchors,
   They laid the gangplank with its end on shore.
   Vasily disembarked on the steep shore,
110   Vasily set out for the steep mountain,
   Vasily couldn't find the miraculous cross,
   Vasily found only a dry bone,
   A dry head, a human bone,*
   Vasily kicked it with his right foot.
115   The head spoke, the human bone:
   "Vasily, don't kick me, the dry bone,
   The dry head, the human bone.
   As a youth I was better than you,
   Better than you and more than a match for you.
120   The Long-Skirted Saracen killed me,

---

*Skull would be a more exact word.

The Two-Eyed Chud killed me.
Vasily, you won't return to Holy Russia,
Vasily, you won't see your mother again,
The honorable widow, Amelfa Timofeyevna."
125   Vasily spat and uttered a spell:
"You were sleeping and saw your own fate in a dream."*
Vasily kicked the head a second time:
"Really head, is the devil stirring you up?
Is the devil stirring you up or is a demon speaking in you?"
130   Then the human head spoke:
"The devil isn't stirring me up, and a demon
   isn't speaking in me,
I was sleeping and I saw you in a dream.
Vasily, you're to lie with me in a single grave,
In a single grave on my right side."
135   Vasily set out for the scarlet ship,
Vasily came to the scarlet ship,
They pulled up the oaken gangplank,
They weighed the steel anchors,
They raised the canvas sails,
140   They set sail for the city of Jerusalem.
They entered the harbor for ships,
They lowered the thin canvas sails,
They cast the steel anchors,
They laid the gangplank with its end on land,
145   They went to the city of Jerusalem,
They entered God's church,
They prayed to the Lord God,
They kissed the Sepulcher of our Lord.
Vasily made his offering,
150   A large offering—forty thousand rubles.
   Vasily went to the River Jordan,
Vasily took off his colorful clothing,
He went into the River Jordan.
An old and aged woman came,
155   She spoke these words herself:

---

* The sense of these lines is that Vasily fears the influence of supernatural forces and tries to counteract them with a magical spell.

"Hail to you, Vasily, Buslav's son!
People here don't bathe in the River Jordan,
They only wash themselves in the River Jordan—
Jesus Christ Himself bathed in the River Jordan.
160   Vasily, you won't return to Holy Russia,
You won't see your own dear mother again,
The honorable widow, Amelfa Timofeyevna."
        Vasily spat and uttered a spell:
"You were sleeping and saw your own fate in a dream."
165   The old and aged woman spoke:
"I was sleeping, and I saw you in a dream."
        Vasily came out of the River Jordan,
Vasily put on his colorful clothing,
Vasily set out for his scarlet ship,
170   Vasily boarded his scarlet ship,
With all his brave druzhina,
They pulled up the oaken gangplank,
They stowed the gangplank along the deck of the ship,
They weighed the steel anchors,
175   They raised the thin canvas sails,
They set out sailing for their tsardom.
        Whether they sailed for a long or a short time,
They approached the Saracen Mountain,
Vasily came on deck of the scarlet ship,
180   He glanced and looked in all directions,
When Vasily saw the miraculous cross,
Vasily spoke these words:
"Hail to you, my brave druzhina!
Brothers, let's disembark for the steep mountain,
185   Let's pray to the miraculous cross and to God."
        All his brave druzhina didn't disobey him,
They lowered the thin canvas sails,
They cast the steel anchors,
They set out, the brothers, for the steep mountain.
190   They went to the steep mountain,
They approached the steep mountain,
They couldn't find the miraculous cross,
They found a gray grieving stone,
The stone was thirty elbows in width,

195 The stone was forty elbows in length,
  The stone was three elbows in height.
   Vasily, Buslav's son, then spoke:
  "Hail to you, my brave druzhina!
  Let's jump across the stone,
200 Let's jump forward and then jump back.
  One of us, Potanya, is small,
  Potanya is small and lame,
  He can jump forward but can't jump back."
  They jumped across the stone,
205 They jumped forward and jumped back.
   Vasily, Buslav's son, then spoke:
  "That's no honor or praise for a youth,
  That's no merit for a bogatyr.
  Let's jump the length of the stone,
210 Let's jump forward and then jump back.
  One of us, Potanya, is lame,
  He can jump forward but can't jump back."
   They jumped the length of the stone,
  They jumped forward and jumped back.
215 Vasily, Buslav's son, then jumped,
  But Vasily fell on his white chest,
  He fell and crushed his white chest,
  Vasily's tongue still moved in his head:
  "Hail to you, my brave druzhina!
220 Please make me a coffin of white oak,
  Find the dry human bone,
  Lay the bone with me in a single coffin,
  In a single coffin, on the right side."
   They made a coffin of white oak,
225 They found the bone, the human head,
  They wrapped it in white patterned silk,
  They laid them in the white coffin,
  They covered them with the coffin lid,
  They dug a deep grave for them,
230 They lowered them into the deep grave,
  They covered it with shifting yellow sand.
  At their nimble feet they placed a miraculous cross,
  On the cross they inscribed a learned inscription:

"Here lie two daring good youths,
235   Two strong and mighty Russian bogatyrs,
One is Vasily, Ignaty's son,*
The other is Vasily, Buslav's son,
The Long-Skirted Saracen killed them,
The Two-Eyed Chud killed them."
240   The druzhina went to the scarlet ship,
They pulled up the oaken gangplank,
They stowed it along the deck of the ship,
They weighed the steel anchors,
They took the pennant off the mast,
245   They took the bright eyes out of the ship,
They took off the black brows,
The master of the ship had passed away,
The very Vasily Buslayevich.
They raised the thin canvas sails,
250   They set out sailing for their tsardom.
        At that time Vasily's mother,
The honorable widow, Amelfa Timofeyevna,
Was waiting for Vasily Buslayevich,
She was looking through a spyglass.
255   The scarlet ship was sailing from beyond the sea,
The ship was not what it was before and not
                what it was of old,
There was no pennant on the ship,
There were no bright eyes on the ship,
There were no black brows on the ship.
260   Amelfa Timofeyevna wept,
She wept bitter tears.
"It's obvious there's no master on the ship,
No young Vasily Buslayevich."
        Vasily's mother set off walking,
265   The honorable widow, Amelfa Timofeyevna,
She went to God's church
To hold an honorable requiem
For the young Vasily Buslayevich.

---

*In the epic bearing his name, Vasily Ignatyev saves Kiev from a Tatar attack.

IV

EPICS WITH BIBLICAL
OR RELIGIOUS SUBJECTS

∼ 24 ∽

Tsar Solomon and Vasily Okulovich

his song represents an example of how written and oral traditions may interact. As Vs.F. Miller (1897–1924, 3: 174–202) and A.N. Veselovskii (1872) have shown in their comparative studies, a cycle of medieval apocryphal stories about the Biblical King Solomon, common in the Near East, Western Europe, and Russia, often consisted of two parts. The first involves Solomon's childhood and the building of the temple in Jerusalem, while the second concerns his marriage and the abduction of his wife. In Russian manuscripts composed in the seventeenth and eighteenth centuries, King Por or Kitovras may be Solomon's adversary. Although the written versions differ considerably in their details and some have been strongly influenced by oral versions, essentially Por abducts Solomon's wife Solomonida out of revenge because Solomon, before he married, had seduced Por's wife and had kept a token from her that he later sent to Por. The plot is further complicated by the fact that Solomonida may willingly contact Por and ask him to come for her. She drinks a potion that apparently causes her death, but Solomon, incredulous, tests her by branding her arm, receives no reaction, and only then buries her in a crypt from which Por takes her away and revives her. Solomon may send out scouts to find out where his wife is and, having located her, goes to the area with an army that he leaves nearby. Solomon may then go to his wife disguised as a pilgrim, but she recognizes him and reveals him to Por, who prepares to hang Solomon but grants him a last request to blow his horn three times at the gallows. Solomon's army responds to the signal, saves him, and hangs the offenders.

While many elements of the story about Solomon occur in the oral tales, ballads, and epics of various peoples, they have been transformed in the Russian oral epic, which relates only the abduction of Solomon's wife. This song, which has been termed a "bylina-novella" and whose origin has been ascribed to fourteenth-century Novgorod, has been recorded in more than fifty variants. Vasily Okulovich usually becomes Solomon's opponent, revenge is not mentioned as a motive, Vasily's "henchman" Tarakashka kidnaps Solomonida, and she is carried away by deceit after she has been given a sleeping potion. Only later, after becoming reconciled to her situation, does Solomonida deliberately betray her husband. The nickname of "Tarakashka," who does not appear in the written tales, comes from the word "cockroach" (*tarakan*), while his family name, "Zamoryanin," indicates that he is an overseas, or foreign, merchant.

To a considerable extent, the story about the abduction of Solomon's wife has been adapted to the language and poetics of the Russian epic. The song opens with a feast where Tsar Vasily Okulovich, just like Prince Vladimir in the epic "Dunai," complains that he alone is not married, describes an ideal bride, and asks for advice. Tarakashka responds and points out that the only suitable person is married but that he can abduct her from her husband. The depiction of Tarakashka's ship resembles the one in the epic "Solovei Budimirovich." Under the pretext of persuading Solomonida to inspect his goods and to allow them to pass customs, Tarakashka bribes her with gifts, lures her to his ships, gives her a "potion of forgetfulness," kidnaps her, and takes her to Vasily Okulovich, who promptly marries her. The conversion to a Kievan epic remains incomplete because no typical Russian heroes or figures are involved and the action does not occur in Kiev but in Jerusalem and in some other place, such as in Tsargrad, the Old Russian name for Constantinople.

Solomon in the Russian epic has preserved the features of the wise Biblical King Solomon; he interprets dreams, solves riddles, and predicts the future. Thus he explains Solomonida's dream, foretelling that she will be tempted by another man: "You were sleeping and also saw a dream." This passage is expressed more clearly in other variants than in the translated song. While Solomon is being taken to his execution, he foretells the fate of his enemies: "A steed is pulling the front wheels, / But why is the devil pulling the rear wheels?" This cryptic statement can be explained as follows: the front wheels represent Solomon himself (he is being carried by a steed), but the rear wheels symbolize Solomonida, Vasily Okulovich, and Tarakashka (they are being carried by the devil). The steed will take Solomon to safety, but the devil will take the others to their deaths. In the gallows scene, Solomon speaks allegorically about the approach of his army, a motif that is widespread in several traditions and genres.

Although Solomonida is an unfaithful wife who also betrays her religious faith, she basically is an adventuress who takes advantage of every situation (Putilov 1971a: 170–86). She is not a sorceress, but she is clever enough to be wary of the "wise and sly" Solomon and wants him executed immediately. Tarakashka tempts Solomonida to abandon her religion when he says "Our faith is better than yours, / On Wednesdays and Fridays we don't fast." Solomon, who is presented as a Russian Orthodox tsar, observes the customs of the Orthodox Church—Wednesdays and Fridays are fast days. Tarakashka emerges as a one of the most diabolic figures appearing in Russian epics.

The members of the expedition of B.M. and Iu.M. Sokolov recorded the song included in this anthology during an expedition to Karelia in 1927 from the singer I.V. Sivtsev. His variant is somewhat disjointed in the way that it abruptly moves from place to place and also in the way it omits details about Solomon's arrival near Tsargrad and about his disguise as a wandering pilgrim. On the other hand, Sivtsev includes a certain amount of humor, irony, and satire, especially in the comic scene where Solomonida hides her "lover husband" in a chest and sits on top of him.

---

๙ Tsar Solomon and Vasily Okulovich ๛

Source: Iu.M. Sokolov, *Onega Bylinas* (Moscow, 1948), no. 208.

In the glorious city of Tsargrad,
At the Tsar's, at Vasily Okulovich's,
A feast of honor was being held
For many princes and boyars,
5   For many Tatars and Ulans.*
The bright day was inclining toward evening,
The tsar had enjoyed himself well and thoroughly.
The tsar came forward and spoke:
"Many, many of you princes and boyars,
10   And all you strong and mighty bogatyrs,
And all you Tatars and Ulans,
All of you in Tsargrad are married,
The maids and widows have been given in marriage,
But I, the handsome Vasily, am still a bachelor.
15   Don't you know someone equal to me,
Someone equal and comparable to me?
In body she should be as graceful as a swan's wing,
Her walk should be like that of a doe with golden horns,
Her face should be like white snow,
20   Her brows should be like black sable,
Her eyes should be like those of a bright falcon—
There shouldn't be another such woman in this world."
All at the feast fell silent and just kept sitting,
The highest ranks hid behind the middle ones,
25   The middle ranks hid behind the lowest ones,
And the lowest ones had no answer for the Tsar.
Tarakashka Zamoryanin stood up
From behind the neighboring table,
He said this himself to the Tsar:

---

*A name for Tatar officials or dignitaries.

30 "Hail to you, my handsome Vasily Okulovich!
I've been far away beyond the blue sea,
There I saw the Tsaritsa Solomonida.
In body she's like a swan's wing,
Her walk is like that of a doe with golden horns,
35 Her face is like white snow,
Her eyes are like those of a bright falcon,
Her brows are like black sable—
There shouldn't be another such woman in this world."
  "You're stupid, Tarakashka Zamoryanin!
40 How can one take a wife from a living husband?"
  "I know how to take a wife away from a living husband.
Just build three scarlet ships,
Decorate the bows and sterns like a serpent,
Decorate the sides like a wild beast,
45 Put a cypress mast in each ship,
On the masts put birds of paradise
So that they would sing and perform tunes,
Would perform tunes from Jerusalem,
So that there would be amusement for Tsargrad,
50 So that the amusement would be regal,
So that it would cloud reason in a reckless head.
Also sir, you should give an order:
Put a cypress mast in each ship,
Cover each place for the eyes
55 With the whole fur of a Pechoran fox
And with the whole fur of a Siberian dog.
Also sir, you should give another order:
Brew a lot of the best vodka,
Brew a lot of sleeping potion,
60 And give me some scribes and accountants,
And give me some workers and entertainers
For the trip to Tsargrad.
I'll bring back Tsaritsa Solomonida."
Tarakashka soon got ready
65 And he set out for the blue sea.
  Near the city of Jerusalem
Solomon was leaving for the open field,
He had come to say goodbye to the Tsaritsa.

Then the Tsaritsa spoke these words:
70   "Hail to you, my wise Tsar Solomon Vataseyevich!
Last night I slept very little,
But in my dreams I saw very much.
From your garden, from your green garden,
A white swan was carried away.
75   Last night I slept very little,
I slept very little but saw very much in my dreams.
A barrel from Novgorod started rolling
And fell apart in the middle of a hut."
Solomon himself knew how to interpret dreams:
80   "You're beautiful, Tsaritsa Solomonida!
You were sleeping and you also saw a dream."
He said goodbye and rode to the open field.
Tarakashka took his honorable gifts,
He went to the Tsaritsa and paid his respects:*
85   "You're beautiful, Tsaritsa Solomonida!
Please accept these honorable gifts from me.
Give me some scribes and accountants
So that I can trade now in Jerusalem."
She gave him some scribes and accountants,
90   Tarakashka took them to the first ship,
He served them some sleeping potion.
Tarakashka took them to the second ship,
He served them some of the best vodka.
Then the scribes got drunk.
95   Tarakashka went to the Tsaritsa and complained:
"You're beautiful, Tsaritsa Solomonida!
You didn't give me either scribes or accountants,
You gave me tavern riff-raff.
It's as though they all had never drunk green wine,
100   They're lying around like peasant swine."
The Tsaritsa herself got up,
She took a force of nearly five hundred.
Tarakashka took her to the first ship,
He served her some of the best vodka.

---

*The singer might have explained that Tarakashka arrived with his ships in the "seaport" of Jerusalem.

105 Tarakashka took her to the second ship,
He served her some sleeping potion,
And then the Tsaritsa got drunk.
She spoke these words herself:
"Where is your ivory bed?
110 Where are your down featherbeds?"
Tarakashka took her to the third ship,
To the bedroom, to the dark bedroom.
Then the Tsaritsa fell asleep.
　　Tarakashka yelled in a shrill voice:
115 "Hail to you, my brothers and my workers!
Raise the linen sails
And quickly make a run to the blue sea."
They raised the linen sails,
They quickly made a run to the blue sea,
120 They soon were close to Tsargrad.
Then the Tsaritsa woke up,
She spoke these words herself:
"You're stupid, Tarakashka, merchant Zamoryanin!
If you're taking me for yourself, then I won't marry you,
(*Obviously he wasn't handsome . . .*)*
125 But if you're taking me for a friend, then I'll marry him."
　　"You're beautiful, Tsaritsa Solomonida!
I'm not taking you for myself but for my friend,
For the Tsar, for Vasily Okulovich.
Our faith is better than yours,
130 On Wednesdays and on Fridays we don't fast."
This faith pleased her very much.
　　They pulled into a harbor for ships,
Tsar Vasily Okulovich met them,
He took the Tsaritsa by her white hands,
135 He kissed her on her sweet lips,
They were taken to God's church,
And they were married as in that country,
And they started living and passing their lives together.
　　Tsar Solomon arrived from the open field—

---

*An inserted remark by the singer.

140   Tsaritsa Solomonida wasn't there.
              He collected one army of forty thousand
              And a second of forty thousand all in mail.
              Then the Tsar set out around the blue sea.
              He left his army in some nearby groves,
145   And he gave his army instructions:
              "Hail to you, my brothers and my warriors!
              When I'm close to death, to a quick death,
              Rescue me from a quick death!
              The first time I blow my aurochs' horn,
150   Quickly saddle your good steeds.
              The second time I blow my aurochs' horn,
              Quickly mount your good steeds.
              The third time I blow my aurochs' horn,
              Come to the gallows, to the oaken gallows."
155   The Tsar said goodbye and went to Tsargrad.
                  He came to the Tsaritsa and paid his respects:
              "You're beautiful, Tsaritsa Solomonida!
              Please give me some alms."*
                  The Tsaritsa spoke these words:
160   "I see that you're not a wandering pilgrim,
              I see that you're the wise Tsar Solomon Vataseyevich.
              Please come in my high palace,
              I'll give you something to drink and something to eat."
              Solomon entered the high palace,
165   She gave him something to drink, she fed him,
                    and she honored him greatly.
                  Vasily arrived from the open field,
              He rapped with the silver knocker.
              Then Solomon said these words:
              "You're beautiful, Tsaritsa Solomonida!
170   Where can I go hide now?"
                  She unlocked the double locks,
              She shoved in Solomon the Wise,
              She locked the double locks,
              And she sat down on the new chest.

---

*The singer forgot to describe how Solomon disguises himself as a wandering pilgrim.

175   She spoke these words herself:
        "My handsome Tsar Vasily Okulovich!
        Solomon said that he was sly and wise,
        But now no one is more stupid than Solomon,
        He's sitting under a woman's asshole."
180   "You're beautiful, Tsaritsa Solomonida!
        Please show me Solomon the Wise."
            She spoke these words herself:
        "Hail to you, wise Tsar Vasily Okulovich!
        Solomon is still sly and wise,
185   Please grant him a quick death."
            Then Solomon spoke these words:
        "My handsome Tsar Vasily Okulovich!
        Please don't execute me like a dog,
        Please execute me like a tsar,
190   Please set up oaken gallows for me in the field,
        Hang three silken nooses on it,
        A first noose made of black silk,
        A second noose made of white silk,
        A third noose made of red silk.
195   Put my reckless head in the first,
        Put my right hand in the second,
        Put my left hand in the third—
        That's the way they execute tsars like a tsar."
            They set up oaken gallows in the field,
200   They got into a carriage and rode off.
        Then Solomon spoke these words:
        "A steed is pulling the front wheels,
        But why is the devil pulling the rear wheels?"
        No one could guess the meaning of these words.
205   They arrived at the oaken gallows,
        Tarakashka, the merchant Zamoryanin, got out,
        Tsar Vasily Okulovich got out,
        Tsaritsa Solomonida got out,
        Solomon Vataseyevich got out,
210   And he spoke these words himself:
        "Hail to you, my handsome Tsar Vasily Okulovich!
        Let me blow my aurochs's horn one time."
            Then everyone at the gallows grinned:

"They told us that Solomon was sly and wise,
215   But now the time has come for Solomon to die,
And he wants to play for time before dying."
He blew his aurochs's horn the first time,
His whole army became alarmed,
The mother earth trembled awhile.
220   Vasily became afraid and scared:
"Hail to you, my wise Tsar Solomon Vataseyevich!
What's that stomping and jingling in the field?"
        "Don't be afraid, Vasily, don't be scared.
Out of my garden, out of my green garden,
225   A bird has flown in the dark forest,
It's beating its wings against the dark forest."
He blew his aurochs' horn a second time,
His whole army became alarmed,
All the mother earth trembled awhile.
230   Then Tsar Vasily Okulovich spoke these words:
"My wise Tsar Solomon Vataseyevich!
Is a steed stomping and jingling in the open field?"
        "Don't be afraid, Vasily, don't be scared,
You see my steeds, my steeds have left their stalls,
235   And they're only beating their hooves against
                the damp earth."
He blew his aurochs' horn a third time,
His whole army rushed around them,
Like gray wolves it dashed around them.
The army took down Solomon the Wise
240   From the noose on the oaken gallows.
Then they put Vasily Okulovich
In the noose made of red silk,
They put Tsaritsa Solomonida
In the noose made of black silk,
245   And they put in Tarakashka Zamoryanin.
*(If my father were alive, he would have sung the song
wonderfully! He learned the song from my grandfather,
Ivan Pavlovich, and perhaps from my great-grandfather
Pavel himself.)*

✌ 25 ✎

Forty Pilgrims and One

*T*he song "Forty Pilgrims and One" belongs to what are called "religious verses" (*dukhovnye stikhi*) in Russian (Selivanov 1995). These verses involve a variety of lyric and narrative genres devoted to religious themes, represent a mixture of written and oral features, and were created by several groups over a period of centuries. By the time they were first recorded in the beginning of the nineteenth century, they were performed mainly by wandering pilgrims (*kaliki perekhozhie*). They were often blind or handicapped, in many instances were organized into professional fraternities or guilds, roamed from holy place to holy place in Russia seeking alms, and performed their songs, especially on religious holidays, at churches, monasteries, and fairs. However, in medieval Rus from the eleventh to the fourteenth centuries, religious pilgrims comprised all classes, traveled to Tsargrad (Constantinople) or the Holy Land, as a rule formed groups that chose a leader for themselves (an *ataman*), and may have received special dispensations from the church (Liatskii 1912: iii–liv). During their journey, they accepted rules of conduct that subjected violators to severe punishment. Religious verses were derived in particular from the Bible, apocrypha, church writings, saints' lives, and legends.

The song "Forty Pilgrims and One" represents an example of a narrative religious verse that not only combines religious themes with the features of oral epics but also was performed by epic singers (Vs.F. Miller 1897–1924, 2: 211–55; B.M. Sokolov 1913). The song concerns pilgrims who, with their traditional garb, staff, and bag, make a trip to the Holy Land from Kievan Rus. While pilgrims occasionally appear, sometimes in disguise, in epics such as "Potyk," they are the central figures in this song, which has been recorded in forty-two variants. The work has been adapted to the Kievan cycle, much of the action takes place in or near Kiev, and Vladimir, Apraxia, Alyosha, Dobrynya, and sometimes Ilya Muromets appear among the characters. In some variants the pilgrims are portrayed as "mighty bogatyrs" who may demand alms in a terrifyingly shrill voice. The pilgrims may also have been bogatyrs who have killed and robbed much of their lives and who have decided to atone for their sins by making a pilgrimage to Jerusalem. The bylina "Vasily Buslayev Travels to Jerusalem" may perhaps be an example of such repentance.

In the translated variant nothing is stated about the background of the pilgrims except that they are somehow connected with two northern monasteries. Before leaving for the Holy Land, they choose Kasyan (or Mikhailo) as their ataman and take vows to observe strict behavior. On their way they meet Prince Vladimir and are sent by him to Princess Apraxia, who is called "Apraxevna" in the selected recording. She honors them with a feast but afterward asks Kasyan to spend the evening alone with her. After his refusal, she arranges for Vladimir's silver drinking goblet to be slipped into Kasyan's bag. Soon after the pilgrims leave, Alyosha and Dobrynya are ordered to search them, with the result that the goblet is discovered in Kasyan's bag and he is punished by being buried up to his shoulders. The other pilgrims complete their pilgrimage to the Holy Land, return to the same spot six months later, discover that Kasyan is still alive, and, because of this miracle, again accept him as their ataman. The pilgrims are invited to a feast by Prince Vladimir, who receives them and Kasyan warmly. After Kasyan learns that Apraxia has been afflicted with a putrid disease, he exorcises her ailment; she asks his forgiveness, and the pilgrims leave. Some variants relate how Apraxia visits Kasyan three times during the night, but her advances are rejected by him each time. Only in a few recordings does Apraxia develop a disease; and the song may end with Kasyan's execution or may continue when he is resurrected and rejoins his comrades for the journey. In some cases, Saint Nicholas comes to help the main character, as occurs in the songs "Sadko" and "Potyk."

The most obvious association of "Forty Pilgrims and One" is with the Old Testament story of Joseph, his temptation by the wife of Potiphar, and the planting of a cup in the bag of one of Joseph's brothers after they visit him at the Pharaoh's court. This represents a widespread story about a woman whose love is rejected and who in revenge accuses the person she has accosted of theft. Within the Russian tradition, two other possible sources also exist. The general theme about the pilgrimage in the Russian song, but not the temptation, has been ascribed to a legend inserted in one of the chronicles under the year 1163. The legend describes how forty pilgrims traveled from Novgorod to Jerusalem and brought home a chalice that became a sacred object in Rus. Pilgrimages to the Holy Land, especially from Novgorod, were common in the twelfth century, when the Crusaders ruled Palestine. The story inserted in the chronicles betrays some epic elements, indicating that it probably had already circulated in oral form. The "Life of Saint Mikhail the Monk," in which a Greek saint is tempted by a Muslim queen, was a common Slavic saint's life and has also been considered as a source of this song.

Although the place names vary considerably, those mentioned in the selected variant are historical in origin. The Yefimyev Hermitage represents the Savior's Yefimyev Monastery, which was located near the North Russian city of Vologda and existed from the fifteenth century through the seventeenth. The Bogolyubov Monastery was located near the city of Vladimir northeast of Moscow and was founded in the twelfth century.

Kasyan, whose name is rarely encountered in Russian, is the central person in this religious verse. Already at the feast with Apraxia he is depicted as a saint with rays streaming from his face as though from the sun. He endures his tribulations without complaint, miraculously survives after being buried in the ground for six months, and, with his breath or spirit, cleanses Apraxia both of her disease and of her sin. It should be mentioned that the Russian word *dukh* can mean spirit, breath, or smell, all of which are applicable in the passage where Apraxia's affliction is described and she is cured by Kasyan (lines 309 to 325). Kasyan lives up to the ascetic ideal of the wandering pilgrims and is rewarded for his zeal by being restored to life. Several other characters are briefly but succinctly portrayed. Apraxia is presented in a negative light, just as she is in the epics about Tugarin and Churila; Alyosha is petty and conniving; and Dobrynya behaves like a courteous diplomat.

The text selected for this anthology appears in the collection of Kirsha Danilov, was taken down in the middle of the eighteenth century in Western Siberia, and represents the oldest variant of this song.

❧ Forty Pilgrims and One ❧

Source: Kirsha Danilov, *Ancient Russian Poems* (Moscow, 1977), pp. 121–29.

From the Yefimyev Hermitage,
From the Bogolyubov Monastery,
Pilgrims were preparing to leave
For the holy city of Jerusalem,
5   Forty pilgrims and one.
They stood in a single circle,
They were thinking a single thought,
A single but deep thought,
They were choosing their senior ataman,
10   The young Kasyan, Mikhaila's son.
The young Kasyan, Mikhaila's son,
Laid down a solemn vow
For all those stout youths:
"We have to walk, brothers, the road isn't short,
15   We have to walk to the city of Jerusalem
To pray at the Holy of Holies,
To kiss the Grave of our Lord,
To bathe in the River Jordan,
To touch the Incorruptible Shroud.
20   We have to walk past towns and villages,
Past cities and their suburbs.
This is what the vow lays down:
'He who steals or he who lies,
Or he who gives in to lechery
25   And doesn't tell the senior ataman,
And the ataman finds out about this matter,
That one's to be left alone in the open field
And to be buried up to his shoulders in the damp earth.' "
And the vow was signed this way,
30   And white hands were laid upon it.
The ataman was Kasyan, Mikhaila's son,

The junior ataman was his dear brother,
The young Mikhaila Mikhailovich.
    The pilgrims started walking to the city of Jerusalem.
35   They had walked for an entire week,
They had walked for a long time,
They had already approached the city of Kiev,
Above the River Cherega.
On the islands, on the hunting islands,
40   Of Grand Prince Vladimir,
They came out of the dense forest,
Vladimir the Prince was coming toward them.
He was riding after game,
He was shooting geese, white swans,
45   And small migratory ducks,
He was chasing all the foxes and hares.
He happened to be riding nearby,
Then the wandering pilgrims saw him,
They stood in a single circle,
50   They stuck their sticks and staffs in the ground
And on them hung their bags.
The pilgrims shouted in shrill voices—
The mother damp earth shook,
The tops fell from the trees,
55   The steed under the Prince fell on its knees,
The bogatyrs fell off their steeds,
Spirya started shaking,
And Syoma started fidgeting.
    Vladimir the Prince barely roused himself,
60   He looked at the daring good youths,
They bowed to him,
To Grand Prince Vladimir,
They asked him for holy alms,
Something the youths could save their souls with.
65   Gracious Vladimir the Prince then answered them:
"Hail to you, my wandering pilgrims!
We have only the bread we brought with us,
I don't happen to have any money with me,
I, the Prince, am riding after game,
70   After hares and after foxes,

After sables and after martens,
And I'm shooting geese, white swans,
And small migratory ducks.
Please go to the city of Kiev

75   To my darling, Princess Apraxevna.
She's the daughter and princess of an honorable family,
She'll give you drink and food, good youths,
She'll provide you gold and silver for the road."
        The pilgrims didn't take counsel for long,

80   They started walking toward the city of Kiev.
They arrived in the city of Kiev,
In the middle of the Prince's courtyard
They stuck their sticks and staffs into the ground,
On them they hung their bags

85   And small pouches of patterned velvet.
The pilgrims shouted in shrill voices—
The tops came off the palaces,
The center beams fell from the halls,
Beverages were shaken in the cellars.

90   The pilgrims stood in a single circle,
They asked for holy alms
From the young Princess Apraxevna.
        The young Princess was frightened,
And she trembled terribly,

95   She sent the stewards and cupbearers
To invite the pilgrims into the bright hall.
Then the stewards and cupbearers came,
They bowed and paid their respects
To the young Kasyan Mikhailov

100   And to all his comrades,
And they asked them to come take bread in the bright hall
With the young Princess Apraxevna.
        Then Kasyan didn't disobey,
He went to the hall, to the bright hall,

105   They prayed to the Savior's image,
They bowed to the young Princess.
Having folded her arms as Turkish women do,
The young Princes Apraxevna
Was there with her nannies and her nurses,

110   And with her pretty servant girls.
       The young Kasyan, Mikhaila's son,
       Sat down in the place of honor.
       As though from the sun, from the bright sun,
       Great rays were streaming
115   From his youthful face.
       Then all the good youths,
       The wandering pilgrims,
       Were seated at the decorated tables.
       The stewards and the cupbearers
120   Were hurrying and urging on
       All their servants,
       They brought tasty dishes,
       They brought drinks of mead.
       The wandering pilgrims
125   Were sitting at the decorated tables,
       They quickly ate the tasty dishes,
       And drank the drinks of mead,
       And they sat for a time, an hour or two.
       During the third hour they got up,
130   Having gotten up, they prayed to God,
       They bowed in thanks for the hospitality
       To the young Princess Apraxevna
       And to all the stewards and the cupbearers.
       And then they still were expecting
135   That the young Princess Apraxevna
       Would provide them with gold and silver for the road,
       To go to the city of Jerusalem.
       But the young Princess Apraxevna
       Didn't have that in mind or thought.
140   She sent Alyosha Popovich
       To persuade their ataman
       And all the wandering pilgrims
       Not to leave on this day and on this date.
       Alyosha tried to persuade
145   The young Kasyan Mikhailovich to stay,
       Alyosha invited him to the Princess Apraxevna
       To stay with her for the long evening,
       To speak amusing words,

And to sit alone with her in her bedroom.
150   For the young Kasyan, Mikhaila's son,
His youthful heart grew troubled,
He refused Alyosha Popovich,
He wouldn't go for the long evening
To the young Princess Apraxevna
155   To speak amusing words.
        The Princess grew angry at this,
She sent Alyosha Popovich
To slit Kasyan's pouch of patterned velvet
And to shove in a silver goblet,
160   The goblet the Prince drinks from after coming home.
Alyosha was keen witted,
He unstitched the pouch of patterned velvet,
He shoved in the silver goblet
And sewed the pouch up smoothly
165   So that you couldn't see a thing.
        With this the pilgrims set out on their journey,
The pilgrims set out from the wide courtyard,
They didn't say goodbye to the young Princess,
The pilgrims walked and didn't look back.
170   They had gone about ten versts
From the capital city of Kiev,
The young Princess Apraxevna
Sent Alyosha in pursuit of them.
The young Alyosha Popovich
175   Overtook the pilgrims in the open field,
Alyosha had no inborn courtesy,
He started quarreling with the pilgrims,
He denounced them as thieves and robbers:
"Pilgrims, you roam through the Christian world,
180   You steal something and call it your own.
You've stolen from the Princess Apraxevna,
You've carried away a silver goblet,
The goblet the Prince drinks from after coming home!"
The pilgrims didn't allow him,
185   The young Alyosha Popovich,
They didn't allow him to search them.
The young Alyosha Popovich grumbled,

He set out riding to the city of Kiev
And thus he arrived in the capital city of Kiev.
190   At the same time and at the same hour
The Prince arrived from the open field
And with him the young Dobrynya Nikitich.
The young Princess Apraxevna
Summoned Dobrynya Nikitich,
195   She sent him after the pilgrims,
After Kasyan Mikhailovich.
Then Dobrynya didn't disobey,
He quickly rode to the open field,
Dobrynya had inborn and well-trained courtesy,
200   He overtook the pilgrims in the open field,
He dismounted his steed and bowed:
"Hail to you, Kasyan Mikhailovich!
Don't provoke the wrath of Prince Vladimir!
Order the wandering pilgrims to search each other
205   To see if there's someone stupid among you!"
The young Kasyan, Mikhaila's son,
Stood the pilgrims in a single circle
And he ordered them to search each other
From the youngest to the oldest,
210   From the oldest to the highest person,
To him, the young Kasyan Mikhailovich.
The goblet didn't turn up anywhere—
But it happened to be in the young Kasyan's possession.
His brother, the young Mikhaila Mikhailovich,
215   Carried out the solemn vow,
They buried the ataman up to his shoulders
in the damp earth,
They left him alone in the open field,
The young Kasyan Mikhailovich,
They returned the silver goblet
220   To the young Dobrynya Nikitich,
Then the young Kasyan Mikhailovich
Was written down as the guilty party.*

---

*Kasyan's name is written down to indicate the guilty person in a report to Prince
Vladimir.

Dobrynya set out riding to the city of Kiev,
And the pilgrims started walking to the city of Jerusalem.
225   The young Kasyan, Mikhaila's son,
Said goodbye to them, the pilgrims.
        When Dobrynya came to Kiev
To the young Princess Apraxevna,
He brought the silver goblet.
230   The guilty person was named—
The young Kasyan, Mikhaila's son.
From that time and hour the Princess fell sick
            with a bad affliction,
She was covered with large sores and took to her bed.
        The pilgrims were walking to the city of Jerusalem,
235   They walked ahead for three months.
When they came to the city of Jerusalem,
They prayed at the Holy of Holies,
They kissed the Grave of our Lord,
They bathed in the River Jordan,
240   They touched the Incorruptible Shroud,
And the youths accomplished everything.
They celebrated a mass with prayers
For their youthful well-being,
They each made a bow for Kasyan Mikhailovich.
245   Then the pilgrims didn't linger,
They started walking to the city of Kiev
And to the gracious Prince Vladimir,
And they walked back about two months.
They didn't happen upon that place,
250   They passed by a little to the side of him,
The young Kasyan Mikhailovich.
The sound of a soft voice reached them,
Then the pilgrims halted,
They tried to remember that place,
255   Little by little they advanced
And saw the young Kasyan, Mikhaila's son.
He waved with his arm and shouted with his voice.
The daring good youths approached him,
At first the ataman, his own brother,
260   Mikhaila Mikhailovich,

Then all came and bowed to him,
They greeted him.
Kasyan gave them his right hand,
And they kissed his hand,
265   They exchanged kisses with him,
And all went over to him.
        The young Kasyan, Mikhaila's son,
Sprang out of the damp earth,
Like a bright falcon out of a warm nest.
270   And they all, the youths, were amazed,
The good youths couldn't see
His youthful face,
His youthful curls reached to his very waist.
Kasyan wasn't there a short time—
275   He was in the ground six months,
And six months would be half a year.
        Then the pilgrims started walking to the city of Kiev,
To gracious Prince Vladimir.
They reached the miraculous cross of Lebanon,
280   They stood in a single circle,
They stuck their sticks and staffs in the ground,
And the pilgrims stood there quietly.
The young Mikhaila Mikhailovich
Ruled them again as their ataman,
285   He sent a quick young fellow
To report to Prince Vladimir:
"Would he invite us to come for dinner?"
Vladimir the Prince happened to be at home,
He sent his key keepers and chest keepers
290   To bow and greet the pilgrims,
The pilgrims were to come for dinner,
The young Kasyan in particular.
And then the key keepers and chest keepers
Came to the pilgrims and greeted them,
295   They bowed and asked them to come
                to the Prince's for dinner.
        The pilgrims came to the wide courtyard,
In the middle of the Prince's courtyard
Vladimir the Prince then greeted him,

The young Kasyan Mikhailovich.
300   Vladimir took him by his white hands
And led him into the bright hall.
      Then the young Kasyan Mikhailovich
Asked Prince Vladimir
About the young Princess Apraxevna:
305   "Hail to you, sir, Vladimir the Prince!
Is your Princess Apraxevna well?"
      Vladimir the Prince scarcely uttered a word:
"We haven't visited her for a week or two."
      The young Kasyan wasn't squeamish about that,
310   He and the Prince went to her bedroom,
The Prince walked and held his nose,
This meant nothing to the young Kasyan,
He wasn't afraid of any bad smell.
They opened the doors of the bright hall,
315   They threw open the windows with a wooden frame,
Then the Princess asked for forgiveness,
Because she had spoken false words.
The young Kasyan, Mikhaila's son,
Blew with his holy breath
320   On the young Princess Apraxevna,
Her smell and vileness were no more,
Kasyan protected her with his holy hand,
He forgave the sins of her female flesh,
She had wanted to sin and she had suffered,
325   She had lain in shame for half a year.
      The young Kasyan, Mikhaila's son,
Went to Prince Vladimir in the bright hall,
He prayed to the Savior's image
With his wandering pilgrims,
330   They sat down at the decorated tables,
They started drinking and eating and enjoying themselves.
When the middle of the day had come,
The pilgrims had drunk their fill,
Drunk their fill and eaten their fill.
335   Vladimir the Prince was very sad,
The pilgrims were getting ready for their trip,
Vladimir the Prince then asked them

To stay and to remain awhile that day with him.
The young Princess Apraxevna

340 Had shed her scabs and vileness.
Soon she cleaned herself up,
She cleaned herself up and dressed,
Then she came to them at the table
With her nannies and nurses

345 And with her pretty serving girls.
She greeted the young Kasyan
Without disgrace and without shame,
But she kept her sin in mind.
    The young Kasyan, Mikhaila's son,

350 Waved his right hand
Over the tasty dishes,
He protected and blessed the meal with a sign of the cross.
They drank and ate, and they amused themselves.
    Then the young Kasyan, Mikhaila's son,

355 Took a little book* out of his bag,
He looked and showed the date and said:
"Brothers, we've been eating and drinking
    and enjoying ourselves,
The third day is already coming to an end,
And it's time for us youths to go on our way."

360   The pilgrims stood up on their nimble feet,
They prayed to the Savior's image
And bowed to Prince Vladimir
And to the young Princess Apraxevna
For their hospitality,

365 And the pilgrims said goodbye to Prince Vladimir
And to the young Princess Apraxevna.
They got ready and set out on their way
To the Bogolyubov Monastery
And to the Yefimyev Hermitage.

370   This was the old song, and these were the deeds.

---

*The little book was probably a diary or chronicle about the pilgrimage.

~ V ~

HISTORICAL SONGS OF THE SIXTEENTH CENTURY

❧ 26 ❧

Ivan the Terrible and His Sons

*T*he work "Ivan the Terrible and His Sons," or, as it may also be called, "The Wrath of Ivan the Terrible Against His Son," is an example of the genre called the "historical song," which emerged toward the end of a creative epic tradition and became fully developed in the sixteenth century (Putilov 1960; Sokolova 1960; Stief 1953). A cycle of such songs is devoted to the reign and personality of Ivan IV, also known as Ivan the Terrible, who ruled Muscovite Russia from 1533 to 1584 and, in 1547, was the first grand prince to be crowned tsar. The epithet "terrible" at the time indicated respect rather than fear; in songs, Ivan the Terrible is often addressed simply as "Ivan Vasilyevich." All the main characters in this work were historical in origin. Ivan the Terrible had two sons, named Ivan and Fyodor; their mother, Anastasia Romanovna, was the tsar's first wife, whom he married in 1547. Nikita Romanovich was her brother; he was an important adviser at court and belonged to the Romanov family, one of whose members, Mikhail, was elected tsar in 1613 at the end of the Time of Troubles (1598–1613). Malyuta Skuratov was one of the leaders of the *oprichnina,* a separate state administration that Ivan the Terrible created in 1565 to deal with suspected "treachery" or internal resistance to his rule, especially by the boyars or older aristocracy. The members of the oprichnina numbered several thousand, wore black clothing, and carried a broom as a symbol that they were "sweeping away treachery." Today one might apply the term "secret police" to describe the oprichnina, which conducted a reign of terror against the population until the organization was abolished in 1572.

The approximately seventy recorded variants of the song can be divided into three basic versions. The first, "extensive version," one example of which has been translated here, presents a broad political picture of

358 HISTORICAL SONGS OF THE SIXTEENTH CENTURY

the time and concentrates on an accusation of treachery involving the two sons, Ivan and Fyodor. The second, "short version" focuses on one son, usually Fyodor, whose mere report about treachery provokes the tsar's wrath. The third and least common "special version" presents other motivations for the conflict between the tsar and his son.

Some variants of the first version open with a lyrical introduction that mentions how Ivan was crowned tsar and refers to the capture of the Tatar cities of Kazan (1552) and Astrakhan (1556) east of Moscow on the Volga River. Many recordings open directly with a feast at which Ivan boasts about how he has eradicated "treachery" from the cities of Pskov and Novgorod and soon will do so in Moscow. Although other cites may be mentioned, Novgorod is the central one because in 1570 the tsar carried out a punitive expedition to the city, killing many inhabitants among all levels of the population, exiling many to distant parts of Russia, and bringing others to Moscow, where they were tortured to reveal the names of alleged collaborators. Several hundred people were publicly executed later that year in Moscow. In the sixteenth century, Pskov and Novgorod, located in the northwestern border area south of present-day St. Petersburg, had close relations with the then large and influential state of Lithuania. Ivan the Terrible suspected particularly Novgorod of treacherous dealings with Lithuania.

In most variants, Ivan the Terrible's son Ivan denounces his brother Fyodor at a feast for protecting people instead of killing them in Novgorod. The Tsar immediately orders Malyuta Skuratov to execute Fyodor for treachery. At this point the song diverges from historical facts. While it is correct that the Tsarevich Ivan and Malyuta took part in the ravage of Novgorod, Fyodor was only thirteen at the time and did not participate in the expedition. The singer of the selected song also somewhat confuses the relative ages of the two sons, Ivan actually being the older and Fyodor the younger. Furthermore, Fyodor, just as he is depicted in the song, was known for his piety and his passivity both before and while he was tsar from 1584 to 1598. Another fictitious element concerns the sons' mother Anastasia Romanovna, who could not have interceded for Fyodor because she died in 1560, ten years before the events in Novgorod. Her brother Nikita Romanovich, on the other hand, was influential as an adviser to Ivan the Terrible and later as a regent for Fyodor. Nikita Romanovich appears in other historical songs about this epoch, particularly in "Kostryuk," and is an idealized father figure and wise counselor.

The execution scene may be treated in various ways by singers, who may or may not state that the tsar demands tangible proof of the execution. Thus Nikita may offer a groom as a substitute victim, or he may kill Malyuta Skurlatov, whom the singer in the translated variant may call Malyuta Skurlatovich. The final scene at church during state mourning for the supposedly executed Fyodor shows Ivan the Terrible repenting his action and then rejoicing that his son is alive. Especially effective is the passage where Nikita and Fyodor come dressed in colorful clothes while everyone else wears black. Nikita is well aware of Ivan the Terrible's sudden shifts of mood and chooses his words carefully to tell Ivan that his son is still alive. No information has been found to confirm the existence of "Mikita's estate," which Nikita Romanovich requests at the end as a reward, but the estate would appear to be a refuge, perhaps for people fleeing from persecution by the oprichnina. However, in the middle of the sixteenth century there existed the so-called "Tarkhan deeds," according to which some feudal lords were allowed to collect taxes and to conduct their own judicial court independently of the state.

Although in the past most investigators considered that the song "Ivan the Terrible and His Sons" was directly connected with the fact that the tsar killed his son Ivan in a rage in 1581, more recently V.Ia. Propp (1958a) and B.N. Putilov (1960: 198–218) have pointed out inconsistencies in this interpretation. Although it is true that the son Ivan supported the policies of his father and took part in the devastation of Novgorod, the son Fyodor did not. Consequently, the key episodes about the denunciation and execution of Fyodor are fictitious. Even within the context of the song itself, Ivan the Terrible does not personally kill his son, Tsaritsa Anastasia Romanovna saves her son, and in the end father and son are reconciled. Furthermore, the work focuses on the suspicious atmosphere and the preoccupation with treachery that reached its height during the time of the oprichnina from 1565 to 1572, whereas the Tsarevich Ivan was killed later, in 1581. Although this song mirrors many historical events, realia, and personages, at its basis nevertheless lies an imaginative work of oral literature that poetically generalizes and interprets a particular period in Russian history.

The song "Ivan the Terrible and His Sons" shares several features, stylistic elements, and the long epic line with the bylina. The opening feast, boasting, description of Anastasia Romanovna rushing through Moscow, and Nikita Romanovich's hasty ride to the spot of the execution constitute traditional pattern scenes in epics. In addition, the con-frontation of father and son is a common subject in epics; Anastasia Romanovna also corresponds to an "epic mother." The presence of such characteristics to some extent can be explained by the fact that a majority of the recordings have been taken down from epic performers in far northwestern Russia, where the epic tradition was still viable at the end of the nineteenth century and beginning of the twentieth. De-spite such shared features, "Ivan the Terrible and His Sons" essentially does not represent an epic but a historical song, which differs in sev-eral ways from epics and injects a new content into the old epic form. The recent rather than the distant past is depicted, actual historical people are involved rather than bogatyrs, and the story in part concerns the devastation of a Russian city by a Russian ruler rather than a battle with an invading enemy force. Ivan the Terrible, unlike Prince Vladi-mir in epics, is an energetic and decisive leader; the plot is also much more terse and concentrated than usually is the case in an epic. Besides this, the political atmosphere of the 1560s and 1570s and the psycho-logical state of Ivan the Terrible occupy a central place in this many-faceted song. The result is a remarkable achievement of oral poetry that provides an insightful study into Ivan the Terrible's complex and contradictory character, showing how he impulsively shifted from rage to repentance and from despair to joy.

P.N. Rybnikov collected this song in the 1860s from Vasily Lazarev in Olonets Province.

✨ Ivan the Terrible and His Sons ✨

Source: P.N. Rybnikov, *Songs,* vol. 2 (Petrozavodsk, 1990), no. 109.

When the Terrible Tsar Ivan Vasilyevich ascended
   the throne,
Then he captured famous Pskov,
He captured Pskov and also Novgorod,
And he burst out bragging at a feast:
5   "I banished treachery from Pskov,
And I banished treachery from Novgorod,
But treachery must still be banished from stone Moscow."
   His younger son then spoke to him,
The young Ivan Ivanovich:
10   "Father, you've bragged in vain,
You didn't banish treachery from Pskov,
You didn't banish treachery from Novgorod,
You can't banish it from stone Moscow.
You're eating and drinking with treachery,
15   And you're been taking council with it at the same table."
   Ivan Vasilyevich then screamed:
"Bring treachery before my eyes,
But if you don't bring treachery before my eyes,
I'll chop off your reckless head,
20   I won't let you live even one short hour."
   Then Ivan grew thoughtful:
If he would speak against a prince or boyar,
He would spill blood in vain,
But he had to speak against his own dear brother,
25   Against the younger Fyodor Tsarevich:
"Terrible Tsar Ivan Vasilyevich!
Whichever streets* you rode by, father,
In those streets not even a chicken was left alive.

---

*Novgorod was divided into administrative units called "streets" and "ends."

And whichever streets Malyuta Skurlatovich rode by,
30   In those streets not even a chicken was left alive.
But whichever streets Fyodor Ivanovich rode by,
He closed them off with iron gratings,*
And he signed announcements
That the streets had been executed and destroyed,
35   But those streets remained unexecuted and undestroyed."
The Terrible Tsar Ivan Vasilyevich screamed:
"Where are my merciless executioners?
Take the young Fyodor Tsarevich,
Lead him beyond the Moscow River
40   To the linden block, to the sharp saber."
Malyuta, the son of Skurlata, took him
Beyond the Mother Moscow River
To the linden block, to the sharp saber.
A white doe wasn't running through the city,
45   The faithful tsaritsa† was running
In a thin white nightgown without a belt,
Without shoes and only in stockings,
To her own dear brother,
To Prince Nikita Romanovich.
50   Prince Nikita Romanovich was sitting at table.
He was sitting and eating a meal,
He spoke these words himself:
"What are you here for, uninvited guest?"
And she spoke these words:
55   "You, my own dear brother,
Prince Nikita Romanovich!
The early morning dawn has gone out,
Our bright sun has dimmed!
Malyuta, the son of Skurlata, has led
60   Young Fyodor Tsarevich beyond the Moscow River
To the linden block, to the sharp saber,
To chop off his reckless head."
Prince Nikita Romanovich

---

*Although the meaning of the line is not clear, it appears that Fyodor barricaded some "streets" so that the people living there would not be touched.
†Anastasia Romanovna, Ivan's first wife.

Jumped up from behind the oaken table,
65   He jumped across the oaken table,
He pulled his shoes on his bare feet,
He threw his hat on one ear,
He grabbed his marten coat by a sleeve,
He ran to the stableyard,
70   He took the very best steed,
He mounted it unbridled and unsaddled,
He started riding through the city beyond the Moscow River.
     He shouted at the top of his lungs and waved his hat:
"Stop, people, stand aside,
75   Clear the path, clear the wide road,
For me to ride beyond the Mother Moscow River,
To the linden block, to the sharp saber."
     And he shouted across the Moscow River
          to Malyuta Skurlatov:
"Dog, you've bitten off more than you can chew,
80   You'll choke on what you're eating!"
     Malyuta's heart then sank,
His right arm froze,
His left leg started shaking.
The prince came to the linden block, to the sharp saber,
85   He dismounted his good steed,
He lifted the young Fyodor Tsarevich
From the linden block by his right hand,
He kissed him on his sweet lips,
And he gave up to Malyuta Skurlatov
90   His beloved groom,
Who was face for face and shoulder for shoulder
And hair for hair matched with Fyodor Tsarevich.
     Ivan Vasilyevich tolled the mourning bell,*
So that everyone would go to church in black clothes.
95   Prince Nikita Romanovich
Dressed himself and his nephew
In clothes finer than those of everyone else.
He approached the Terrible Tsar Ivan Vasilyevich,

---

*After a rapid transition in time and place, the song shows how Ivan the Terrible has arranged state mourning for Fyodor.

He bowed to him and greeted him:
100 "Greetings, Terrible Tsar Ivan Vasilyevich,
Together with your beloved family,
And with two bright falcon-sons,
And with all the princes and boyars!"
The Terrible Tsar Ivan Vasilyevich spoke:
105 "Prince Nikita Romanovich!
Before you were an old friend to me,
Now you've become an old cur to me.
Don't you know the misfortune hanging over me,
Don't you know the misfortune, or are you mocking me?"
110 Nikita Romanovich then spoke:
"Will there be forgiveness for the guilty person?"
The Terrible Tsar Ivan Vasilyevich then spoke to him:
"I'd be glad to forgive him, but he's no longer alive!"
Nikita Romanovich revealed
115 The young Fyodor Tsarevich:
"Here's your own dear son,
The young Fyodor Tsarevich."
"Prince Nikita Romanovich!
Before you were an old friend to me,
120 But now you're my dear father.
Do you want cities and their suburbs
Or countless treasure of pure gold?"
Prince Nikita Romanovich spoke to him:
"I don't want cities and their suburbs,
125 I have enough treasure for myself.
Give me Mikita's estate,
So that Mikita's estate would be known
From now on and forever:
Whoever steals a steed and escapes to my estate—
130 God will forgive him;
Whoever makes off with another's wife
and escapes to my estate—
God will forgive him;
Whoever kills a person and escapes to my estate—
God will forgive him."
135 Then the Terrible Tsar gave him the estate
That he wanted.

✺ 27 ✺

Kostryuk

*T*he song "Kostryuk" is another example of the genre called historical song, which fully emerged in the sixteenth century and initially reflected events during the reign of Ivan IV (Putilov 1960: 144–70; Sokolova 1960: 37–48). He ruled Muscovite Russia from 1533 to 1584, is also known as Ivan the Terrible, and in folklore is often addressed as "Ivan Vasilyevich" (see the introduction to the song "Ivan the Terrible and His Sons"). The main figures appearing in "Kostryuk" are historical in origin. In 1561 Ivan IV married his second wife, Marya Temryukovna, who was the daughter of a Kabardinian or Circassian prince, the Kabardinans being a people that lived in the northwestern Caucasus. One of her brothers, Mikhail, came with her to the wedding in Moscow, where he stayed, became a member of court, served in the oprichnina, and was executed in 1571. A second brother, Mamstryuk, from whom the name "Kostryuk" in the song is derived, came to Moscow after the wedding in 1565 but visited only for a short time. Nikita Romanovich, who is depicted in songs about this period as a "wise counselor," was the brother of Ivan's first wife, Anastasia, who died in 1560. Although some investigators have tried to connect the main event in "Kostryuk" with Mamstryuk or with other historical figures later in the seventeenth century, most folklorists believe that the episode was fictitious and that no specific person or occasion was involved. The song "Kostryuk," which has been collected over one hundred times in many parts of Russia, exists in a less common "epic version" and in a more popular "historical version." A variant of the historical version has been chosen for translation.

The historical song "Kostryuk," similarly to "Ivan the Terrible and His Sons," contains elements from the older Kievan epic. Traditional epic motifs or pattern scenes such as bride taking in a foreign land, a feast at court where one person refuses to take part, a challenge to a fight by a foreign adversary, the appeal for a bogatyr to defend a Russian city, and the duel itself are examples. However, the way these features are treated and the outcome of the fight differ greatly from those in such a heroic epic as "Ilya Muromets and Kalin Tsar." Unlike Prince Vladimir, who is fainthearted in dealing with Kalin Tsar, Ivan the Terrible is master of the situation. Although Ivan sends a group to Lithuania to obtain a bride by force, in Russian epics Lithuania is often depicted as a foreign country in general rather than any particular place. Furthermore, other variants of "Kostryuk" may instead mention the Golden Horde, that is, the Tatars on the Volga. The ensuing banquet held in honor of Marya Temryukovna's brother really represents a wedding feast where, in some recordings, Kostryuk may be much more menacing and may threaten to reimpose Tatar rule over Moscow. In the translated variant, after Kostryuk makes his challenge for a wrestling match, Ivan, rather than getting involved himself, asks his brother-in-law Nikita Romanovich to make a public appeal for someone to wrestle with Kostryuk. At this point in a Kievan epic, one would expect that a lone bogatyr would come forward to defend the city and Russian honor, but in "Kostryuk" two lower-class antiheroes appear, one small and the other lame. They cautiously ask whether they would be punished if they harm the tsar's brother-in-law, but Nikita gives them no definite answer. As usually would be the case in an epic, Kostryuk wants to fight to the death, but the unassuming pair of Russian challengers insists on a less drastic condition—the victor will strip the defeated person naked and shame him publicly. Depending on the recording, the fight, a traditional and sometimes ritualistic wrestling match, may be described in more or less detail, but the outcome is always the same—Kostryuk loses and is disgraced. In the ending, Marya Temryukovna may complain to Ivan the Terrible about the treatment of her brother, who then leaves Moscow in great bitterness. Thus the historical song "Kostryuk" in several ways deliberately parodies a heroic epic by lowering the tone and by inverting typical epic features. In a broader sense, this work can be interpreted as a parodistic farewell to the period of the Tatar yoke in Russian history.

As several musicologists and folklorists have pointed out, the melody as well as the distinctive "playful" performance manner often associated with "Kostryuk" also contribute to its innate humorous quality. However, "Kostryuk" is not an isolated instance of such satiric, comic, or grotesque treatment of a subject in Russian folklore; it is connected with a diverse group of satirical songs, such as the nebylitsa or the skomoroshina, that are usually connected with the skomorokhs (Ivleva 1972). The fact that "Kostryuk" is composed in the short epic line rather than in the long line used in most bylinas also emphasizes the distinctive character of the work (Bailey 1978: 92–94). The song about Kostryuk represents an imaginative combination of elements from a Kievan epic, history of the sixteenth century, and low comedy.

The variant selected for translation was collected by A. Kharitonov in Shenkursk District of Archangel Province and was first published in P.V. Kireevskii's collection.

✎ Kostryuk ✎

Source: Songs, Collected by P.V. Kireevskii, vol. 6 (Moscow, 1864), pp. 138–43.

    In our Holy Russia,
In Holy Russia, in stone Moscow,
There lived, there was a Tsar, Ivan Vasilyevich.
Tsar Ivan Vasilyevich wanted to get married,
5   In the distant Lithuanian land,
To Marya Temryukovna, to the daughter
Of the Lithuanian king.
Tsar Ivan collected his mighty army,
He sent it to the Lithuanian land.
10   The army went to the Lithuanian land,
The army took away Marya Temryukovna,
And to boot took three hundred Tatars.
Kostryuk-Mastryuk set out riding,
Temryuk's son set out riding,
15   The young Circassian.
    The young people arrived in stone Moscow,
Tsar Ivan Vasilyevich held

A feast of honor for his brother-in-law,
For Kostryuk-Mastryuk, Temryuk's son.
20 Kostryuk-Mastryuk sat at table,
He didn't eat any food, he didn't drink any beer or mead,
He didn't take any green wine,
He didn't carve the white swan,
He held a grudge against someone.
25 Tsar Ivan Vasilyevich then spoke:
"Hail to you, Kostryuk-Mastryuk,
Hail to you, Temryuk's son,
Young Circassian!
Why aren't you eating any food?
30 Why aren't you drinking any beer or mead?
Why aren't you taking any green wine?
Why aren't you carving the white swan?
Do you hold a grudge against someone?"
Kostryuk-Mastryuk then answered:
35 "Terrible Tsar Ivan Vasilyevich!
I'm not eating any food,
I'm not drinking any beer or mead,
I'm not taking any green wine,
I'm not carving the white swan,
40 Because I hold a grudge against you.
I want to ask you, Tsar,
Whether you have in stone Moscow
Any skillful wrestlers
To wrestle like a Tatar
45 With Kostryuk-Mastryuk,
With the Tsar's own brother-in-law?"
Tsar Ivan Vasilyevich then spoke:
"Hail to you, my uncle,
Dear Nikita Romanovich!
50 Uncle, please go
To the main porch,
Stand on the gray grieving stone,
Start shouting, Uncle,
As long as your reckless head can,
55 So that they'll hear you in stone Moscow.
Ask for a wrestler,

We need a wrestler
To wrestle like a Tatar,
With Kostryuk-Mastryuk,
60   With my own brother-in-law."
     His uncle went out,
Dear Nikita Romanovich,
To the main porch,
His uncle climbed up
65   On the gray grieving stone,
His uncle started shouting
As loud as his reckless head could
So that they'd hear him in stone Moscow.
From a tiny little hut,
70   From a tiny little courtyard
Ran two young fellows:
Vasenka the Little
And Potanyushko the Cripple.
They ran, these fellows,
75   To the sovereign's palace,
To the main porch.
     Vasenka then spoke,
Vasenka the Little spoke:
"Hail to you, dear Uncle,
80   Dear Nikita Romanovich!
What do you need, dear Uncle,
What are you asking for, dear Uncle?"
     "Hail to you, my Vasenka,
Hail to you, my Vasenka the Little!
85   We need a wrestler
To wrestle like a Tatar
With Kostryuk-Mastryuk,
With the Tsar's own brother-in-law."
     "Nikita Romanovich!
90   How can you wrestle with him?
He's the Tsar's own brother-in-law,
The Tsar mustn't have anyone to blame."
     The uncle answered,
Dear Nikita Romanovich:
95   "If only God would help,

No blame would be placed upon you!"
    They told Kostryuk at table,
They told Mastryuk at table:
"The Tsar has a wrestler outside!"
100   Kostryuk jumped up from the table,
He ran outside,
He ran to wrestle,
He kicked a bench with his foot.
    His sister spoke to him,
105   Marya Temryukovna:
"Hail to you, my brother,
Hail to you, Kostryuk-Mastryuk,
Hail to you, Temryuk's son,
Young Circassian!
110   Don't go wrestle!
Your first misfortune is—
You jumped up rudely from the table,
You kicked the bench with your foot."
Kostryuk-Mastryuk didn't listen,
115   He ran outside,
He ran to wrestle.
    Vasenka was walking around,
Vasenka the Little was strolling around:
"Hail to you, Kostryuk-Mastryuk,
120   Hail to you, Temryuk's son,
Young Circassian!
How will we wrestle?
For our reckless heads
Or for our colorful clothing?"
125   Kostryuk-Mastryuk then spoke:
"We will wrestle
For our reckless heads!"
    Vasenka said to him:
"I don't want to wrestle with you
130   For our reckless heads:
You're the Tsar's own brother-in-law,
The Tsar mustn't have anyone to blame.
We will wrestle
For our colorful clothing.

135   The one who wins
    Can strip the other,
    Can let the other go in shame."
        Vasenka grabbed Kostryuk,
    Vasenka threw Kostryuk against the ground,
140   Vasenka pressed him to the ground with his knee,
    He stripped Kostryuk,
    And let him go naked in shame.
        Kostryuk-Mastryuk then ran
    To the sovereign's palace,
145   He, the wretch, then tried to cover his shame.
    His sister ran to meet him,
    She carried colorful clothing.
        Kostryuk then dressed himself,
    He got ready to leave Moscow:
150   "Tsar Ivan Vasilyevich!
    We don't do things that way at home,
    We don't wrestle that way at home,
    In Moscow the one who wins
    Can strip the other
155   And can let him go in shame,
    In ridicule before honest people!"
        The Terrible Tsar then said,
    Tsar Ivan Vasilyevich:
    "Don't be angry, Kostryuk-Mastryuk,
160   This wasn't ordered by me,
    My uncle ordered this,
    My dear Nikita Romanovich."
        "Thanks to you, my brother-in-law,
    Tsar Ivan Vasilyevich,
165   In your stone Moscow!
    God forbid that I stay any longer
    In your stone Moscow,
    Neither I nor my children!"

❧ VI ❧
SKOMOROSHINA

28

Agafonushka

*A*ppearing only in the eighteenth-century collection of Kirsha Danilov, the song "Agafonushka" contains several parodic, satiric, and humorous inversions of epics, most of which were recorded later as separate short works. The title is an affectionate form of the masculine name Agafon, which in the past was a fairly common Russian name. B.M. Dobrovolskii and V.V. Korguzalov (1981: 594–95) have divided this "anti-epic" into two broad sections: (1) lines 1–47, consisting of several illogically connected parodies, and (2) lines 48–72, belonging to the epic subgenre *nebylitsa* (Ivleva 1972). The opening (lines 1–7) inverts the beginning of the bylina about Solovei Budimirovich in Danilov's volume by turning a broad and expansive spatial setting into specific places in a peasant house. Thus the initial lines of that song, "High, high is the sky, / Deep, deep is the ocean-sea," in "Agafonushka" become "The high height—was a stove under the ceiling, / The deep depth—was under the floor." The next episode (lines 8–19) can be called a "mock epic" since the depiction of a duel between two bogatyrs is transformed into a battle between a mother-in-law and her daughter-in-law who, in place of a hero's weapons, use assorted household items. Instead of defeating an enemy of Kiev or slaying a monster, the women kill "one scrawny chicken." The following short section (lines 20–26) offers a parody on the idealized clothing of a bogatyr, in particular the exaggerated description of the dress and buttons that Dyuk wears in the bylina bearing his name. The remaining lines in the first part constitute a series of impossible situations and conclude with another inversion of an epic battle. The last part, as is typical for a nebylitsa, contains a chain of absurdities such as "A gray pig wove a nest" or "Ships were cruising through the open field." Thus "Agafonushka" presents a combination of disparate episodes that have little logical development and have no clear motivation. The traditional raised tone, language, characters, descriptions, and actions in Russian epics have been turned inside out and have been replaced with objects and features from everyday peasant life. The last line, "This was the old song—these were the deeds," concludes many of the bylinas in Kirsha Danilov's collection. It should be mentioned that "Agafonushka," probably because of its satiric and parodic character, contains some passages whose meaning is unclear even to a person closely familiar with the language of Russian folklore.

✍ Agafonushka ✎

Source: Kirsha Danilov, *Ancient Russian Poems,* 2nd ed. (Moscow, 1977), pp. 141–42.

On the Don, on the Don—in a hut on a house,
On steep banks—on a stove on firewood,
The high height—was under the ceiling,
The deep depth—was under the floor,
5   And the wide plain—was a hearth before the stove,
The open field—was under the benches,
The blue sea—was the water in the washtub.
    Near the white city wall—near the millstone,
There was shooting—with spindles,
10   The canons and muskets—were clay pots,
The planted banners—were brooms,
The sharp sabers—were kokoshniks,*
The heavy maces—were shemshuras,†
These shemshuras belonged to women from Tyumen.‡
15   A mother-in-law battled and fought with her
        daughter-in-law,

---

*A traditional woman's headpiece, which was often pointed on top.
†A kind of kokoshnik.
‡A city in Western Siberia.

Making an attack on the city millstone,
Over a pie and over barley bread,
They battled and fought all day till evening,
They killed one scrawny chicken.
20   To this fight and to this great battle
Ran out a strong and mighty bogatyr—
The young Agafonushka, Nikita's son.
His fur coat—was made of pig's tails,
It was trimmed with pain and lined with fever,
25   The buttons—were boils and sores,
The buttonholes—were itchy scabs.
      At that time an old man was lying on a plank bed,*
He was counting his army—he shit in his pants.
An old woman—young in mind—
30   Sat down to shit—she sang songs.
The blind ran—they saw with their rears,
The headless ran—they sang songs,
The holeless ran—they farted,
The noseless ran—they sniffed.
35   Then an armless person stole something in a shed,
The armless one put it in a naked man's shirt.
A tongueless one—was taken to torture,
The hanged ones—listened,
Those slashed to death—escaped into the forest.
40   To this fight, to this great battle,
Then ran out three mighty bogatyrs.
The head of the first mighty bogatyr—
Was smashed through with pancakes,
The legs of the second mighty bogatyr—
45   Were broken with straw,
The belly of the third mighty bogatyr—
Was ripped through with guts.
      At the same time and at the same hour,
Brothers, on the sea a barn was burning
50   With turnips, with boiled turnips.
In the middle of the blue Khvalynsk Sea—

---

*A sleeping shelf above the stove in a peasant house.

Was growing a thick oak.
On that thick damp oak—
A gray pig wove a nest,
55   It wove a nest on the oak,
And it raised children—grayish piglets,
Piglets with small stripes.
They ran everywhere on the oak,
They looked in the water—they wanted to drown,
60   They looked in the field—they wanted to run away.
Ships were cruising through the open field,
A gray wolf was sitting at the helm,
A red fox was egging him on:
"Keep to the right, keep to the left, then go where you want."
65   They looked at the sky—they wanted to fly away.
High up there a mare was flying in overalls,
A devil saw a bear flying,
It was carrying a brown cow in its claws,
In a mortar a chicken gave birth to a lamb,
70   Under the hearth a cow laid an egg,
In a pen a sheep gave birth to a calf.
      This was the old song—these were the deeds.

✌ 29 ✌

About the Merchant Terenty

*A*s a song in verse, "About the Merchant Terenty" has been recorded just five times, but as a prose tale, it has been collected many times in Russian folklore (Smirnov and Smolitskii 1978: 445–46). The most complete variant, which has been translated here, appears in Kirsha Danilov's collection, which was taken down in the middle of the eighteenth century. Basically this is an anecdote about how an old husband, with the aid of clever helpers, catches his unfaithful young wife with her lover and punishes them. The Russian version is set in the city of Novgorod and involves Terenty, who is an old husband and a rich merchant, and his young wife, Avdotya. She complains about an "ailment" and sends her credulous husband for a doctor or sorcerer to treat her. In the city, Terenty runs into some skomorokhs near the Exaltation of the Cross Church. They first tease him in good humor but then decide to help him when he promises to give a hundred rubles to anyone who will cure his wife's ailment. The perceptive skomorokhs, who here are called "merry youths," take him to buy a bag and club, hire a porter to carry him in the bag, and go to Terenty's home, where they tell his wife that he has died. She is happy to hear that the "whore's son" is dead and invites the skomorokhs in, whereupon they sing a song telling Terenty to cure his wife's ailment with the club.

This comic tale, which is composed in the same short epic line as the playful historical song "Kostryuk," belongs to a varied group of satiric, humorous, and grotesque works, such as the *skomoroshina* and the *nebylitsa,* that are usually attributed to the skomorokhs. L.M. Ivleva (1972) surveys the divergent definitions and interpretations of this group of Russian songs. While some folklorists deny that such works represent bylinas, others regard them as a subgenre that can most fully be understood only within the context of Russian epics. Yet other scholars believe that "Terenty" is a unique work in the Russian tradition, but they nevertheless point out that it resembles the French fabliaux. These anonymous tales flourished in the twelfth and thirteenth centuries, were also composed in a short eight-syllable line, and represented amusing anecdotes or jokes in verse. They were frequently concerned with outlandish sexual escapades, depicted stupid husbands and deceitful wives, were commonly misogynous in tone, and often concluded with a moral. In keeping with the low style and subject matter of the fabliaux, the Russian work about the rich merchant Terenty treats the wife negatively, makes fun of the naive husband, and amounts to low comedy. Just like the song called "The Journey of Vavilo with the Skomorokhs," which has not been included in this anthology, the one about "Terenty" represents an apology or defense of the skomorokhs. In an ironical but farcical way, they help maintain social morality and are rewarded "for their great truth," the concluding words perhaps being an inverted "moral" to end the tale. Small but imaginative aspects of the song are revealed in the elaborate description of Terenty's home, the way that the wife but not the husband controls the keys to the family money, the feigned naiveness of the skomorokhs, and the personification of the "ailment" that crawls away from the vengeful husband at the end.

About the Merchant Terenty

Source: Kirsha Danilov, *Ancient Russian Poems* (Moscow, 1977), pp. 15–19.

In the capital Novgorod,
On Yuryev Street,
In Terentyev District,
There lived, there was a rich merchant,
5   By name Terenty.
    His courtyard was a whole verst long,
Around the yard there was an iron stockade,
On each post there was a cupola,
And on each there also was a pearl.
10   The gates were carved,
The jambs were made of crystal,
The threshold was made of walrus tusk.
A building stood in the middle of the yard,
The walls were covered with gray beaver pelts,
15   The ceiling was covered with black sable furs,
The main beam was finely chiseled,
The stove was glazed,
The floor was made of brick.
A bed stood on the floor,
20   The bed was made of ivory,
On the bed lay a featherbed,
On the featherbed lay a pillow,
On the pillow lay the young wife,
Avdotya Ivanovna.
25   Since evening she's been sick and ill,
Since midnight she's been ailing all over.
The ailment spread in her head,
Pain broke out in her spine,
The ailment moved toward her heart,
30   A bit lower than her navel,
But a bit higher than her knees,

Between her legs, fiddle-de-dee.
    The young wife spoke,
Avdotya Ivanovna:
35   "Hail to you, rich merchant,
By name Terenty!
Take my golden keys,
Open the bound trunk,
Take out a hundred rubles in coins
40   Go get some doctors,
Go look for some sorcerers."
    And then Terenty
Obeyed his wife,
He loved his wife.
45   He took her golden keys,
He opened the bound trunk,
He took out a hundred rubles in coins
And went to get some doctors.
    When Terenty came
50   To the Exaltation of the Cross,
To the lively guelder-rose bridge,
Terenty was met by merry skomorokhs.
The skomorokhs were courteous people,
The skomorokhs were polite,
55   They bowed low to Terenty:
"Greetings, rich merchant,
By name Terenty!
Until now not a peep's been heard from you,
Until now not a bit of you's been seen,
60   But now, Terenty,
You're roaming through the open field,
Like a cow gone astray,
Like a crow flown astray."
    He didn't get angry at these words,
65   Terenty spoke to them:
"Hail to you, skomorokhs, young men!
I myself, Terenty, didn't go astray,
And a steed didn't carry the rich man astray,
Want and need led him astray . . .
70   I have a young wife,

Avdotya Ivanovna.
Since evening she's been sick and ill,
Since midnight she's been ailing all over.
The ailment spread in her head,
75   Pain broke out in her spine,
The ailment moved toward her heart,
A bit lower than her navel,
But a bit higher than her knees,
Between her legs, fiddle-de-dee.
80   Whoever will relieve the ailments,
Whoever will drive the ailments away
From my young wife,
From Avdotya Ivanovna,
Will receive a hundred rubles in coins
85   From me, less one coin."
      The merry young men figured things out,
They glanced at each other
And grinned at each other:
"Hail to you, Terenty!
90   What will you pay us for our labors?"
      "I'll give you a hundred rubles!"
      They led him, Terenty,
Through famous Novgorod,
They took him, Terenty,
95   To some trading stalls,
They bought a silken sack,
They gave two grosh for the sack.
They went to other trading stalls,
They bought a red club,
100   A cudgel strapped with leather
And half filled with lead.
They gave ten altyns for it.
They put Terenty
In the silken sack,
105   A porter put it on his shoulders.
They went, the skomorokhs,
To Terenty's courtyard.
      The wary young wife
Glanced out the window:

110   "Hail to you, my merry young men!
     Why are you coming to the courtyard
     When the master isn't in the house?"
         The merry young men then spoke:
     "Hail to you, young wife,
115   Avdotya Ivanovna!
     We bear greetings to you
     From a rich merchant,
     By name Terenty!"
         She suddenly exclaimed:
120   "Hail to you, my merry young men!
     Where did you see him
     And where did you hear about him?"
         The merry young men then answered:
     "We heard him,
125   We saw him for certain
     By the Exaltation of the Cross,
     By the lively guelder-rose bridge.
     His head was lying alone
     And the crows were pecking his ass."
130   The young wife then spoke,
     Avdotya Ivanovna:
     "Merry skomorokhs!
     Go to the bright hall,
     Sit down on the benches,
135   Play your guslis
     And sing a song
     About the rich merchant,
     About the old whore's son,
     By name Terenty—
140   Don't let him be seen again in this house!"
         The merry skomorokhs
     Sat down on the benches,
     They played their guslis,
     They sang a song.
145   "Listen, silken sack
     On the porter's shoulders,
     Listen, Terenty, the merchant,
     To what they say about you,

To what your young wife says,
150 Avdotya Ivanovna,
About her old husband Terenty,
About the old whore's son—
'Don't let you be seen again in this house!'
Stir, silken sack,
155 On the porter's shoulders,
Stand up, Terenty,
You have to cure your young wife!
Take the red club,
The cudgel strapped with leather,
160 Go, Terenty,
Through your bright hall
Along the brick floor
To the white curtain,
To the bed of ivory,
165 To the down featherbed,
And cure, Terenty,
Cure your young wife,
Avdotya Ivanovna!"
    Terenty stood up,
170 He grabbed the red club,
The cudgel strapped with leather
And half filled with lead.
He walked, Terenty,
Through his bright hall
175 Behind the white curtain
To the bed of ivory.
He started curing his young wife,
Avdotya Ivanovna.
He knocked the kerchief off her head,
180 Terenty looked
At the bed of ivory,
At the down featherbed—
The ailment stirred
Under the sable blanket.
185 He, Terenty,
Chased that ailment away
With his cudgel strapped with leather.

The ailment foolishly jumped out the window,
It nearly broke its head,
190 It crawled on all fours,
It barely crawled away from the window.
It left, the ailment,
A caftan of patterned silk,
A vest of silk woven with gold,
195 And five hundred rubles in coins.
　　Then Terenty
Also gave the merry young men
Another hundred rubles
For their great truth.

VII

BALLAD

↪ 30 ↩

The Mother of Prince Mikhailo Kills His Wife

*I*n Russian folklore, ballads form a transitional genre between epics and lyric songs in regard to their kind of melody, mode of performance (solo versus chorus), and linguistic idiom or style. A distinction is made between the older and more traditional Russian ballads and the newer, urban ballads that started appearing in the eighteenth century. Unlike the ballads in many West European countries, the older Russian ballads were unrhymed, had no stanza form, and had no refrain. In the far north, mainly women performed ballads as part of their repertory, which also might include epics. The translated song represents an example of the older type of Russian ballad.

The plot of the song about Prince Mikhailo can be stated in relatively few words. While he is away from home, his mother kills his wife during childbirth in the bathhouse. After his horse stumbles, the Prince returns home, looks for his wife, finally learns from the servants that his mother has killed his wife and child, finds their bodies, and commits suicide. The ballad belongs to an international subject about a conflict between a mother-in-law and her daughter-in-law, the setting for the murder in a bathhouse apparently being a Russian modification. About seventy variants of this song have been collected.

As D.M. Balashov (1966) and A.V. Kulagina (1977) have observed, the ballad about Prince Mikhailo contains a combination of personages that is typical for this genre in Russian folklore: (1) lovers who passively accept their fate (the Prince and his wife); (2) the evildoers (here the mother) who manipulate them and cause their death; and (3) outsiders (the servants) who observe the events and may comment on them. In the ending, attention is focused on the evildoers, who are left to face the consequences of their actions, usually repent their deeds, and may also be deeply affected by grief. This kind of ballad is usually centered around some kind of family conflict (mother-in-law and daughter-in-law). At the same time, the story is universalized so that it becomes essentially timeless and placeless (no specific place-names or historical events); deals with the fate of several stereotyped characters (mother, son, and son's wife); represents a public genre, since the community (servants) witnesses a family drama; and ends tragically with the murder or suicide of a young couple.

Although Russian ballads are usually rather short compared to epics and are focused on one or two terse but highly emotional and dramatic high points, this variant of the song about Prince Mikhailo becomes fairly long (154 lines), largely because of several repeated passages. Rapid transitions in time or place may take place between parts of the story, as, for example, when Mikhailo suddenly returns home or when the time between his marriage and the birth of his child is compressed. Such ballads may contain bad portents or prophetic dreams, which, according to the logic of the genre, are always realized with the worst possible results. In the song about Mikhailo, such an omen occurs when his horse stumbles while he is away from home, and, as one would expect in the world of the ballad, the Prince immediately understands the meaning of the sign. In most of these characteristics, a traditional ballad differs considerably from a Russian epic.

Although the main incidents related in this work are immediately evident, in keeping with the sometimes mysterious background of plots in the ballads, no explanation is offered about why the Prince twice leaves home nor are any details provided about his marriage or his wife's family. While these elements can only be surmised, the motivation of the mother's hatred for the Princess and her violent acts, however briefly alluded to, can be attributed to the Prince's violation of a social code—he married without asking his mother's permission and without receiving her blessing. Only through the mother's words, and especially through her actions, does it become evident that she was insulted when she was not asked to take part in such an important family matter as choosing a wife for her son. Not only does the mother vent her displeasure on the young Princess by killing her, but she slanders her by suggesting to the Prince that his wife has been going to evening parties or gatherings for unmarried young people at a neighbor's.

The variant that has been selected for this anthology shows how singers may incorporate elements from ethnography and from a local landscape into a folk song, in this instance from the Russian North. For example, childbirth was not allowed in the family home but was relegated to the bathhouse, which was a separate building and was associated with its own set of beliefs and superstitions. One suspects that elements of an ancient birth ritual in a bathhouse may be hinted at in this ballad. The description about how the mother-in-law places the bodies of the Princess and her child in a coffin (more precisely, a hollowed-out log) and pushes it into the sea may partly reflect an old North Russian burial custom, according to which a deceased was placed in a coffin and was left in the woods without being buried. In this regard, one might point out how the same motif receives a different resolution in a magic tale, where the wife and child are sealed in a barrel and thrown into the sea, only to be rescued eventually in a happy ending. The mysterious and perhaps magical "gray stone" is not simply a murder weapon; it is also widely encountered in Russian folklore as a symbol of death and grief. At the very end of the song, the mother is described as wandering among water plants along a shore and looking for the bodies of her family, perhaps another indication of a northern landscape, which consists of numerous lakes, waterways, and swamps. The Kvalynsk Sea, an older name for the Caspian Sea, is out of place in a northern song but often represents "sea" in general in Russian folklore.

A.D. Grigorev recorded this ballad in 1901 in Archangel Province on the Mezen River from the woman performer A.V. Potrukhova.

The Mother of Prince Mikhailo Kills His Wife

Source: A.D. Grigorev, *Archangel Bylinas and Historical Songs,* vol. 3
(St. Petersburg, 1910), no. 330.

Mikhailo, the young Prince, set out
To roam in the open field.
He left, he didn't ask for his mother's blessing,
He married, he didn't ask for her permission.
5   He brought the young princess
To his dear mother:
"Hail to you, my dear mother!
Take the young princess,
Lead her to the high chambers,
10   To the wide summer bedrooms.
Give the princess food and drink:
Three kinds of sweet mead
And the tastiest dishes."
His dear mother spoke to him:
15   "You set out, you didn't ask for my blessing,
You married, you didn't ask for my permission."
Then Mikhailo, the young Prince, decided
To roam in the open field.
He asked for his mother's blessing:
20   "Hail to you, my dear mother!
Take the young princess,
Give her food and drink,
Mead and the tastiest dishes."
Then Mikhailo, the young Prince, left,
25   Then he left to roam in the open field.
His young princess,
In the high chambers,
In the wide summer bedrooms,
Burst into tears.

30	Mikhailo's dear mother
	Barely saw him off—
	She stoked the steaming bathhouse,
	She heated a gray stone,
	A gray stone with fiery lights
35	And with small sparks.
	She called the young princess
	To wash herself in the steaming bathhouse.
	The young princess went
	To wash herself in the steaming bathhouse,
40	She burst into tears.
	Mikhailo's dear mother
	Laid his young princess down
	On a white log bench
	Toward the window with a wooden frame.
45	She heated a gray stone,
	She put it on the princess's white breasts,
	She scorched out of her womb
	A little infant.
	She swaddled the infant
50	In colorful swaddling clothes,
	In silken bands.
	She laid the young princess
	With her little infant
	Into a white-oak coffin,
55	On the coffin she fastened
	Three iron hoops,*
	She lowered the coffin
	Into the blue Khvalynsk Sea.
	Mikhailo's steed stumbled,
60	Its legs gave way,
	He sensed that something was wrong at home.
	He came back home,
	He ran into the high chambers,
	Into the wide summer bedrooms:
65	"Hail to you, my dear mother,

*In the original, lines 52–53 and 54–55 form single doubled lines that have been divided to preserve the otherwise short verse of the ballad.

Where's my young princess?"
    "Your young princess—
She's proud and haughty:
She'd leave—she wouldn't tell me,
70   She'd come—she wouldn't ask permission.
Now your young princess
Is at a neighbor's gathering."
    He rushed and dashed
To the neighbor's gathering—
75   The young princess wasn't there
At the neighbor's gathering.
He rushed and dashed
To his dear mother:
"Hail to you, my dear mother,
80   Where's my young princess?"
    "Your young princess—
She'd come—she wouldn't ask permission,
She'd leave—she wouldn't tell me.
Now she's in the high chambers,
85   Now she's in the wide summer bedrooms."
    He rushed and dashed
Into the high chambers,
Into the wide summer bedrooms—
He didn't find his princess.
90   He rushed and dashed
To his faithful servants:
"Hail to you, my faithful servants!
Where's the young princess?"
    The faithful servants answered:
95   "Your dear mother
Barely saw you off,
She stoked the steaming bathhouse,
She heated a gray stone
With fiery lights and with small sparks,
100   She called the young princess
To wash herself in the steaming bathhouse.
The young princess went
To wash herself in the steaming bathhouse,
She burst into tears.

105   Your dear mother
Laid your young princess down
On a white log bench
Toward the window with a wooden frame,
And on her white breasts
110   She laid a gray stone
With fiery lights and with small sparks.
She scorched out of her womb
A little infant,
She swaddled the infant,
115   In colorful swaddling clothes,
In silken bands.
She put the young princess
With her little infant
In a white-oak coffin.
120   On the coffin she fastened
Three iron hoops,
She lowered the coffin
Into the blue Khvalynsk Sea."
        Then Mikhailo, the young Prince,
125   Rushed and dashed,
He also took a silken net,
He also took his faithful servants.
He cast his net once—
Then the coffin wasn't snagged,
130   He cast his net twice—
He threw too far,
He cast his net thrice—
Then he snagged the coffin.
From the coffin he unfastened
135   The three iron hoops,
He saw in the coffin
His young princess
And his little infant.
On the coffin he fastened
140   The three iron hoops,
He lowered this coffin
Into the blue Khvalynsk Sea.
He also rushed and dashed

After the coffin,
145   He threw himself after the coffin
Into the blue Khvalynsk Sea,
The faithful servants were left alone.
    His dear mother
Was roaming up to her knees in mud:
150   "I've committed a terrible sin,
I've destroyed three souls:
The first soul was sinless,
The second soul was innocent,
The third soul was in vain."

Glossary

altyn: Three-kopeck piece.

Apraxia/Apraxevna: Usually the wife of Prince Vladimir but occasionally his daughter or niece.

ataman: Originally the term for a Cossack chieftain.

aurochs: A fierce and large European wild ox that became extinct in the sixteenth century. Its enormous horns were used as sacral objects and as drinking cups.

baba: A word for a peasant woman, now derogatory in the literary language.

bogatyr: The name for a hero in Russian epics.

bogatyrka: Warrior woman.

boyar: A member of the aristocracy in Kievan and Muscovite Rus.

bratchina: An institution or fraternity that was pagan in origin but in modern times was attached to a parish church and gave feasts on religious holidays, ostensibly for collecting donations.

Burko/Burushko: A traditional name for a magic bay horse, often encountered in epics and magic tales. Also see "Kosmatushko."

Chernava: Often the name for a young servant woman in epics. She may appear at a crucial time for the hero and may help him.

Circassian: Usually in the phrase "Circassian saddle" as an indication of quality. The Circassians are a people that live in the northern Caucasus.

cross of Lebanon: An obscure reference that may refer to the Levant, Lebanon, or cedar of Lebanon; usually implies a holy cross with magic qualities.

Dolgopoly: A rarely met bogatyr whose name means "long skirts," as in the tails of a coat.

druzhina: A prince's or bogatyr's retinue.

elbow: A unit of measure amounting to about two feet.

girth: A measure of how much a person could put his or her arms around.

Golden Horde: The rather late name for the Tatars along the Volga River.

golden wedding crowns: During the Russian Orthodox wedding ceremony, golden crowns are held above the couple's heads.

gray/white burning/grieving stone: A mysterious symbol suggesting grief, misfortune, and death.

grivna: Ten-kopeck piece.

grosh: Two-kopeck piece.

gusli: A stringed instrument that resembled a psaltery and was plucked.

hat of the Greek land: A hat that pilgrims worn, especially after visiting holy places in Greece.

horde: Usually refers to the Tatar Golden Horde but may also refer to any group of people.

kalach: The finest bread made of white flour.

kaliki perekhozhie: Wandering religious pilgrims, who in the nineteenth century performed their songs on church holidays and at fairs, begging for alms.

Kosmatushko: The name for a shaggy horse, often suggesting a magic horse. Compare "Burushko."

Khvalynsk Sea: An older name for the Caspian Sea.

Latyr/Alatyr stone: A legendary holy stone that occasionally appears in Russian folklore.

Lithuania: The name often indicates a foreign country in general in epics.

Mother of God: The name for the Virgin Mary in the Orthodox Church.

oprichnina: A separate administration of the state that Ivan the Terrible created to deal with suspected treachery. The oprichnina existed from 1565 to 1572.

Pochai or Pochaina River: A river that emptied into the Dnieper River in ancient Kiev but has long since disappeared; by legend the place where the population was baptized in 988. In epics the river may be an ominous spot marking the boundary between two worlds.

Podolian land: The Podolia region is located in west-central Ukraine. In epics Podolia may represent another name for a foreign country in general.

polyanitsa: This noun has several possible meanings: bogatyr, group of bogatyrs, or woman warrior.

pood: A measure of weight that equaled thirty-six English pounds.

Prince Vladimir: The central Kievan prince around whom Russian heroes are grouped in epics, but without any implication of any specific prince.

radunitsa: The Tuesday of the week after Easter, when people commemorated their ancestors by visiting the cemetery.

religious verses: Songs on various religious subjects that were performed by wandering pilgrims.

sazhen: A unit of measure amounting to about seven feet.

seven kinds of silk: Silk of the finest quality, perhaps with magic associations because of the sacred numeral "seven."

shako: A military hat in the eighteenth and nineteenth centuries, an anachronism in the bylina.

Shemakhan silk: Shemakha was a city in the northern Causasus. The epithet denotes something of eastern origin and of high quality.

skomorokh: The medieval Russian minstrel.

skomoroshina: The general name for a group of satirical songs that have been attributed to the skomorokhs.

Smorodina: A river where a hero may meet his adversary; it may mark the boundary between the world of the living and world of the dead.

Sorochinsk Mountains: Literally, the "Saracen Mountains."

span: The amount that a "hand" can reach, or about nine inches.

sworn brother/blood brother: In Russian this may indicate that the two people have exchanged crosses.

Tatar Yoke: The Russian term indicating the period of Tatar domination beginning about 1240 with the fall of Kiev and ending sometime in the first part of the sixteenth century.

tsar's tavern: In certain periods, all alcohol was sold through establishments controlled by the government, an expression that came into existence only after the crowning of the first tsar in 1547.

tsarevich: The tsar's son.

tsarevna: The tsar's daughter.

tsaritsa: The tsar's wife.

Tsargrad: The older Russian name for Constantinople before the city was captured by the Turks and renamed Istanbul.

Turkish Sea: In Russian folklore, the Turkish Sea represents the Black Sea.

ulan: A name for a Tatar official or dignitary.

verst: A measure of length amounting to about two-thirds of a mile.

Varangian Sea: An old name for the Baltic Sea.

voyevoda: An archaic term for a general or for the governor of a city.

willow bush: The willow bush is often a symbol of death.

yarlyk: A document in which a Tatar Khan granted privileges to a Russian prince; may mean simply "letter."

Bibliography

Only a selection of the most significant anthologies of Russian epics and studies about them have been included. The bibliography has been divided into three parts: scholarly studies, collections of Russian epics, and dictionaries. The titles of works in Russian have been followed with an English translation.

1. Scholarly Studies

Afanasev, A.N. 1865–69. *Poeticheskie vozzreniia slavian na prirodu* [The Slavs' poetic views of nature]. 3 vols. Moscow. Reprint, Moscow: Indrik, 1994.

Alexander, Alex E. 1973. *Bylina and Fairy Tale: The Origins of Russian Heroic Poetry.* The Hague: Mouton.

Anikin, V.P. 1984. *Byliny: Metod vyiasneniia istoricheskoi khronologii variantov* [Bylinas: Method for the elucidation of the historical chronology of variants]. Moscow: Moskovskii universitet.

Arant, Patricia. 1967. "Formulaic Style and the Russian Bylina." *Indiana Slavic Studies* 4: 7–51.

—————. 1990. *Compositional Techniques of the Russian Oral Epic, the Bylina.* New York: Garland.

Astakhova, A.M. 1938. "Bylinnoe tvorchestvo severnykh krestian" [The bylina creation of the northern peasants]. In *Byliny Severa.* Vol. 1, pp. 7–105. Moscow, Leningrad: AN SSSR.

—————. 1948. *Russkii bylinnyi epos na Severe* [The Russian epic in the north]. Petrozavodsk: Gosudarstvennoe izdatelstvo Karelo-Finskoi SSR.

—————. 1966. *Byliny: Itogi i problemy izucheniia* [Bylinas: Summary and problems of study]. Moscow, Leningrad: Nauka.

Avizhanskaia, S.A. 1947. "Boi ottsa s synom v russkom epose" [The battle between father and son in the Russian epic]. *Vestnik Leningradskogo universiteta* 3: 142–44.

Azbelev, S.N. 1971. "Byliny ob otrazhenii tatarskogo nashestviia" [Bylinas about the repulse of the Tatar attack]. *Russkii folklor* 12: 162–80.

—————. 1982. *Istorizm bylin i spetsifika folklora* [The historism of bylinas and the features of folklore]. Leningrad: Nauka.

Bailey, James. 1978. "The Metrical Typology of Russian Narrative Folk Meters."

In *American Contributions to the Eighth International Congress of Slavists,* ed. Henrik Birnbaum. Vol. 1, pp. 82–103. Columbus, OH: Slavica.

———. 1993. *Three Russian Lyric Folk Song Meters.* Columbus: Slavica.

Balashov, D.M. 1966. *Istoriia razvitiia zhanra russkoi ballady* [The history of the development of the Russian ballad]. Petrozavodsk: Karelskoe knizhnoe izdatelstvo.

———. 1976. " 'Dunai' " [Dunai]. *Russkii folklor* 16: 95–114.

Chadwick, N. Munro, and N. Kershaw Chadwick. 1936. "Russian Oral Literature." In *The Growth of Literature.* Vol. 2, pp. 3–296. New York: Macmillan.

Chettéoui, Wilfred. 1942. *Un Rapsode russe: Rjabinin le père.* Paris: Librairie ancienne Honoré Champion.

Chicherov, V.I. 1982. *Shkoly skazitelei Zaonezhia* [Schools of narrators in Zaonezhie]. Moscow: Nauka.

Chistov, K.V. 1963. *Sovremennye problemy tekstologii russkogo folklora* [Contemporary problems of the textology of Russian folklore]. Moscow: AN SSSR.

———. 1980. *Russkie skaziteli Karelii* [Russian narrators of Karelia]. Petrozavodsk: Kareliia.

Dmitrieva, S.I. 1975. *Geograficheskoe rasprostranenie russkikh bylin* [The geographic distribution of Russian bylinas]. Moscow: Nauka.

Dobrovolskii, B.M., and V.V. Korguzalov. 1981. *Byliny: Russkii muzykalnyi epos* [Bylinas: The Russian musical epic]. Moscow: Sovetskii kompozitor.

Fedotov, G. 1935. *Stikhi dukhovnye* [Religious verses]. Paris: YMCA Press.

Findeizen, Nik. 1928. *Ocherki po istorii muzyki v Rossii s drevneishikh vremen do kontsa XVIII veka* [Essays on the history of music in Russia from the most ancient times to the end of the eighteenth century]. Vol. 2. Moscow, Leningrad: Muzsektor.

Froianov, I.Ia., and Iu.I. Iudin. 1990. "Istoricheskie realii v byline o Diuke" [Historical realia in the bylina about Diuk]. *Russkaia literatura* 2: 3–31.

———. 1993. *Drama drevnei semi v russkoi bylevoi poezii* [Drama of an ancient family in Russian epic poetry]. St. Petersburg: Kubik.

———. 1995. "Istoricheskie cherty v bylinakh o Churile Plenkoviche" [Historical features in the bylinas about Churila Plenkovich]. *Russkii folklor* 28: 146–77.

Gatsak, V.M. 1973. "Metaforicheskaia antiteza v sravnitelno-istoricheskom osveshchenii" [Metaphoric antithesis in a comparative and historical light]. In *Istoriia, kultura, etnografiia i folklor slavianskikh narodov,* ed. I.A. Khrenov et al., pp. 286–306. Moscow: Nauka.

———. 1977. "Problema folkloristicheskogo perevoda eposa" [Problem of the folkloristic translation of an epic]. In *Folklore: Izdanie eposa,* ed. A.A. Petrosian, pp. 182–96. Moscow: Nauka.

———. 1989. *Ustnaia epicheskaia traditsia vo vremeni* [Oral epic tradition in time]. Moscow: Nauka.

Gilferding, A.F. [1873] 1949. "Olonetskaia guberniia i ee narodnye rapsody" [Olonets Province and its folk rhapsodists]. In *Onezhskie byliny, zapisannye Aleksandrom Fedorovichem letom 1871 goda.* 4th ed. Vol. 1, pp. 29–84. Moscow, Leningrad: AN SSSR.

Gorelov, A.A. 1995. "Kirsha Danilov—realnoe istoricheskoe litso" [Kirsha Danilov—Real historical person]. *Russkii folklor* 28: 97–110.

Gromyko, M.M. 1984. "Obychai pobratimstva v bylinakh" [Custom of blood brotherhood in bylinas]. In *Folklor i etnografiia,* ed. B.N. Putilov, pp. 116–25. Leningrad: Nauka.

Iarkho, B.I. 1910. "Epicheskie elementy, priurochennye k imeni 'Mikhaila Potyka' " [Epic elements attached to the name 'Mikhail Potyk']. *Etnograficheskoe obozrenie* 3–4: 49–79.

Iudin, Iu.I. 1975. *Geroicheskie byliny* [Heroic bylinas]. Moscow: Nauka.

Ivanov, V.V., and V.N. Toporov. 1974. *Issledovaniia v oblasti slavianskikh drevnostei* [Investigations of Slavic antiquities]. Moscow: Nauka.

Ivanova, T.G. 1982. "Klassicheskie sobraniia bylin v svete tekstologii" [Classic collections of bylinas in the light of textology]. *Russkaia literatura* 1: 135–48.

———. 1993a. *Russkaia folkloristika nachala XX veka v biograficheskikh ocherkakh* [Russian folkloristics at the beginning of the twentieth century in biographical essays]. St. Petersburg: Dmitrii Bulanin.

———. 1993b. "Russkie byliny v angliiskikh perevodakh" [Russian bylinas in English translations]. *Russkii folklor* 27: 313–23.

———. comp. 1987. *Russkii folklor: Bibliograficheskii ukazatel 1976–1980* [Russian folklore: Bibliographic index 1976–1980]. Leningrad: AN SSSR.

———. comp. 1993. *Russkii folklor: Bibliograficheskii ukazatel 1981-1985* [Russian folklore: Bibliographic index 1981–1985]. St. Petersburg: Biblioteka RAN.

Ivleva, L.M. 1972. "Skomoroshiny" [Skomoroshinas]. In *Slavianskii folklor,* ed. B.N. Putilov and V.K. Sokolova, pp. 110–24. Moscow: Nauka.

Jakobson, Roman. 1949. "The Vseslav Epic." In *Russian Epic Studies,* ed. Roman Jakobson and Ernest J. Simmons, pp. 13–86. Philadelphia: American Folklore Society.

Khalanskii, M.G. 1885. *Velikorusskie byliny kievskogo tsikla* [Great Russian bylinas of the Kiev cycle]. Warsaw: Zemkevich.

Korguzalov, V.V. 1966. "Struktury skazitelskoi rechi v russkom epose" [The structures of the narrator's speech in the Russian epic." *Russkii folklor* 10: 127–48.

———. 1994. "Novyi opyt rekonstruktsii napevov sbornika Kirshi Danilova" [New attempt at reconstruction of the melodies in the collection of Kirsha Danilov]. *Izvestiia RAN, Seriia literatury iazyka* 53, no. 4: 41–52.

Korobka, N.I. 1910. "Chudesnoe derevo i veshchaia ptitsa" (The miraculous tree and the prophetic bird). *Zhivaia starina* 1: 189–203.

Kotliarevskii, A.A. 1889. "Skandinavskii korabl na Rusi" [The Scandinavian ship in Rus]. In *Sochineniia.* Vol. 2. *Sbornik Otdeleniia russkogo iazyka i slovesnosti* 48: 555–69.

Krafčik, Patricia A. 1976. "The Russian Negative Simile: An Expression of Folkloric Fantasy." *Slavic and East European Journal* 20, no.1: 18–26.

Krinichnaia, N.A. 1995. *Zhil v Kizhskoi volosti krestianin . . .* [A peasant lived in Kizhi District]. St. Petersburg: Gosudarstvennyi istoriko-arkhitekturnyi i etnograficheskii muzei-zapovednik 'Kizhi.'

Kulagina, A.V. 1977. *Russkaia narodnaia ballada* [The Russian folk ballad]. Moscow: Moskovskii universitet.

Liashchenko, A.I. 1922. "Bylina o Solove Budimiroviche i saga o Garalde" [The bylina about Solovei Budimirovich and the saga about Garald]. In *Sertum*

Bibliologicum v chest prezidenta Russkogo bibliologicheskogo obshchestva A.I. Maleina, pp. 94–136. St. Petersburg: Gosudarstrennoe izdatelstvo.

Liatskii, E.A. 1912. *Stikhi dukhovnye* [Religious verses]. St. Petersburg.

Likhachev, D.S. 1949. "Letopisnye izvestiia ob Aleksandre Popoviche" [Chronicle information about Alexander Popovich]. *Trudy Otdela drevnei russkoi literatury* 7: 17–51.

———. 1967. "Epicheskoe vremia bylin" [Epic time of the bylinas]. In *Poetika drevnerusskoi literatury*, pp. 230–43. Leningrad: Nauka.

Lipets, R.S. 1969. *Epos i drevniaia Rus* [The epic and ancient Rus]. Moscow: Nauka.

———. 1972. "Obraz drevnego tura i otgoloski ego kulta v bylinax" [Image of the ancient aurochs and echoes of its cult in bylinas]. In *Slavianskii folklor*, ed. B.N. Putilov and V.K. Sokolova, pp. 82–109. Moscow: Nauka.

Loboda, A.M. 1904. *Russkie byliny o svatovstve* [Russian bylinas about bride taking]. Kiev: Korchak-Novitskii.

Lord, Albert B. 1965. *The Singer of Tales*. New York: Atheneum.

Machinskii, D.A. 1981. " 'Dunai' russkogo folklora na fone vostochno-slavianskoi istorii i mifologii" ['Dunai' of Russian folklore on the background of East Slavic history and mythology]. In *Russkii Sever*, ed. K.V. Chistov and T.A. Bernshtam, pp. 110–71. Leningrad: Nauka.

Maksimov, S.V. 1989. "Nishchaia bratiia" [Brotherhood of the poor]. In *Po russkoi zemle*, pp. 17–128. Moscow: Sovetskaia Rossiia.

Mazon, André. 1932. "Svjatogor ou Saint-Mont le Géant." *Revue des études slaves* 12: 160–201.

Meletinskii, E.M. 1963. *Proiskhozhdenie geroicheskogo eposa* [Origin of the heroic epic]. Moscow: Vostochnaia literatura.

Miller, Orest F. 1869. *Ilia Muromets i bogatyrstvo kievskoe* [Ilya Muromets and the Kievan bogatyrs]. St. Petersburg: Mikhailov.

Miller, Vs.F. 1892. *Ekskursy v oblast russkogo narodnogo eposa* [Excusions into the Russian folk epic]. Moscow: Levenson.

———. 1897–1924. *Ocherki russkoi narodnoi slovesnosti* [Essays on Russian folk literature]. 3 vols. Moscow: Sytin (1897), Gosudarstvennoe izdatelstvo (1914).

Novichkova, T.A. 1982. "K istolkovaniiu byliny o Potyke" [Toward an interpretation of the bylina about Potyk]. *Russkaia literatura* 4: 152–63.

———. 1987. "Buslaev i Novgorodtsy" [Buslaev and the Novgorodians]. *Russkaia literatura* 1: 157–68.

———. 1989. "Puteshestvie Vasiliia Buslaeva v Ierusalim" [The journey of Vasily Buslayev to Jerusalem]. *Russkii folklor* 25: 3–13.

Novikov, Iu.A. 1995. *Bylina i kniga: Ukazatel zavisimykh ot knigi bylinnykh tekstov* [Bylina and book: Index of bylina texts dependent on a book]. Vilnius: Vilniusskii pedagogicheskii universitet.

Oinas, Felix J. 1984. *Essays on Russian Folklore and Mythology*. Columbus: Slavica.

———. 1987. "Hunting in Russian Byliny Revisited." *Slavic and East European Journal* 31, no. 3: 420–24.

Oinas, Felix, J., and Stephen Soudakoff, eds. and trans. 1975. *The Study of Russian Folklore*. The Hague: Mouton.

Plisetskii, M.M. 1962. *Istorizm russkikh bylin* [Historicism of Russian bylinas]. Moscow: Vysshaia shkola.

Polívka, Georg. 1903. "Zu der Erzählung von der undankbaren Gattin." *Zeitschrift des Vereins für Volkskunde* 13: 399–412.

Popov, A.A. 1854. "Piry i bratchiny" [Feasts and fraternities]. *Arkhiv istoriko-iuridicheskikh svedenii, otnosiashchikhsia do Rossii* 1, no. 2: 19–41.

Propp, V.Ia. 1958a. "Pesnia o gneve Groznogo na syna" [Song about the rage of Ivan the Terribla against his son]. *Vestnik Leningradskogo universiteta* 14, no. 3: 75–103.

————. 1958b. *Russkii geroicheskii epos* [The Russian heroic epic]. 2nd ed. Moscow: Khudozhestvennaia literatura.

Propp, V.Ia., and B.N. Putilov. 1958. "Epicheskaia poeziia russkogo naroda" [Epic poetry of the Russian people]. In *Byliny v dvukh tomakh*. Vol. 1., pp. iii–lxiv. Moscow: Khudozhestvennaia literatura.

Putilov, B.N. 1960. *Russkii istoriko-pesennyi folklor XIII-XVI vekov* [Russian historical-sung folklore of the thirteenth to the sixteenth centuries]. Moscow, Leningrad: AN SSSR.

————. 1963. "Sovremennaia folkloristika i problemy tekstologii" [Contemporary folkloristics and problems of textology]. *Russkaia literatura* 1: 100–14.

————. 1968. "Problemy zhanrovoi tipologii i siuzhetnykh sviazei v russkom i iuzhnoslavianskom epose" [Problems of genre typology and plot connections in the Russian and South Slavic epic]. In *Istoriia, kultura, folklor i etnografiia slavianskikh narodov*, ed. I.A. Khrenov et al., pp. 213–39. Moscow: Nauka.

————. 1971a. *Russkii i iuzhnoslavianskii geroicheskii epos* [The Russian and South Slavic heroic epic]. Moscow: Nauka.

————. 1971b. "Siuzhetnaia zamknutost i vtoroi siuzhetnyi plan v slavianskom epose" [Plot enclosure and plot background in the Slavic epic]. In *Slavianskii i balkanskii folklor*, ed. I.M. Sheptunov, pp. 75–94. Moscow: Nauka.

————. 1972. "Ob epicheskom podtekste" [About the epic subtext]. In *Slavianskii folklor*, ed. B.N. Putilov and V.K. Sokolova, pp. 3–17. Moscow: Nauka.

————. 1976. *Metodologiia sravnitelno-istoricheskogo izucheniia folklora* [Methodology of the comparative-historical study of folklore]. Leningrad: Nauka.

————. 1986. "Byliny—russkii klassicheskii epos" [Bylinas—The Russian classical epic]. In *Byliny*, pp. 5–46. Leningrad: Sovetskii pisatel.

————. 1988. *Geroicheskii epos i deistvitelnost* [The heroic epic and reality]. Leningrad: Nauka.

Riasanovsky, Nicholas V. 1993. *A History of Russia*. 5th ed. New York: Oxford University Press.

Rybakov, B.A. 1963. *Drevniaia Rus: Skazaniia, byliny, letopisi* [Ancient Rus: Legends, bylinas, and chronicles]. Moscow: AN SSSR.

Rybnikov, P.N. [1864] 1989. "Zametka sobiratelia" [Collector's note]. In *Pesni, sobrannye P.N. Rybnikovym*. Vol. 1, pp. 47–83. Petrozavodsk: Kareliia.

Selivanov, F.M. 1977. *Poetika bylin* [The poetics of bylinas]. Pt. 1. Moscow: Moskovskii universitet.

————. 1986. "Ustoichivost i izmeniaemost obraznoi sistemy v byline o Stavre Godinoviche" [Stability and variability of the imagery system in the bylina about Stavr Godinovich]. In *Traditsii russkogo folklora,* ed. V.P. Anikin, pp. 25–68. Moscow: Moskovskii universitet.

———. 1990. *Khudozhestvennye sravneniia russkogo pesennogo eposa* [Artistic comparisons of the Russian sung epic]. Moscow: Nauka.

———. 1995. *Russkie narodnye dukhovnye stikhi* [Russian folk religious verses]. Moscow: Mariiskii gosudarstvennyi universitet.

Shaw, J. Thomas. 1996. " 'Otritsatelnoe sravnenie' [Negative Analogy]: A Note on Terminology.' " In *Collected Works.* Vol. 2, pp. 232–35. Los Angeles: Carl Schlachs, Jr.

Skaftymov, D.P. [1924] 1994. *Poetika i genezis bylin* [Poetics and genesis of the bylinas]. Saratov: Saratovskii universitet.

Smirnov, Iu.I. 1974. *Slavianskie epicheskie traditsii* [Slavic epic traditions]. Moscow: Nauka.

Smolitskii, V.G. 1963. "Iz istorii russkogo geroicheskogo eposa" [From the history of the Russian heroic epic]. *Sovetskaia etnografiia* 5: 7–19.

———. 1972. "Bylina o Sviatogore" [The bylina about Sviatogor]. In *Slavianskii folklor,* ed. B.N. Putilov and V.K. Sokolova, pp. 71–81. Moscow: Nauka.

Sokolov, B.M. 1913. "Istoriia starin o 40 kalikakh so kalikoiu" [History of the old tales about forty and one pilgrims]. *Russkii filologicheskii vestnik* 69, no. 1: 84–95; 69, no. 2: 426–41; 70, no. 3: 134–43; 70, no. 4: 291–313.

———. 1923. "Epicheskie skazaniia o zhenitbe kniazia Vladimira" [Epic legends about the marriage of Prince Vladimir]. *Uchenye zapiski Gosudarstvennogo saratovskogo universiteta* 1, no. 3: 69–122.

Sokolov, Boris and Jurij. 1932. "À la recherche des bylines." *Revue des études slaves* 12: 202–15.

Sokolov, Iu.M. 1927. "Po sledam Rybnikova i Gilferdinga" [In the steps of Rybnikov and Gilferding]. *Khudozhestvennyi folklor* 2–3: 3–33.

———. 1950. "The Byliny." In *Russian Folklore,* pp. 291–341. New York: Macmillan.

Sokolova, V.K. 1960. *Russkie istoricheskie pesni XVI–XVIII vv.* [Russian historical songs from the sixteenth through the eighteenth centuries]. Moscow: AN SSSR.

Stasov, V.V. 1894. "Proiskhozhdenie russkikh bylin" [Origin of Russian epics]. In *Sobranie sochinenii.* Vol. 3, pp. 948–1268. St. Petersburg: Samokhdov.

Stief, Carl. 1953. *Studies in the Russian Historical Song.* Copenhagen: Rosenkilde and Bagger.

Sumtsov, N.F. 1893. "Muzh na svadbe svoei zheny" [The husband at his wife's marriage]. *Etnograficheskoe obozrenie* 4: 1–25.

Tatishchev, V.N. [1768] 1962. *Istoriia rossiiskaia* [Russian history]. Vol. 1. Moscow, Leningrad: AN SSSR.

Tikhonravov, N.S. 1898. "Kaleki perekhozhie" [Wandering pilgrims]. In *Sochineniia N.S. Tikhonravova.* Vol. 1, pp. 324–58. Moscow: Sabashnikov.

Toporkov, A.L. 1997. *Teoriia mifa v russkoi filologicheskoi nauke XIX veka* [The theory of myth in Russian philological scholarship of the nineteenth century]. Moscow: Indrik.

Vasilev, M.I. 1990. "O prichinakh neravnomernogo geograficheskogo rasprostraneniia russkikh bylin" [About the reasons for the uneven geographic distribution of Russian bylinas]. *Sovetskaia geografiia* 3: 76–82.

Vasileva, E.E. 1979. "Kompozitsiia odnostrochnykh epicheskikh napevov po sobiraniiu A.D. Grigoreva" [The composition of one-line epic melodies according to the collection of A.D. Grigorev]. In *Problemy muzykalnoi nauki,* ed. M.E. Tarakanov et al., Vol. 4, pp. 145–63. Moscow: Sovetskii kompozitor.

————. 1989. "Etnomuzykovedcheskaia problematika russkogo eposa" [Ethnomusicological problems of the Russian epic]. In *Muzyka eposa,* ed. I.I. Zemtsovskii, pp. 44–68. Ioshkar-Ola: Soiuz kompozitorov.

Vernadsky, George. 1976. *Kievan Russia.* New Haven: Yale University.

Veselovskii, A.N. 1872. *Slavianskie skazaniia o Solomone i Kitovrase i zapadnye legendy o Morolfe i Merline* [Slavic legends about Solomon and Kitovras, and western legends about Morolfe and Merline]. St. Petersburg: Demankov.

————. 1879–91. "Razyskaniia v oblasti russkogo dukhovnogo stikha I" [Research on Russian religious verses]. *Sbornik Otdeleniia russkogo iazyka i slovesnosti* 20, no. 6 (1879); "II," 21, no. 2 (1880); "III–V," 28, no. 2 (1881); "VI–X," 32, no. 4 (1883); "XI–XVII," 46, no. 6 (1889); "XVIII–XXIV," 53, no. 6 (1891).

————. 1881–84. "Iuzhno-russkie byliny I–II" [South Russian bylinas]. *Sbornik Otdeleniia russkogo iazyka i slovesnosti* 22, no. 2 (1881); "III–XI," 36, no. 3 (1884).

————. 1885–90. "Melkie zametki k bylinam I–IV" [Some remarks about bylinas]. *Zhurnal Ministerstva narodnogo prosveshcheniia* no. 242 (December 1885): 166–98; "V–VII," no. 255 (May 1888): 74–90; "VIII–XII," no. 263 (June 1889): 32–46; "XIII–XV," no. 268 (March 1890): 1–55; "XVI–XVII," no. 269 (May 1890): 56–73]; "XVIII," no. 306 (August 1890): 235–77.

————. 1940. *Istoricheskaia poetika* [Historical poetics]. Ed. V.M. Zhirmunskii. Leningrad: Khudozhestvennaia literatura.

Weiher, Eckhard. 1972. *Der negative Verglich in der russischen Volkspoesie.* Munich: Fink.

Zemtsovsky, Izaly and Alma Kunanbaeva. 1997. "Communism and Folklore." In *Folklore and Traditional Music in the Former Soviet Union and Eastern Europe,* ed. James Porter, pp. 3–23, 42–44. Los Angeles: Department of Ethnomusicology UCLA.

Zguta, Russell 1972. "Kievan 'Byliny': Their Enigmatic Disappearance from Kievan Territory." *Journal of the Folklore Institute* 9: 185–93.

————. 1978. *Russian Minstrels: A History of the Skomorokhs.* Philadelphia: University of Pennsylvania.

Zhirmunskii, V.M. 1979. "Epicheskoe tvorchestvo slavianskikh narodov i problemy sravnitelnogo izucheniia eposa" [Epic creations of the Slavic peoples and problems of the comparative study of the epic]. In *Sravnitelnoe literaturovedenie: Vostok i zapad.* Leningrad: Nauka. 192–280.

2. Collections of Russian Epics

Alexander, Alex E. 1975. *Russian Folklore.* Belmont: Nordland.

Astakhova, A.M. 1938–51. *Byliny Severa* [Bylinas of the north]. 2 vols. Moscow, Leningrad: AN SSSR.

————. 1958. *Ilya Muromets* [Ilia Muromets]. Moscow, Leningrad: AN SSSR.

———— et al. 1961. *Byliny Pechory i Zimnego berega* [Bylinas of Pechora and the Winter Shore]. Moscow, Leningrad: AN SSSR.

Bazanov, V. 1939. *Byliny P.I. Riabinina-Andreeva* [The Bylinas of P.I. Riabinin-Andreev]. Petrozavodsk: Kargoizdat.

Chadwick, N. Kershaw. [1932] 1964. *Russian Heroic Poetry.* New York: Russell and Russell.

Cherniaeva, N.G. 1981. *Russkie epicheskie pesni Karelii* [Russian epic songs of Karelia]. Petrozavodsk: Kareliia.

Costello, D.P., and I.P. Foote. 1967. *Russian Folk Literature.* Oxford: Oxford on the Clarendon.

Danilov, Kirsha. 1977. *Drevnie rossiiskie stikhotvoreniia, sobrannye Kirsheiu Danilovym* [Ancient Russian poems collected by Kirsha Danilov]. Ed. A.P. Evgeneva and B.N. Putilov. 2nd ed. Moscow, Leningrad: Nauka.

Gilferding, A.F. [1873] 1949–51. *Onezhskie byliny, zapisannye A.F. Gilferdingom letom 1871 goda* [Onega bylinas, recorded by A.F. Gilferding in the summer of 1871]. 4th ed., 3 vols. Moscow, Leningrad: AN SSSR.

Grigorev, A.D. 1904–39. *Arkhangelskie byliny i istoricheskie pesni, sobrannye A. D. Grigorevym v 1899-1901 gg.* [Archangel bylinas and historical songs collected by A.D. Grigorev from 1899 to 1901]. Vol. 1, Moscow: 1904; vol. 2, Prague: 1939; vol. 3, St. Petersburg: 1910.

Guliaev, S.I. 1939 [1988]. *Byliny i pesni Altaia* [Bylinas and songs of the Altai]. Barnaul: Altaiskoe Knizhnoe izdatelstvo.

Kireevskii, P.V. 1860–74. *Pesni, sobrannye P.V. Kireevskim* [Songs collected by P.V. Kireevskii]. Vols. 1–10. Moscow.

Kolpakova, N.P., et al. 1967. *Pesennyi folklor Mezeni* [The sung folklore of Mezen]. Leningrad: Nauka.

Linevskii, A.M. 1948. *Skazitel F.A. Konashkov* [The Narrator F.A. Konashkov]. Petrozavodsk: Gosudarstvennoe izdatelstvo Karelo-Finskoi SSR.

Listopadov, A.M. 1949–54. *Pesni donskikh kazakov* [Songs of the Don Cossacks]. Vols. 1–5. Moscow: Muzgiz.

Markov, A.V. 1901. *Belomorskie byliny, zapisannye A. Markovym* [White Sea bylinas recorded by A. Markov]. Moscow: Ethnograficheskii otdel obshchestva liubitelei estestvoznaniia i etnografii.

Onchukov, N.E. 1904. *Pechorskie byliny* [Pechora bylinas]. St. Petersburg: Sokolov and Pastor.

Parilova, G.N., and A.D. Soimonov. 1941. *Byliny pudozhskogo kraia* [Bylinas of Pudoga Region]. Petrozavodsk: Gosudarstvennoe izdatelstvo Karelo-Finskoi SSR.

Propp, V.Ia., and B.N. Putilov. 1958. *Byliny v dvukh tomakh* [Bylinas in two volumes]. 2 vols. Moscow: Khudozhestvennaia literatura.

Putilov, B.N. 1986. *Byliny* [Bylinas]. Leningrad: Sovetskii pisatel.

Rybnikov, P.N. [1861–67] 1989–91. *Pesni, sobrannye P.N. Rybnikovym* [Songs collected by P.N. Rybnikov]. 3 vols. Petrozavodsk: Kareliia.

Smirnov, Iu.I. 1991. *Russkaia epicheskaia poeziia Sibiri i Dalnego Vostoka* [Russian epic poetry of Siberia and the Far East]. Novosibirsk: Nauka.

Smirnov, Iu.I., and V.G. Smolitskii. 1974. *Dobrynia Nikitich i Alesha Popovich* [Dobrynia Nikitich and Alesha Popovich]. Moscow: Nauka.

————. 1978. *Novgorodskie byliny* [Novgorod bylinas]. Moscow: Nauka.

Sokolov, Iu.M. 1948. *Onezhskie byliny* [Onega bylinas]. Ed. V. Chicherov. Moscow: Gosudarstvennyi literaturnyi muzei.

3. Dictionaries

Barkhudarov, S.G., et al., eds. *Slovar russkogo iazyka XI–XVII vv.* 23 vols. to date. Moscow: Nauka, 1975–96.

Chernyshev, V.I., et al., eds. *Slovar sovremennogo russkogo literaturnogo iazyka.* 17 vols. Moscow, Leningrad: AN SSSR, 1950–65.

Dal, Vladimir. *Tolkovyi slovar zhivogo velikorusskogo iazyka.* 3rd ed., 4 vols. St. Petersburg, Moscow: Volf, 1903–09. Reprint, Moscow: Progress and Univers, 1994.

Dopolnenie k opytu oblastnogo velikorusskogo slovaria. St. Petersburg: Akademiia nauk, 1858. Reprint, Leipzig: Zentralantiquariat, 1970.

Evgeneva, A.P., et al., eds. *Slovar russkogo iazyka v chetyrekh tomakh.* 2nd ed., 4 vols. Moscow: Russkii iazyk, 1981–84.

Filin, F.P., et al., eds. *Slovar russkikh narodnykh govorov.* 29 vols. to date. Moscow, Leningrad: Nauka, 1965–95.

Opyt oblastnogo velikorusskogo slovaria. St. Petersburg: Akademiia nauk, 1852. Reprint, Leipzig: Zentralantiquariat, 1970.

Slovar tserkovno-slavianskogo i russkogo iazyka, sostavlennyi Vtorym otdeleniem AN. 4 vols. St. Petersburg: Akademiia nauk, 1847.

Sreznevskii, I.I. *Materialy dlia slovaria drevnerusskogo iazyka.* 3 vols. Moscow, 1893–03. Reprint, Moscow: Gosudarstvennoe izdatelstvo inostrannykh i natsionalnykh slovarei, 1958.

Ushakov, D.N., et al., eds. *Tolkovyi slovar russkogo iazyka.* 4 vols. Moscow: OGIZ, 1935–40.

About the Editors

For nearly thirty years, until his retirement in 1995, **James Bailey** taught courses on Russian language, literature, poetics, and folklore in the Slavic Department at the University of Wisconsin–Madison. At various times he served as chair of the Slavic Department, Russian Area Studies, and the Folklore Program. He has published studies of Russian poetics, literature, and folklore, including, most recently, a book entitled *Three Russian Lyric Folk Song Meters*.

Tatyana Ivanova has served as a folklorist in the Folklore Section of the Institute of Russian Literature, Russian Academy of Sciences, in St. Petersburg, Russia, since 1979. In 1996 she was appointed head of the Manuscript Section at the Institute. She is a specialist in the Russian epic, has published many articles about Russian folklore, and has compiled four volumes in the series on the basic bibliography of Russian folklore. Recently she published a book entitled *Russian Folklorists at the Beginning of the Twentieth Century in Bibliographic Essays*.